GRANADA FROM THE BANKS OF XENIL.

FRONTISPIECE—Irving Vol. Three

A CHRONICLE OF
THE CONQUEST OF GRANADA

WASHINGTON IRVING

WITH FRONTISPIECE

Fredonia Books
Amsterdam, The Netherlands

A Chronicle of
the Conquest of Granada

by
Washington Irving

ISBN 1-58963-264-8

Fredonia Books
Amsterdam, The Netherlands
http://www.fredoniabooks.com

CONQUEST OF GRANADA

CONTENTS

(3)

APPENDIX

A CHRONICLE OF THE

CONQUEST OF GRANADA

BY FRAY ANTONIO AGAPIDA

INTRODUCTION

ALTHOUGH the following Chronicle bears the name of
the venerable Fray Antonio Agapida, it is rather a super-
structure reared upon the fragments which remain of his
work. It may be asked, Who is this same Agapida, who is
cited with such deference, yet whose name is not to be found
in any of the catalogues of Spanish authors? The question
is hard to answer: he appears to have been one of the many
indefatigable authors of Spain, who have filled the libraries
of convents and cathedrals with their tomes, without ever
dreaming of bringing their labors to the press. He evidently
was deeply and accurately informed of the particulars of the
wars between his countrymen and the Moors—a tract of history but too much overgrown with the weeds of fable. His
glowing zeal, also, in the cause of the Catholic faith, entitles
him to be held up as a model of the good old orthodox chroniclers, who recorded with such pious exultation the united
triumphs of the cross and the sword. It is deeply to be
regretted, therefore, that his manuscripts, deposited in the
libraries of various convents, have been dispersed during the
late convulsions in Spain, so that nothing is now to be met
of them but disjointed fragments. These, however, are too
precious to be suffered to fall into oblivion, as they contain
many curious facts not to be found in any other historian.
In the following work, therefore, the manuscript of the

(7)

worthy Fray Antonio will be adopted, wherever it exists entire; but will be filled up, extended, illustrated and corroborated, by citations from various authors, both Spanish and Arabian, who have treated of the subject.   Those who may wish to know how far the work is indebted to the chronicle of Fray Antonio Agapida may readily satisfy their curiosity by referring to his manuscript fragments, which are carefully preserved in the library of the Escurial.

Before entering upon the history, it may be as well to notice the opinions of certain of the most learned and devout historiographers of former times, relative to this war.

Marinus Siculus, historian to Charles V., pronounces it a war to avenge the ancient injuries received by the Christians from the Moors, to recover the kingdom of Granada, and to extend the name and honor of the Christian religion.*

Estevan de Garibay, one of the most distinguished among the Spanish historians, regards the war as a special act of divine clemency toward the Moors; to the end that those barbarians and infidels, who had dragged out so many centuries under the diabolical oppression of the absurd sect of Mahomet, should at length be reduced to the Christain faith.†

Padre Mariana, also, a venerable Jesuit and the most renowned historian of Spain, considers the past domination of the Moors as a scourge inflicted on the Spanish nation for its iniquities, but the triumphant war with Granada as the reward of heaven for its great act of propitiation in establishing the glorious tribunal of the Inquisition!   No sooner (says the worthy father) was this holy office opened in Spain than there instantly shone forth a resplendent light.   Then it was that, through divine favor, the nation increased in power, and became competent to overthrow and trample down the Moorish domination.‡

Having thus cited high and venerable authority for con-

---

* Lucio Marino Siculo, Cosas Memorabiles de España, lib. 20.
† Garibay, Compend. Hist. España, lib. 18, c. 22.
‡ Mariana, Hist. España, lib. 25, c. 1.

sidering this war in the light of one of those pious enterprises denominated crusades, we trust we have said enough to engage the Christian reader to follow us into the field, and to stand by us to the very issue of the encounter.

CHAPTER ONE

OF THE KINGDOM OF GRANADA, AND THE TRIBUTE WHICH IT PAID TO THE CASTILIAN CROWN

THE history of those bloody and disastrous wars which have caused the downfall of mighty empires (observes Fray Antonio Agapida), has ever been considered a study highly delectable and full of precious edification. What then must be the history of a pious crusade, waged by the most Catholic of sovereigns, to rescue from the power of the Infidels one of the most beautiful but benighted regions of the globe? Listen, then, while, from the solitude of my cell, I relate the events of the conquest of Granada, where Christian knight and turbaned Infidel disputed, inch by inch, the fair land of Andalusia, until the crescent, that symbol of heathenish abomination, was cast down, and the blessed cross, the tree of our redemption, erected in its stead.

Nearly eight hundred years were past and gone, since the Arabian invaders had sealed the perdition of Spain, by the defeat of Don Roderick, the last of her Gothic kings. Since that disastrous event, kingdom after kingdom had been gradually recovered by the Christian princes, until the single but powerful territory of Granada alone remained under domination of the Moors.

This renowned kingdom was situated in the southern part of Spain, bordering on the Mediterranean Sea, and defended on the land side by lofty and rugged mountains, locking up within their embraces deep, rich and verdant valleys, where the sterility of the surrounding heights was repaid by prodigal fertility. The city of Granada lay in the center of the kingdom, sheltered as it were in the lap of the Sierra Nevada, or chain of snowy mountains. It covered two lofty hills, and a deep valley which divides them, through which flows the river Darro. One of these hills was crowned by the royal palace and fortress of the Alhambra, capable of containing forty thousand men within its walls and towers. There is a Moorish tradition, that the king who built this mighty pile was skilled in the occult sciences, and furnished himself with gold and silver for the purpose by means of alchemy.* Certainly, never was there an edifice accomplished in a superior style of barbaric magnificence; and the stranger who, even at the present day, wanders among its silent and deserted courts and ruined halls, gazes with astonishment at its gilded and fretted domes and luxurious decorations, still retaining their brilliancy and beauty in defiance of the ravages of time.

Opposite to the hill on which stood the Alhambra was its rival hill, on the summit of which was a spacious plain, covered with houses and crowded with inhabitants. It was commanded by a fortress called the Alcazaba. The declivities and skirts of these hills were covered with houses to the number of seventy thousand, separated by narrow streets and small squares, according to the custom of Moorish cities. The houses had interior courts and gardens, refreshed by fountains and running streams, and set out with oranges, citrons, and pomegranates, so that, as the edifices of the city rose above each other on the sides of the hill, they presented a mingled appearance of city and grove, delightful to the eye. The whole was surrounded by high walls, three leagues in circuit, with twelve gates, and fortified by a thousand and thirty towers. The elevation of the city, and the neighborhood of the Sierra Nevada crowned with perpetual snows, tempered the fervid rays of summer; so that, while other cities were panting with the sultry and stifling heat of the dog-days, the most salubrious breezes played through the marble halls of Granada.

---

*Zurita. lib. 20. c. 42.

The glory of the city, however, was its vega or plain, which spread out to a circumference of thirty-seven leagues, surrounded by lofty mountains. It was a vast garden of delight, refreshed by numerous fountains, and by the silver windings of the Xenil. The labor and ingenuity of the Moors had diverted the waters of this river into thousands of rills and streams, and diffused them over the whole surface of the plain. Indeed, they had wrought up this happy region to a degree of wonderful prosperity, and took a pride in decorating it, as if it had been a favorite mistress. The hills were clothed with orchards and vineyards, the valleys embroidered with gardens, and the wide plains covered with waving grain. Here were seen in profusion the orange, the citron, the fig and pomegranate, with great plantations of mulberry trees, from which was produced the finest of silk. The vine clambered from tree to tree; the grapes hung in rich clusters about the peasant's cottage, and the groves were rejoiced by the perpetual song of the nightingale. In a word, so beautiful was the earth, so pure the air, and so serene the sky of this delicious region, that the Moors imagined the paradise of their prophet to be situated in that part of the heaven which overhung the kingdom of Granada.*

This rich and populous territory had been left in quiet possession of the Infidels, on condition of an annual tribute to the sovereign of Castile and Leon of two thousand doblas or pistoles of gold, and sixteen hundred Christian captives; or, in default of captives, an equal number of Moors to be surrendered as slaves; all to be delivered in the city of Cordova.†

At the era at which this chronicle commences, Ferdinand and Isabella, of glorious and happy memory, reigned over the united kingdoms of Castile, Leon, and Aragon; and Muley Aben Hassan sat on the throne of Granada. This Muley Aben Hassan had succeeded to his father Ismael in

---

* Juan Botero Benes. Relaciones Universales del Mundo.
† Garibay. Compend., lib. 4, c. 25.

1465, while Henry IV., brother and immediate predecessor
of Queen Isabella, was king of Castile and Leon. He was
of the illustrious lineage of Mohammed Aben Alaman, the
first Moorish king of Granada, and was the most potent of
his line. He had in fact augmented in power, in consequence
of the fall of other Moorish kingdoms, which had been conquered by the Christians. Many cities and strong places of
those kingdoms, which lay contiguous to Granada, had refused to submit to Christian vassalage, and had sheltered
themselves under the protection of Muley Aben Hassan.
His territories had thus increased in wealth, extent, and
population, beyond all former example, and contained fourteen cities and ninety-seven fortified towns, besides numerous
unwalled towns and villages, defended by formidable castles.
The spirit of Muley Aben Hassan swelled with his possessions.

The tribute of money and captives had been regularly
paid by his father Ismael; and Muley Aben Hassan had on
one occasion attended personally in Cordova at the payment. He had witnessed the taunts and sneers of the
haughty Castilians; and so indignant was the proud son of
Afric at what he considered a degradation of his race, that
his blood boiled whenever he recollected the humiliating
scene.

When he came to the throne he ceased all payment of the
tribute; and it was sufficient to put him in a transport of
rage only to mention it. "He was a fierce and warlike
Infidel," says the Catholic Fray Antonio Agapida; "his
bitterness against the holy Christian faith had been signalized in battle, during the life-time of his father; and the
same diabolical spirit of hostility was apparent in his ceasing
to pay this most righteous tribute."

CHAPTER TWO

HOW THE CATHOLIC SOVEREIGNS SENT TO DEMAND ARREARS OF TRIBUTE OF THE MOOR, AND HOW THE MOOR REPLIED

IN the year 1478, a Spanish courtier, of powerful frame and haughty demeanor, arrived at the gates of Granada, as ambassador from the Catholic monarchs, to demand the arrears of tribute. His name was Don Juan de Vera, a zealous and devout knight, full of ardor for the faith and loyalty for the crown. He was gallantly mounted, armed at all points, and followed by a moderate but well-appointed retinue.

The Moorish inhabitants looked jealously at this small but proud array of Spanish chivalry, as it paraded, with that stateliness possessed only by Spanish cavaliers, through the renowned gate of Elvira. They were struck with the stern and lofty demeanor of Don Juan de Vera, and his sinewy frame, which showed him formed for hardy deeds of arms; and they supposed he had come in search of distinction, by defying the Moorish knights in open tourney, or in the famous tilt with reeds, for which they were so renowned; for it was still the custom of the knights of either nation to mingle in these courteous and chivalrous contests, during the intervals of war. When they learned, however, that he was come to demand the tribute so abhorrent to the ears of the fiery monarch, they observed that it well required a warrior of his apparent nerve to execute such an embassy.

Muley Aben Hassan received the cavalier in state, seated on a magnificent divan, and surrounded by the officers of his court, in the Hall of Ambassadors, one of the most sumptuous apartments of the Alhambra. When De Vera had delivered his message, a haughty and bitter smile curled the lip of the fierce monarch. "Tell your sovereigns," said he, "that the kings of Granada, who used to pay tribute in money to the

Castilian crown, are dead. Our mint at present coins nothing but blades of scimiters and heads of lances." *

The defiance couched in this proud reply was heard with stern and lofty courtesy by Don Juan de Vera, for he was a bold soldier and a devout hater of the Infidels; and he saw iron war in the words of the Moorish monarch. He retired from the audience chamber with stately and ceremonious gravity, being master of all points of etiquette. As he passed through the Court of Lions, and paused to regard its celebrated fountain, he fell into a discourse with the Moorish courtiers on certain mysteries of the Christian faith. The arguments advanced by those Infidels (says Fray Antonio Agapida) awakened the pious indignation of this most Christian knight and discreet ambassador; but still he restrained himself within the limits of lofty gravity, leaning on the pommel of his sword, and looking down with ineffable scorn upon the weak casuists around him. The quick and subtle Arabian witlings redoubled their light attacks upon this stately Spaniard, and thought they had completely foiled him in the contest; but the stern Juan de Vera had an argument in reserve, for which they were but little prepared; for, on one of them, of the race of the Abencerrages, daring to question, with a sneer, the immaculate conception of the Blessed Virgin, the Catholic knight could no longer restrain his ire. Raising his voice of a sudden, he told the Infidel he lied; and, raising his arm at the same time, he smote him on the head with his sheathed sword.

In an instant the Court of Lions glistened with the flash of arms, and its fountains would have been dyed with blood, had not Muley Aben Hassan overheard the tumult, and forbade all appeal to arms, pronouncing the person of the ambassador sacred while within his territories. The Abencerrage treasured up the remembrance of the insult until an hour of vengeance should arrive, and the ambassador prayed our

---

* Garibay. Compend. lib. 40, c. 29. Conde. Hist. de les Arabes, p. 4, c. 34.

blessed lady to grant him an opportunity of proving her immaculate conception on the head of this turbaned Infidel.*

Notwithstanding this occurrence, Don Juan de Vera was treated with great distinction by Muley Aben Hassan; but nothing could make him unbend from his stern and stately reserve. Before his departure, a scimiter was sent to him by the king; the blade of the finest Damascus steel, the hilt of agate enriched with precious stones, and the guard of gold. De Vera drew it, and smiled grimly as he noticed the admirable temper of the blade. "His majesty has given me a trenchant weapon," said he; "I trust a time will come when I may show him that I know how to use his royal present." The reply was considered as a compliment, of course; the bystanders little knew the bitter hostility that lay couched beneath.

Don Juan de Vera and his companions, during their brief sojourn at Granada, learned the force and situation of the Moor, with the eyes of practiced warriors. They saw that he was well prepared for hostilities. His walls and towers were of vast strength, in complete repair, and mounted with lombards and other heavy ordnance. His magazines were well stored with all the munitions of war: he had a mighty host of foot-soldiers, together with squadrons of cavalry, ready to scour the country and carry on either defensive or predatory warfare. The Christian warriors noted these things without dismay; their hearts rather glowed with emulation, at the thoughts of encountering so worthy a foe. As they slowly pranced through the streets of Granada, on their departure, they looked round with eagerness on its stately palaces and sumptuous mosques; on its alcayceria or bazaar, crowded with silks and cloth of silver and gold, with jewels and precious stones, and other rich merchandise, the

---

* The Curate of Los Palacios also records this anecdote, but mentions it as happening on a subsequent occasion, when Don Juan de Vera was sent to negotiate for certain Christian captives. There appears every reason, however, to consider Fray Antonio Agapida most correct in the period to which he refers it.

luxuries of every clime; and they longed for the time when all this wealth should be the spoil of the soldiers of the faith, and when each tramp of their steeds might be fetlock deep in the blood and carnage of the Infidels.

Don Juan de Vera and his little band pursued their way slowly through the country, to the Christian frontier. Every town was strongly fortified. The vega was studded with towers of refuge for the peasantry; every.pass of the mountain had its castle of defense, every lofty height its watchtower. As the Christian cavaliers passed under the walls of the fortresses, lances and scimiters flashed from their battlements, and the turbaned sentinels seemed to dart from their dark eyes glances of hatred and defiance. It was evident that a war with this kingdom must be one of doughty peril and valiant enterprise; a war of posts, where every step must be gained by toil and bloodshed, and maintained with the utmost difficulty. The warrior spirit of the cavaliers kindled at the thoughts, and they were impatient for hostilities; "not," says Antonio Agapida, "for any thirst for rapine and revenge, but from that pure and holy indignation which every Spanish knight entertained at beholding this beautiful dominion of his ancestors defiled by the footsteps of Infidel usurpers. It was impossible," he adds, "to contemplate this delicious country, and not long to see it restored to the dominion of the true faith, and the sway of the Christian monarchs."

When Don Juan de Vera returned to the Castilian court, and reported the particulars of his mission, and all that he had heard and seen in the Moorish territories, he was highly honored and rewarded by King Ferdinand; and the zeal he had shown in vindication of the sinless conception of the Blessed Virgin was not only applauded by that most Catholic of sovereigns, but gained him great favor and renown among all pious cavaliers and reverend prelates.

CHAPTER THREE

HOW THE MOOR DETERMINED TO STRIKE THE FIRST BLOW
IN THE WAR

THE defiance thus hurled at the Castilian sovereigns by
the fiery Moorish king would at once have been answered by
the thunder of their artillery; but they were embroiled, at
that time, in a war with Portugal, and in contests with their
own factious nobles. The truce, therefore, which had existed
for many years between the nations, was suffered to continue;
the wary Ferdinand reserving the refusal to pay tribute as
a fair ground for war, whenever the favorable moment to
wage it should arrive.

In the course of three years, the war with Portugal was
terminated, and the factions of the Spanish nobles were, for
the most part, quelled. The Castilian sovereigns now turned
their thoughts to what, from the time of the union of their
crowns, had been the great object of their ambition—the conquest of Granada, and the complete extirpation of the Moslem
power from Spain. Ferdinand, whose pious zeal was quickened by motives of temporal policy, looked with a craving
eye at the rich territory of the Moor, studded with innumerable towns and cities. He determined to carry on the war
with cautious and persevering patience, taking town after
town and fortress after fortress, and gradually plucking away
all the supports, before he attempted the Moorish capital.
"I will pick out the seeds, one by one, of this pomegranate,"
said the wary Ferdinand.*

Muley Aben Hassan was aware of the hostile intentions
of the Catholic monarch, but felt confident in his means of
resisting them. He had amassed great wealth, during a
tranquil reign; he had strengthened the defenses of his king-

---

* Granada is the Spanish term for *pomegranate.*

dom, and had drawn large bodies of auxiliary troops from
Barbary, besides making arrangements with the African
princes to assist him with supplies, in case of emergency.
His subjects were fierce of spirit, stout of heart, and valiant
of hand.   Inured to the exercises of war, they could fight
skillfully on foot, but, above all, were dexterous horsemen,
whether heavily armed and fully appointed, or lightly
mounted *a la geneta*, with simply lance and target.   They
were patient of fatigue, hunger, thirst, and nakedness;
prompt for war, at the first summons of their king, and te-
nacious in defense of their towns and possessions.

Thus amply provided for war, Muley Aben Hassan determined to be beforehand with the politic Ferdinand, and
to be the first to strike a blow.   In the truce which existed
between them there was a singular clause, permitting either
party to make sudden inroads and assaults upon towns and
fortresses, provided they were done furtively and by stratagem, without display of banners or sound of trumpet, or
regular encampment, and that they did not last above three
days.*   This gave rise to frequent enterprises of a hardy and
adventurous character, in which castles and strongholds were
taken by surprise and carried sword in hand.   A long time
had elapsed, however, without any outrage of the kind on
the part of the Moors; and the Christian towns on the frontiers had all, in consequence, fallen into a state of the most
negligent security.

Muley Aben Hassan cast his eyes round to select his
object of attack, when information was brought him that
the fortress of Zahara was but feebly garrisoned and scantily
supplied, and that its alcayde was careless of his charge.
This important post was on the frontier, between Ronda and
Medina Sidonia, and was built on the crest of a rocky mountain, with a strong castle perched above it, upon a cliff, so
high that it was said to be above the flight of birds or drift

---

*Zurita.   Annales de Aragon, l. 20, c. 41.   Mariana.   Hist. de
Espana, l. 25, c. 1.

of clouds. The streets and many of the houses were mere excavations wrought out of the living rock. The town had but one gate, opening to the west, and defended by towers and bulwarks. The only ascent to this cragged fortress was by roads cut in the rock, and so rugged as in many places to resemble broken stairs. Such was the situation of the mountain fortress of Zahara, which seemed to set all attack at defiance, insomuch that it had become so proverbial throughout Spain, that a woman of forbidding and inaccessible virtue was called a Zahareña. But the strongest fortress and sternest virtue have weak points and require unremitting vigilance to guard them: let warrior and dame take warning from the fate of Zahara.

CHAPTER FOUR

EXPEDITION OF MULEY ABEN HASSAN AGAINST THE FORTRESS OF ZAHARA

It was in the year of Our Lord one thousand four hundred and eighty-one, and but a night or two after the festival of the most blessed Nativity, that Muley Aben Hassan made his famous attack upon Zahara. The inhabitants of the place were sunk in profound sleep; the very sentinel had deserted his post and sought shelter from a tempest which had raged for three nights in succession; for it appeared but little probable that an enemy would be abroad during such an uproar of the elements. But evil spirits work best during a storm (observes the worthy Antonio Agapida), and Muley Aben Hassan found such a season most suitable for his diabolical purposes. In the midst of the night, an uproar arose within the walls of Zahara, more awful than the raging of the storm. A fearful alarm cry—"The Moor! the Moor!" resounded through the streets, mingled with the clash of arms, the shriek of anguish, and the shout of victory. Muley Aben Hassan, at the head of a powerful force, had hurried from

Granada and passed unobserved through the mountains in the obscurity of the tempest. While the storm pelted the sentinel from his post, and howled round tower and battlement, the Moors had planted their scaling-ladders and mounted securely into both town and castle. The garrison was unsuspicious of danger, until battle and massacre burst forth within its very walls. It seemed to the affrighted inhabitants as if the fiends of the air had come upon the wings of the wind and possessed themselves of tower and turret. The war cry resounded on every side, shout answering shout, above, below, on the battlements of the castle, in the streets of the town—the foe was in all parts wrapped in obscurity, but acting in concert by the aid of preconcerted signals. Starting from sleep, the soldiers were intercepted and cut down as they rushed from their quarters; or, if they escaped, they knew not where to assemble or where to strike. Wherever lights appeared, the flashing scimiter was at its deadly work, and all who attempted resistance fell beneath its edge.

In a little while the struggle was at an end. Those who were not slain took refuge in the secret places of their houses, or gave themselves up as captives. The clash of arms ceased; and the storm continued its howling, mingled with the occasional shout of the Moorish soldiery roaming in search of plunder. While the inhabitants were trembling for their fate, a trumpet resounded through the streets, summoning them all to assemble, unarmed, in the public square. Here they were surrounded by soldiery, and strictly guarded, until daybreak. When the day dawned, it was piteous to behold this once prosperous community, who had laid down to rest in peaceful security, now crowded together without distinction of age, or rank, or sex, and almost without raiment, during the severity of a wintry storm. The fierce Muley Aben Hassan turned a deaf ear to all their prayers and remonstrances, and ordered them to be conducted captives to Granada. Leaving a strong garrison in both town and castle, with orders to put them in a complete state of defense, he returned, flushed with victory, to his capital, entering it at the head of his troops, laden with spoil, and bearing in triumph the banners and pennons taken at Zahara.

While preparations were making for jousts and other festivities, in honor of this victory over the Christians, the captives of Zahara arrived—a wretched train of men, women and children, worn out with fatigue and haggard with despair, and driven like cattle into the city gates by a detachment of Moorish soldiery.

Deep was the grief and indignation of the people of Granada at this cruel scene. Old men, who had experienced the calamities of warfare, anticipated coming troubles. Mothers clasped their infants to their breasts, as they beheld the hapless females of Zahara, with their children expiring in their arms. On every side the accents of pity for the sufferers were mingled with execrations of the barbarity of the king. The preparations for festivity were neglected; and the viands, which were to have feasted the conquerors, were distributed among the captives.

The nobles and alfaquis, however, repaired to the Alhambra to congratulate the king; for, whatever storms may rage in the lower regions of society, rarely do any clouds, but clouds of incense, rise to the awful eminence of the throne. In this instance, however, a voice rose from the midst of the obsequious crowd, that burst like thunder upon the ears of Aben Hassan. "Woe! woe! woe! to Granada!" exclaimed the voice; "its hour of desolation approaches. The ruins of Zahara will fall upon our heads; my spirit tells me that the end of our empire is at hand!" All shrunk back aghast, and left the denouncer of woe standing alone in the center of the hall. He was an ancient and hoary man, in the rude attire of a dervise. Age had withered his form without quenching the fire of his spirit, which glared in baleful luster from his eyes. He was (say the Arabian historians), one of those holy men termed santons, who pass their lives in hermitages, in fasting, meditation and prayer, until they attain to the purity of saints and the foresight of prophets. "He was," says the indignant Fray Antonio

Agapida, "a son of Belial, one of those fanatic Infidels possessed by the devil, who are sometimes permitted to predict the truth to their followers; but with the proviso that their predictions shall be of no avail."

The voice of the santon resounded through the lofty hall of the Alhambra and struck silence and awe into the crowd of courtly sycophants. Muley Aben Hassan alone was unmoved; he eyed the hoary anchorite with scorn as he stood dauntless before him, and treated his predictions as the ravings of a maniac. The santon rushed from the royal presence, and, descending into the city, hurried through its streets and squares, with frantic gesticulations. His voice was heard in every part in awful denunciation. "The peace is broken! the exterminating war is commenced. Woe! woe! woe! to Granada! its fall is athand! desolation shall dwell in its palaces; its strong men shall fall beneath the sword, its children and maidens shall be led into captivity. Zahara is but a type of Granada!"

Terror seized upon the populace, for they considered these ravings as the inspirations of prophecy. They hid themselves in their dwellings, as in a time of general mourning; or, if they went abroad, it was to gather together in knots in the streets and squares, to alarm each other with dismal forebodings, and to curse the rashness and cruelty of the fierce Aben Hassan.

The Moorish monarch heeded not their murmurs. Knowing that his exploit must draw upon him the vengeance of the Christians, he now threw off all reserve, and made attempts to surprise Castellan and Elvira, though without success. He sent alfaquis, also, to the Barbary powers, informing them that the sword was drawn, and inviting them to aid in maintaining the kingdom of Granada and the religion of Mahomet against the violence of unbelievers.

CHAPTER FIVE

EXPEDITION OF THE MARQUES OF CADIZ AGAINST ALHAMA

GREAT was the indignation of King Ferdinand, when he heard of the storming of Zahara—more especially as it had anticipated his intention of giving the first blow in this eventful war. He valued himself upon his deep and prudent policy; and there is nothing which politic monarchs can less forgive than thus being forestalled by an adversary. He immediately issued orders to all the adelantados and alcaydes of the frontiers to maintain the utmost vigilance at their several posts, and to prepare to carry fire and sword into the territories of the Moors.

Among the many valiant cavaliers who rallied round the throne of Ferdinand and Isabella, one of the most eminent in rank and renowned in arms was Don Roderigo Ponce de Leon, Marques of Cadiz. As he was the distinguished champion of this holy war, and commanded in most of its enterprises and battles, it is meet that some particular account should be given of him. He was born in 1443, of the valiant lineage of the Ponces, and from his earliest youth had rendered himself illustrious in the field. He was of the middle statúre, with a muscular and powerful frame, capable of great exertion and fatigue. His hair and beard were red and curled, his countenance was open and magnanimous, of a ruddy complexion, and slightly marked with the small-pox. He was temperate, chaste, valiant, vigilant; a just and generous master to his vassals; frank and noble in his deport‧ ment toward his equals; loving and faithful to his friends; fierce and terrible, yet magnanimous, to his enemies. He was considered the mirror of chivalry of his times, and compared by contemporary historians to the immortal Cid.

The Marques of Cadiz had vast possessions in the most fertile parts of Andalusia, including many towns and castles, and could lead forth an army into the field from his own vassals and dependents. On receiving the orders of the king, he burned to signalize himself by some sudden incursion into the kingdom of Granada that should give a brilliant commencement to the war, and should console the sovereigns for the insult they had received in the capture of Zahara. As his estates lay near to the Moorish frontiers, and were subject to sudden inroads, he had always in his pay numbers of adalides or scouts and guides, many of them converted Moors. These he sent out in all directions, to watch the movements of the enemy, and to procure all kinds of information important to the security of the frontier. One of these spies came to him one day in his town of Marchena, and informed him that the Moorish town of Alhama was slightly garrisoned and negligently guarded, and might be taken by surprise. This was a large, wealthy, and populous place within a few leagues of Granada. It was situated on a rocky height, nearly surrounded by a river, and defended by a fortress to which there was no access but by a steep and cragged ascent. The strength of its situation, and its being embosomed in the center of the kingdom, had produced the careless security which now invited attack.

To ascertain fully the state of the fortress, the marques dispatched secretly a veteran soldier, who was highly in his confidence. His name was Ortega de Prado, a man of great activity, shrewdness, and valor, and captain of escaladors, or those employed to scale the walls of fortresses in time of attack. Ortega approached Alhama one moonless night, and paced along its walls with noiseless step, laying his ear occasionally to the ground or to the wall. Every time, he distinguished the measured tread of a sentinel, and now and then the challenge of the night-watch going its rounds. Finding the town thus guarded, he clambered to the castle —there all was silent. As he ranged its lofty battlements between him and the sky he saw no sentinel on duty. He noticed certain places where the wall might be ascended by scaling-ladders; and, having marked the hour of relieving guard, and made all necessary observations, he retired without being discovered.

Ortega returned to Marchena, and assured the Marques of Cadiz of the practicability of scaling the castle of Alhama, and taking it by surprise. The marques had a secret conference with Don Pedro Henriquez, adelantado of Andalusia; Don Diego de Merlo, commander of Seville; and Sancho de Avila, alcayde of Carmona, who all agreed to aid him with their forces. On an appointed day the several commanders assembled at Marchena with their troops and retainers. None but the leaders knew the object or destination of the enterprise; but it was enough to rouse the Andalusian spirit to know that a foray was intended into the country of their old enemies, the Moors. Secrecy and celerity were necessary for success. They set out promptly, with three thousand genetes or light cavalry, and four thousand infantry. They chose a route but little traveled, by the way of Antiquera, passing with great labor through rugged and solitary defiles of the sierra or chain of mountains of Alzerifa, and left all their baggage on the banks of the river Yeguas, to be brought after them. Their march was principally in the night; all day they remained quiet; no noise was suffered in their camp, and no fires were made, lest the smoke should betray them. On the third day they resumed their march as the evening darkened, and forcing themselves forward at as quick a pace as the rugged and dangerous mountain roads would permit, they descended toward midnight into a small deep valley, only half a league from Alhama. Here they made a halt, fatigued by this forced march, during a long dark evening toward the end of February.

The Marques of Cadiz now explained to the troops the object of the expedition. He told them it was for the glory of the most holy faith, and to avenge the wrongs of their countrymen of Zahara; and that the rich town of Alhama, full of wealthy spoil, was the place to be attacked. The troops were roused to new ardor by these words, and desired to be led forthwith to the assault. They arrived close to

***2

Alhama about two hours before daybreak. Here the army remained in ambush, while three hundred men were dispatched to scale the walls and get possession of the castle. They were picked men, many of them alcaydes and officers, men who preferred death to dishonor. This gallant band was guided by the escalador Ortega de Prado, at the head of thirty men with scaling-ladders. They clambered the ascent to the castle in silence, and arrived under the dark shadow of its towers without being discovered. Not a light was to be seen, not a sound to be heard; the whole place was wrapped in profound repose.

Fixing their ladders, they ascended cautiously and with noiseless step. Ortega was the first that mounted upon the battlements, followed by one Martin Galindo, a youthful esquire, full of spirit and eager for distinction. Moving stealthily along the parapet to the portal of the citadel, they came upon the sentinel by surprise. Ortega seized him by the throat, brandished a dagger before his eyes, and ordered him to point the way to the guard-room. The Infidel obeyed, and was instantly dispatched, to prevent his giving an alarm. The guard-room was a scene rather of massacre than combat. Some of the soldiery were killed while sleeping, others were cut down almost without resistance, bewildered by so unexpected an assault: all were dispatched, for the scaling party was too small to make prisoners or to spare. The alarm spread throughout the castle, but by this time the three hundred picked men had mounted the battlements. The garrison, startled from sleep, found the enemy already masters of the towers. Some of the Moors were cut down at once, others fought desperately from room to room, and the whole castle resounded with the clash of arms, the cries of the combatants, and the groans of the wounded. The army in ambush, finding by the uproar that the castle was surprised, now rushed from their concealment, and approached the walls with loud shouts, and sound of kettle-drums and trumpets, to increase the confusion and dismay of the garrison. A violent conflict took place in the court of the castle, where several of the scaling party sought to throw open the gates to admit their countrymen. Here fell two valiant alcaydes, Nicholas de Roja and Sancho de Avila; but they fell honorably, upon a heap of slain. At length Ortega de Prado succeeded in throwing open a postern, through which the Marques of Cadiz, the adelantado of Andalusia, and Don Diego de Merlo, entered with a host of followers, and the citadel remained in full possession of the Christians.

As the Spanish cavaliers were ranging from room to room, the Marques of Cadiz, entering an apartment of superior richness to the rest, beheld, by the light of a silver lamp, a beautiful Moorish female, the wife of the alcayde of the castle, whose husband was absent, attending a wedding-feast at Velez Malaga. She would have fled at the sight of a Christian warrior in her apartment, but, entangled in the covering of the bed, she fell at the feet of the marques, imploring mercy. The Christian cavalier, who had a soul full of honor and courtesy toward the sex, raised her from the floor, and endeavored to allay her fears; but they were increased at the sight of her female attendants pursued into the room by the Spanish soldiery. The marques reproached his soldiers with their unmanly conduct, and reminded them that they made war upon men, not on defenseless women. Having soothed the terrors of the females by the promise of honorable protection, he appointed a trusty guard to watch over the security of their apartment.

The castle was now taken; but the town below it was in arms. It was broad day, and the people, recovered from their panic, were enabled to see and estimate the force of the enemy. The inhabitants were chiefly merchants and tradespeople; but the Moors all possessed a knowledge of the use of weapons, and were of brave and warlike spirit. They confided in the strength of their walls, and the certainty of speedy relief from Granada, which was but about eight leagues distant. Manning the battlements and towers, they discharged showers of stones and arrows, whenever the part of the Christian army, without the walls, attempted to approach. They barricadoed the entrances of their streets, also, which opened toward the castle; stationing men expert at the crossbow and arquebuse. These kept up a constant fire upon the gate of the castle, so that no one could sally forth without being instantly shot down. Two valiant cavaliers, who attempted to lead forth a party in defiance of this fatal tempest, were shot dead at the very portal.

The Christians now found themselves in a situation of great peril. Re-enforcements must soon arrive to the enemy from Granada; unless, therefore, they gained possession of the town in the course of the day, they were likely to be surrounded and beleaguered, without provisions, in the castle. Some observed that, even if they took the town, they should not be able to maintain possession of it. They proposed, therefore, to make booty of everything valuable, to sack the castle, set it on fire, and make good their retreat to Seville.

The Marques of Cadiz was of different counsel. "God has given the citadel into Christian hands," said he; "He will no doubt strengthen them to maintain it. We have gained the place with difficulty and bloodshed; it would be a stain upon our honor to abandon it through fear of imaginary dangers." The adelantado and Don Diego de Merlo joined in his opinion; but without their earnest and united remonstrances the place would have been abandoned; so exhausted were the troops by forced marches and hard fighting, and so apprehensive of the approach of the Moors of Granada.

The strength and spirits of the party within the castle were in some degree restored by the provisions which they found. The Christian army beneath the town, being also refreshed by a morning's repast, advanced vigorously to the attack of the walls. They planted their scaling-ladders, and, swarming up, sword in hand, fought fiercely with the Moorish soldiery upon the ramparts.

In the meantime, the Marques of Cadiz, seeing that the gate of the castle, which opened toward the city, was completely commanded by the artillery of the enemy, ordered a large breach to be made in the wall, through which he might lead his troops to the attack; animating them, in this perilous moment, by assuring them that the place should be given up to plunder, and its inhabitants made captives.

The breach being made, the marques put himself at the head of his troops, and entered sword in hand. A simultaneous attack was made by the Christians in every part—by the ramparts, by the gate, by the roofs and walls which connected the castle with the town. The Moors fought valiantly in their streets, from their windows, and from the tops of their houses. They were not equal to the Christians in bodily strength, for they were for the most part peaceful men, of industrious callings, and enervated by the frequent use of the warm bath; but they were superior in number, and unconquerable in spirit; old and young, strong and weak, fought with the same desperation. The Moors fought for property, for liberty, for life. They fought at their thresholds and their hearths, with the shrieks of their wives and children ringing in their ears, and they fought in the hope that each moment would bring aid from Granada. They regarded neither their own wounds nor the deaths of their companions; but continued fighting until they fell, and seemed as if, when they could no longer contend, they would block up the thresholds of their beloved homes with their mangled bodies. The Christians fought for glory, for revenge, for the holy faith, and for the spoil of these wealthy Infidels. Success would place a rich town at their mercy; failure would deliver them into the hands of the tyrant of Granada.

The contest raged from morning until night, when the Moors began to yield. Retreating to a large mosque near the walls, they kept up so galling a fire from it with lances, crossbows, and arquebuses, that for some time the Christians dared not approach. Covering themselves, at length, with bucklers and mantelets* to protect them from the deadly

---

* Mantelet—a movable parapet, made of thick planks, to protect troops, when advancing to sap or assault a walled place.

shower, they made their way to the mosque, and set fire to the doors. When the smoke and flames rolled in upon them, the Moors gave all up as lost. Many rushed forth desperately upon the enemy, but were immediately slain; the rest surrendered themselves captives.

The struggle was now at an end; the town remained at the mercy of the Christians; and the inhabitants, both male and female, became the slaves of those who made them prisoners. Some few escaped by a mine or subterranean way, which led to the river, and concealed themselves, their wives and children, in caves and secret places; but in three or four days were compelled to surrender themselves through hunger.

The town was given up to plunder, and the booty was immense. There were found prodigious quantities of gold and silver, and jewels, and rich silks, and costly stuffs of all kinds; together with horses and beeves, and abundance of grain and oil, and honey, and all other productions of this fruitful kingdom; for in Alhama were collected the royal rents and tributes of the surrounding country; it was the richest town in the Moorish territory, and, from its great strength and its peculiar situation, was called the key to Granada.

Great waste and devastation were committed by the Spanish soldiery; for, thinking it would be impossible to keep possession of the place, they began to destroy whatever they could not take away. Immense jars of oil were broken, costly furniture shattered to pieces, and magazines of grain broken open, and their contents scattered to the winds. Many Christian captives, who had been taken at Zahara, were found buried in a Moorish dungeon, and were triumphantly restored to light and liberty; and a renegado Spaniard, who had often served as guide to the Moors in their incursions into the Christian territories, was hanged on the highest part of the battlements, for the edification of the army.

CHAPTER SIX

HOW THE PEOPLE OF GRANADA WERE AFFECTED, ON HEAR-
ING OF THE CAPTURE OF ALHAMA; AND HOW THE
MOORISH KING SALLIED FORTH TO REGAIN IT

A MOORISH horseman had spurred across the vega, nor
reined his panting steed until he alighted at the gate of the
Alhambra. He brought tidings to Muley Aben Hassan of
the attack upon Alhama.

"The Christians," said he, "are in the land. They came
upon us, we know not whence or how, and scaled the walls
of the castle in the night. There has been dreadful fighting
and carnage in its towers and courts; and when I spurred
my steed from the gate of Alhama the castle was in possession of the unbelievers."

Muley Aben Hassan felt for a moment as if swift retribution had come upon him for the woes he had inflicted upon
Zahara. Still he flattered himself that this had only been
some transient inroad of a party of marauders intent upon
plunder; and that a little succor, thrown into the town, would
be sufficient to expel them from the castle, and drive them
from the land. He ordered out, therefore, a thousand of his
chosen cavalry, and sent them in all speed to the assistance
of Alhama. They arrived before its walls the morning after
its capture: the Christian standards floated upon its towers,
and a body of cavalry poured forth from its gates and came
wheeling down into the plain to receive them.

The Moorish horsemen turned the reins of their steeds
and galloped back for Granada. They entered its gates in
tumultuous confusion, spreading terror and lamentation by
their tidings. "Alhama is fallen! Alhama is fallen!" exclaimed they; "the Christians garrison its walls; the key of
Granada is in the hands of the enemy!"

When the people heard these words they remembered the denunciation of the santon. His prediction seemed still to resound in every ear, and its fulfillment to be at hand. Nothing was heard throughout the city but sighs and wailings. "Woe is me, Alhama!" was in every mouth; and this ejaculation of deep sorrow and doleful foreboding came to be the burden of a plaintive ballad, which remains until the present day.*

Many aged men, who had taken refuge in Granada from other Moorish dominions which had fallen into the power of the Christians, now groaned in despair at the thoughts that war was to follow them into this last retreat, to lay waste this pleasant land, and to bring trouble and sorrow upon their declining years. The women were more loud and vehement in their grief; for they beheld the evils impending over their children, and what can restrain the agony of a mother's heart? Many of them made their way through the halls of the Alhambra into the presence of the king, weeping, and wailing, and tearing their hair. "Accursed be the day," cried they, "that thou hast lighted the flame of war in our land! May the holy Prophet bear witness before Allah that we and our children are innocent of this act! Upon thy head, and upon the heads of thy posterity, until the end of the world, rest the sin of the desolation of Zahara!" †

Muley Aben Hassan remained unmoved amid all this storm; his heart was hardened (observes Fray Antonio Agapida), like that of Pharaoh, to the end that, through his blind violence and rage, he might produce the deliverance of the land from its heathen bondage. In fact, he was a bold and fearless warrior, and trusted soon to make this blow recoil upon the head of the enemy. He had ascertained that the captors of Alhama were but a handful: they were in the center of his dominions, within a short distance of his capital.

---

* The mournful little Spanish romance of "Ay de mi, Alhama!" is supposed to be of Moorish origin, and to embody the grief of the people of Granada on this occasion.

† Garibay, lib. 40, c. 29.

They were deficient in munitions of war, and provisions for sustaining a siege. By a rapid movement he might surround them with a powerful army, cut off all aid from their countrymen, and entrap them in the fortress they had taken.

To think was to act with Muley Aben Hassan; but he was prone to act with too much precipitation. He immediately set forth in person, with three thousand horse and fifty thousand foot, and in his eagerness to arrive at the scene of action would not wait to provide artillery and the various engines required in a siege. "The multitude of my forces," said he, confidently, "will be sufficient to overwhelm the enemy."

The Marques of Cadiz, who thus held possession of Alhama, had a chosen friend and faithful companion in arms among the most distinguished of the Christian chivalry. This was Don Alonzo de Cordova, senior and lord of the house of Aguilar, and brother of Gonsalvo of Cordova, afterward renowned as grand captain of Spain. As yet Alonzo de Aguilar was the glory of his name and race—for his brother was but young in arms. He was one of the most hardy, valiant, and enterprising of the Spanish knights, and foremost in all service of a perilous and adventurous nature. He had not been at hand to accompany his friend Ponce de Leon, Marques of Cadiz, in his inroad into the Moorish territory; but he hastily assembled a number of retainers, horse and foot, and pressed forward to join the enterprise. Arriving at the river Yeguas, he found the baggage of the army still upon its banks, and took charge of it to carry it to Alhama. The Marques of Cadiz heard of the approach of his friend, whose march was slow in consequence of being encumbered by the baggage. He was within but a few·leagues of Alhama, when scouts came hurrying into the place, with intelligence that the Moorish king was at hand with a powerful army. The Marques of Cadiz was filled with alarm lest De Aguilar should fall into the hands of the enemy. Forgetting his own danger, and thinking only of that of his friend, he dispatched a well-mounted messenger to ride full speed, and warn him not to approach.

The first determination of Alonzo de Aguilar, when he heard that the Moorish king was at hand, was to take a strong position in the mountains, and await his coming. The madness of an attempt with his handful of men to oppose an immense army was represented to him with such force as to induce him to abandon the idea; he then thought of throwing himself into Alhama, to share the fortunes of his friend; but it was now too late. The Moor would infallibly intercept him, and he should only give the marques the additional distress of beholding him captured beneath his walls. It was even urged upon him that he had no time for delay, if he would consult his own safety, which could only be insured by an immediate retreat into the Christian territory. This last opinion was confirmed by the return of scouts, who brought information that Muley Aben Hassan had received notice of his movements, and was rapidly advancing in quest of him. It was with infinite reluctance that Don Alonzo de Aguilar yielded to these united and powerful reasons. Proudly and sullenly he drew off his forces, laden with the baggage of the army, and made an unwilling retreat toward Antiquera. Muley Aben Hassan pursued him for some distance through the mountains, but soon gave up the chase and turned with his forces upon Alhama.

As the army approached the town they beheld the fields strewn with the dead bodies of their countrymen, who had fallen in defense of the place, and had been cast forth and left unburied by the Christians. There they lay, mangled, and exposed to every indignity; while droves of half-famished dogs were preying upon them, and fighting and howling over their hideous repast.* Furious at the sight, the Moors, in the first transports of their rage, attacked those ravenous animals: their next measure was to vent their fury upon the Christians. They rushed like madmen to the walls,

----

* Pulgar. Cronicæ.

applied scaling-ladders in all parts, without waiting for the necessary mantelets and other protections—thinking, by attacking suddenly and at various points, to distract the enemy and overcome them by the force of numbers.

The Marques of Cadiz, with his confederate commanders, distributed themselves along the walls to direct and animate their men in the defense. The Moors, in their blind fury, often assailed the most difficult and dangerous places. Darts, stones, and all kinds of missiles, were hurled down upon their defenseless heads. As fast as they mounted they were cut down, or dashed from the battlements, their ladders overturned, and all who were on them precipitated headlong below.

Muley Aben Hassan stormed with passion at the sight; he sent detachment after detachment to scale the walls—but in vain; they were like waves rushing upon a rock, only to dash themselves to pieces. The Moors lay in heaps beneath the wall, and among them many of the bravest cavaliers of Granada. The Christians, also, sallied frequently from the gates, and made great havoc in the irregular multitude of assailants.

On one of these occasions, the party was commanded by Don Juan de Vera, the same pious and high-handed knight who had borne the embassy to Muley Aben Hassan, demanding tribute. As this doughty cavalier, after a career of carnage, was slowly retreating to the gate, he heard a voice loudly calling after him in furious accents. "Turn back! turn back!" cried the voice; "thou who canst insult in hall, prove that thou canst combat in the field." Don Juan de Vera turned, and beheld the same Abencerrage whom he had struck with his sword in the Alhambra, for scoffing at the immaculate conception of the Blessed Virgin. All his holy zeal and pious indignation rekindled at the sight; he put lance in rest, and spurred his steed to finish this doctrinal dispute. Don Juan de Vera was a potent and irresistible arguer with his weapon; and he was aided (says Fray Antonio Agapida) by the peculiar virtue of his cause. At the very

first encounter, his lance entered the mouth of the Moor, and
hurled him to the earth, never more to utter word or breath.
Thus (continues the worthy friar) did this scoffing Infidel
receive a well-merited punishment, through the very organ
with which he had offended; and thus was the immaculate
conception miraculously vindicated from his foul aspersions.

The vigorous and successful defense of the Christians
now made Muley Aben Hassan sensible of his error in hurrying from Granada without the proper engines for a siege.
Destitute of all means to batter the fortifications, the town
remained uninjured, defying the mighty army which raged
and roamed before it. Incensed at being thus foiled, Muley
Aben Hassan gave orders to undermine the walls. The
Moors advanced with shouts to the attempt. They were received with a deadly fire from the ramparts, which drove
them from their works. Repeatedly were they repulsed,
and repeatedly did they return to the charge. The Christians not merely galled them from the battlements, but issued
forth and cut them down in the excavations they were attempting to form. The contest lasted throughout a whole
day, and by evening two thousand Moors were either killed
or wounded.

Muley Aben Hassan now abandoned all hope of carrying
the place by assault, and attempted to distress it into terms
by turning the channel of the river which runs by its walls.
On this stream the inhabitants depended for their supply of
water; the place being destitute of fountains and cisterns,
from which circumstance it is called Alhama *la seca*, or "the
dry."

A desperate conflict ensued on the banks of the river, the
Moors endeavoring to plant palisades in its bed to divert the
stream, and the Christians striving to prevent them. The
Spanish commanders exposed themselves to the utmost danger to animate their men, who were repeatedly driven back
into the town. The Marques of Cadiz was often up to his
knees in the stream, fighting hand to hand with the Moors.
The water ran red with blood, and was encumbered with

dead bodies. At length, the overwhelming numbers of the Moors gave them the advantage, and they succeeded in diverting the greater part of the water. The Christians had to struggle severely to supply themselves from the feeble rill which remained. They sallied to the river by a subterraneous passage; but the Moorish cross-bowmen stationed themselves on the opposite bank, keeping up a heavy fire upon the Christians, whenever they attempted to fill their vessels from the scanty and turbid stream. One party of the Christians had, therefore, to fight, while another drew water. At all hours of the day and night this deadly strife was maintained, until it seemed as if every drop of water were purchased with a drop of blood.

In the meantime, the sufferings in the town became intense. None but the soldiery and their horses were allowed the precious beverage so dearly earned, and even that in quantities that only tantalized their wants. The wounded, who could not sally to procure it, were almost destitute; while the unhappy prisoners, shut up in the mosques, were reduced to frightful extremities. Many perished raving mad, fancying themselves swimming in boundless seas, yet unable to assuage their thirst. Many of the soldiers lay parched and panting along the battlements, no longer able to draw a bowstring or hurl a stone; while above five thousand Moors, stationed upon a rocky height which overlooked part of the town, kept up a galling fire into it with slings and crossbows; so that the Marques of Cadiz was obliged to heighten the battlements by using the doors from the private dwellings.

The Christian cavaliers, exposed to this extreme peril, and in imminent danger of falling into the hands of the enemy, dispatched fleet messengers to Seville and Cordova, entreating the chivalry of Andalusia to hasten to their aid. They sent, likewise, imploring assistance from the king and queen, who at that time held their court in Medina del Campo. In the midst of their distress, a tank, or cistern, of water, was fortunately discovered in the city, which gave temporary relief to their sufferings.

CHAPTER SEVEN

HOW THE DUKE OF MEDINA SIDONIA, AND THE CHIVALRY OF ANDALUSIA, HASTENED TO THE RELIEF OF ALHAMA

THE perilous situation of the Christian cavaliers, pent up and beleaguered within the walls of Alhama, spread terror among their friends and anxiety throughout all Andalusia. Nothing, however, could equal the anguish of the Marchioness of Cadiz, the wife of the gallant Roderigo Ponce de Leon. In her deep distress, she looked round for some powerful noble, who had the means of rousing the country to the assistance of her husband. No one appeared more competent for the purpose than Don Juan de Guzman, the Duke of Medina Sidonia. He was one of the most wealthy and puissant grandees of Spain; his possessions extended over some of the most fertile parts of Andalusia, embracing towns, and seaports, and numerous villages. Here he reigned in feudal state, like a petty sovereign, and could at any time bring into the field an immense force of vassals and retainers.

The Duke of Medina Sidonia, and the Marques of Cadiz, however, were at this time deadly foes. An hereditary feud existed between them, which had often arisen to bloodshed and open war; for as yet the fierce contests between the proud and puissant Spanish nobles had not been completely quelled by the power of the crown, and in this respect they exerted a right of sovereignty, in leading their vassals against each other in open field.

The Duke of Medina Sidonia would have appeared, to many, the very last person to whom to apply for aid of the Marques of Cadiz; but the marchioness judged of him by the standard of her own high and generous mind. She knew him to be a gallant and courteous knight, and had already experienced the magnanimity of his spirit, having been relieved by him when besieged by the Moors in her husband's fortress of Arcos. To the duke, therefore, she applied in this moment of sudden calamity, imploring him to furnish succor to her husband. The event showed how well noble spirits understand each other. No sooner did the duke receive this appeal from the wife of his enemy than he generously forgot all feeling of animosity, and determined to go in person to his succor. He immediately dispatched a courteous letter to the marchioness, assuring her that in consideration of the request of so honorable and estimable a lady, and to rescue from peril so valiant a cavalier as her husband, whose loss would be great, not only to Spain, but to all Christendom, he would forego the recollection of all past grievances, and hasten to his relief with all the forces he could raise.

The duke wrote at the same time to the alcaydes of his towns and fortresses, ordering them to join him forthwith at Seville, with all the forces they could spare from their garrisons. He called on all the chivalry of Andalusia to make a common cause in the rescue of those Christian cavaliers, and he offered large pay to all volunteers who would resort to him with horses, armor, and provisions. Thus all who could be incited by honor, religion, patriotism, or thirst of gain, were induced to hasten to his standard, and he took the field with an army of five thousand horse and fifty thousand foot.* Many cavaliers of distinguished name accompanied him in this generous enterprise. Among these was the redoubtable Alonzo de Aguilar, the chosen friend of the Marques of Cadiz, and with him his younger brother, Gonsalvo Fernandez de Cordova, afterward renowned as the grand captain; Don Roderigo Giron, also, Master of the order of Calatrava, together with Martin Alonzo de Montemayor, and the Marques de Villena, esteemed the best lance in Spain. It was a gallant and splendid army, comprising the flower of Spanish

---

* Cronica de los Duques de Medina Sidonia, por Pedro de Medina. MS.

chivalry, and poured forth in brilliant array from the gates
of Seville, bearing the great standard of that ancient and
renowned city.

Ferdinand and Isabella were at Medina del Campo, when
tidings came of the capture of Alhama. The king was at
mass when he received the news, and ordered *Te Deum* to be
chanted for this signal triumph of the holy faith. When the
first flush of triumph had subsided, and the king learned the
imminent peril of the valorous Ponce de Leon and his companions, and the great danger that this stronghold might
again be wrested from their grasp, he resolved to hurry in
person to the scene of action. So pressing appeared to him
the emergency that he barely gave himself time to take a
hasty repast while horses were providing, and then departed
at furious speed for Andalusia, leaving a request for the
queen to follow him.* He was attended by Don Beltram de
la Cueva, Duke of Albuquerque, Don Inigo Lopez de Mendoza, Count of Tendilla, and Don Pedro Mauriques, Count
of Trevino, with a few more cavaliers of prowess and distinction. He traveled by forced journeys, frequently changing his jaded horses, being eager to arrive in time to take
command of the Andalusian chivalry. When he arrived
within five leagues of Cordova, the Duke of Albuquerque
remonstrated with him upon entering, with such incautious
haste, into the enemy's country. He represented to him
that there were troops enough assembled to succor Alhama,
and that it was not for him to venture his royal person in
doing what could be done by his subjects; especially as he
had such valiant and experienced captains to act for him.
"Besides, sire," added the duke, "your majesty should be-
think you that the troops about to take the field are mere
men of Andalusia, whereas your illustrious predecessors
never made an inroad into the territory of the Moors without being accompanied by a powerful force of the stanch and
iron warriors of old Castile."

---

* Illescas. Hist. Pontifical.

"Duke," replied the king, "your counsel might have been good had I not departed from Medina with the avowed determination of succoring these cavaliers in person. I am now near the end of my journey, and it would be beneath my dignity to change my intention, before even I had met with an impediment. I shall take the troops of this country who are assembled, without waiting for those of Castile, and, with the aid of God, shall prosecute my journey." [*]

As King Ferdinand approached Cordova, the principal inhabitants came forth to receive him. Learning, however, that the Duke of Medina Sidonia was already on the march, and pressing forward into the territory of the Moors, the king was all on fire to overtake him, and to lead in person the succor to Alhama. Without entering Cordova, therefore, he exchanged his weary horses for those of the inhabitants who had come forth to meet him, and pressed forward for the army. He dispatched fleet couriers in advance, requesting the Duke of Medina Sidonia to await his coming, that he might take command of the forces.

Neither the duke nor his companions in arms, however, felt inclined to pause in their generous expedition, and gratify the inclination of the king. They sent back missives, representing that they were far within the enemy's frontier, and it was dangerous either to pause or turn back. They had likewise received pressing entreaties from the besieged to hasten their speed, setting forth their great sufferings, and their hourly peril of being overwhelmed by the enemy.

The king was at Ponton del Maestre when he received these missives. So inflamed was he with zeal for the success of this enterprise that he would have penetrated into the kingdom of Granada with the handful of cavaliers who accompanied him, but they represented the rashness of such a journey, through the mountainous defiles of a hostile country, thickly beset with towns and castles. With some diffi-

---

[*] Pulgar. Cronica, p. 3, c. 2.

culty, therefore, he was dissuaded from his inclination, and prevailed upon to await tidings from the army in the frontier city of Antiquera.

CHAPTER EIGHT

SEQUEL OF THE EVENTS AT ALHAMA

WHILE all Andalusia was thus in arms, and pouring its chivalry through the mountain passes of the Moorish frontier, the garrison of Alhama was reduced to great extremity, and in danger of sinking under its sufferings before the promised succor could arrive. The intolerable thirst that prevailed in consequence of the scarcity of water, the incessant watch that had to be maintained over the vast force of enemies without, and the great number of prisoners within, and the wounds which almost every soldier had received in the incessant skirmishes and assaults, had worn grievously both flesh and spirit. The noble Ponce de Leon, Marques of Cadiz, still animated the soldiery, however, by word and example, sharing every hardship and being foremost in every danger; exemplifying that a good commander is the vital spirit of an army.

When Muley Aben Hassan heard of the vast force that was approaching under the command of the Duke of Medina Sidonia, and that Ferdinand was coming in person with additional troops, he perceived that no time was to be lost: Alhama must be carried by one powerful attack, or abandoned entirely to the Christians.

A number of Moorish cavaliers, some of the bravest youth of Granada, knowing the wishes of the king, proposed to undertake a desperate enterprise, which, if successful, must put Alhama in his power. Early one morning, when it was scarcely the gray of the dawn, about the time of changing the watch, these cavaliers approached the town, at a place considered inaccessible, from the steepness of the rocks on which the wall was founded; which, it was supposed, elevated the battlements beyond the reach of the longest scaling-ladder. The Moorish knights, aided by a number of the strongest and most active escaladors, mounted these rocks, and applied the ladders, without being discovered; for, to divert attention from them, Muley Aben Hassan made a false attack upon the town in another quarter.

The scaling party mounted with difficulty, and in small numbers; the sentinel was killed at his post, and seventy of the Moors made their way into the streets before an alarm was given. The guards rushed to the walls to stop the hostile throng that was still pouring in. A sharp conflict, hand to hand and man to man, took place on the battlements, and many on both sides fell. The Moors, whether wounded or slain, were thrown headlong without the walls; the scaling-ladders were overturned, and those who were mounting were dashed upon the rocks, and from thence tumbled upon the plain. Thus, in a little while, the ramparts were cleared by Christian prowess, led on by that valiant knight Don Alonzo Ponce, the uncle, and that brave esquire Pedro Pineda, nephew of the Marques of Cadiz.

The walls being cleared, these two kindred cavaliers now hastened with their forces in pursuit of the seventy Moors who had gained an entrance into the town. The main party of the garrison being engaged at a distance resisting the feigned attack of the Moorish king, this fierce band of Infidels had ranged the streets almost without opposition, and were making their way to the gates to throw them open to the army.* They were chosen men from among the Moorish forces, several of them gallant knights of the proudest families of Granada. Their footsteps through the city were in a manner printed in blood, and they were tracked by the bodies of those they had killed and wounded. They had attained the gate; most of the guard had fallen beneath their scimiters: a moment more, and Alhama would have been thrown open to the enemy.

---

* Zurita. lib. 20. c. 43.

Just at this juncture Don Alonzo Ponce and Pedro de Pineda reached the spot with their forces. The Moors had the enemy in front and rear; they placed themselves back to back, with their banner in the center. In this way they fought with desperate and deadly determination, making a rampart around them with the slain. More Christian troops arrived, and hemmed them in; but still they fought without asking for quarter. As their numbers decreased, they serried their circle still closer, defending their banner from assault; and the last Moor died at his post, grasping the standard of the Prophet. This standard was displayed from the walls, and the turbaned heads of the Moors were thrown down to the besiegers.*

Muley Aben Hassan tore his beard with rage at the failure of this attempt, and at the death of so many of his chosen cavaliers. He saw that all further effort was in vain; his scouts brought word that they had seen from the heights the long columns and flaunting banners of the Christian army approaching through the mountains. To linger would be to place himself between two bodies of the enemy. Breaking up his camp, therefore, in all haste, he gave up the siege of Alhama, and hastened back to Granada; and the last clash of his cymbals scarce died upon the ear from the distant hills, before the standard of the Duke of Sidonia was seen emerging in another direction from the defiles of the mountains.

When the Christians in Alhama beheld their enemies retreating on one side and their friends advancing on the other, they uttered shouts of joy and hymns of thanksgiving, for it was as a sudden relief from present death. Harassed by several weeks of incessant vigil and fighting, suffering from scarcity of provisions and almost continual thirst, they resembled skeletons rather than living men. It was a noble and gracious sight to behold the meeting of those two ancient foes, the Duke of Medina Sidonia and the Marques of Cadiz.

---

* Pedro de Pineda received the honor of knighthood from the hand of King Ferdinand, for his valor on this occasion (Alonzo Ponce was already knight).—See Zuñiga, Annales of Seville, lib. 12, an. 1482.

When the marques beheld his magnanimous deliverer approaching, he melted into tears; all past animosities only gave the greater poignancy to present feelings of gratitude and admiration; they clasped each other in their arms, and from that time forward were true and cordial friends.

While this generous scene took place between the commanders a sordid contest arose among their troops. The soldiers who had come to the rescue claimed a portion of the spoils of Alhama; and so violent was the dispute that both parties seized their arms. The Duke of Medina Sidonia interfered, and settled the question with his characteristic magnanimity. He declared that the spoil belonged to those who had captured the city. "We have taken the field," said he, "only for honor, for religion, and for the rescue of our countrymen and fellow Christians, and the success of our enterprise is a sufficient and a glorious reward. If we desire booty, there are sufficient Moorish cities yet to be taken to enrich us all." The soldiers were convinced by the frank and chivalrous reasoning of the duke; they replied to his speech by acclamations, and the transient broil was happily appeased.

The Marchioness of Cadiz, with the forethought of a loving wife, had dispatched her major domo with the army with a large supply of provisions. Tables were immediately spread beneath the tents, where the marques gave a banquet to the duke and the cavaliers who had accompanied him, and nothing but hilarity prevailed in this late scene of suffering and death.

A garrison of fresh troops was left in Alhama; and the veterans who had so valiantly captured and maintained it, returned to their homes, burdened with precious booty. The marques and duke, with their confederate cavaliers, repaired to Antiquera, where they were received with great distinction by the king, who honored the Marques of Cadiz with signal marks of favor. The duke then accompanied his late enemy, but now most zealous and grateful friend, the Marques of Cadiz, to his town of Marchena, where he received the reward of his generous conduct, in the thanks and blessings of the marchioness. The marques celebrated a sumptuous feast in honor of his guest; for a day and night, his palace was thrown open and was the scene of continual revel and festivity. When the duke departed for his estates at St. Lucar, the marques attended him for some distance on his journey; and when they separated, it was as the parting scene of brothers. Such was the noble spectacle exhibited to the chivalry of Spain, by these two illustrious rivals. Each reaped universal renown from the part he had performed in the campaign; the marques, from having surprised and captured one of the most important and formidable fortresses of the kingdom of Granada; and the duke, from having subdued his deadliest foe by a great act of magnanimity.

CHAPTER NINE

EVENTS AT GRANADA, AND RISE OF THE MOORISH KING
BOABDIL EL CHICO

THE Moorish king, Aben Hassan, returned baffled and disappointed from before the walls of Alhama, and was received with groans and smothered execrations by the people of Granada. The prediction of the santon was in every mouth, and appeared to be rapidly fulfilling; for the enemy was already strongly fortified in Alhama, in the very heart of the kingdom. The disaffection, which broke out in murmurs among the common people, fermented more secretly and dangerously among the nobles. Muley Aben Hassan was of a fierce and cruel nature; his reign had been marked with tyranny and bloodshed, and many chiefs of the family of the Abencerrages, the noblest lineage among the Moors, had fallen victims to his policy or vengeance. A deep plot was now formed to put an end to his oppressions and dispossess him of the throne. The situation of the royal household favored the conspiracy.

Muley Aben Hassan, though cruel, was uxorious; that is

to say, he had many wives, and was prone to be managed by
them by turns. He had two queens in particular whom he
had chosen from affection. One, named Ayxa, was a Moorish female; she was likewise termed in Arabic, La Horra,
or the chaste, from the spotless purity of her character.
While yet in the prime of her beauty, she bore a son to Aben
Hassan, the expected heir to his throne. The name of this
prince was Mahomet Abdalla, or, as he has more generally
been termed among historians, Boabdil. At his birth, the
astrologers, according to custom, cast his horoscope: they
were seized with fear and trembling when they beheld the
fatal portents revealed to their science. "Allah Achbar! God
is great!" exclaimed they; "He alone controls the fate of empires. It is written in the heavens that this prince shall sit
upon the throne of Granada, but that the downfall of the
kingdom shall be accomplished during his reign." From
this time, the prince was ever regarded with aversion by his
father; and the series of persecutions which he suffered, and
the dark prediction which hung over him from his infancy,
procured him the surname of El Zogoybi, or "the unfortunate." He is more commonly known by the appellation
of El Chico (the younger), to distinguish him from a usurp-
ing uncle.

The other favorite queen of Aben Hassan was named
Fatima, to which the Moors added the appellation of La Zoraya, or the light of dawn, from her effulgent beauty. She
was a Christian by birth, the daughter of the commander
Sancho Ximenes de Solis, and had been taken captive in her
tender youth.* The king, who was well stricken in years at
the time, became enamored of the blooming Christian maid;
he made her his sultana, and, like most old men who marry
in their dotage, resigned himself to her management. Zoraya became the mother of two princes, and her anxiety for
their advancement seemed to extinguish every other natural
feeling in her breast. She was as ambitious as she was

---

* Cronica del Gran Cardinal, cap. 71.   Salazar.

beautiful, and her ruling desire became to see one of her sons seated upon the throne of Granada. For this purpose, she made use of all her arts, and of the complete ascendency she had over the mind of her cruel husband, to undermine his other children in his affections, and to fill him with jealousies of their designs. Muley Aben Hassan was so wrought upon by her machinations that he publicly put several of his sons to death, at the celebrated fountain of Lions, in the court of the Alhambra—a place signalized in Moorish history as the scene of many sanguinary deeds.

The next measure of Zoraya was against her rival sultana, the virtuous Ayxa. She was past the bloom of her beauty, and had ceased to be attractive in the eyes of her husband. He was easily persuaded to repudiate her, and to confine her and her son in the tower of Comares, one of the principal towers of the Alhambra. As Boabdil increased in years, Zoraya beheld in him a formidable obstacle to the pretensions of her sons; for he was universally considered heir-apparent to the throne. The jealousies, suspicions and alarms of his tiger-hearted father were again excited; he was reminded, too, of the prediction that fixed the ruin of the kingdom during the reign of this prince. Muley Aben Hassan impiously set the stars at defiance: "The sword of the executioner," said he, "shall prove the falsehood of these lying horoscopes, and shall silence the ambition of Boabdil, as it has the presumption of his brothers."

The sultana Ayxa was secretly apprised of the cruel design of the old monarch. She was a woman of talents and courage, and, by means of her female attendants, concerted a plan for the escape of her son. A faithful servant was instructed to wait below the Alhambra, in the dead of the night, on the banks of the river Darro, with a fleet Arabian courser. The sultana, when the castle was in a state of deep repose, tied together the shawls and scarfs of herself and her female attendants, and lowered the youthful prince from the tower of Comares.* He made his way in safety down the

* Salazar. Cronica del Gran Cardinal, cap. 71.

steep rocky hill to the banks of the Darro, and, throwing himself on the Arabian courser, was thus spirited off to the city of Guadix in the Alpuxarras. Here he lay for some time concealed, until, gaining adherents, he fortified himself in the place, and set the machinations of his tyrant father at defiance. Such was the state of affairs in the royal household of Granada, when Muley Aben Hassan returned foiled from his expedition against Alhama. The faction, which had secretly formed among the nobles, determined to depose the old king Aben Hassan, and to elevate his son Boabdil to the throne. They concerted their measures with the latter, and an opportunity soon presented to put them in practice. Muley Aben Hassan had a royal country palace called Alixares, in the vicinity of Granada, to which he resorted occasionally to recreate his mind, during this time of perplexity. He had been passing one day among its bowers, when, on returning to the capital, he found the gates closed against him, and his son Mahomet Abdalla, otherwise called Boabdil, proclaimed king. "Allah Achbar! God is great!" exclaimed old Muley Aben Hassan; "it is in vain to contend against what is written in the book of fate. It was predestined that my son should sit upon the throne—Allah forefend the rest of the prediction!" The old monarch knew the inflammable nature of the Moors, and that it was useless to attempt to check any sudden blaze of popular passion. "A little while," said he, "and this rash flame will burn itself out, and the people when cool will listen to reason." So he turned his steed from the gate, and repaired to the city of Baza, where he was received with great demonstrations of loyalty. He was not a man to give up his throne without a struggle. A large part of the kingdom still remained faithful to him; he trusted that the conspiracy in the capital was but transient and partial, and that by suddenly making his appearance in its streets, at the head of a moderate force, he should awe the people again into allegiance. He took his measures with that combination of dexterity and daring which formed his character, and arrived one night under

***3

the walls of Granada, with five hundred chosen followers. Scaling the walls of the Alhambra, he threw himself with sanguinary fury into its silent courts. The sleeping inmates were roused from their repose only to fall by the exterminating scimiter. The rage of Aben Hassan spared neither age, nor rank, nor sex; the halls resounded with shrieks and yells, and the fountains ran red with blood. The alcayde, Aben Cimixer, retreated to a strong tower, with a few of the garrison and inhabitants. The furious Aben Hassan did not lose time in pursuing him; he was anxious to secure the city, and to wreak his vengeance on its rebellious inhabitants. Descending with his bloody band into the streets, he cut down the defenseless inhabitants, as, startled from their sleep, they rushed forth to learn the cause of the alarm. The city was soon completely roused; the people flew to arms; lights blazed in every street, revealing the scanty numbers of this band, that had been dealing such fatal vengeance in the dark. Muley Aben Hassan had been mistaken in his conjectures; the great mass of the people, incensed by his tyranny, were zealous in favor of his son. A violent, but transient conflict took place in the streets and squares; many of the followers of Aben Hassan were slain; the rest driven out of the city; and the old monarch, with the remnant of his band, retreated to his loyal city of Malaga.

Such was the commencement of those great internal feuds and divisions, which hastened the downfall of Granada. The Moors became separated into two hostile factions, headed by the father and the son, and several bloody encounters took place between them: yet they never failed to act with all their separate force against the Christians, as a common enemy, whenever an opportunity occurred.

CHAPTER TEN

ROYAL EXPEDITION AGAINST LOXA

KING FERDINAND held a council of war at Cordova, where it was deliberated what was to be done with Alhama. Most of the council advised that it should be demolished, inasmuch as, being in the center of the Moorish kingdom, it would be at all times liable to attack, and could only be maintained by a powerful garrison and at a vast expense. Queen Isabella arrived at Cordova in the midst of these deliberations and listened to them with surprise and impatience. "What!" said she, "shall we destroy the first fruits of our victories? shall we abandon the first place we have wrested from the Moors? Never let us suffer such an idea to occupy our minds. It would give new courage to the enemy, arguing fear or feebleness in our councils. You talk of the toil and expense of maintaining Alhama. Did we doubt, on undertaking this war, that it was to be a war of infinite cost, labor, and bloodshed? And shall we shrink from the cost, the moment a victory is obtained, and the question is merely to guard or abandon its glorious trophy? Let us hear no more about the destruction of Alhama; let us maintain its walls sacred, as a stronghold granted us by Heaven, in the center of this hostile land; and let our only consideration be how to extend our conquest and capture the surrounding cities."

The language of the queen infused a more lofty and chivalrous spirit into the royal council. Preparations were immediately made to maintain Alhama at all risk and expense; and King Ferdinand appointed as alcayde Luis Fernandez Puerto Carrero, senior of the house of Palma, supported by Diego Lopez de Ayola, Pero Ruiz de Alarcon, and Alonzo Ortis, captains of four hundred lances, and a body of one thousand foot; supplied with provisions for three months.

Ferdinand resolved also to lay siege to Loxa, a city of great strength, at no great distance from Alhama. For this purpose, he called upon all the cities and towns of Andalusia and Estramadura, and the domains of the orders of Santiago, Calatrava, and Alcantara, and of the priory of St. Juan, and the kingdom of Toledo, and beyond to the cities of Salamanca, Tero, and Valladolid, to furnish, according to their repartimientos or allotments, a certain quantity of bread, wine, and cattle, to be delivered at the royal camp before Loxa, one-half at the end of June, and one-half in July. These lands, also, together with Biscay and Guipiscoa, were ordered to send re-enforcements of horse and foot, each town furnishing its quota; and great diligence was used in providing bombards, powder, and other warlike munitions.

The Moors were no less active in their preparations, and sent missives into Africa, entreating supplies, and calling upon the Barbary princes to aid them in this war of the faith. To intercept all succor, the Castilian sovereigns stationed an armada of ships and galleys in the Straits of Gibraltar, under the command of Martin Diaz de Mina and Carlos de Valera, with orders to scour the Barbary coast and sweep every Moorish sail from the sea.

While these preparations were making, Ferdinand made an incursion, at the head of his army, into the kingdom of Granada, and laid waste the vega, destroying its hamlets and villages, ravaging the fields of grain, and driving away the cattle.

It was about the end of June that King Ferdinand departed from Cordova to sit down before the walls of Loxa. So confident was he of success, that he left a great part of the army at Ecija, and advanced with but five thousand cavalry and eight thousand infantry. The Marques of Cadiz, a warrior as wise as he was valiant, remonstrated against employing so small a force, and indeed was opposed to the measure altogether, as being undertaken precipitately and without sufficient preparation. King Ferdinand, however, was influenced by the counsel of Don Diego de Merlo, and was eager to strike a brilliant and decided blow. A vain-glorious confidence prevailed, about this time, among the Spanish cavaliers; they overrated their own prowess, or rather they undervalued and despised their enemy. Many of them believed that the Moors would scarcely remain in their city, when they saw the Christian troops advancing to assail it. The Spanish chivalry, therefore, marched gallantly and fearlessly, and almost carelessly, over the border, scantily supplied with the things needful for a besieging army, in the heart of an enemy's country. In the same negligent and confident spirit, they took up their station before Loxa.

The country around was broken and hilly, so that it was extremely difficult to form a combined camp. The river Xenil, which runs by the town, was compressed between high banks, and so deep as to be fordable with extreme difficulty; and the Moors had possession of the bridge. The king pitched his tents in a plantation of olives, on the banks of the river; the troops were distributed in different encampments on the heights, but separated from each other by deep rocky ravines, so as to be incapable of yielding each other prompt assistance. There was no room for the operation of the cavalry. The artillery, also, was so injudiciously placed as to be almost entirely useless. Alonzo of Aragon, Duke of Villahermosa, and illegitimate brother of the king, was present at the siege, and disapproved of the whole arrangement. He was one of the most able generals of his time, and especially renowned for his skill in battering fortified places. He recommended that the whole disposition of the camp should be changed, and that several bridges should be thrown across the river. His advice was adopted, but slowly and negligently followed, so that it was rendered of no avail. Among other oversights in this hasty and negligent expedition, the army had no supply of baked bread; and, in the hurry of encampment, there was no time to erect fur-naces. Cakes were therefore hastily made and baked on the coals, and for two days the troops were supplied in this irregular way.

King Ferdinand felt, too late, the insecurity of his position, and endeavored to provide a temporary remedy. There was a height near the city, called by the Moors Santo Albohacen, which was in front of the bridge. He ordered several of his most valiant cavaliers to take possession of this height, and to hold it as a check upon the enemy and a protection to the camp. The cavaliers chosen for this distinguished and perilous post were the Marques of Cadiz, the Marques of Villena, Don Roderigo Tellez Giron, Master of Calatrava, his brother the Count of Urena, and Don Alonzo de Aguilar. These valiant warriors, and tried companions in arms, led their troops with alacrity to the height, which soon glittered with the array of arms, and was graced by several of the most redoubtable pennons of warlike Spain.

Loxa was commanded at this time by an old Moorish alcayde, whose daughter was the favorite wife of Boabdil el Chico. The name of this Moor was Ibrahim Ali Atar, but he was generally known among the Spaniards as Alatar. He had grown gray in border warfare, was an implacable enemy of the Christians, and his name had long been the terror of the frontier. He was in the ninetieth year of his age, yet indomitable in spirit, fiery in his passions, sinewy and powerful in frame, deeply versed in warlike stratagem, and accounted the best lance in all Mauritania. He had three thousand horsemen under his command, veteran troops, with whom he had often scoured the borders; and he daily expected the old Moorish king, with re-enforcements.

Old Ali Atar had watched from his fortress every movement of the Christian army, and had exulted in all the errors of its commanders: when he beheld the flower of Spanish chivalry glittering about the height of Albohacen, his eye flashed with exultation. ''By the aid of Aliah,'' said he, ''I will give those pranking cavaliers a rouse.''

Ali Atar, privately, and by night, sent forth a large body of his chosen troops, to lie in ambush near one of the skirts of Albohacen. On the fourth day of the siege, he sallied across the bridge and made a feint attack upon the height.

The cavaliers rushed impetuously forth to meet him, leaving their encampment almost unprotected. Ali Atar wheeled and fled, and was hotly pursued. When the Christian cavaliers had been drawn a considerable distance from their encampment, they heard a vast shout behind them, and, looking round, beheld their encampment assailed by the Moorish force which had been placed in ambush and which had ascended a different side of the hill. The cavaliers desisted from the pursuit and hastened to prevent the plunder of their tents. Ali Atar, in his turn, wheeled and pursued them; and they were attacked in front and rear, on the summit of the hill. The contest lasted for an hour; the height of Albohacen was red with blood; many brave cavaliers fell, expiring among heaps of the enemy. The fierce Ali Atar fought with the fury of a demon, until the arrival of more Christian forces compelled him to retreat into the city. The severest loss to the Christians, in this skirmish, was that of Roderigo Tellez Giron, Master of Calatrava. As he was raising his arm to make a blow, an arrow pierced him just beneath the shoulder, at the open part of the corselet. He fell instantly from his horse, but was caught by Pedro Gasca, a cavalier of Avila, who conveyed him to his tent where he died. The king and queen, and the whole kingdom, mourned his death, for he was in the freshness of his youth, being but twenty-four years of age, and had proved himself a gallant and high-minded cavalier. A melancholy group collected about his corpse, on the bloody height of Albohacen: the knights of Calatrava mourned him as a commander; the cavaliers who were encamped on the height lamented him as their companion in arms, in a service of peril; while the Count de Urena grieved over him with the tender affection of a brother.

King Ferdinand now perceived the wisdom of the opinion of the Marques of Cadiz, and that his force was quite insufficient for the enterprise. To continue his camp in its present unfortunate position would cost him the lives of his bravest cavaliers, if not a total defeat, in case of re-enforcements to the enemy. He called a council of war, late in the evening of Saturday; and it was determined to withdraw the army, early the next morning, to Rio Frio, a short distance from the city, and there wait for additional troops from Cordova.

The next morning, early, the cavaliers on the height of Albohacen began to strike their tents. No sooner did Ali Atar behold this than he sallied forth to attack them. Many of the Christian troops, who had not heard of the intention to change the camp, seeing the tents struck and the Moors sallying forth, supposed that the enemy had been re-enforced in the night, and that the army was on the point of retreating. Without stopping to ascertain the truth or to receive orders, they fled in dismay, spreading confusion through the camp; nor did they halt until they had reached the Rock of the Lovers, about seven leagues from Loxa.*

The king and his commanders saw the imminent peril of the moment, and made face to the Moors, each commander guarding his quarter and repelling all assaults, while the tents were struck and the artillery and ammunition conveyed away. The king, with a handful of cavaliers, galloped to a rising ground, exposed to the fire of the enemy, calling upon the flying troops and endeavoring in vain to rally them. Setting upon the Moors, he and his cavaliers charged them so vigorously that they put a squadron to flight, slaying many with their swords and lances, and driving others into the river, where they were drowned. The Moors, however, were soon re-enforced and returned in great numbers. The king was in danger of being surrounded, and twice owed his safety to the valor of Don Juan de Ribera, Senior of Montemayor.

The Marques of Cadiz beheld, from a distance, the peril of his sovereign. Summoning about seventy horsemen to follow him, he galloped to the spot, threw himself between the king and the enemy, and, hurling his lance, transpierced one of the most daring of the Moors. For some time, he

* Pulgar. Cronica.

remained with no other weapon than his sword; his horse was wounded by an arrow, and many of his followers slain; but he succeeded in beating off the Moors, and rescuing the king from imminent jeopardy, whom he then prevailed upon to retire to less dangerous ground.

The marques continued, throughout the day, to expose himself to the repeated assaults of the enemy; he was ever found in the place of the greatest danger, and through his bravery a great part of the army and camp was preserved from destruction.*

It was a perilous day for the commanders; for in a retreat of the kind it is the noblest cavaliers who most expose themselves to save their people. The Duke of Medina Celi was struck to the ground, but rescued by his troops. The Count de Tendilla, whose tents were nearest to the city, received several wounds, and various other cavaliers of the most distinguished note were exposed to fearful jeopardy. The whole day was passed in bloody skirmishings, in which the hidalgos and cavaliers of the royal household distinguished themselves by their bravery; at length, the encampments being all broken up, and most of the artillery and baggage removed, the bloody height of Albohacen was abandoned and the neighborhood of Loxa evacuated. Several tents, a quantity of provisions, and a few pieces of artillery were left upon the spot, from the want of horses and mules to carry them off.

Ali Atar hung upon the rear of the retiring army, and harassed it until it reached Rio Frio; from thence Ferdinand returned to Cordova, deeply mortified, though greatly benefited, by the severe lesson he had received, which served to render him more cautious in his campaigns and more diffident of fortune. He sent letters to all parts, excusing his retreat, imputing it to the small number of his forces, and the circumstance that many of them were quotas sent from various cities, and not in royal pay; in the meantime, to console his

---

* Cura de los Palacios. c. 58.

troops for their disappointment, and to keep up their spirits, he led them upon another inroad to lay waste the vega of Granada.

CHAPTER ELEVEN

HOW MULEY ABEN HASSAN MADE A FORAY INTO THE LANDS OF MEDINA SIDONIA, AND HOW HE WAS RECEIVED

OLD Muley Aben Hassan had mustered an army, and marched to the relief of Loxa; but arrived too late—the last squadron of Ferdinand had already passed over the border. "They have come and gone," said he, "like a summer cloud, and all their vaunting has been mere empty thunder." He turned to make another attempt upon Alhama, the garrison of which was in the utmost consternation at the retreat of Ferdinand, and would have deserted the place had it not been for the courage and perseverance of the alcayde Luis Fernandez Puerto Carrero. That brave and loyal commander cheered up the spirits of his men, and kept the old Moorish king at bay, until the approach of Ferdinand, on his second incursion into the vega, obliged him to make an unwilling retreat to Malaga.

Muley Aben Hassan felt that it would be in vain, with his inferior force, to oppose the powerful army of the Christian monarch. But to remain idle and see his territories laid waste would ruin him in the estimation of his people. "If we cannot parry," said he, "we can strike; if we cannot keep our own lands from being ravaged, we can ravage the lands of the enemy." He inquired and learned that most of the chivalry of Andalusia, in their eagerness for a foray, had marched off with the king, and left their own country almost defenseless. The territories of the Duke of Medina Sidonia were particularly unguarded: here were vast plains of pasturage, covered with flocks and herds—the very country for a hasty inroad. The old monarch had a bitter grudge against the duke, for having foiled him at Alhama. "I'll give this cavalier a lesson," said he, exultingly, "that will cure him of his love of campaigning." So he prepared in all haste for a foray into the country about Medina Sidonia.

Muley Aben Hassan sallied out of Malaga with fifteen hundred horse and six thousand foot, and took the way by the seacoast, marching through Estiponia, and entering the Christian country between Gibraltar and Castellar. The only person that was likely to molest him on this route was one Pedro de Vargas; a shrewd, hardy, and vigilant soldier, alcayde of Gibraltar, and who lay ensconced in his old warrior rock as in a citadel. Muley Aben Hassan knew the watchful and daring character of the man, but had ascertained that his garrison was too small to enable him to make a sally, or at least to insure him any success. Still he pursued his march with great silence and caution; sent parties in advance to explore every pass where a foe might lie in ambush; cast many an anxious eye toward the old rock of Gibraltar, as its cloud-capped summit was seen towering in the distance on his left; nor did he feel entirely at ease until he had passed through the broken and mountainous country of Castellar, and descended into the plains. Here he encamped on the banks of the Celemin. From hence he sent four hundred corredors or fleet horsemen, armed with lances, who were to station themselves near Algeziras, and to keep a strict watch across the bay, upon the opposite fortress of Gibraltar. If the alcayde attempted to sally forth, they were to waylay and attack him, being almost four times his supposed force; and were to send swift tidings to the camp. In the meantime, two hundred corredors were sent to scour that vast plain called the Campina de Tarifa, abounding with flocks and herds; and two hundred more were to ravage the lands about Medina Sidonia. Muley Aben Hassan remained with the main body of the army, as a rallying point, on the banks of the Celemin.

The foraging parties scoured the country to such effect that they came driving vast flocks and herds before them, enough to supply the place of all that had been swept from the vega of Granada. The troops which had kept watch upon the rock of Gibraltar returned with word that they had not seen a Christian helmet stirring. The old king congratulated himself upon the secrecy and promptness with which he had conducted his foray, and upon having baffled the vigilance of Pedro de Vargas.

Muley Aben Hassan had not been so secret as he imagined; the watchful Pedro de Vargas had received notice of his movements. His garrison was barely sufficient for the defense of the place, and he feared to take the field and leave his fortress unguarded. Luckily, at this juncture, there arrived in the harbor of Gibraltar a squadron of the armed galleys stationed in the Strait, and commanded by Carlos de Valera. The alcayde immediately prevailed upon him to guard the place during his absence, and sallied forth at midnight with seventy horse. He made for the town of Castellar, which is strongly posted on a steep height, knowing that the Moorish king would have to return by this place. He ordered alarm-fires to be lighted upon the mountains, to give notice that the Moors were on the ravage, that the peasants might drive their flocks and herds to places of refuge; and he sent couriers, riding like mad, in every direction, summoning the fighting men of the neighborhood to meet him at Castellar.

Muley Aben Hassan saw, by the fires blazing about the mountains, that the country was rising. He struck his tents and pushed forward as rapidly as possible for the border; but he was incumbered with booty, and with the vast cavalgada swept from the pastures of the Campina de Tarifa. His scouts brought him word that there were troops in the field, but he made light of the intelligence, knowing that they could only be those of the alcayde of Gibraltar, and that he had not more than a hundred horsemen in his garrison. He threw in advance two hundred and fifty of his bravest troops, and with them the alcaydes of Marabella and Casares. Behind this vanguard was a great cavalgada of cattle; and in the rear marched the king, with the main force of his little army.

It was near the middle of a sultry summer day that they approached Castellar. De Vargas was on the watch, and beheld, by an immense cloud of dust, that they were descending one of the heights of that wild and broken country. The vanguard and rear guard were above half a league asunder, with the cavalgada between them; and a long and close forest hid them from each other. De Vargas saw that they could render but little assistance to each other in case of a sudden attack, and might be easily thrown in confusion. He chose fifty of his bravest horsemen, and, making a circuit, took his post secretly in a narrow glen opening into a defile between two rocky heights, through which the Moors had to pass. It was his intention to suffer the vanguard and the cavalgada to pass, and to fall upon the rear.

While thus lying perdue, six Moorish scouts, well mounted and well armed, entered the glen, examining every place that might conceal an enemy. Some of the Christians advised that they should slay these six men, and retreat to Gibraltar. "No," said De Vargas, "I have come out for higher game than these; and I hope, by the aid of God and Santiago, to do good work this day. I know these Moors well, and doubt not but that they may readily be thrown into confusion."

By this time the six horsemen approached so near that they were on the point of discovering the Christian ambush. De Vargas gave the word, and ten horsemen rushed forth upon them: in an instant four of the Moors rolled in the dust; the other two put spurs to their steeds, and fled toward their army, pursued by the ten Christians. About eighty of the Moorish vanguard came galloping to the relief of their companions; the Christians turned and fled toward their ambush. De Vargas kept his men concealed until the fugitives and their pursuers came clattering pell-mell into the glen. At a signal trumpet his men sallied forth with great heat and in close array. The Moors almost rushed upon their weapons before they perceived them; forty of the Infidels were overthrow, the rest turned their backs. "Forward!"

cried De Vargas; "let us give the vanguard a brush before it can be joined by the rear." So saying, he pursued the flying Moors down hill, and came with such force and fury upon the advance guard as to overturn many of them at the first encounter. As he wheeled off with his men the Moors discharged their lances; upon which he returned to the charge, and made great slaughter. The Moors fought valiantly for a short time, until the alcaydes of Marabella and Casares were slain, when they gave way and fled for the rear guard. In their flight, they passed through the cavalgada of cattle, threw the whole in confusion, and raised such a cloud of dust that the Christians could no longer distinguish objects. Fearing that the king and the main body might be at hand, and finding that De Vargas was badly wounded, they contented themselves with despoiling the slain and taking above twenty-eight horses, and then retreated to Castellar.

When the routed Moors came flying back upon the rear guard, Muley Aben Hassan feared that the people of Xeres were in arms. Several of his followers advised him to abandon the cavalgada, and retreat by another road. "No," said the old king, "he is no true soldier who gives up his booty without fighting." Putting spurs to his horse, he galloped forward through the center of the cavalgada, driving the cattle to the right and left. When he reached the field of battle, he found it strewed with the bodies of upward of one hundred Moors, among which were those of the two alcaydes. Enraged at the sight, he summoned all his crossbowmen and cavalry, pushed on to the very gates of Castellar, and set fire to two houses close to the walls. Pedro de Vargas was too severely wounded to sally forth in person; but he ordered out his troops and there was brisk skirmishing under the walls, until the king drew off and returned to the scene of the recent encounter. Here he had the bodies of the principal warriors laid across mules, to be interred honorably at Malaga; the rest of the slain were buried on the field of battle. Then, gathering together the scattered cavalgada, he paraded it slowly, in an immense line, past the walls of Castellar, by way of taunting his foe.

With all his fierceness, old Muley Aben Hassan had a gleam of warlike courtesy, and admired the hardy and sol- dierlike character of Pedro de Vargas. He summoned two Christian captives, and demanded what were the revenues of the alcayde of Gibraltar. They told him that, among other things, he was entitled to one out of every drove of cattle that passed his boundaries. "Allah forbid," cried the old monarch, "that so brave a cavalier should be defrauded of his dues."

He immediately chose twelve of the finest cattle from the twelve droves which formed the cavalgada. These he gave in charge to an alfaqui, to deliver to Pedro de Vargas. "Tell him," said he, "that I crave his pardon for not having sent these cattle sooner; but I have this moment learned the nat- ure of his rights, and I hasten to satisfy them, with the punctuality due to so worthy a cavalier. Tell him, at the same time, that I had no idea the alcayde of Gibraltar was so active and vigilant in collecting his tolls."

The brave alcayde relished the stern, soldierlike pleasan- try of the old Moorish monarch. He ordered a rich silken vest, and a scarlet mantle, to be given to the alfaqui, and dismissed him with great courtesy. "Tell his majesty," said he, "that I kiss his hands for the honor he has done me, and regret that my scanty force has not permitted me to give him a more signal reception, on his coming into these parts. Had three hundred horsemen, whom I have been promised from Xeres, arrived in time, I might have served up an entertainment more befitting such a monarch. I trust, however, they will arrive in the course of the night, in which case his majesty may be sure of a royal regale at the dawning."

Muley Aben Hassan shook his head when he received the reply of De Vargas. "Allah preserve us," said he, "from any visitation of these hard riders of Xeres! a handful of troops, acquainted with the wild passes of these mountains, may destroy an army encumbered as ours is with booty."

It was some relief to the king, however, to learn that the hardy alcayde of Gibraltar was too severely wounded to take the field in person. He immediately beat a retreat, with all speed, before the close of day, hurrying with such precipitation that the cavalgada was frequently broken, and scattered among the rugged defiles of the mountains; and above five thousand of the cattle turned back, and were regained by the Christians. Muley Aben Hassan returned triumphantly with the residue to Malaga, glorying in the spoils of the Duke of Medina Sidonia.

King Ferdinand was mortified at finding his incursion into the vega of Granada counterbalanced by this inroad into his dominions, and saw that there were two sides to the game of war, as to all other games. The only one who reaped real glory in this series of inroads and skirmishings was Pedro de Vargas, the stout alcayde of Gibraltar.*

CHAPTER TWELVE

FORAY OF SPANISH CAVALIERS AMONG THE MOUNTAINS OF MALAGA

THE foray of old Muley Aben Hassan had touched the pride of the Andalusian chivalry, and they determined on retaliation. For this purpose, a number of the most distinguished cavaliers assembled at Antiquera, in the month of March, 1483. The leaders of the enterprise were the gallant Marques of Cadiz; Don Pedro Henriquez, adelantado of Andalusia; Don Juan de Silva, Count of Cifuentes, and bearer of the royal standard, who commanded in Seville; Don Alonzo de Cardenas, Master of the religious and military order of Santiago; and Don Alonzo de Aguilar. Several other cavaliers of note hastened to take part in the enterprise; and in a little while about twenty-seven hundred horse and several companies of foot were assembled within the old

---

* Alonzo de Paleneca. l. 28. c. 3.

warlike city of Antiquera, comprising the very flower of
Andalusian chivalry.

A council of war was held by the chiefs to determine in
what quarter they should strike a blow. The rival Moorish
kings were waging civil war with each other in the vicinity
of Granada; and the whole country lay open to inroads.
Various plans were proposed by the different cavaliers. The
Marques of Cadiz was desirous of scaling the walls of Zahara
and regaining possession of that important fortress. The
Master of Santiago, however, suggested a wider range and
a still more important object. He had received information
from his adalides, who were apostate Moors, that an incursion might be safely made into a mountainous region near
Malaga, called the Axarquia. Here were valleys of pasture
land well stocked with flocks and herds; and there were numerous villages and hamlets, which would be an easy prey.
The city of Malaga was too weakly garrisoned, and had too
few cavalry, to send forth any force in opposition; nay, he
added, they might even extend their ravages to its very
gates, and peradventure carry that wealthy place by sudden
assault.

The adventurous spirits of the cavaliers were inflamed by
this suggestion; in their sanguine confidence they already
beheld Malaga in their power, and they were eager for the
enterprise. The Marques of Cadiz endeavored to interpose
a little cool caution. He likewise had apostate adalides, the
most intelligent and experienced on the borders; among
these, he placed especial reliance on one named Luis Amar,
who knew all the mountains and valleys of the country. He
had received from him a particular account of these mountains of the Axarquia.* Their savage and broken nature
was a sufficient defense for the fierce people who inhabited

---

*Pulgar, in his Chronicle, reverses the case, and makes the Marques
of Cadiz recommend the expedition to the Axarquia; but Fray Antonio
Agapida is supported in his statement by that most veracious and contemporary chronicler, Andreas Bernaldes, curate of Los Palacios.

them, who, manning their rocks, and their tremendous passes, which were often nothing more than the deep dry beds of torrents, might set whole armies at defiance. Even if vanquished they afforded no spoil to the victor. Their houses were little better than bare walls, and they would drive off their scanty flocks and herds to the fastnesses of the mountains.

The sober counsel of the marques, however, was over-ruled. The cavaliers, accustomed to mountain warfare, considered themselves and their horses equal to any wild and rugged expedition, and were flushed with the idea of terminating their foray by a brilliant assault upon Malaga.

Leaving all heavy baggage at Antiquera, and all such as had horses too weak for this mountain scramble, they set forth, full of spirit and confidence. Don Alonzo de Aguilar, and the adelantado of Andalusia, led the squadron of advance. The Count of Cifuentes followed, with certain of the chivalry of Seville. Then came the battalion of the most valiant Roderigo Ponce de Leon, Marques of Cadiz; he was accompanied by several of his brothers and nephews, and many cavaliers, who sought distinction under his banner; and this family band attracted universal attention and applause, as they paraded in martial state through the streets of Antiquera. The rear guard was led by Don Alonzo Cardenas, Master of Santiago, and was composed of the knights of his order, and the cavaliers of Ecija, with certain men-at-arms of the Holy Brotherhood, whom the king had placed under his command. The army was attended by a great train of mules, laden with provisions for a few days' supply, until they should be able to forage among the Moorish villages. Never did a more gallant and self-confident little army tread the earth. It was composed of men full of health and vigor, to whom war was a pastime and delight. They had spared no expense in their equipments, for never was the pomp of war carried to a higher pitch than among the proud chivalry of Spain. Cased in armor richly inlaid and embossed, decked with rich surcoats and waving plumes, and

superbly mounted on Andalusian steeds, they pranced out
of Antiquera with banners flying and their various devices
and armorial bearings ostentatiously displayed; and, in the
confidence of their hopes, promised the inhabitants to enrich
them with the spoils of Malaga.

In the rear of this warlike pageant followed a peaceful
band, intent upon profiting by the anticipated victories.
They were not the customary wretches that hover about
armies to plunder and strip the dead, but goodly and sub-
stantial traders from Seville, Cordova, and other cities of
traffic. They rode sleek mules, and were clad in goodly raiment, with long leathern purses at their girdles, well filled
with pistoles and other golden coin. They had heard of the
spoils wasted by the soldiery at the capture of Alhama, and
were provided with moneys to buy up the jewels and precious stones, the vessels of gold and silver, and the rich silks
and cloths, that should form the plunder of Malaga. The
proud cavaliers eyed these sons of traffic with great disdain,
but permitted them to follow for the convenience of the troops,
who might otherwise be overburdened with booty.

It had been intended to conduct this expedition with great
celerity and secrecy; but the noise of their preparations had
already reached the city of Malaga. The garrison, it is true,
was weak; but it possessed a commander who was himself a
host. This was Muley Abdallah, commonly called El Zagal,
or the valiant. He was younger brother of Muley Aben
Hassan, and general of the few forces which remained faithful to the old monarch. He possessed equal fierceness of
spirit with his brother, and surpassed him in craft and vigilance. His very name was a war-cry among his soldiery,
who had the most extravagant opinion of his prowess.

El Zagal suspected that Malaga was the object of this
noisy expedition. He consulted with old Bexir, a veteran
Moor, who governed the city. "If this army of marauders
should reach Malaga," said he, "we should hardly be able
to keep them without its walls. I will throw myself, with a
small force, into the mountains; rouse the peasantry, take

possession of the passes, and endeavor to give these Spanish cavaliers sufficient entertainment upon the road."

It was on a Wednesday that the pranking army of high-mettled warriors issued forth from the ancient gates of Antiquera. They marched all day and night, making their way, secretly as they supposed, through the passes of the mountains. As the tract of country they intended to maraud was far in the Moorish territories, near the coast of the Mediterranean, they did not arrive there until late in the following day. In passing through these stern and lofty mountains, their path was often along the bottom of a barranco, or deep rocky valley, with a scanty stream dashing along it, among the loose rocks and stones which it had broken and rolled down in the time of its autumnal violence. Sometimes their road was a mere rambla, or dry bed of a torrent, cut deep into the mountains and filled with their shattered fragments. These barrancos and ramblas were overhung by immense cliffs and precipices, forming the lurking-places of ambuscades during the wars between the Moors and Spaniards, as in after times they have become the favorite haunts of robbers to waylay the unfortunate traveler.

As the sun went down, the cavaliers came to a lofty part of the mountains, commanding to the right a distant glimpse of a part of the fair vega of Malaga, with the blue Mediterranean beyond; and they hailed it with exultation as a glimpse of the promised land. As the night closed in, they reached the chain of little valleys and hamlets locked up among these rocky heights, and known among the Moors by the name of the Axarquia. Here their vaunting hopes were destined to meet with the first disappointment. The inhabitants had heard of their approach; they had conveyed away their cattle and effects, and, with their wives and children, had taken refuge in the towers and fastnesses of the mountains.

Enraged at their disappointment, the troops set fire to the deserted houses, and pressed forward, hoping for better fortune as they advanced. Don Alonzo de Aguilar, and the other cavaliers in the vanguard, spread out their forces to lay waste the country; capturing a few lingering herds of cattle, with the Moorish peasants who were driving them to some place of safety.

While this marauding party carried fire and sword in the advance, and lighted up the mountain cliffs with the flames of the hamlets, the Master of Santiago, who brought up the rear guard, maintained strict order, keeping his knights together in martial array, ready for attack or defense, should an enemy appear. The men-at-arms of the Holy Brotherhood attempted to roam in quest of booty; but he called them back, and rebuked them severely.

At length they came to a part of the mountain completely broken up by barrancos and ramblas, of vast depth, and shagged with rocks and precipices. It was impossible to maintain the order of march; the horses had no room for action, and were scarcely manageable, having to scramble from rock to rock, and up and down frightful declivities, where there was scarce footing for a mountain goat. Passing by a burning village, the light of the flames revealed their perplexed situation. The Moors, who had taken refuge in a watch-tower on an impending height, shouted with exultation when they looked down upon these glistening cavaliers struggling and stumbling among the rocks. Sallying forth from their tower, they took possession of the cliffs which overhung the ravine, and hurled darts and stones upon the enemy. It was with the utmost grief of heart that the good Master of Santiago beheld his brave men falling like helpless victims around him, without the means of resistance or revenge. The confusion of his followers was increased by the shouts of the Moors, multiplied by the echoes of every crag and cliff, as if they were surrounded by innumerable foes. Being entirely ignorant of the country, in their struggles to extricate themselves they plunged into other glens and defiles, where they were still more exposed to danger. In this extremity, the Master of Santiago dispatched messengers in search of succor. The Marques of Cadiz, like a loyal companion in arms, hastened to his aid with his cavalry; his approach checked the assaults of the enemy, and the master was at length enabled to extricate his troops from the defile.

In the meantime, Don Alonzo de Aguilar and his companions, in their eager advance, had likewise got entangled in deep glens and the dry beds of torrents, where they had been severely galled by the insulting attacks of a handful of Moorish peasants, posted on the impending precipices. The proud spirit of De Aguilar was incensed at having the game of war thus turned upon him, and his gallant forces domineered over by mountain boors, whom he had thought to drive, like their own cattle, to Antiquera. Hearing, however, that his friend the Marques of Cadiz, and the Master of Santiago, were engaged with the enemy, he disregarded his own danger, and, calling together his troops, returned to assist them, or rather to partake their perils. Being once more assembled together, the cavaliers held a hasty council, amid the hurling of stones and the whistling of arrows; and their resolves were quickened by the sight, from time to time, of some gallant companion in arms laid low. They determined that there was no spoil in this part of the country to repay for the extraordinary peril; and that it was better to abandon the herds they had already taken, which only embarrassed their march, and to retreat with all speed to less dangerous ground.

The adalides or guides were ordered to lead the way out of this place of carnage. These, thinking to conduct them by the most secure route, led them by a steep and rocky pass, difficult for the foot-soldiers, but almost impracticable to the cavalry. It was overhung with precipices from whence showers of stones and arrows were poured upon them, accompanied by savage yells which appalled the stoutest heart. In some places they could pass but one at a time, and were often transpierced, horse and rider, by the Moorish darts, impeding the progress of their comrades by their dying struggles. The surrounding precipices were lighted up by a thousand alarm-fires; every crag and cliff had its flame, by the light of which they beheld their foes, bounding from rock to rock, and looking more like fiends than mortal men.

Either through terror and confusion, or through real ignorance of the country, their guides, instead of conducting them out of the mountains, led them deeper into their fatal recesses. The morning dawned upon them in a narrow rambla, its bottom formed of broken rocks, where once had raved along the mountain torrent; while above there beetled great arid cliffs, over the brows of which they beheld the turbaned heads of their fierce and exulting foes.   What a different appearance did the unfortunate cavaliers present from that of the gallant band that marched so vauntingly out of Antiquera!   Covered with dust, and blood, and wounds, and haggard with fatigue and horror, they looked like victims rather than like warriors.   Many of their banners were lost, and not a trumpet was heard to rally up their sinking spirits.   The men turned with imploring eyes to their commanders; while the hearts of the cavaliers were ready to burst with rage and grief, at the merciless havoc made among their faithful followers.

All day they made ineffectual attempts to extricate themselves from the mountains.   Columns of smoke rose from the heights, where, in the preceding night, had blazed the alarm-fire.   The mountaineers assembled from every direction; they swarmed at every pass, getting in the advance of the Christians, and garrisoning the cliffs like so many towers and battlements.

Night closed again upon the Christians, when they were shut up in a narrow valley traversed by a deep stream, and surrounded by precipices which seemed to reach the skies, and on which blazed and flared the alarm-fires.   Suddenly a new cry was heard resounding along the valley: "El Zagal! El Zagal!" echoed from cliff to cliff.   "What cry is that?" said the Master of Santiago.   "It is the war-cry of El Zagal, the Moorish general," said an old Castilian soldier; "he must be coming in person, with the troops of Malaga."

The worthy master turned to his knights: "Let us die," said he, "making a road with our hearts, since we cannot

with our swords. Let us scale the mountain, and sell our
lives dearly, instead of staying here to be tamely butchered.''

So saying, he turned his steed against the mountain, and
spurred him up its flinty side. Horse and foot followed his
example, eager, if they could not escape, to have at least a
dying blow at the enemy. As they struggled up the height,
a tremendous storm of darts and stones was showered upon
them by the Moors. Sometimes a fragment of rock came
bounding and thundering down, plowing its way through the
center of their host. The foot-soldiers, faint with weariness
and hunger, or crippled by wounds, held by the tails and
manes of the horses to aid them in their ascent; while the
horses, losing their foothold among the loose stones, or receiving some sudden wound, tumbled down the steep declivity, steed, rider, and soldier, rolling from crag to crag, until
they were dashed to pieces in the valley. In this desperate
struggle the alferez or standard-bearer of the master, with
his standard, was lost; as were many of his relations and his
dearest friends. At length he succeeded in attaining the crest
of the mountain; but it was only to be plunged in new difficulties. A wilderness of rocks and rugged dells lay before
him, beset by cruel foes. Having neither banner nor trumpet
by which to rally his troops, they wandered apart, each intent upon saving himself from the precipices of the mountains, and the darts of the enemy. When the pious Master
of Santiago beheld the scattered fragments of his late gallant
force, he could not restrain his grief. ''O God!'' exclaimed
he, ''great is Thine anger this day against Thy servants.
Thou hast converted the cowardice of these Infidels into desperate valor, and hast made peasants and boors victorious
over armed men of battle.''

He would fain have kept with his foot-soldiers, and, gathering them together, have made head against the enemy;
but those around him entreated him to think only of his personal safety. To remain was to perish without striking a
blow; to escape was to preserve a life that might be devoted
to vengeance on the Moors. The master reluctantly yielded

to the advice. "O Lord of hosts!" exclaimed he again, "from Thy wrath do I fly; not from these Infidels: they are but instruments in Thy hands, to chastise us for our sins." So saying, he sent the guides in the advance, and, putting spurs to his horse, dashed through a defile of the mountains, before the Moors could intercept him. The moment the master put his horse to speed, his troops scattered in all directions. Some endeavored to follow his traces, but were confounded among the intricacies of the mountain. They fled hither and thither, many perishing among the precipices, others being slain by the Moors, and others taken prisoners.

The gallant Marques of Cadiz, guided by his trusty adalid, Luis Amar, had ascended a different part of the mountain. He was followed by his friend, Don Alonzo de Aguilar, the adelantado, and the Count of Cifuentes; but, in the darkness and confusion, the bands of these commanders became separated from each other. When the marques attained the summit, he looked around for his companions in arms; but they were no longer following him, and there was no trumpet to summon them. It was a consolation to the marques, however, that his brothers, and several of his relations, with a number of his retainers, were still with him: he called his brothers by name, and their replies gave comfort to his heart.

His guide now led the way into another valley, where he would be less exposed to danger: when he had reached the bottom of it, the marques paused to collect his scattered followers, and to give time for his fellow-commanders to rejoin him. Here he was suddenly assailed by the troops of El Zagal, aided by the mountaineers from the cliffs. The Christians, exhausted and terrified, lost all presence of mind; most of them fled, and were either slain or taken captive. The marques and his valiant brothers, with a few tried friends, made a stout resistance. His horse was killed under him; his brothers, Don Diego and Don Lope, with his two nephews, Don Lorenzo and Don Manuel, were one by one swept from his side, either transfixed with darts and lances by the soldiers of El Zagal, or crushed by stones from the

VOL. III.   * * *4

heights.   The marques was a veteran warrior, and had been
in many a bloody battle; but never before had death fallen
so thick and close around him.   When he saw his remaining
brother, Don Beltram, struck out of his saddle by a fragment
of a rock, and his horse running wildly about without his
rider, he gave a cry of anguish and stood bewildered and
aghast.   A few faithful followers surrounded him, and entreated him to fly for his life.   He would still have remained,
to have shared the fortunes of his friend Don Alonzo de
Aguilar, and his other companions in arms; but the forces of
El Zagal were between him and them, and death was whistling by on every wind.   Reluctantly, therefore, he consented
to fly.   Another horse was brought him: his faithful adalid
guided him by one of the steepest paths, which lasted for
four leagues; the enemy still hanging on his traces, and
thinning the scanty ranks of his followers.   At length the
marques reached the extremity of the mountain defiles, and,
with a haggard remnant of his men, escaped by dint of hoof
to Antiquera.

The Count of Cifuentes, with a few of his retainers, in
attempting to follow the Marques of Cadiz, wandered into a
narrow pass, where they were completely surrounded by the
band of El Zagal.   Finding all attempts at escape impossible,
and resistance vain, the worthy count surrendered himself
prisoner, as did also his brother Don Pedro de Silva, and the
few of his retainers who survived.

The dawn of day found Don Alonzo de Aguilar, with a
handful of his followers, still among the mountains.   They
had attempted to follow the Marques of Cadiz, but had been
obliged to pause and defend themselves against the thicken-
ing forces of the enemy.   They at length traversed the mountain, and reached the same valley where the marques had
made his last disastrous stand.   Wearied and perplexed, they
sheltered themselves in a natural grotto, under an overhanging rock, which kept off the darts of the enemy; while a bub-
bling fountain gave them the means of slaking their raging
thirst, and refreshing their exhausted steeds.   As day broke,

the scene of slaughter unfolded its horrors. There lay the noble brothers and nephews of the gallant marques, transfixed with darts or gashed and bruised with unseemly wounds; while many other gallant cavaliers lay stretched out dead and dying around, some of them partly stripped and plundered by the Moors. De Aguilar was a pious knight, but his piety was not humble and resigned, like that of the worthy Master of Santiago. He imprecated holy curses upon the Infidels, for having thus laid low the flower of Christian chivalry; and he vowed in his heart bitter vengeance upon the surrounding country.

By degrees, the little force of De Aguilar was augmented by numbers of fugitives, who issued from caves and chasms, where they had taken refuge in the night. A little band of mounted knights was gradually formed; and the Moors having abandoned the heights to collect the spoils of the slain, this gallant but forlorn squadron was enabled to retreat to Antiquera.

This disastrous affair lasted from Thursday evening, throughout Friday, the twenty-first of March, the festival of St. Benedict. It is still recorded in Spanish calendars as the defeat of the mountains of Malaga; and the spot where the greatest slaughter took place is pointed out to the present day, and is called *la Cuesta de la Matanza*, or The Hill of the Massacre. The principal leaders who survived returned to Antiquera. Many of the knights took refuge in Alhama and other towns; many wandered about the mountains for eight days, living on roots and herbs, hiding themselves during the day and sallying forth at night. So enfeebled and disheartened were they that they offered no resistance if attacked. Three or four soldiers would surrender to a Moorish peasant; and even the women of Malaga sallied forth and made prisoners. Some were thrown into the dungeons of frontier towns, others led captive to Granada; but by far the greater number were conducted to Malaga, the city they had threatened to attack. Two hundred and fifty principal cavaliers, alcaydes, commanders, and hidalgos, of generous blood,

were confined in the Alcazaba or citadel of Malaga, to await
their ransom; and five hundred and seventy of the common
soldiery were crowded in an inclosure or courtyard of the
Alcazaba, to be sold as slaves.*

Great spoils were collected of splendid armor and weapons
taken from the slain, or thrown away by the cavaliers in
their flight; and many horses, magnificently caparisoned,
together with numerous standards—all which were paraded
in triumph into the Moorish towns.

The merchants also, who had come with the army, intending to traffic in the spoils of the Moors, were themselves made
objects of traffic. Several of them were driven like cattle,
before the Moorish viragos, to the market of Malaga; and in
spite of all their adroitness in trade, and their attempts to
buy themselves off at a cheap ransom, they were unable
to purchase their freedom without such draughts upon their
money-bags at home as drained them to the very bottom.

CHAPTER THIRTEEN

EFFECTS OF THE DISASTERS AMONG THE MOUNTAINS OF MALAGA

THE people of Antiquera had scarcely recovered from the
tumult of excitement and admiration, caused by the departure of the gallant band of cavaliers upon their foray, when
they beheld the scattered wrecks flying for refuge to their
walls. Day after day, and hour after hour, brought some
wretched fugitive, in whose battered plight, and haggard
woebegone demeanor, it was almost impossible to recognize
the warrior whom they had lately seen to issue so gayly and
gloriously from their gates.

The arrival of the Marques of Cadiz, almost alone, covered with dust and blood, his armor shattered and defaced,

---

* Cura de los Palacios.

his countenance the picture of despair, filled every heart with
sorrow, for he was greatly beloved by the people. The multitude asked where was the band of brothers which had rallied round him as he went forth to the field; and when they
heard that they had, one by one, been slaughtered at his
side, they hushed their voices, or spake to each other only in
whispers as he passed, gazing at him in silent sympathy. No
one attempted to console him in so great an affliction, nor did
the good marques speak ever a word, but, shutting himself
up, brooded in lonely anguish over his misfortune. It was
only the arrival of Don Alonzo de Aguilar that gave him a
gleam of consolation, for, amid the shafts of death that had
fallen so thickly among his family, he rejoiced to find that his
chosen friend and brother in arms had escaped uninjured.

For several days every eye was turned, in an agony of
suspense, toward the Moorish border, anxiously looking, in
every fugitive from the mountains, for the lineaments of
some friend or relation, whose fate was yet a mystery. At
length every hope and doubt subsided into certainty; the
whole extent of this great calamity was known, spreading
grief and consternation throughout the land, and laying desolate the pride and hopes of palaces. It was a sorrow that
visited the marble hall and silken pillow. Stately dames
mourned over the loss of their sons, the joy and glory of
their age; and many a fair cheek was blanched with woe
that had lately mantled with secret admiration. "All Andalusia," says a historian of the time, "was overwhelmed by
a great affliction; there was no drying of the eyes which wept
in her." *

Fear and trembling reigned, for a time, along the frontier. Their spear seemed broken, their buckler cleft in
twain: every border town dreaded an attack, and the mother
caught her infant to her bosom when the watch-dog howled
in the night, fancying it the war-cry of the Moor. All, for
a time, seemed lost; and despondency even found its way to

---

* Cura de los Palacios.

the royal breasts of Ferdinand and Isabella, amid the splendors of their court.

Great, on the other hand, was the joy of the Moors, when they saw whole legions of Christian warriors brought captive into their towns, by rude mountain peasantry. They thought it the work of Allah in favor of the faithful. But when they recognized, among the captives thus dejected and broken down, some of the proudest of Christian chivalry; when they saw several of the banners and devices of the noblest houses of Spain, which they had been accustomed to behold in the foremost of the battle, now trailed ignominiously through their streets; when, in short, they witnessed the arrival of the Count of Cifuentes, the royal standard-bearer of Spain, with his gallant brother Don Pedro de Silva, brought prisoners into the gates of Granada, there were no bounds to their exultation. They thought that the days of their ancient glory were about to return, and that they were to renew their career of triumph over the unbelievers.

The Christian historians of the time are sorely perplexed to account for this misfortune; and why so many Christian knights, fighting in the cause of the holy faith, should thus miraculously, as it were, be given captive to a handful of Infidel boors; for we are assured that all this rout and destruction was effected by five hundred foot and fifty horse, and those mere mountaineers without science or discipline.* "It was intended," observes one historiographer, "as a lesson to their confidence and vainglory; overrating their own prowess, and thinking that so chosen a band of chivalry had but to appear in the land of the enemy and conquer. It was to teach them that the race is not to the swift, nor the battle to the strong, but that God alone giveth the victory."

The worthy father Fray Antonio Agapida, however, asserts it to be a punishment for the avarice of the Spanish warriors. They did not enter the kingdom of the Infidels with the pure spirit of Christian knights, zealous only for the

---

* Cura de los Palacios.

glory of the faith, but rather as greedy men of traffic, to
enrich themselves by vending the spoils of the Infidels. Instead of preparing themselves by confession and communion,
and executing their testaments, and making donations and
bequests to churches and convents, they thought only of ar-
ranging bargains and sales of their anticipated booty. Instead of taking with them holy monks to aid them with their
prayers, they were followed by a train of trading men, to
keep alive their worldly and sordid ideas, and to turn what
ought to be holy triumphs into scenes of brawling traffic.
Such is the opinion of the excellent Agapida, in which he is
joined by that most worthy and upright of chroniclers, the
curate of Los Palacios. Agapida comforts himself, however,
with the reflection that this visitation was meant in mercy
to try the Castilian heart, and to extract from its present
humiliation the elements of future success, as gold is ex-
tracted from amid the impurities of earth; and in this reflection he is supported by the venerable historian Pedro Abarca,
of the society of Jesuits.*

CHAPTER FOURTEEN

HOW KING BOABDIL EL CHICO MARCHED OVER THE BORDER

THE defeat of the Christian cavaliers among the mountains of Malaga, and the successful inroad of Muley Aben
Hassan into the lands of Medina Sidonia, had produced a
favorable effect on the fortunes of the old monarch. The
inconstant populace began to shout forth his name in the
streets, and to sneer at the inactivity of his son Boabdil el
Chico. The latter, though in the flower of his age, and distinguished for vigor and dexterity in jousts and tournaments,
had never yet fleshed his weapon in the field of battle; and
it was murmured that he preferred the silken repose of

* Abarca. Annales de Aragon, Rey 30, cap. 2, § 7.

the cool halls of the Alhambra to the fatigue and danger of the foray and the hard encampments of the mountains.

The popularity of these rival kings depended upon their success against the Christians, and Boabdil el Chico found it necessary to strike some signal blow to counterbalance the late triumph of his father. He was further incited by the fierce old Moor, his father-in-law, Ali Atar, alcayde of Loxa, with whom the coals of wrath against the Christians still burned among the ashes of age, and had lately been blown into a flame by the attack made by Ferdinand on the city under his command.

Ali Atar informed Boabdil that the late discomfiture of the Christian knights had stripped Andalusia of the prime of her chivalry and broken the spirit of the country. All the frontier of Cordova and Ecija now lay open to inroad; but he especially pointed out the city of Lucena as an object of attack, being feebly garrisoned, and lying in a country rich in pasturage, abounding in cattle and grain, in oil and wine. The fiery old Moor spoke from thorough information; for he had made many an incursion into these parts, and his very name was a terror throughout the country. It had become a by-word in the garrison of Loxa to call Lucena the garden of Ali Atar, for he was accustomed to forage its fertile territories for all his supplies.

Boabdil el Chico listened to the persuasions of this veteran of the borders. He assembled a force of nine thousand foot and seven hundred horse, most of them his own adherents, but many the partisans of his father; for both factions, however they might fight among themselves, were ready to unite in any expedition against the Christians. Many of the most illustrious and valiant of the Moorish nobility assembled round his standard, magnificently arrayed in sumptuous armor and rich embroidery, as though they were going to a festival or a tilt of canes, rather than an enterprise of iron war. Boabdil's mother, the Sultana Ayxa la Horra, armed him for the field, and gave him her benediction as she girded his scimiter to his side. His favorite wife Morayma wept, as she thought of the evils that might befall him. "Why dost thou weep, daughter of Ali Atar?" said the high-minded Ayxa: "these tears become not the daughter of a warrior nor the wife of a king. Believe me, there lurks more danger for a monarch within the strong walls of a palace than within the frail curtains of a tent. It is by perils in the field that thy husband must purchase security on his throne."

But Morayma still hung upon his neck, with tears and sad forebodings; and when he departed from the Alhambra, she betook herself to her mirador, which looks out over the vega. From thence she watched the army, as it went, in shining order, along the road which leads to Loxa; and every burst of warlike melody that came swelling on the breeze was answered by a gush of sorrow.

As the royal cavalcade issued from the palace and descended through the streets of Granada, the populace greeted their youthful sovereign with shouts, and anticipated success that should wither the laurels of his father. In passing through the gate of Elvira, however, the king accidentally broke his lance against the arch. At this, certain of his nobles turned pale, and entreated him to turn back, for they regarded it as an evil omen. Boabdil scoffed at their fears, for he considered them mere idle fancies; or rather (says Fray Antonio Agapida), he was an incredulous pagan, puffed up with confidence and vainglory. He refused to take another spear, but drew forth his scimiter and led the way (adds Agapida) in an arrogant and haughty style, as though he would set both heaven and earth at defiance. Another evil omen was sent to deter him from his enterprise; arriving at the rambla, or dry ravine of Beyro, which is scarcely a bow-shot from the city, a fox ran through the whole army and close by the person of the king; and, though a thousand bolts were discharged at it, escaped uninjured to the mountains. The principal courtiers about Boabdil now reiterated their remonstrances against proceeding; for they considered these occurrences as mysterious portents of disasters to their army; the king, however, was not to be dismayed but continued to march forward.*

At Loxa, the royal army was re-enforced by old Ali Atar, with the chosen horsemen of his garrison, and many of the bravest warriors of the border towns. The people of Loxa shouted with exultation, when they beheld Ali Atar, armed at all points, and once more mounted on his Barbary steed, which had often borne him over the borders. The veteran warrior, with nearly a century of years upon his head, had all the fire and animation of youth, at the prospect of a foray, and careered from rank to rank with the velocity of an Arab of the desert. The populace watched the army, as it paraded over the bridge and wound into the passes of the mountains; and still their eyes were fixed upon the pennon of Ali Atar, as if it bore with it an assurance of victory.

The Moorish army entered the Christian frontier by forced marches, hastily ravaging the country, driving off the flocks and herds, and making captives of the inhabitants. They pressed on furiously, and made the latter part of their march in the night, that they might elude observation and come upon Lucena by surprise. Boabdil was inexperienced in the art of war, but he had a veteran counselor in his old father-in-law; for Ali Atar knew every secret of the country, and, as he prowled through it, his eye ranged over the land, uniting, in its glare, the craft of the fox with the sanguinary ferocity of the wolf. He had flattered himself that their march had been so rapid as to outstrip intelligence, and that Lucena would be an easy capture; when suddenly he beheld alarm-fires blazing upon the mountains. "We are discovered," said he to Boabdil el Chico; "the country will be up in arms; we have nothing left but to strike boldly for Lucena; it is but slightly garrisoned, and we may carry it by assault before it can receive assistance." The king approved of his counsel and they marched rapidly for the gate of Lucena.

* Marmol. Rebel. de los Moros. lib. 1, c. xii, fol. 14.

CHAPTER FIFTEEN

DON DIEGO DE CORDOVA, Count of Cabra, was in the castle of Vaena, which, with the town of the same name, is situated on a lofty sun-burned hill on the frontier of the kingdom of Cordova, and but a few leagues from Lucena. The range of mountains of Horquera lie between them. The castle of Vaena was strong, and well furnished with arms, and the count had a numerous band of vassals and retainers; for it behooved the noblemen of the frontiers, in those times, to be well prepared with man and horse, with lance and buckler, to resist the sudden incursions of the Moors. The Count of Cabra was a hardy and experienced warrior, shrewd in council, prompt in action, rapid and fearless in the field. He was one of the bravest cavaliers for an inroad, and had been quickened and sharpened, in thought and action, by living on the borders.

On the night of the 20th of April, 1483, the count was about to retire to rest, when the watchman from the turret brought him word that there were alarm-fires on the mountains of Horquera, and that they were made on the signal-tower overhanging the defile through which the road passes to Cabra and Lucena.

The count ascended the battlement, and beheld five lights blazing on the tower—a sign that there was a Moorish army attacking some place on the frontier. The count instantly ordered the alarm-bells to be sounded, and dispatched couriers to rouse the commanders of the neighboring towns. He ordered all his retainers to prepare for action, and sent a trumpet through the town, summoning the men to assemble at the castle-gate at daybreak, armed and equipped for the field.

Throughout the remainder of the night the castle re-sounded with the din of preparation. Every house in the town was in equal bustle; for in these frontier towns every house had its warrior, and the lance and buckler were ever hanging against the wall, ready to be snatched down for instant service. Nothing was heard but the din of armorers, the shoeing of steeds, and furbishing up of weapons; and, all night long, the alarm-fires kept blazing on the mountains.

When the morning dawned, the Count of Cabra sallied forth at the head of two hundred and fifty cavaliers, of the best families of Vaena, all well appointed, exercised in arms, and experienced in the warfare of the borders. There were, besides, twelve hundred foot-soldiers, all brave and well sea-soned men of the same town. The count ordered them to hasten forward, whoever could make most speed, taking the road to Cabra, which was three leagues distant. That they might not loiter on the road, he allowed none of them to break their fast until they arrived at that place. The provi-dent count dispatched couriers in advance, and the little army, on reaching Cabra, found tables spread with food and refreshments, at the gates of the town. Here they were joined by Don Alonzo de Cordova, Senior of Zuheros.

Having made a hearty repast, they were on the point of resuming their march, when the count discovered that, in the hurry of his departure from home, he had forgotten to bring the standard of Vaena, which for upward of eighty years had always been borne to battle by his family. It was now noon, and there was not time to return; he took, there-fore, the standard of Cabra, the device of which is a goat, and which had not been seen in the wars for the last half century. When about to depart, a courier came galloping at full speed, bringing missives to the count from his nephew, Don Diego Hernandez de Cordova, Senior of Lucena and alcayde de los Donzeles, entreating him to hasten to his aid, as his town was beset by the Moorish king Boabdil el Chico, with a powerful army, who were actually setting fire to the gates.

The count put his little army instantly in movement for Lucena, which is only one league from Cabra; he was fired with the idea of having the Moorish king in person to contend with. By the time he reached Lucena, the Moors had desisted from the attack and were ravaging the surrounding country. He entered the town with a few of his cavaliers, and was received with joy by his nephew, whose whole force consisted but of eighty horse and three hundred foot. Don Diego Hernandez de Cordova was a young man, yet he was a prudent, careful, and capable officer. Having learned, the evening before, that the Moors had passed the frontiers, he had gathered within his walls all the women and children from the environs; had armed the men, sent couriers in all directions for succor, and had lighted alarm-fires on the mountains.

Boabdil had arrived with his army at daybreak, and had sent in a message threatening to put the garrison to the sword if the place were not instantly surrendered. The messenger was a Moor of Granada, named Hamet, whom Don Diego had formerly known: he contrived to amuse him with negotiation, to gain time for succor to arrive. The fierce old Ali Atar, losing all patience, had made an assault upon the town, and stormed like a fury at the gate; but had been repulsed. Another and more serious attack was expected in the course of the night.

When the Count de Cabra had heard this account of the situation of affairs, he turned to his nephew with his usual alacrity of manner, and proposed that they should immediately sally forth in quest of the enemy. The prudent Don Diego remonstrated at the rashness of attacking so great a force with a mere handful of men. "Nephew," said the count, "I came from Vaena with a determination to fight this Moorish king, and I will not be disappointed."

"At any rate," replied Don Diego, "let us wait but two hours, and we shall have re-enforcements which have been promised me from Rambla, Santaella, Montilla, and other places in the neighborhood." "If we await these," said the hardy count, "the Moors will be off and all our trouble will have been in vain. You may await them, if you please; I am resolved on fighting."

The count paused for no reply; but, in his prompt and rapid manner, sallied forth to his men. The young alcayde de los Donzeles, though more prudent than his ardent uncle, was equally brave; he determined to stand by him in his rash enterprise, and, summoning his little force, marched forth to join the count, who was already on the move. They then proceeded together in quest of the enemy.

The Moorish army had ceased ravaging the country and were not to be seen—the neighborhood being hilly and broken with deep ravines. The count dispatched six scouts on horseback to reconnoiter, ordering them to return with all speed when they should have discovered the enemy, and by no means to engage in skirmishing with stragglers. The scouts, ascending a high hill, beheld the Moorish army in a valley behind it, the cavalry ranged in five battalions keeping guard, while the foot-soldiers were seated on the grass making a repast. They returned immediately with the intelligence.

The count now ordered the troops to march in the direction of the enemy. He and his nephew ascended the hill, and saw that the five battalions of Moorish cavalry had been formed into two, one of about nine hundred lances, the other of about six hundred. The whole force seemed prepared to march for the frontier. The foot-soldiers were already under way, with many prisoners and a great train of mules and beasts of burden laden with booty. At a distance was Boabdil el Chico: they could not distinguish his person, but they knew him by his superb white charger, magnificently caparisoned, and by his being surrounded by a numerous guard, sumptuously armed and attired. Old Ali Atar was careering about the valley with his usual impatience, hurrying the march of the loitering troops.

The eyes of the Count de Cabra glistened with eager joy as he beheld the royal prize within his reach. The immense disparity of their forces never entered into his mind. "By

Santiago!" said he to his nephew, as they hastened down the hill, "had we waited for more forces, the Moorish king and his army would have escaped us!"

The count now harangued his men, to inspirit them to this hazardous encounter. He told them not to be dismayed at the number of Moors, for God often permitted the few to conquer the many; and he had great confidence, that, through the divine aid, they were that day to achieve a signal victory which should win them both riches and renown. He commanded that no man should hurl his lance at the enemy, but should keep it in his hands and strike as many blows with it as he could. He warned them, also, never to shout except when the Moors did; for, when both armies shouted together, there was no perceiving which made the most noise and was the strongest. He desired his uncle Lope de Mendoza, and Diego Cabrera, alcayde of Menica, to alight and enter on foot in the battalion of infantry, to animate them to the combat. He appointed, also, the alcayde of Vaena and Diego de Clavijo, a cavalier of his household, to remain in the rear, and not to permit any one to lag behind, either to despoil the dead, or for any other purpose.

Such were the orders given by this most adroit, active and intrepid cavalier, to his little army, supplying, by admirable sagacity and subtle management, the want of a more numerous force. His orders being given, and all arrangements made, he threw aside his lance, drew his sword, and commanded his standard to be advanced against the enemy.

CHAPTER SIXTEEN

THE BATTLE OF LUCENA

THE Moorish king had descried the Spanish forces at a distance, although a slight fog prevented his seeing them distinctly and ascertaining their numbers. His old father-in-law, Ali Atar, was by his side, who, being a veteran marauder, was well acquainted with all the standards and armorial bearings of the frontiers. When the king beheld the ancient and long-disused banner of Cabra emerging from the mist, he turned to Ali Atar and demanded whose ensign it was. The old borderer was for once at a loss, for the banner had not been displayed in battle in his time. "Sire," replied he, after a pause, "I have been considering that standard, but do not know it. It appears to be a dog, which device is borne by the towns of Baeza and Ubeda. If it be so, all Andalusia is in movement against you; for it is not probable that any single commander or community would venture to attack you. I would advise you, therefore, to retire."

The Count de Cabra in winding down the hill toward the Moors found himself on much lower ground than the enemy: he ordered in all haste that his standard should be taken back, so as to gain the vantage ground. The Moors, mistaking this for a retreat, rushed impetuously toward the Christians. The latter, having gained the height proposed, charged down upon them at the same moment, with the battle-cry of "Santiago!" and, dealing the first blows, laid many of the Moorish cavaliers in the dust.

The Moors, thus checked in their tumultuous assault, were thrown into confusion, and began to give way, the Christians following hard upon them. Boabdil el Chico endeavored to rally them. "Hold! hold! for shame!" cried he; "let us not fly, at least until we know our enemy." The Moorish chivalry were stung by this reproof, and turned to make front, with the valor of men who feel that they are fighting under their monarch's eye.

At this moment, Lorenzo de Porres, alcayde of Luque, arrived with fifty horse and one hundred foot, sounding an Italian trumpet from among a copse of oak trees, which concealed his force. The quick ear of old Ali Atar caught the note. "That is an Italian trumpet," said he to the king; "the whole world seems in arms against your majesty!"

The trumpet of Lorenzo de Porres was answered by that of the Count de Cabra, in another direction, and it seemed to the Moors as if they were between two armies. Don Lorenzo, sallying from among the oaks, now charged upon the enemy: the latter did not wait to ascertain the force of this new foe; the confusion, the variety of alarms, the attacks from opposite quarters, the obscurity of the fog, all conspired to deceive them as to the number of their adversaries. Broken and dismayed, they retreated fighting; and nothing but the presence and remonstrance of the king prevented their retreat from becoming a headlong flight.

This skirmishing retreat lasted for about three leagues. Many were the acts of individual prowess between Christian and Moorish knights, and the way was strewed with the flower of the king's guards and of his royal household. At length they came to the rivulet of Mingonzales, the verdant banks of which were covered with willows and tamarisks. It was swollen by recent rain, and was now a deep and turbid torrent.

Here the king made a courageous stand with a small body of cavalry, while his baggage crossed the stream. None but the choicest and most loyal of his guards stood by their monarch, in this hour of extremity. The foot-soldiers took to flight the moment they passed the ford; many of the horsemen, partaking of the general panic, gave reins to their steeds and scoured for the frontier. The little host of devoted cavaliers now serried their forces in front of their monarch, to protect his retreat. They fought hand to hand with the Christian warriors, disdaining to yield or to ask for quarter. The ground was covered with the dead and dying. The king, having retreated along the river banks, and gained some distance from the scene of combat, looked back, and saw the loyal band at length give way. They crossed the ford, followed pell mell by the enemy, and several of them were struck down into the stream.

The king now dismounted from his white charger, whose color and rich caparison made him too conspicuous, and endeavored to conceal himself among the thickets which fringed the river. A soldier of Lucena, named Martin Hurtado, discovered him and attacked him with a pike. The king defended himself with scimiter and target, until another soldier assailed him, and he saw a third approaching. Perceiving that further resistance would be vain, he drew back and called upon them to desist, offering them a noble ransom. One of the soldiers rushed forward to seize him, but the king struck him to the earth with a blow of his scimiter.

Don Diego Fernandez de Cordova coming up at this moment, the men said to him, "Senor, here is a Moor that we have taken, who seems to be a man of rank and offers a large ransom."

"Slaves!" exclaimed King Boabdil, "you have not taken me. I surrender to this cavalier."

Don Diego received him with knightly courtesy. He perceived him to be a person of high rank; but the king concealed his quality, and gave himself out as the son of Aben Aleyzar, a nobleman of the royal household.* Don Diego gave him in charge of five soldiers, to conduct him to the castle of Lucena; then, putting spurs to his horse, he hastened to rejoin the Count de Cabra, who was in hot pursuit of the enemy. He overtook him at a stream called Rianaul; and they continued to press on the skirts of the flying army during the remainder of the day. The pursuit was almost as hazardous as the battle; for, had the enemy at any time recovered from their panic, they might, by a sudden reaction, have overwhelmed the small force of their pursuers. To guard against this peril, the wary count kept his battalion always in close order, and had a body of a hundred chosen lancers in the advance. The Moors kept up a Parthian retreat; several times they turned to make battle; but, seeing this solid body of steeled warriors pressing upon them, they again took to flight.

The main retreat of the army was along the valley watered by the Xenil, and opening through the mountains of Algaringo to the city of Loxa. The alarm-fires of the

---

* Garibay, lib. 40, c. 31.

preceding night had roused the country; every man snatched sword and buckler from the wall, and the towns and villages poured forth their warriors to harass the retreating foe. Ali Atar kept the main force of the army together, and turned fiercely from time to time upon his pursuers; he was like a wolf, hunted through the country he had often made desolate by his maraudings.

The alarm of this invasion had reached the city of Antiquera, where were several of the cavaliers who had escaped from the carnage in the mountains of Malaga. Their proud minds were festering with their late disgrace, and their only prayer was for vengeance on the Infidels. No sooner did they hear of the Moor being over the border than they were armed and mounted for action. Don Alonzo de Aguilar led them forth—a small body of but forty horsemen, but all cavaliers of prowess and thirsting for revenge. They came upon the foe on the banks of the Xenil, where it winds through the valleys of Cordova. The river, swelled by the late rains, was deep and turbulent, and only fordable at certain places. The main body of the army was gathered in confusion on the banks, endeavoring to ford the stream, protected by the cavalry of Ali Atar.

No sooner did the little band of Alonzo de Aguilar come in sight of the Moors than fury flashed from their eyes. "Remember the mountains of Malaga!" they cried to each other, as they rushed to combat. Their charge was desperate, but was gallantly resisted. A scrambling and bloody fight ensued, hand to hand and sword to sword, sometimes on land, sometimes in the water. Many were lanced on the banks; others, throwing themselves into the river, sunk with the weight of their armor, and were drowned; some, grappling together, fell from their horses, but continued their struggle in the waves, and helm and turban rolled together down the stream. The Moors were far greater in number, and among them were many warriors of rank; but they were disheartened by defeat, while the Christians were excited even to desperation.

Ali Atar alone preserved all his fire and energy amid his reverses. He had been enraged at the defeat of the army, the loss of the king, and the ignominious flight he had been obliged to make through a country which had so often been the scene of his exploits; but to be thus impeded in his flight, and harassed and insulted by a mere handful of warriors, roused the violent passions of the old Moor to perfect frenzy. He had marked Don Alonzo de Aguilar dealing his blows (says Agapida) with the pious vehemence of a righteous knight, who knows that in every wound inflicted upon the Infidels he is doing God service. Ali Atar spurred his steed along the bank of the river to come upon Don Alonzo by surprise. The back of the warrior was toward him; and, collecting all his force, the Moor hurled his lance to transfix him on the spot. The lance was not thrown with the usual accuracy of Ali Atar; it tore away a part of the cuirass of Don Alonzo, but failed to inflict a wound. The Moor rushed upon Don Alonzo with his scimiter; but the latter was on the alert, and parried his blow. They fought desperately upon the borders of the river, alternately pressing each other into the stream, and fighting their way again up the bank. Ali Atar was repeatedly wounded; and Don Alonzo, having pity on his age, would have spared his life; he called upon him to surrender. "Never," cried Ali Atar, "to a Christian dog!" The words were scarce out of his mouth when the sword of Don Alonzo clove his turbaned head and sank deep into the brain. He fell dead without a groan; his body rolled into the Xenil, nor was it ever found and recognized.* Thus fell Ali Atar, who had long been the terror of Andalusia. As he had hated and warred upon the Christians all his life, so he died in the very act of bitter hostility.

The fall of Ali Atar put an end to the transient stand of the cavalry. Horse and foot mingled together in the desperate struggle across the Xenil; and many were trampled down, and perished beneath the waves. Don Alonzo and

---

* Cura de los Palacios.

his band continued to harass them until they crossed the frontier; and every blow struck home to the Moors seemed to lighten the load of humiliation and sorrow which had weighed heavy on their hearts.

In this disastrous rout the Moors lost upward of five thousand killed and made prisoners; many of whom were of the most noble lineages of Granada: numbers fled to rocks and mountains, where they were subsequently taken.

This battle was called by some the battle of Lucena; by others, the battle of the Moorish king, because of the capture of Boabdil. Twenty-two banners fell into the hands of the Christians and were carried to Vaena, and hung up in the church; where (says a historian of after times) they remain to this day. Once a year, on the day of St. George, they are borne about in procession by the inhabitants, who at the same time give thanks to God for this signal victory granted to their forefathers.

Great was the triumph of the Count de Cabra, when, on returning from the pursuit of the enemy, he found that the Moorish king had fallen into his hands. When the unfortunate Boabdil was brought before him, however, and he beheld him a dejected captive, whom but shortly before he had seen in royal splendor, surrounded by his army, the generous heart of the count was touched by sympathy. He said everything that became a courteous and Christian knight to comfort him; observing that the same mutability of things which had suddenly destroyed his recent prosperity might cause his present misfortunes as rapidly to pass away; since in this world nothing is stable, and even sorrow has its allotted term.

––––––

CHAPTER SEVENTEEN

LAMENTATIONS OF THE MOORS FOR THE BATTLE OF LUCENA

THE sentinels looked out from the watch-towers of Loxa, along the valley of the Xenil, which passes through the mountains of Algaringo. They looked to behold the king returning in triumph, at the head of his shining host, laden with the spoil of the unbeliever. They looked to behold the standard of their warlike idol, the fierce Ali Atar, borne by the chivalry of Loxa, ever foremost in the wars of the border.

In the evening of the 21st of April, they descried a single horseman urging his faltering steed along the banks of the Xenil. As he drew near, they perceived by the flash of arms that he was a warrior, and on nearer approach, by the richness of his armor and the caparison of his steed, they knew him to be a warrior of rank.

He reached Loxa faint and aghast; his Arabian courser covered with foam, and dust, and blood, panting and staggering with fatigue, and gashed with wounds. Having brought his master in safety he sunk down and died before the gate of the city. The soldiers at the gate gathered round the cavalier as he stood mute and melancholy by his expiring steed; they knew him to be the gallant Cidi Caleb, nephew of the chief alfaqui of the Albaycin of Granada. When the people of Loxa beheld this noble cavalier thus alone, haggard and dejected, their hearts were filled with fearful forebodings.

"Cavalier," said they, "how fares it with the king and army?"

He cast his hand mournfully toward the land of the Christians. "There they lie!" exclaimed he. "The heavens have fallen upon them. All are lost! all dead!" *

Upon this there was a great cry of consternation among the people, and loud wailings of women; for the flower of the youth of Loxa were with the army.

An old Moorish soldier, scarred in many a border battle, stood leaning on his lance by the gateway. "Where is Ali Atar?" demanded he eagerly. "If he lives the army cannot be lost."

"I saw his turban cleaved by the Christian sword," replied Cidi Caleb. "His body is floating in the Xenil."

* Cura de los Palacios.

When the soldier heard these words he smote his breast and threw dust upon his head; for he was an old follower of Ali Atar.

The noble Cidi Caleb gave himself no repose, but mounting another steed, hastened to carry the disastrous tidings to Granada. As he passed through the villages and hamlets he spread sorrow around; for their chosen men had followed the king to the wars.

When he entered the gates of Granada, and announced the loss of the king and army, a voice of horror went throughout the city. Every one thought but of his own share in the general calamity, and crowded round the bearer of ill tidings. One asked after a father, another after a brother, some after a lover, and many a mother after her son. His replies were still of wounds and death. To one he replied, "I saw thy father pierced with a lance, as he defended the person of the king." To another, "Thy brother fell wounded under the hoofs of the horses; but there was no time to aid him, for the Christian cavalry were upon us." To another, "I saw the horse of thy lover, covered with blood and galloping without his rider." To another, "Thy son fought by my side on the banks of the Xenil: we were surrounded by the enemy, and driven into the stream. I heard him cry upon Allah, in the midst of the waters: when I reached the other bank he was no longer by my side."

The noble Cidi Caleb passed on, leaving all Granada in lamentation; he urged his steed up the steep avenue of trees and fountains that leads to the Alhambra, nor stopped until he arrived before the gate of Justice. Ayxa, the mother of Boabdil, and Morayma, his beloved and tender wife, had daily watched from the tower of the Comares to behold his triumphant return. Who shall describe their affliction when they heard the tidings of Cidi Caleb? The sultana Ayxa spake not much, but sat as one entranced in woe. Every now and then a deep sigh burst forth, but she raised her eyes to heaven: "It is the will of Allah!" said she, and with these words endeavored to repress the agonies of a mother's sorrow. The tender Morayma threw herself on the earth, and gave way to the full turbulence of her feelings, bewailing her husband and her father. The high-minded Ayxa rebuked the violence of her grief: "Moderate these transports, my daughter," said she; "remember magnanimity should be the attribute of princes; it becomes not them to give way to clamorous sorrow, like common and vulgar minds." But Morayma could only deplore her loss with the anguish of a tender woman. She shut herself up in her mirador, and gazed all day, with streaming eyes, upon the vega. Every object before her recalled the causes of her affliction. The river Xenil, which ran shining amid the groves and gardens, was the same on whose banks had perished her father, Ali Atar; before her lay the road to Loxa, by which Boabdil had departed, in martial state, surrounded by the chivalry of Granada. Ever and anon she would burst into an agony of grief. "Alas! my father!" she would exclaim; "the river runs smiling before me that covers thy mangled remains; who will gather them to an honored tomb, in the land of the unbeliever? And thou, oh Boabdil, light of my eyes! joy of my heart! life of my life! woe the day, and woe the hour, that I saw thee depart from these walls. The road by which thou hast departed is solitary; never will it be gladdened by thy return! the mountain thou hast traversed lies like a cloud in the distance, and all beyond it is darkness."

The royal minstrels were summoned to assuage the sorrows of the queen: they attuned their instruments to cheerful strains; but in a little while the anguish of their hearts prevailed, and turned their songs to lamentations.

"Beautiful Granada!" they exclaimed, "how is thy glory faded! The Vivarambla no longer echoes to the tramp of steed and sound of trumpet; no longer is it crowded with thy youthful nobles, eager to display their prowess in the tourney and the festive tilt of reeds. Alas! the flower of thy chivalry lies low in a foreign land! the soft note of the lute is no longer heard in thy moonlit streets; the lively castanet is silent upon thy hills; and the graceful dance of the Zambra is no more seen beneath thy bowers. Behold, the Alhambra is forlorn and desolate! in vain do the orange and myrtle breathe their perfumes into its silken chambers; in vain does the nightingale sing within its groves; in vain are its marble halls refreshed by the sound of fountains and the gush of limpid rills. Alas! the countenance of the king no longer shines within those halls: the light of the Alhambra is set forever!''

Thus all Granada, say the Arabian chroniclers, gave itself up to lamentation: there was nothing but the voice of wailing from the palace to the cottage. All joined to deplore their youthful monarch, cut down in the freshness and promise of his youth; many feared that the prediction of the astrologers was about to be fulfilled, and that the downfall of the kingdom would follow the death of Boabdil; while all declared that, had he survived, he was the very sovereign calculated to restore the realm to its ancient prosperity and glory.

CHAPTER EIGHTEEN

HOW MULEY ABEN HASSAN PROFITED BY THE MISFORTUNES OF HIS SON BOABDIL

An unfortunate death atones, with the world, for a multitude of errors. While the populace thought their youthful monarch had perished in the field, nothing could exceed their grief for his loss, and their adoration of his memory; when, however, they learned that he was still alive, and had surrendered himself captive to the Christians, their feelings underwent an instant change. They decried his talents as a commander, his courage as a soldier; they railed at his expedition, as rash and ill conducted; and they reviled him for not having dared to die on the field of battle, rather than surrender to the enemy.

The alfaquis, as usual, mingled with the populace and artfully guided their discontents. ''Behold,'' exclaimed they, "the prediction is accomplished which was pronounced at the birth of Boabdil. He has been seated on the throne, and the kingdom has suffered downfall and disgrace by his defeat and captivity. Comfort yourselves, oh Moslems! The evil day has passed by; the fates are satisfied; the scepter which has been broken in the feeble hand of Boabdil is destined to resume its former power and sway in the vigorous grasp of Aben Hassan."

The people were struck with the wisdom of these words: they rejoiced that the baleful prediction, which had so long hung over them, was at an end; and declared that none but Muley Aben Hassan had the valor and capacity necessary for the protection of the kingdom in this time of trouble.

The longer the captivity of Boabdil continued the greater grew the popularity of his father. One city after another renewed allegiance to him; for power attracts power, and fortune creates fortune. At length he was enabled to return to Granada, and establish himself once more in the Alhambra. At his approach, his repudiated spouse, the sultana Ayxa, gathered together the family and treasures of her captive son, and retired, with a handful of the nobles, into the Albaycin, the rival quarter of the city, the inhabitants of which still retained feelings of loyalty to Boabdil. Here she fortified herself, and held the semblance of a court in the name of her son. The fierce Muley Aben Hassan would have willingly carried fire and sword into this factious quarter of the capital, but he dared not confide in his new and uncertain popularity. Many of the nobles detested him for his past cruelty; and a large portion of the soldiery, beside many of the people of his own party, respected the virtues of Ayxa la Horra, and pitied the misfortunes of Boabdil.

Granada therefore presented the singular spectacle of two sovereignties within the same city. The old king fortified himself in the lofty towers of the Alhambra, as much against his own subjects as against the Christians; while Ayxa, with the zeal of a mother's affection, which waxes warmer and warmer toward her offspring when in adversity, still maintained the standard of Boabdil on the rival fortress of the Alcazaba, and kept his powerful faction alive within the walls of the Albaycin.

CHAPTER NINETEEN

CAPTIVITY OF BOABDIL EL CHICO

THE unfortunate Boabdil remained a prisoner, closely guarded, in the castle of Vaena. From the towers of his prison he beheld the town below filled with armed men; and the lofty hill on which it was built, girdled by massive walls and ramparts, on which a vigilant watch was maintained night and day. The mountains around were studded with watch-towers, overlooking the lonely roads which led to Granada, so that a turban could not stir over the border without the alarm being given and the whole country put on the alert. Boabdil saw that there was no hope of escape from such a fortress, and that any attempt to rescue him would be equally in vain. His heart was filled with anxiety, as he thought on the confusion and ruin which his captivity must cause in his affairs; while sorrows of a softer kind overcame his fortitude, as he thought on the evils it might bring upon his family.

The Count de Cabra, though he maintained the most vigilant guard over his royal prisoner, yet treated him with profound deference; he had appointed the noblest apartments in the castle for his abode, and sought in every way to cheer him during his captivity. A few days only had passed away when missives arrived from the Castilian sovereigns. Ferdinand had been transported with joy at hearing of the capture of the Moorish monarch, seeing the deep and politic uses that might be made of such an event; but the magnanimous spirit of Isabella was filled with compassion for the unfortunate captive. Their messages to Boabdil were full of sympathy and consolation, breathing that high and gentle courtesy which dwells in noble minds.

This magnanimity in his foe cheered the dejected spirit of the captive monarch. "Tell my sovereigns, the king and queen," said he to the messenger, "that I cannot be unhappy, being in the power of such high and mighty princes, especially since they partake so largely of that grace and goodness which Allah bestows upon the mónarchs whom he greatly loves. Tell them further that I had long thought of submitting myself to their sway to receive the kingdom of Granada from their hands, in the same manner that my ancestor received it from King John II., father to the gracious queen. My greatest sorrow, in this my captivity, is that I must appear to do that from force which I would fain have done from inclination."

In the meantime, Muley Aben Hassan, finding the faction of his son still formidable in Granada, was anxious to consolidate his power by gaining possession of the person of Boabdil. For this purpose he sent an embassy to the Catholic monarchs, offering large terms for the ransom, or rather the purchase, of his son; proposing, among other conditions, to release the Count of Cifuentes and nine other of his most distinguished captives, and to enter into a treaty of confederacy with the sovereigns. Neither did the implacable father make any scruple of testifying his indifference whether his son were delivered up alive or dead, so that his person were placed assuredly within his power.

The humane heart of Isabella revolted at the idea of giving up the unfortunate prince into the hands of his most unnatural and inveterate enemy: a disdainful refusal was therefore returned to the old monarch, whose message had been couched in a vaunting spirit. He was informed that the Castilian sovereigns would listen to no proposals of peace from Muley Aben Hassan, until he should lay down his arms, and offer them in all humility.

Overtures in a different spirit were made by the mother of Boabdil, the Sultana Ayxa la Horra, with the concurrence of the party which still remained faithful to him. It was thereby proposed that Mahomet Abdalla, otherwise called

Boabdil, should hold his crown as vassal to the Castilian sovereigns, paying an annual tribute, and releasing seventy
Christian captives annually, for five years: that he should,
moreover, pay a large sum, upon the spot, for his ransom,
and at the same time give freedom to four hundred Christians to be chosen by the king: that he should also engage to
be always ready to render military aid, and should come to
the Cortes, or assemblage of nobles and distinguished vassals
of the crown, whenever summoned. His only son, and the
sons of twelve distinguished Moorish houses, were to be
delivered as hostages.

King Ferdinand was at Cordova when he received this
proposition. Queen Isabella was absent at the time. He
was anxious to consult her in so momentous an affair; or
rather, he was fearful of proceeding too precipitately, and
not drawing from this fortunate event all the advantage of
which it was susceptible. Without returning any reply,
therefore, to the mission, he sent missives to the castle of
Vaena, where Boabdil remained in courteous durance of the
brave Count de Cabra, ordering that the captive monarch
should be brought to Cordova.

The Count de Cabra set out with his illustrious prisoner;
but when he arrived at Cordova King Ferdinand declined
seeing the Moorish monarch. He was still undetermined
what course to pursue—whether to retain him prisoner, set
him at liberty on ransom, or treat him with politic magnanimity; and each course would require a different kind of
reception. Until this point should be resolved, therefore, he
gave him in charge to Martin de Alarcon, alcayde of the ancient fortress of Porcuna, with orders to guard him strictly,
but to treat him with the distinction and deference due unto
a prince. These commands were strictly obeyed; and, with
the exception of being restrained in his liberty, the monarch
was as nobly entertained as he could have been in his regal
palace at Granada.

In the meantime, Ferdinand availed himself of this critical moment, while Granada was distracted with factions and

dissensions, and before he had concluded any treaty with Boabdil, to make a puissant and ostentatious inroad into the very heart of the kingdom, at the head of his most illustrious nobles. He sacked and destroyed several towns and castles, and extended his ravages to the very gates of Granada. Old Muley Aben Hassan did not venture to oppose him. His city was filled with troops, but he was uncertain of their affection. He dreaded that, should he sally forth, the gates of Granada might be closed against him by the faction of the Albaycin.

The old Moor stood on the lofty tower of the Alhambra (says Antonio Agapida), grinding his teeth, and foaming like a tiger shut up in his cage, as he beheld the glittering battalions of the Christians wheeling about the vega, and the standard of the cross shining forth from among the smoke of Infidel villages and hamlets. The most Catholic king (continues Agapida) would gladly have continued this righteous ravage, but his munitions began to fail. Satisfied, therefore, with having laid waste the country of the enemy, and insulted old Muley Aben Hassan in his very capital, he returned to Cordova covered with laurels and his army laden with spoils; and now bethought himself of coming to an immediate decision in regard to his royal prisoner.

CHAPTER TWENTY

OF THE TREATMENT OF BOABDIL BY THE CASTILIAN SOVEREIGNS

A STATELY convention was held by King Ferdinand in the ancient city of Cordova, composed of several of the most reverend prelates and renowned cavaliers of the kingdom, to determine upon the fate of the unfortunate Boabdil.

Don Alonzo de Cardenas, the worthy Master of Santiago, was one of the first who gave his counsel. He was a pious and zealous knight, rigid in his devotion to the faith; and his holy zeal had been inflamed to peculiar vehemence since his disastrous crusade among the mountains of Malaga. He inveighed with ardor against any compromise or compact with the Infidels: the object of this war, he observed, was not the subjection of the Moors, but their utter expulsion from the land; so that there might no longer remain a single stain of Mahometanism throughout Christian Spain. He gave it as his opinion, therefore, that the captive king ought not to be set at liberty.

Roderigo Ponce de Leon, the valiant Marques of Cadiz, on the contrary, spoke warmly for the release of Boabdil. He pronounced it a measure of sound policy, even if done without conditions. It would tend to keep up the civil war in Granada, which was as a fire consuming the entrails of the enemy, and effecting more for the interests of Spain, without expense, than all the conquests of its arms.

The grand cardinal of Spain, Don Pedro Gonzalez de Mendoza, coincided in opinion with the Marques of Cadiz. Nay (added that pious prelate and politic statesman), it would be sound wisdom to furnish the Moor with men and money, and all other necessaries, to promote the civil war in Granada: by this means would be produced great benefit to the service of God, since we are assured by His infallible word that "a kingdom divided against itself cannot stand." *

Ferdinand weighed these counsels in his mind, but was slow in coming to a decision; he was religiously attentive to his own interests (observes Fray Antonio Agapida), knowing himself to be but an instrument of Providence in this holy war, and that, therefore, in consulting his own advantage he was promoting the interests of the faith. The opinion of Queen Isabella relieved him from his perplexity. That high-minded princess was zealous for the promotion of the faith, but not for the extermination of the Infidels. The Moorish kings had held their thrones as vassals to her progenitors; she was content at present to accord the same privi-

---

* Salazar. Cronica del Gran Cardinal, p. 188.

lege, and that the royal prisoner should be liberated on condition of becoming a vassal to the crown. By this means might be effected the deliverance of many Christian captives, who were languishing in Moorish chains.

King Ferdinand adopted the magnanimous measure recommended by the queen; but he accompanied it with several shrewd conditions; exacting tribute, military services, and safe passage and maintenance for Christian troops, throughout the places which should adhere to Boabdil. The captive king readily submitted to these stipulations, and swore, after the manner of his faith, to observe them with exactitude. A truce was arranged for two years, during which the Castilian sovereigns engaged to maintain him on his throne, and to assist him in recovering all places which he had lost during his captivity.

When Boabdil el Chico had solemnly agreed to this arrangement, in the castle of Porcuna, preparations were made to receive him in Cordova in regal style. Superb steeds richly caparisoned, and raiment of brocade, and silk, and the most costly cloths, with all other articles of sumptuous array, were furnished to him and fifty Moorish cavaliers, who had come to treat for his ransom, that he might appear in state befitting the monarch of Granada and the most distinguished vassal of the Castilian sovereigns. Money also was advanced to maintain him in suitable grandeur, during his residence at the Castilian court and his return to his dominions. Finally, it was ordered by the sovereigns that when he came to Cordova all the nobles and dignitaries of the court should go forth to receive him.

A question now arose among certain of those ancient and experienced men, who grow gray about a court in the profound study of forms and ceremonials, with whom a point of punctilio is as a vast political right, and who contract a sublime and awful idea of the external dignity of the throne. Certain of these court sages propounded the momentous question, whether the Moorish monarch, coming to do homage as a vassal, ought not to kneel and kiss the hand of the king.

This was immediately decided in the affirmative, by a large number of ancient cavaliers accustomed (says Antonio Agapida) to the lofty punctilio of our most dignified court and transcendent sovereigns. The king, therefore, was informed by those who arranged the ceremonies, that when the Moorish monarch appeared in his presence, he was expected to extend his royal hand to receive the kiss of homage.

"I should certainly do so," replied King Ferdinand, "were he at liberty, and in his own kingdom; but I certainly shall not do so, seeing that he is a prisoner and in mine."

The courtiers loudly applauded the magnanimity of this reply; though many condemned it in secret, as savoring of too much generosity toward an Infidel; and the worthy Jesuit, Fray Antonio Agapida, fully concurs in their opinion.

The Moorish king entered Cordova with his little train of faithful knights, and escorted by all the nobility and chivalry of the Castilian court. He was conducted, with great state and ceremony, to the royal palace. When he came in presence of Ferdinand, he knelt and offered to kiss his hand, not merely in homage as his subject, but in gratitude for his liberty. Ferdinand declined the token of vassalage, and raised him graciously from the earth. An interpreter began, in the name of Boabdil, to laud the magnanimity of the Castilian monarch, and to promise the most implicit submission. "Enough," said King Ferdinand, interrupting the interpreter in the midst of his harangue; "there is no need of these compliments. I trust in his integrity, that he will do everything becoming a good man and a good king." With these words he received Boabdil el Chico into his royal friendship and protection.

CHAPTER TWENTY-ONE

RETURN OF BOABDIL FROM CAPTIVITY

In the month of August, a noble Moor, of the race of the Abencerrages, arrived with a splendid retinue at the city of

Cordova, bringing with him the son of Boabdil el Chico, and other of the noble youth of Granada, as hostages for the fulfillment of the terms of ransom. When the Moorish king beheld his son, his only child, who was to remain in his stead, a sort of captive in a hostile land, he folded him in his arms and wept over him. "Woe the day that I was born!" exclaimed he, "and evil the stars that presided at my birth! Well was I called El Zogoybi, or the unlucky; for sorrow is heaped upon me by my father, and sorrow do I transmit to my son!" The afflicted heart of Boabdil, however, was soothed by the kindness of the Christian sovereigns, who received the hostage prince with a tenderness suited to his age, and a distinction worthy of his rank. They delivered him in charge to the worthy alcayde Martin de Alarcon, who had treated his father with such courtesy during his confinement in the castle of Porcuna, giving orders that, after the departure of the latter, his son should be entertained with great honor and princely attention in the same fortress.

On the 2d of September, a guard of honor assembled at the gate of the mansion of Boabdil to escort him to the frontiers of his kingdom. He pressed his child to his heart at parting, but he uttered not a word; for there were many Christian eyes to behold his emotion. He mounted his steed, and never turned his head to look again upon the youth; but those who were near him observed the vehement struggle that shook his frame, wherein the anguish of the father had wellnigh subdued the studied equanimity of the king.

Boabdil el Chico and King Ferdinand sallied forth, side by side, from Cordova, amid the acclamations of a prodigious multitude. When they were a short distance from the city, they separated, with many gracious expressions on the part of the Castilian monarch, and many thankful acknowledgments from his late captive, whose heart had been humbled by adversity. Ferdinand departed for Guadalupe and Boabdil for Granada. The latter was accompanied by a guard of honor; and the viceroys of Andalusia, and the generals on the frontier, were ordered to furnish him with escorts, and to show him all possible honor on his journey. In this way he was conducted in royal state through the country he had entered to ravage, and was placed in safety in his own dominions.

He was met on the frontier by the principal nobles and cavaliers of his court, who had been secretly sent by his mother, the Sultana Ayxa, to escort him to the capital. The heart of Boabdil was lifted up for a moment, when he found himself on his own territories, surrounded by Moslem knights, with his own standards waving over his head; and he began to doubt the predictions of the astrologers: he soon found cause, however, to moderate his exultation. The loyal train which had come to welcome him was but scanty in number, and he missed many of his most zealous and obsequious courtiers. He had returned, indeed, to his kingdom, but it was no longer the devoted kingdom he had left. The story of his vassalage to the Christian sovereigns had been made use of by his father to ruin him with the people. He had been represented as a traitor to his country, a renegado to his faith, and as leagued with the enemies of both, to subdue the Moslems of Spain to the yoke of Christian bondage. In this way, the mind of the public had been turned from him; the greater part of the nobility had thronged round the throne of his father in the Alhambra; and his mother, the resolute Sultana Ayxa, with difficulty maintained her faction in the opposite towers of the Alcazaba.

Such was the melancholy picture of affairs given to Boabdil by the courtiers who had come forth to meet him. They even informed him that it would be an enterprise of difficulty and danger to make his way back to the capital and regain the little court which still remained faithful to him in the heart of the city. The old tiger, Muley Aben Hassan, lay couched within the Alhambra, and the walls and gates of the city were strongly guarded by his troops. Boabdil shook his head at these tidings. He called to mind the ill omen of his breaking his lance against the gate of Elvira, when issuing forth so vaingloriously with his army, which he now saw clearly had foreboded the destruction of that army on which he had so confidently relied. "Henceforth," said he, "let no man have the impiety to scoff at omens."

Boabdil approached his capital by stealth, and in the night, prowling about its walls, like an enemy seeking to destroy rather than a monarch returning to his throne. At length he seized upon a postern-gate of the Albaycin—that part of the city which had always been in his favor; he passed rapidly through the streets before the populace were aroused from their sleep, and reached in safety the fortress of the Alcazaba. Here he was received into the embraces of his intrepid mother and his favorite wife Morayma. The transports of the latter, on the safe return of her husband, were mingled with tears; for she thought of her father, Ali Atar, who had fallen in his cause, and of her only son, who was left a hostage in the hands of the Christians.

The heart of Boabdil, softened by his misfortunes, was moved by the changes in everything round him; but his mother called up his spirit. "This," said she, "is no time for tears and fondness. A king must think of his scepter and his throne, and not yield to softness like common men. Thou hast done well, my son, in throwing thyself resolutely into Granada; it must depend upon thyself whether thou remain here a king or a captive."

The old king Muley Aben Hassan had retired to his couch that night, in one of the strongest towers of the Alhambra; but his restless anxiety kept him from repose. In the first watch of the night, he heard a shout faintly rising from the quarter of the Albaycin, which is on the opposite side of the deep valley of the Darro. Shortly afterward, horsemen came galloping up the hill that leads to the main gate of the Alhambra, spreading the alarm that Boabdil had entered the city and possessed himself of the Alcazaba.

In the first transports of his rage, the old king would have struck the messenger to earth. He hastily summoned his counselors and commanders, exhorting them to stand by him in this critical moment; and, during the night, made every preparation to enter the Albaycin sword in hand in the morning.

In the meantime, the Sultana Ayxa had taken prompt and vigorous measures to strengthen her party. The Albaycin was the part of the city filled by the lower orders. The return of Boabdil was proclaimed throughout the streets, and large sums of money were distributed among the populace. The nobles, assembled in the Alcazaba, were promised honors and rewards by Boabdil, as soon as he should be firmly seated on the throne. These well-timed measures had the customary effect; and, by daybreak, all the motley populace of the Albaycin were in arms.

A doleful day succeeded. All Granada was a scene of tumult and horror. Drums and trumpets resounded in every part; all business was interrupted; the shops were shut, the doors barricadoed. Armed bands paraded the streets, some shouting for Boabdil and some for Muley Aben Hassan. When they encountered each other, they fought furiously and without mercy; every public square became a scene of battle. The great mass of the lower orders was in favor of Boabdil, but it was a multitude without discipline or lofty spirit; part of the people was regularly armed, but the greater number had sallied forth with the implements of their trade. The troops of the old king, among whom were many cavaliers of pride and valor, soon drove the populace from the squares. They fortified themselves, however, in the streets and lanes, which they barricadoed. They made fortresses of their houses, and fought desperately from the windows and the roofs, and many a warrior of the highest blood of Granada was laid low by plebeian hands and plebeian weapons, in this civic brawl.

It was impossible that such violent convulsions should last long, in the heart of a city. The people soon longed for repose, and a return to their peaceful occupations; and the cavaliers detested these conflicts with the multitude, in which there were all the horrors of war without its laurels. By the interference of the alfaquis, an armistice was at length effected. Boabdil was persuaded that there was no dependence upon the inconstant favor of the multitude, and was prevailed upon to quit a capital where he could only maintain a precarious seat upon his throne by a perpetual and bloody struggle. He fixed his court at the city of Almeria, which was entirely devoted to him, and which, at that time, vied with Granada in splendor and importance. This compromise of grandeur for tranquillity, however, was sorely against the counsels of his proud-spirited mother, the Sultana Ayxa. Granada appeared, in her eyes, the only legitimate seat of dominion; and she observed, with a smile of disdain, that he was not worthy of being called a monarch who was not master of his capital.

CHAPTER TWENTY-TWO

FORAY OF THE MOORISH ALCAYDES AND BATTLE OF LOPERA

Though Muley Aben Hassan had regained undivided sway over the city of Granada, and the alfaquis, by his command, had denounced his son Boabdil as an apostate, and as one doomed by heaven to misfortune, still the latter had many adherents among the common people. Whenever, therefore, any act of the old monarch was displeasing to the turbulent multitude, they were prone to give him a hint of the slippery nature of his standing, by shouting out the name of Boabdil el Chico. Long experience had instructed Muley Aben Hassan in the character of the inconstant people over whom he ruled. "Allah Achbar!" exclaimed he, "God is great; but a successful inroad into the country of the unbelievers will make more converts to my cause than a thousand texts of the Koran, expounded by ten thousand alfaquis."

At this time King Ferdinand was absent from Andalusia on a distant expedition with many of his troops. The moment was favorable for a foray, and Muley Aben Hassan cast about his thoughts for a leader to conduct it. Ali Atar, the terror of the border, the scourge of Andalusia, was dead; but there was another veteran general, scarce inferior to him for predatory warfare. This was old Bexir, the gray and crafty alcayde of Malaga; and the people under his command were ripe for an expedition of the kind. The signal defeat and slaughter of the Spanish knights in the neighboring mountains had filled the people of Malaga with vanity and self-conceit. They had attributed to their own valor the defeat which had been caused by the nature of the country. Many of them wore the armor and paraded in public with the horses of the unfortunate cavaliers slain on that occasion, which they vauntingly displayed as the trophies of their boasted victory. They had talked themselves into a contempt for the chivalry of Andalusia, and were impatient for an opportunity to overrun a country defended by such troops. This, Muley Aben Hassan considered a favorable state of mind to insure a daring inroad, and he sent orders to old Bexir to gather together his people and the choicest warriors of the borders, and to carry fire and sword into the very heart of Andalusia. The wary old Bexir immediately dispatched his emissaries among the alcaydes of the border towns, calling upon them to assemble with their troops at the city of Ronda, close upon the Christian frontier.

Ronda was the most virulent nest of Moorish depredators in the whole border country. It was situated in the midst of the wild Serrania, or chain of mountains of the same name, which are uncommonly lofty, broken and precipitous. It stood on an almost isolated rock, nearly encircled by a deep valley, or rather chasm, through which ran the beautiful river called Rio Verde. The Moors of this city were the most active, robust, and warlike of all the mountaineers, and their very children discharged the crossbow with unerring aim. They were incessantly harassing the rich plains of Andalusia; their city abounded with Christian spoils, and their deep dungeons were crowded with Christian captives, who might sigh in vain for deliverance from this impregnable fortress. Such was Ronda in the time of the Moors; and it has ever retained something of the same character, even to the present day. Its inhabitants continue to be among the boldest, fiercest, and most adventurous of the Andalusian mountaineers; and the Serrania de Ronda is famous as the most dangerous resort of the bandit and the contrabandista.

Hamet Zeli, surnamed El Zegri, was the commander of this belligerent city and its fierce inhabitants. He was of the tribe of the Zegries, and one of the most proud and daring of that warlike race. Besides the inhabitants of Ronda, he had a legion of African Moors in his immediate service. They were of the tribe of the Comares, mercenary troops, whose hot African blood had not yet been tempered by the softer living of Spain, and whose whole business was to fight. These he kept always well armed and well appointed. The rich pasturage of the valley of Ronda produced a breed of horses famous for strength and speed; no cavalry, therefore, was better mounted than the band of Comares. Rapid on the march, fierce in the attack, it would sweep down upon the Andalusian plains like a sudden blast from the mountains, and pass away as suddenly, before there was time for pursuit.

There was nothing that stirred up the spirit of the Moors of the frontiers more thoroughly than the idea of a foray. The summons of Bexir was gladly obeyed by the alcaydes of the border towns, and in a little while there was a force of fifteen hundred horse and four thousand foot, the very pith and marrow of the surrounding country, assembled within the walls of Ronda. The people of the place anticipated with eagerness the rich spoils of Andalusia that were soon to crowd their gates; throughout the day, the city resounded with the noise of kettle-drum and trumpet; the high-mettled steeds stamped and neighed in their stalls, as if they shared the impatience for the foray; while the Christian captives sighed, as the varied din of preparation reached to their rocky dungeons, denoting that a fresh ravage was preparing against their countrymen.

The Infidel host sallied forth full of spirits, anticipating an easy ravage and abundant booty. They encouraged each other in a contempt for the prowess of the foe. Many of the warriors of Malaga and of some of the mountain towns had insultingly arrayed themselves in the splendid armor of the Christian knights slain or taken prisoners in the famous massacre, and some of them rode the Andalusian steeds which had been captured on that occasion.

The wary Bexir had concerted his plans so secretly and expeditiously that the Christian towns of Andalusia had not the least suspicion of the storm that had gathered beyond the mountains. The vast and rocky range of the Serrania de Ronda extended like a screen, covering all their movements from observation.

The army made its way as rapidly as the rugged nature of the mountains would permit, guided by Hamet el Zegri, the bold alcayde of Ronda, who knew every pass and defile: not a drum, nor the clash of a cymbal, nor the blast of a trumpet, was permitted to be heard. The mass of war rolled quietly on as the gathering cloud to the brow of the mountains, intending to burst down like the thunderbolt upon the plain.

Never let the most wary commander fancy himself secure from discovery; for rocks have eyes, and trees have ears, and the birds of the air have tongues, to betray the most secret enterprise. There chanced at this time to be six Christian scouts prowling about the savage heights of the Serrania de Ronda. They were of that kind of lawless ruffians who infest the borders of belligerent countries, ready at any time to fight for pay, or prowl for plunder. The wild mountain passes of Spain have ever abounded with loose rambling vagabonds of the kind—soldiers in war, robbers in peace; guides, guards, smugglers, or cut-throats, according to the circumstances of the case.

These six marauders (says Fray Antonio Agapida) were

on this occasion chosen instruments, sanctified by the right-eousness of their cause. They were lurking among the mountains to entrap Moorish cattle or Moorish prisoners, both of which were equally salable in the Christian market. They had ascended one of the loftiest cliffs, and were looking out like birds of prey, ready to pounce upon anything that might offer in the valley, when they descried the Moorish army emerging from a mountain glen. They watched it in silence as it wound below them, remarking the standards of the various towns and the pennons of the commanders. They hovered about it on its march, skulking from cliff to cliff, until they saw the route by which it intended to enter the Christian country. They then dispersed, each making his way by the secret passes of the mountains to some different alcayde, that they might spread the alarm far and wide and each get a separate reward.

One hastened to Luis Fernandez Puerto Carrero, the same valiant alcayde who had repulsed Muley Aben Hassan from the walls of Alhama, and who now commanded at Ecija, in the absence of the Master of Santiago. Others roused the town of Utrera, and the places of that neighborhood, putting them all on the alert.

Puerto Carrero was a cavalier of consummate vigor and activity. He immediately sent couriers to the alcaydes of the neighboring fortresses; to Herman Carrello, captain of a body of the Holy Brotherhood, and to certain knights of the order of Alcantara. Puerto Carrero was the first to take the field. Knowing the hard and hungry service of these border scampers, he made every man take a hearty repast, and see that his horse was well shod and perfectly appointed. Then all being refreshed and in valiant heart, he sallied forth to seek the Moors. He had but a handful of men, the retainers of his household and troops of his captaincy; but they were well armed and mounted, and accustomed to the sudden rouses of the border; men whom the cry of "Arm and out! to horse and to the field!" was sufficient at any time to put in a fever of animation.

While the northern part of Andalusia was thus on the alert, one of the scouts had hastened southward to the city of Xeres, and given the alarm to the valiant Marques of Cadiz. When the marques heard that the Moor was over the border, and that the standard of Malaga was in the advance, his heart bounded with a momentary joy; for he remembered the massacre in the mountains, where his valiant brothers had been mangled before his eyes. The very authors of his calamity were now at hand, and he flattered himself that the day of vengeance had arrived. He made a hasty levy of his retainers and of the fighting men of Xeres, and hurried off with three hundred horse and two hundred foot, all resolute men and panting for revenge.

In the meantime, the veteran Bexir had accomplished his march, as he imagined, undiscovered. From the openings of the craggy defiles, he pointed out the fertile plains of Andalusia, and regaled the eyes of his soldiery with the rich country they were about to ravage. The fierce Comares of Ronda were flushed with joy at the sight; and even their steeds seemed to prick up their ears and snuff the breeze, as they beheld the scenes of their frequent forays.

When they came to where the mountain defile opened into the low land, Bexir divided his force into three parts: one, composed of foot-soldiers and of such as were weakly mounted, he left to guard the pass, being too experienced a veteran not to know the importance of securing a retreat; a second body he placed in ambush, among the groves and thickets on the banks of the river Lopera; the third, consisting of light cavalry, he sent forth to ravage the Campina, or great plain of Utrera. Most of this latter force was composed of the fiery Comares of Ronda, mounted on the fleet steeds bred among the mountains. It was led by the bold alcayde Hamet el Zegri, who was ever eager to be foremost in the forage. Little suspecting that the country on both sides was on the alarm, and rushing from all directions to close upon them in rear, this fiery troop dashed forward until they came within two leagues of Utrera. Here they scattered themselves about the plain, careering round the great herds of cattle and flocks of sheep, and sweeping them into droves, to be hurried to the mountains.

While they were thus dispersed in every direction, a troop of horse and body of foot from Utrera came suddenly upon them. The Moors rallied together in small parties, and endeavored to defend themselves; but they were without a leader, for Hamet el Zegri was at a distance, having, like a hawk, made a wide circuit in pursuit of prey. The marauders soon gave way and fled toward the ambush on the banks of the Lopera, being hotly pursued by the men of Utrera.

When they reached the Lopera, the Moors in ambush rushed forth with furious cries; and the fugitives, recovering courage from this re-enforcement, rallied and turned upon their pursuers. The Christians stood their ground, though greatly inferior in number. Their lances were soon broken, and they came to sharp work with sword and scimiter. The Christians fought valiantly, but were in danger of being overwhelmed. The bold Hamet had collected a handful of his scattered Comares, and, leaving his prey, had galloped toward the scene of action. His little troop of horsemen had reached the crest of a rising ground at no great distance, when trumpets were heard in another direction, and Luis Fernandez Puerto Carrero and his followers came galloping into the field, and charged upon the Infidels in flank.

The Moors were astounded at finding war thus breaking upon them, from various quarters of what they had expected to find an unguarded country. They fought for a short time with desperation, and resisted a vehement assault from the knights of Alcantara, and the men at-arms of the Holy Brotherhood. At length the veteran Bexir was struck from his horse by Puerto Carrero and taken prisoner, and the whole force gave way and fled. In their flight, they separated, and took two roads to the mountains, thinking, by dividing their forces, to distract the enemy. The Christians

were too few to separate. Puerto Carrero kept them together, pursuing one division of the enemy with great
slaughter. This battle took place at the fountain of the fig-
tree, near to the Lopera. Six hundred Moorish cavaliers
were slain and many taken prisoners. Much spoil was collected on the field, with which the Christians returned in
triumph to their homes.

The larger body of the enemy had retreated along a road
leading more to the south, by the banks of the Guadalete.
When they reached that river, the sound of pursuit had died
away, and they rallied to breathe and refresh themselves on
the margin of the stream. Their force was reduced to about
a thousand horse, and a confused multitude of foot. While
they were scattered and partly dismounted on the banks of
the Guadalete, a fresh storm of war burst upon them from
an opposite direction. It was the Marques of Cadiz, leading
on his household troops and the fighting men of Xeres.
When the Christian warriors came in sight of the Moors,
they were roused to fury at beholding many of them arrayed
in the armor of the cavaliers who had been slain among the
mountains of Malaga. Nay, some who had been in that
defeat beheld their own armor, which they had cast away in
their flight, to enable themselves to climb the mountains.
Exasperated at the sight, they rushed upon the foe with the
ferocity of tigers rather than the temperate courage of cavaliers. Each man felt as if he were avenging the death of a
relative, or wiping out his own disgrace. The good marques
himself beheld a powerful Moor bestriding the horse of his
brother Beltran: giving a cry of rage and anguish at the
sight, he rushed through the thickest of the enemy, attacked
the Moor with resistless fury, and after a short combat hurled
him breathless to the earth.

The Moors, already vanquished in spirit, could not withstand the assault of men thus madly excited. They soon
gave way and fled for the defile of the Serrania de Ronda,
where the body of troops had been stationed to secure a retreat. These, seeing them come galloping wildly up the

defile, with Christian banners in pursuit, and the flash of weapons at their deadly work, thought all Andalusia was upon them, and fled without awaiting an attack. The pursuit continued among glens and defiles; for the Christian warriors, eager for revenge, had no compassion on the foe.

When the pursuit was over, the Marques of Cadiz and his followers reposed themselves upon the banks of the Guadalete, where they divided the spoil. Among this were found many rich corselets, helmets, and weapons.—the Moorish trophies of the defeat in the mountains of Malaga. Several were claimed by their owners; others were known to have belonged to noble cavaliers who had been slain or taken prisoners. There were several horses also, richly caparisoned, which had pranced proudly with the unfortunate warriors, as they sallied out of Antiquera upon that fatal expedition. Thus the exultation of the victors was dashed with melancholy, and many a knight was seen lamenting over the helmet or corselet of some loved companion in arms.

The good Marques of Cadiz was resting under a tree on the banks of the Guadalete, when the horse which had belonged to his slaughtered brother Beltran was brought to him. He laid his hand upon the mane and looked wistfully at the empty saddle. His bosom heaved with violent agitation, and his lip quivered and was pale. "Ay de mi! mi hermano!" (woe is me! my brother!) was all that he said; for the grief of a warrior has not many words. He looked round on the field strewn with the bodies of the enemy, and in the bitterness of his woe he felt consoled by the idea that his brother had not been unrevenged.

Note.—"En el despojo de la Batalla se ireron muchas ricas corazas e capacetes, i barberas de las que se habian perdido en el Axarquia, e otras muchas armas, e algunes fueron conocidas de sus Duenos que las havian dejado por fuir, e otras fueron conocidas, que eran mui senaladas de hombres principales que havian quedado muertos e cautivos, i fueron tornados muchos de los mismos Cavallos con sus ricassillas, de los que quedaron en la Axarquia, e fueron conocidos cuios eran."—"Cura de Palacios," cap. 67.

CHAPTER TWENTY-THREE

RETREAT OF HAMET EL ZEGRI, ALCAYDE OF RONDA

THE bold alcayde of Ronda, Hamet el Zegri, had careered wide over the Campina of Utrera, encompassing the flocks and herds, when he heard the burst of war at a distance. There were with him but a handful of his Comares. He saw the scamper and pursuit afar off, and beheld the Christain horsemen spurring madly on toward the ambuscade on the banks of the Lopera. Hamet tossed his hand triumphantly aloft for his men to follow him. "The Christian dogs are ours!" said he, as he put spurs to his horse to take the enemy in rear.

The little band which followed Hamet scarcely amounted to thirty horsemen. They spurred across the plain, and reached a rising ground, just as the force of Puerto Carrero had charged, with sound of trumpet, upon the flank of the party in ambush. Hamet beheld the headlong rout of the army with rage and consternation. He found the country was pouring forth its legions from every quarter, and perceived that there was no safety but in precipitate flight.

But which way to fly? An army was between him and the mountain pass; all the forces of the neighborhood were rushing to the borders; the whole route by which he had come was by this time occupied by the foe. He checked his steed, rose in the stirrups, and rolled a stern and thoughtful eye over the country; then sinking into his saddle, he seemed to commune a moment with himself. Turning quickly to his troop, he singled out a renegado Christian, a traitor to his religion and his king. "Come hither," said Hamet. "Thou knowest all the secret passes of the country." "I do," replied the renegado. "Dost thou know any circuitous route, solitary and untraveled, by which we can pass wide within these troops, and reach the Serrania?" The renegado paused: "Such a route I know, but it is full of peril, for it leads through the heart of the Christian land. " 'Tis well," said Hamet; "the more dangerous in appearance the less it will be suspected. Now hearken to me. Ride by my side. Thou seest this purse of gold, and this scimiter. Take us, by the route thou hast mentioned, safe to the pass of the Serrania, and this purse shall be thy reward; betray us, and this scimiter shall cleave thee to the saddle-bow." *

The renegado obeyed, trembling. They turned off from the direct road to the mountains, and struck southward toward Lebrixa, passing by the most solitary roads, and along those deep ramblas and ravines by which the country is intersected. It was indeed a daring course. Every now and then they heard the distant sound of trumpets, and the alarm-bells of towns and villages, and found that the war was still hurrying to the borders. They hid themselves in thickets, and in the dry beds of rivers, until the danger had passed by, and then resumed their course. Hamet el Zegri rode on in silence, his hand upon his scimiter and his eye upon the renegado guide, prepared to sacrifice him on the least sign of treachery; while his band followed, gnawing their lips with rage at having thus to skulk through a country they had come to ravage.

When night fell, they struck into more practicable roads, always keeping wide of the villages and hamlets, lest the watch-dogs should betray them. In this way, they passed in deep midnight by Areos, crossed the Guadalete, and effected their retreat to the mountains. The day dawned as they made their way up the savage defiles. Their comrades had been hunted up these very glens by the enemy. Every now and then they came to where there had been a partial fight, or a slaughter of the fugitives; and the rocks were red with blood and strewed with mangled bodies. The alcayde of Ronda was almost frantic with rage at seeing

---

* Cura de los Palacios. Ubi sup.

many of his bravest warriors lying stiff and stark, a prey to the hawks and vultures of the mountains. Now and then some wretched Moor would crawl out of a cave or glen, whither he had fled for refuge; for in the retreat many of the horsemen had abandoned their steeds, thrown away their armor, and clambered up the cliffs, where they could not be pursued by the Christian cavalry.

The Moorish army had sallied forth from Ronda amid shouts and acclamations; but wailings were heard within its walls, as the alcayde and his broken band returned without banner or trumpet, and haggard with famine and fatigue. The tidings of their disaster had preceded them, borne by the fugitives of the army. No one ventured to speak to the stern Hamet el Zegri as he entered the city; for they saw a dark cloud gathered upon his brow.

It seemed (says the pious Antonio Agapida) as if Heaven meted out this defeat in exact retribution for the ills inflicted upon the Christian warriors in the heights of Malaga. It was equally signal and disastrous. Of the brilliant array of Moorish chivalry, which had descended so confidently into Andalusia, not more than two hundred escaped. The choicest troops of the frontier were either taken or destroyed; the Moorish garrisons enfeebled; and many alcaydes and cavaliers of noble lineage carried into captivity, who were afterward obliged to redeem themselves with heavy ransoms.

This was called the battle of Lopera, and was fought on the 17th of September, 1483. Ferdinand and Isabella were at Vittoria in old Castile, when they received news of the victory, and· the standards taken from the enemy. They celebrated the event with processions, illuminations, and other festivities. Ferdinand sent to the Marques of Cadiz the royal raiment which he had worn on that day, and conferred on him, and on all those who should inherit his title, the privilege of wearing royal robes on our Lady's day, in September, in commemoration of this victory.

Queen Isabella was equally mindful of the great services of Don Luis Fernandez Puerto Carrero. Besides many en-

comiums and favors, she sent to his wife the royal vestments
and robe of brocade which she had worn on the same day, to
be worn by her, during her life, on the anniversary of that
battle.*

CHAPTER TWENTY-FOUR

OF THE RECEPTION AT COURT OF THE COUNT DE CABRA AND THE ALCAYDE DE LOS DONZELES

IN the midst of the bustle of warlike affairs, the worthy
chronicler Fray Antonio Agapida pauses to note, with curious accuracy, the distinguished reception given to the Count
de Cabra and his nephew, the alcàyde de los Donzeles, at the
stately and ceremonious court of the Castilian sovereigns, in
reward for the capture of the Moorish king Boabdil. The
court (he observes) was held at the time in the ancient Moorish palace of the city of Cordova, and the ceremonials were
arranged by that venerable prelate Don Pedro Gonzalez de
Mendoza, bishop of Toledo and grand cardinal of Spain.

It was on Wednesday, the 14th of October (continues the
precise Antonio Agapida), that the good Count de Cabra,
according to arrangement, appeared at the gate of Cordova.
Here he was met by the grand cardinal and the Duke of Villahermosa, illegitimate brother of the king, together with
many of the first grandees and prelates of the kingdom. By
this august train was he attended to the palace, amid triumphant strains of martial music and the shouts of a prodigious multitude.

When the count arrived in the presence of the sovereigns,
who were seated in state on a dais or raised part of the hall
of audience, they both arose. The king advanced exactly
five steps toward the count, who knelt and kissed his majesty's hand; but the king would not receive him as a mere
vassal, but embraced him with affectionate cordiality. The

---

* Mariana Abarca, Zurita, Pulgar, etc.

queen also advanced two steps, and received the count with
a countenance full of sweetness and benignity: after he had
kissed her hand, the king and queen returned to their thrones,
and, cushions being brought, they ordered the Count de Cabra
to be seated in their presence.   This last circumstance is written in large letters, and followed by several notes of admiration, in the manuscript of the worthy Fray Antonio Agapida,
who considers the extraordinary privilege of sitting in presence of the Catholic sovereigns an honor well worth fighting
for.

The good count took his seat at a short distance from the
king, and near him was seated the Duke of Najera, then the
bishop of Palencia, then the Count of Aguilar, the Count
Luna, and Don Gutierre de Cardonas, senior commander of
Leon.

On the side of the queen were seated the grand cardinal
of Spain, the Duke of Villahermosa, the Count of Monte Rey,
and the bishops of Jaen and Cuenca, each in the order in
which they are named.   The Infanta Isabella was prevented,
by indisposition, from attending the ceremony.

And now festive music resounded through the hall, and
twenty ladies of the queen's retinue entered magnificently
attired; upon which twenty youthful cavaliers, very gay and
galliard in their array, stepped forth, and, each seeking his
fair partner, they commenced a stately dance.   The court in
the meantime (observes Fray Antonió Agapida) looked on
with lofty and becoming gravity.

When the dance was concluded, the king and queen rose
to retire to supper, and dismissed the count with many gracious expressions.   He was then attended by all the grandees
present to the palace of the grand cardinal, where they partook of a sumptuous banquet.

On the following Saturday, the alcayde de los Donzeles
was received, likewise, with great honors; but the ceremonies were so arranged as to be a degree less in dignity
than those shown to his uncle; the latter being considered
the principal actor in this great achievement.   Thus the

grand cardinal and the Duke of Villahermosa did not meet him at the gate of the city, but received him in the palace, and entertained him in conversation until summoned to the sovereigns.

When the alcayde de los Donzeles entered the presence chamber, the king and queen rose from their chairs, but without advancing. They greeted him graciously, and commanded him to be seated next to the Count de Cabra.

The Infanta Isabella came forth to this reception, and took her seat beside the queen. When the court were all seated, the music again sounded through the hall, and the twenty ladies came forth as on the preceding occasion, richly attired, but in different raiment. They danced as before; and the Infanta Isabella, taking a young Portuguese damsel for a partner, joined in the dance. When this was concluded, the king and queen dismissed the alcayde de los Donzeles with great courtesy and the court broke up.

The worthy Fray Antonio Agapida here indulges in a long eulogy on the scrupulous discrimination of the Castilian court, in the distribution of its honors and rewards, by which means every smile, and gesture, and word of the sovereigns, had its certain value, and conveyed its equivalent of joy to the heart of the subject; a matter well worthy the study (says he) of all monarchs, who are too apt to distribute honors with a heedless caprice that renders them of no avail.

On the following Sunday, both the Count de Cabra and the alcayde de los Donzeles were invited to sup with the sovereigns. The court that evening was attended by the highest nobility, arrayed with that cost and splendor for which the Spanish nobility of those days were renowned.

Before supper, there was a stately and ceremonious dance, befitting the dignity of so august a court. The king led forth the queen, in grave and graceful measure; the Count de Cabra was honored with the hand of the Infanta Isabella; and the alcayde de los Donzeles danced with a daughter of the Marques de Astorga.

The dance being concluded, the royal party repaired to

the supper-table, which was placed on an elevated part of the saloon. Here, in full view of the court, the Count de Cabra and the alcayde de los Donzeles supped at the same table with the king, the queen, and the Infanta. The royal family were served by the Marques of Villena. The cupbearer to the king was his nephew Fadrigue de Toledo, son to the Duke of Alva. Don Alexis de Estaniga had the honor of fulfilling that office for the queen, and Tello de Aguilar for the Infanta. Other cavaliers of rank and distinction waited on the count and the alcayde de los Donzeles. At one o'clock, the two distinguished guests were dismissed with many courteous expressions by the sovereigns.

Such (says Fray Antonio Agapida) were the great honors paid at our most exalted and ceremonious court to these renowned cavaliers: but the gratitude of the sovereigns did not end here. A few days afterward, they bestowed upon them large revenues for life, and others to descend to their heirs, with the privilege for them and their descendants to prefix the title of Don to their names. They gave them, moreover, as armorial bearings, a Moor's head crowned, with a golden chain round the neck, in a sanguine field, and twenty-two banners round the margin of the escutcheon. Their descendants, of the houses of Cabra and Cordova, continue to bear these arms at the present day, in memorial of the victory of Lucena and the capture of Boabdil el Chico.*

CHAPTER TWENTY-FIVE

HOW THE MARQUES OF CADIZ CONCERTED TO SURPRISE ZAHARA, AND THE RESULT OF HIS ENTERPRISE

THE valiant Roderigo Ponce de Leon, Marques of Cadiz, was one of the most vigilant of commanders. He kept in

---

*The account given by Fray Antonio Agapida of this ceremonial, so characteristic of the old Spanish court, agrees in almost every particular with an ancient manuscript, made up from the chronicles of the curate of los Palacios and other old Spanish writers.

his pay a number of converted Moors, to serve as adalides or armed guides. These mongrel Christians were of great service in procuring information. Availing themselves of their Moorish character and tongue, they penetrated into the enemy's country, prowled about the castles and fortresses, noticed the state of the walls, the gates and towers, the strength of their garrison, and the vigilance or negligence of their commanders. All this they reported minutely to the marques, who thus knew the state of every fortress upon the frontier, and when it might be attacked with advantage. Besides the various towns and cities over which he held a feudal sway, he had always an armed force about him, ready for the field. A host of retainers fed in his hall, who were ready to follow him to danger and death itself, without inquiring who or why they fought. The armories of his castles were supplied with helms and cuirasses and weapons of all kinds, ready burnished for use; and his stables were filled with hardy steeds that could stand a mountain scamper.

The marques was aware that the late defeat of the Moors on the banks of the Lopera had weakened their whole frontier; for many of the castles and fortresses had lost their alcaydes and their choicest troops. He sent out his warhounds, therefore, upon the range to ascertain where a successful blow might be struck; and they soon returned with word that Zahara was weakly garrisoned and short of provisions.

This was the very fortress which, about two years before, had been stormed by Muley Aben Hassan; and its capture had been the first blow of this eventful war. It had ever since remained a thorn in the side of Andalusia. All the Christians had been carried away captive, and no civil population had been introduced in their stead. There were no women or children in the place. It was kept up as a mere military post, commanding one of the most important passes of the mountains, and was a stronghold of Moorish marauders. The marques was animated by the idea of regaining this fortress for his sovereigns, and wresting from the old

Moorish king this boasted trophy of his prowess. He sent missives, therefore, to the brave Luis Fernandez Puerto Carrero, who had distinguished himself in the late victory, and to Juan Almaraz, captain of the men-at-arms of the Holy Brotherhood, informing them of his designs, and inviting them to meet him with their forces on the banks of the Gaudalete.

It was on the day (says Fray Antonio Agapida) of the glorious apostles St. Simon and Judas, the twenty-eighth of October, in the year of grace one thousand four hundred and eighty-three, that this chosen band of Christian soldiers assembled suddenly and secretly at the appointed place. Their forces, when united, amounted to six hundred horse and fifteen hundred foot. Their gathering place was at the entrance of the defile leading to Zahara. That ancient town, renowned in Moorish warfare, is situated in one of the roughest passes of the Serrania de Ronda. It is built round the craggy cone of a hill, on the lofty summit of which is a strong castle. The country around is broken into deep barrancas or ravines, some of which approach its very walls. The place had until recently been considered impregnable; but (as the worthy Fray Antonio Agapida observes) the walls of impregnable fortresses, like the virtue of self-confident saints, have their weak points of attack.

The Marques of Cadiz advanced with his little army in the dead of the night, marching silently into the deep and dark defiles of the mountains, and stealing up the ravines which extended to the walls of the town. Their approach was so noiseless that the Moorish sentinels upon the walls heard not a voice or a footfall. The marques was accompanied by his old escalador, Ortega de Prado, who had distinguished himself at the scaling of Alhama. This hardy veteran was stationed, with ten men, furnished with scaling-ladders, in a cavity among the rocks, close to the walls. At a little distance, seventy men were hid in a ravine, to be at hand to second him when he should have fixed his ladders. The rest of the troops were concealed in another ravine, commanding a fair approach to the gate of the fortress. A shrewd and wary adalide, well acquainted with the place, was appointed to give signals; and was so stationed that he could be seen by the various parties in ambush, but was hidden from the garrison.

The remainder of the night passed away in profound quiet. The Moorish sentinels could be heard tranquilly patroling the walls, in perfect security. The day dawned, and the rising sun began to shine against the lofty peaks of the Serrania de Ronda. The sentinels looked from their battlements over a savage but quiet mountain country, where not a human being was stirring; they little dreamed of the mischief that lay lurking in every ravine and chasm of the rocks around them. Apprehending no danger of surprise in broad day, the greater part of the soldiers abandoned the walls and towers, and descended into the city.

By orders of the marques, a small body of light cavalry passed along the glen, and, turning round a point of rock, showed themselves before the town: they skirted the fields almost to the gates, as if by way of bravado, and to defy the garrison to a skirmish. The Moors were not slow in replying to it. About seventy horse, and a number of foot who had guarded the walls, sallied forth impetuously, thinking to make easy prey of these insolent marauders. The Christian horsemen fled for the ravine; the Moors pursued them down the hill until they heard a great shouting and tumult behind them. Looking round, they beheld their town assailed, and a scaling party mounting the walls sword in hand. Wheeling about, they galloped furiously for the gate; the Marques of Cadiz and Luis Fernandez Puerto Carrero rushed forth at the same time with their ambuscade, and endeavored to cut them off; but the Moors succeeded in throwing themselves within the walls.

While Puerto Carrero stormed at the gate, the marques put spurs to his horse and galloped to the support of Ortega de Prado and his scaling party. He arrived at a moment of imminent peril, when the party was assailed by fifty Moors, armed with cuirasses and lances, who were on the point of thrusting them from the walls. The marques sprang from his horse, mounted a ladder, sword in hand, followed by a number of his troops, and made a vigorous attack upon the enemy.* They were soon driven from the walls, and the gates and towers remained in possession of the Christians. The Moors defended themselves for a short time in the streets, but at length took refuge in the castle, the walls of which were strong, and capable of holding out until relief should arrive. The marques had no desire to carry on a siege, and he had not provisions sufficient for many prisoners; he granted them, therefore, favorable terms. They were permitted, on leaving their arms behind them, to march out with as much of their effects as they could carry; and it was stipulated that they should pass over to Barbary. The marques remained in the place until both town and castle were put in a perfect state of defense and strongly garrisoned.

Thus did Zahara return once more into possession of the Christians, to the great confusion of old Muley Aben Hassan, who, having paid the penalty of his ill-timed violence, was now deprived of its vaunted fruits. The Castilian sovereigns were so gratified by this achievement of the valiant Ponce de Leon that they authorized him thenceforth to entitle himself Duke of Cadiz and Marques of Zahara. The warrior, however, was so proud of the original title, under which he had so often signalized himself, that he gave it the precedence, and always signed himself, Marques, Duke of Cadiz. As the reader may have acquired the same predilection we shall continue to call him by his ancient title.

---

* Cura de los Palacios. c. 68.

CHAPTER TWENTY-SIX

OF THE FORTRESS OF ALHAMA, AND HOW WISELY IT WAS
GOVERNED BY THE COUNT DE TENDILLA

In this part of his chronicle, the worthy father Fray Antonio Agapida indulges in triumphant exultation over the downfall of Zahara: Heaven sometimes speaks (says he) through the mouths of false prophets for the confusion of the wicked. By the fall of this fortress was the prediction of the santon of Granada in some measure fulfilled, that "the ruins of Zahara should fall upon the heads of the Infidels."

Our zealous chronicler scoffs at the Moorish alcayde, who lost his fortress by surprise in broad daylight; and contrasts the vigilance of the Christian governor of Alhama, the town taken in retaliation for the storming of Zahara.

The important post of Alhama was at this time confided by King Ferdinand to Don Inigo Lopez de Mendoza, Count of Tendilla, a cavalier of noble blood, brother to the grand cardinal of Spain. He had been instructed by the king not merely to maintain his post, but also to make sallies and lay waste the surrounding country. His fortress was critically situated. It was within seven leagues of Granada, and at no great distance from the warlike city of Loxa. It was nestled in the lap of the mountains, commanding the high-road to Malaga and a view over the extensive vega. Thus situated, in the heart of the enemy's country, surrounded by foes ready to assail him, and a rich country for him to ravage, it behooved this cavalier to be forever on the alert. He was in fact an experienced veteran, a shrewd and wary officer, and a commander amazingly prompt and fertile in expedients.

On assuming the command, he found that the garrison consisted but of one thousand men, horse and foot. They were hardy troops, seasoned in rough mountain campaigning, but reckless and dissolute, as soldiers are apt to be when accustomed to predatory warfare. They would fight hard for booty, and then gamble it heedlessly away or squander it in licentious reveling. Alhama abounded with hawking, sharping, idle hangers-on, eager to profit by the vices and follies of the garrison. The soldiers were oftener gambling and dancing beneath the walls than keeping watch upon the battlements; and nothing was heard, from morning till night, but the noisy contest of cards and dice, mingled with the sound of the bolero or fandango, the drowsy strumming of the guitar, and the rattling of the castanets; while often the whole was interrupted by the loud brawl, and fierce and bloody contest.

The Count of Tendilla set himself vigorously to reform these excesses; he knew that laxity of morals is generally attended by neglect of duty, and that the least breach of discipline in the exposed situation of his fortress might be fatal. "Here is but a handful of men," said he; "it is necessary that each man should be a hero."

He endeavored to awaken a proper ambition in the minds of his soldiers, and to instill into them the high principles of chivalry. "A just war," he observed, "is often rendered wicked and disastrous by the manner in which it is conducted; for the righteousness of the cause is not sufficient to sanction the profligacy of the means, and the want of order and subordination among the troops may bring ruin and disgrace upon the best concerted plans." But we cannot describe the character and conduct of this renowned commander in more forcible language than that of Fray Antonio Agapida, excepting that the pious father places in the foreground of his virtues his hatred of the Moors. "The Count de Tendilla," says he, "was a mirror of Christian knighthood—watchful, abstemious, chaste, devout, and thoroughly filled with the spirit of the cause. He labored incessantly and strenuously for the glory of the faith, and the prosperity of their most Catholic majesties; and, above all, he hated the Infidels with a pure and holy hatred. This worthy cavalier discountenanced all idleness, rioting, chambering, and wantonness among his soldiery. He kept them constantly to the exercise of arms, making them adroit in the use of their weapons and management of their steeds, and prompt for the field at a moment's notice. He permitted no sound of lute or harp, or song, or other loose minstrelsy, to be heard in his fortress, debauching the ear and softening the valor of the soldier; no other music was allowed but the wholesome rolling of the drum and braying of the trumpet, and such like spirit-stirring instruments as fill the mind with thoughts of iron war. All wandering minstrels, sharping peddlers, sturdy trulls, and other camp trumpery, were ordered to pack up their baggage, and were drummed out of the gates of Alhama. In place, of such lewd rabble, he introduced a train of holy friars to inspirit his people by exhortation, and prayer, and choral chanting, and to spur them on to fight the good fight of faith. All games of chance were prohibited, except the game of war; and this he labored, by vigilance and vigor, to reduce to a game of certainty. Heaven smiled upon the efforts of this righteous cavalier. His men became soldiers at all points, and terrors to the Moors. The good count never set forth on a ravage without observing the rites of confession, absolution, and communion, and obliging his followers to do the same. Their banners were blessed by the holy friars whom he maintained in Alhama; and in this way success was secured to his arms, and he was enabled to lay waste the land of the heathen.

The fortress of Alhama (continues Fray Antonio Agapida) overlooked from its lofty site a great part of the fertile vega, watered by the Cazin and the Xenil: from this he made frequent sallies, sweeping away the flocks and herds from the pasture, the laborer from the field, and the convoy from the road; so that it was said by the Moors that a beetle could not crawl across the vega without being seen by Count Tendilla. The peasantry, therefore, were fain to betake themselves to watch-towers and fortified hamlets, where they shut up their cattle, garnered their corn, and sheltered their wives and children. Even there they were not safe; the count would storm these rustic fortresses with fire and sword; make captives of their inhabitants; carry off the corn, the oil, the silks, and cattle; and leave the ruins blazing and smoking, within the very sight of Granada.

"It was a pleasing and refreshing sight," continues the good father, "to behold this pious knight and his followers returning from one of these crusades, leaving the rich land of the Infidel in smoking desolation behind them; to behold the long line of mules and asses, laden with the plunder of the Gentiles—the hosts of captive Moors, men, women, and children—droves of sturdy beeves, lowing kine, and bleating sheep; all winding up the steep acclivity to the gates of Alhama, pricked on by the Catholic soldiers. His garrison thus thrived on the fat of the land and the spoil of the Infidel; nor was he unmindful of the pious fathers, whose blessings crowned his enterprises with success. A large portion of the spoil was always dedicated to the church; and the good friars were ever ready at the gate to hail him on his return, and receive the share allotted them. Beside these allotments, he made many votive offerings, either in time of peril or on the eve of a foray; and the chapels of Alhama were resplendent with chalices, crosses, and other precious gifts made by this Catholic cavalier."

Thus eloquently does the venerable Fray Antonio Agapida dilate in praise of the good Count de Tendilla; and other historians of equal veracity, but less unction, agree in pronouncing him one of the ablest of Spanish generals. So terrible in fact did he become in the land that the Moorish peasantry could not venture a league from Granada or Loxa to labor in the fields, without peril of being carried into captivity. The people of Granada clamored against Muley Aben Hassan, for suffering his lands to be thus outraged and insulted, and demanded to have this bold marauder shut up in his fortress. The old monarch was roused by their remonstrances. He sent forth powerful troops of horse, to protect the country, during the season that the husbandmen were abroad in the fields. These troops patroled in formidable squadrons in the neighborhood of Alhama, keeping strict watch upon its gates; so that it was impossible for the Christians to make a sally without being seen and intercepted.

While Alhama was thus blockaded by a roving force of Moorish cavalry, the inhabitants were awakened one night by a tremendous crash that shook the fortress to its foundations. The garrison flew to arms, supposing it some assault of the enemy. The alarm proved to have been caused by the rupture of a portion of the wall, which, undermined by heavy rains, had suddenly given way, leaving a large chasm yawning toward the plain.

The Count de Tendilla was for a time in great anxiety. Should this breach be discovered by the blockading horsemen, they would arouse the country, Granada and Loxa would pour out an overwhelming force, and they would find his walls ready sapped for an assault. In this fearful emergency, the count displayed his noted talent for expedients. He ordered a quantity of linen cloth to be stretched in front of the breach, painted in imitation of stone, and indented with battlements, so as at a distance to resemble the other parts of the wall: behind this screen he employed workmen, day and night, in repairing the fracture. No one was permitted to leave the fortress, lest information of its defenseless plight should be carried to the Moor. Light squadrons of the enemy were seen hovering about the plain, but never approached near enough to discover the deception; and thus, in the course of a few days, the wall was rebuilt stronger than before.

There was another expedient of this shrewd veteran which greatly excites the marvel of Agapida. "It happened," he observes, "that this Catholic cavalier at one time was destitute of gold and silver, wherewith to pay the wages of his troops; and the soldiers murmured greatly, seeing that they had not the means of purchasing necessaries from the people of the town. In this dilemma, what does this most sagacious commander? He takes me a number of little morsels of paper, on the which he inscribes various sums, large and small, according to the nature of the case, and signs me them with his own hand and name. These did he give to the soldiery, in earnest of their pay. 'How!' you will say, 'are soldiers to be paid with scraps of paper?' Even so, I answer, and well paid too, as I will presently make manifest: for the good count issued a proclamation, ordering the inhabitants of Alhama to take these morsels of paper for the full amount thereon inscribed, promising to redeem them at a future time with silver and gold, and threatening severe punishment to all who should refuse. The people, having full confidence in his word, and trusting that he would be as willing to perform the one promise as he certainly was able to perform the other, took those curious morsels of paper without hesitation or demur. Thus, by a subtle and most miraculous kind of alchemy, did this Catholic cavalier turn worthless paper into precious gold, and make his late impoverished garrison abound in money!"

It is but just to add that the Count de Tendilla redeemed his promises like a loyal knight; and this miracle, as it appeared in the eyes of Fray Antonio Agapida, is the first instance on record of paper money, which has since inundated the civilized world with unbounded opulence.

CHAPTER TWENTY-SEVEN

FORAY OF CHRISTIAN KNIGHTS INTO THE TERRITORY OF THE MOORS

THE Spanish cavaliers who had survived the memorable massacre among the mountains of Malaga, although they had repeatedly avenged the death of their companions, yet could not forget the horror and humiliation of their defeat. Nothing would satisfy them but to undertake a second expedition of the kind, to carry fire and sword throughout a wide part of the Moorish territories, and to leave all those regions which had triumphed in their disaster a black and burning monument of their vengeance. Their wishes accorded with the policy of the king, who desired to lay waste the country and destroy the resources of the enemy; every assistance was therefore given to promote and accomplish their enterprise.

In the spring of 1484 the ancient city of Antiquera again resounded with arms; numbers of the same cavaliers who had assembled there so gayly the preceding year again came wheeling into the gates with their steeled and shining warriors, but with a more dark and solemn brow than on that disastrous occasion, for they had the recollection of their slaughtered friends present to their minds, whose deaths they were to avenge.

In a little while there was a chosen force of six thousand horse and twelve thousand foot assembled in Antiquera, many of them the very flower of Spanish chivalry, troops of the established military and religious orders, and of the Holy Brotherhood.

Every precaution had been taken to furnish this army with all things needful for its extensive and perilous inroad. Numerous surgeons accompanied it, who were to attend upon all the sick and wounded, without charge, being paid for their services by the queen. Isabella, also, in her considerate humanity, provided six spacious tents furnished with beds and all things needful for the wounded and infirm. These continued to be used in all great expeditions throughout the war, and were called the Queen's Hospital. The worthy father, Fray Antonio Agapida, vaunts this benignant provision of the queen as the first introduction of a regular camp hospital in campaigning service.

Thus thoroughly prepared, the cavaliers issued forth from Antiquera in splendid and terrible array, but with less exulting confidence and vaunting ostentation than on their former foray; and this was the order of the army. Don Alonzo de Aguilar led the advance guard, accompanied by Don Diego Fernandez de Cordova, the alcayde de los Donzeles, and Luis

Fernandez Puerto Carrero, Count of Palma, with their house-hold troops. They were followed by Juan de Merlo, Juan de Almara, and Carlos de Biezman, of the Holy Brother-hood, with the men-at-arms of their captaincies.

The second battalion was commanded by the Marques of Cadiz and the Master of Santiago, with the cavaliers of San-tiago and the troops of the house of Ponce Leon: with these also went the senior commander of Calatrava and the knights of that order, and various other cavaliers and their retainers.

The right wing of this second battalion was led by Gon-salvo de Cordova, afterward renowned as grand captain of Spain; the left wing, by Diego Lopez de Avila. They were accompanied by several distinguished cavaliers, and certain captains of the Holy Brotherhood, with their men-at-arms.

The Duke of Medina Sidonia and the Count de Cabra commanded the third battalion, with the troops of their re-spective houses. They were accompanied by other com-manders of note, with their forces.

The rear guard was brought up by the senior commander and knights of Alcantara, followed by the Andalusian chiv-alry from Xeres, Ecija, and Carmona.

Such was the army that issued forth from the gates of Antiquera, on one of the most extensive *talas*, or devastating inroads, that ever laid waste the kingdom of Granada.

The army entered the Moorish territory by the way of Alora, destroying all the cornfields, vineyards, and orchards, and plantations of olives, round that city. It then proceeded through the rich valleys and fertile uplands of Coin, Cazara-bonela, Almexia, and Cartama; and in ten days all those fertile regions were a smoking and frightful desert. From hence it pursued its slow and destructive course, like the stream of lava of a volcano, through the regions of Papiana and Alhendin, and so on to the vega of Malaga, laying waste the groves of olives and almonds, and the fields of grain, and destroying every green thing. The Moors of some of these places interceded in vain for their groves and fields, offering to deliver up their Christian captives. One part of the army blockaded the towns, while the other ravaged the surrounding country. Sometimes the Moors sallied forth desperately to defend their property, but were driven back to their gates with slaughter, and their suburbs pillaged and burned. It was an awful spectacle at night to behold the volumes of black smoke mingled with lurid flames that rose from the burning suburbs, and the women on the walls of the town wringing their hands and shrieking at the desolation of their dwellings.

The destroying army, on arriving at the seacoast, found vessels lying off shore laden with all kinds of provisions and munitions for its use, which had been sent from Seville and Xeres: it was thus enabled to continue its desolating career. Advancing to the neighborhood of Malaga, it was bravely assailed by the Moors of that city, and there was severe skirmishing for a whole day; but while the main part of the army encountered the enemy, the rest ravaged the whole vega and destroyed all the mills. As the object of the expedition was not to capture places, but merely to burn, ravage, and destroy, the host, satisfied with the mischief they had done in the vega, turned their backs upon Malaga and again entered the mountains. They passed by Coin, and through the regions of Allazayna, and Gatero, and Alhaurin; all which were likewise desolated. In this way did they make the circuit of that chain of rich and verdant valleys, the glory of those mountains and the pride and delight of the Moors. For forty days did they continue on like a consuming fire, leaving a smoking and howling waste to mark their course, until, weary with the work of destruction, and having fully sated their revenge for the massacre of the Axarquia, they returned in triumph to the meadows of Antiquera.

In the month of June, King Ferdinand took command in person of this destructive army; he increased its force, and added to its means of mischief several lombards and other heavy artillery, intended for the battering of towns, and managed by engineers from France and Germany. With these, the Marques of Cadiz assured the king, he would soon be able to reduce the Moorish fortresses. They were only calculated for defense against the engines anciently used in warfare. Their walls and towers were high and thin, depending for security on their rough and rocky situations. The stone and iron balls thundered from the lombards would soon tumble them in ruins upon the heads of their defenders.

The fate of Alora speedily proved the truth of this opinion. It was strongly posted on a rock washed by a river. The artillery soon battered down two of the towers and a part of the wall. The Moors were thrown into consternation at the vehemence of the assault, and the effect of those tremendous engines upon their vaunted bulwarks. The roaring of the artillery and the tumbling of the walls terrified the women, who beset the alcayde with vociferous supplications to surrender. The place was given up on the 20th of June, on condition that the inhabitants might depart with their effects. The people of Malaga, as yet unacquainted with the power of this battering ordnance, were so incensed at those of Alora, for what they considered a tame surrender, that they would not admit them into their city.

A similar fate attended the town of Setenil, built on a lofty rock and esteemed impregnable. Many times had it been besieged under former Christian kings, but never had it been taken. Even now, for several days the artillery was directed against it without effect, and many of the cavaliers murmured at the Marques of Cadiz for having counseled the king to attack this unconquerable place.*

On the same night that these reproaches were uttered, the marques directed the artillery himself: he leveled the lombards at the bottom of the walls and at the gates. In a little while the gates were battered to pieces, a great breach was effected in the walls, and the Moors were fain to capitulate. Twenty-four Christian captives, who had been taken in the defeat of the mountains of Malaga, were rescued from the dungeons of this fortress, and hailed the Marques of Cadiz as their deliverer.

* Cura de los Palacios.

Needless is it to mention the capture of various other places, which surrendered without waiting to be attacked. The Moors had always shown great bravery and perseverance in defending their towns; they were formidable in their sallies and skirmishes, and patient in enduring hunger and thirst when besieged; but this terrible ordnance, which demolished their walls with such ease and rapidity, overwhelmed them with confusion and dismay, and rendered vain all resistance. King Ferdinand was so struck with the effect of this artillery that he ordered the number of lombards to be increased; and these potent engines had henceforth a great influence on the fortunes of this war.

The last operation of this year, so disastrous to the Moors, was an inroad by King Ferdinand, in the latter part of summer, into the vega, in which he ravaged the country, burned two villages near to Granada, and destroyed the mills near the very gates of the city.

Old Muley Aben Hassan was overwhelmed with dismay at this desolation, which, during the whole year, had been raging throughout his territories, and had now reached to the walls of his capital. His fierce spirit was broken by misfortunes and infirmity; he offered to purchase a peace and to hold his crown as a tributary vassal. Ferdinand would listen to no propositions: the absolute conquest of Granada was the great object of this war, and he was resolved never to rest content without its complete fulfillment. Having supplied and strengthened the garrisons of the places he had taken in the heart of the Moorish territories, he enjoined their commanders to render every assistance to the younger Moorish king, in the civil war against his father. He then returned with his army to Cordova, in great triumph, closing a series of ravaging campaigns, that had filled the kingdom of Granada with grief and consternation.

CHAPTER TWENTY-EIGHT

ATTEMPT OF EL ZAGAL TO SURPRISE BOABDIL IN ALMERIA

DURING this year of sorrow and disaster to the Moors, the younger King Boabdil, most truly called the unfortunate, held a diminished and feeble court in the maritime city of Almeria. He retained little more than the name of king, and was supported in even this shadow of royalty by the countenance and treasures of the Castilian sovereigns. Still he trusted that, in the fluctuation of events, the inconstant nation might once more return to his standard, and replace him on the throne of the Alhambra.

His mother, the high-spirited Sultana Ayxa la Horra, endeavored to rouse him from this passive state. "It is a feeble mind," said she, "that waits for the turn of fortune's wheel; the brave mind seizes upon it and turns it to its purpose. Take the field, and you may drive danger before you; remain cowering at home, and it besieges you in your dwelling. By a bold enterprise you may regain your splendid throne in Granada; by passive forbearance, you will forfeit even this miserable throne in Almeria."

Boabdil had not the force of soul to follow these courageous counsels, and in a little time the evils his mother had predicted fell upon him.

Old Muley Aben Hassan was almost extinguished by age and infirmity. He had nearly lost his sight and was completely bedridden. His brother Abdallah, surnamed El Zagal, or the valiant, the same who had assisted in the massacre of the Spanish chivalry among the mountains of Malaga, was commander-in-chief of the Moorish armies, and gradually took upon himself most of the cares of sovereignty. Among other things, he was particularly zealous in espousing his brother's quarrel with his son; and he prosecuted it with such vehemence that many affirmed there was something more than mere fraternal sympathy at the bottom of his zeal.

The disasters and disgraces inflicted on the country by the Christians during this year had wounded the national feelings of the people of Almeria; and many had felt indignant that Boabdil should remain passive at such a time, or rather, should appear to make a common cause with the enemy. His uncle Abdallah diligently fomented this feeling, by his agents. The same arts were made use of that had been successful, in Granada. Boabdil was secretly but actively denounced by the alfaquis as an apostate, leagued with the Christians against his country and his early faith; the affections of the populace and soldiery were gradually alienated from him, and a deep conspiracy concerted for his destruction.

In the month of February, 1485, El Zagal suddenly appeared before Almeria, at the head of a troop of horse. The alfaquis were prepared for his arrival and the gates were thrown open to him. He entered with his band, and galloped to the citadel. The alcayde would have made resistance; but the garrison put him to death, and received El Zagal with acclamations. El Zagal rushed through the apartments of the Alcazar, but he sought in vain for Boabdil. He found the Sultana Ayxa la Horra in one of the saloons, with Ben Ahagete, a younger brother of the monarch, a valiant Abencerrage, and several attendants, who rallied round them to protect them. "Where is the traitor Boabdil?" exclaimed El Zagal. "I know no traitor more perfidious than thyself," exclaimed the intrepid sultana; "and I trust my son is in safety to take vengeance on thy treason." The rage of El Zagal was without bounds when he learned that his intended victim had escaped. In his fury he slew the prince Ben Ahagete, and his followers fell upon and massacred the Abencerrage and attendants. As to the proud sultana, she was borne away prisoner, and loaded with revilings, as having upheld her son in his rebellion and fomented a civil war.

The unfortunate Boabdil had been apprised of his danger by a faithful soldier, just in time to make his escape. Throwing himself on one of the fleetest horses in his stables, and followed by a handful of adherents, he had galloped in the confusion out of the gates of Almeria. Several of the cavalry of El Zagal, who were stationed without the walls, perceived his flight and attempted to pursue him; their horses were jaded with travel and he soon left them far behind. But, whither was he to fly? Every fortress and castle in the kingdom of Granada was closed against him; he knew not whom among the Moors to trust, for they had been taught to detest him as a traitor and an apostate. He had no alternative but to seek refuge among the Christians, his hereditary enemies. With a heavy heart, he turned his horse's head toward Cordova. He had to lurk, like a fugitive, through a part of his own dominions; nor did he feel himself secure, until he had passed the frontier and beheld the mountain barrier of his country towering behind him. Then it was that he became conscious of his humiliating state—a fugitive from his throne, an outcast from his nation, a king without a kingdom. He smote his breast, in an agony of grief: "Evil indeed," exclaimed he, "was the day of my birth, and truly was I named El Zogoybi, the unlucky."

He entered the gates of Cordova with downcast countenance, and with a train of but forty followers. The sovereigns were absent; but the cavaliers of Andalusia manifested that sympathy in the misfortunes of the monarch that becomes men of lofty and chivalrous souls. They received him with great distinction, attended him with the utmost courtesy, and he was honorably entertained by the civil and military commanders of that ancient city.

In the meantime, El Zagal put a new alcayde over Almeria, to govern in the name of his brother, and, having strongly garrisoned the place, he repaired to Malaga, where an attack of the Christians was apprehended. The young monarch being driven out of the land, and the old monarch blind and bedridden, El Zagal, at the head of the armies, was virtually the sovereign of Granada. The people were pleased with having a new idol to look up to, and a new name to shout forth; and El Zagal was hailed with acclamations, as the main hope of the nation.

CHAPTER TWENTY-NINE

HOW KING FERDINAND COMMENCED ANOTHER CAMPAIGN AGAINST THE MOORS, AND HOW HE LAID SIEGE TO COIN AND CARTAMA

THE great effect of the battering ordnance in demolishing the Moorish fortresses in the preceding year induced King Ferdinand to procure a powerful train for the campaign of 1485, in the course of which he resolved to assault some of the most formidable holds of the enemy. An army of nine thousand cavalry and twenty thousand infantry assembled at Cordova, early in the spring; and the king took the field on the 5th of April. It had been determined, in secret council, to attack the city of Malaga, that ancient and important seaport, on which Granada depended for foreign aid and supplies. It was thought proper previously, however, to get possession of various towns and fortresses in the valleys of Santa Maria and Cartama, through which pass the roads to Malaga.

The first place assailed was the town of Benamáquex. It had submitted to the Catholic sovereigns in the preceding year, but had since renounced its allegiance. King Ferdinand was enraged at the rebellion of the inhabitants. "I will make their punishment," said he, "a terror to others: they shall be loyal through force, if not through faith." The place was carried by storm: one hundred and eight of the principal inhabitants were either put to the sword or hanged on the battlements; the rest were carried into captivity.*

---

* Pulgar, Garibay, Cura de los Palacios.

The towns of Coin and Cartama were besieged on the same day; the first by a division of the army led on by the Marques of Cadiz, the second by another division commanded by Don Alonzo de Aguilar and Luis Fernandez Puerto Carrero, the brave Senior of Palma. The king, with the rest of the army, remained posted between the two places, to render assistance to either division. The batteries opened upon both places at the same time, and the thunder of the lombards was mutually heard from one camp to the other. The Moors made frequent sallies and a valiant defense; but they were confounded by the tremendous uproar of the batteries and the destruction of their walls. In the meantime, the alarm-fires gathered together the Moorish mountaineers of all the Serrania, who assembled in great numbers in the city of Monda, about a league from Coin. They made several attempts to enter the besieged town, but in vain; they were each time intercepted and driven back by the Christians, and were reduced to gaze at a distance in despair on the destruction of the place. While thus situated, there rode one day into Monda a fierce and haughty Moorish chieftain, at the head of a band of swarthy African horsemen: it was Hamet el Zegri, the fiery-spirited alcayde of Ronda, at the head of his band of Comares. He had not yet recovered from the rage and mortification of his defeat on the banks of the Lopera in the disastrous foray of old Bexir, when he had been obliged to steal back furtively to his mountains, with the loss of the bravest of his followers. He had ever since panted for revenge. He now rode among the host of warriors assembled at Monda. "Who among you," cried he, "feels pity for the women and children of Coin, exposed to captivity and death? Whoever he is, let him follow me, who am ready to die as a Moslem for the relief of Moslems." So saying, he seized a white banner, and, waving it over his head, rode forth from the town, followed by the Comares. Many of the warriors, roused by his words and his example, spurred resolutely after his banner. The people of Coin, being prepared for this attempt, sallied forth as they saw the white

VOL. III.   * * *7

banner, and made an attack upon the Christian camp; and in the confusion of the moment, Hamet and his followers galloped into the gates. This re-enforcement animated the besieged, and Hamet exhorted them to hold out obstinately in defense of life and town. As the Comares were veteran warriors, the more they were attacked the harder they fought.

At length a great breach was made in the walls, and Ferdinand, who was impatient of the resistance of the place, ordered the Duke of Naxera and the Count of Benavente to enter with their troops; and as their forces were not sufficient, he sent word to Luis de Cerda, Duke of Medina Celi, to send a part of his people to their assistance.

The feudal pride of the duke was roused at this demand. "Tell my lord the king," said the haughty grandee, "that I have come to succor him with my household troops; if my people are ordered to any place, I am to go with them; but if I am to remain in the camp, my people must remain with me. For the troops cannot serve without their commander, nor their commander without his troops."

The reply of the high-spirited grandee perplexed the cautious Ferdinand, who knew the jealous pride of his powerful nobles. In the meantime, the people of the camp, having made all preparations for the assault, were impatient to be led forward. Upon this, Pero Ruyz de Alarcon put himself at their head, and, seizing their mantas, or portable bulwarks, and their other defenses, they made a gallant assault, and fought their way in at the breach. The Moors were so overcome by the fury of their assault that they retreated fighting to the square of the town. Pero Ruyz de Alarcon thought the place was carried, when suddenly Hamet and his Comares came scouring through the streets with wild war-cries and fell furiously upon the Christians. The latter were in their turn beaten back, and, while attacked in front by the Comares, were assailed by the inhabitants with all kinds of missiles from their roofs and windows. They at length gave way and retreated through the breach. Pero Ruyz de Alarcon still maintained his ground in one of the principal streets

—the few cavaliers that stood by him urged him to fly: "No," said he; "I came here to fight and not to fly." He was presently surrounded by the Comares; his companions fled for their lives; the last they saw of him, he was covered with wounds, but still fighting desperately for the fame of a good cavalier.*

The resistance of the inhabitants, though aided by the valor of the Comares, was of no avail. The battering artillery of the Christians demolished their walls; combustibles were thrown into their town, which set it on fire in various places; and they were at length compelled to capitulate. They were permitted to depart with their effects, and the Comares with their arms. Hamet el Zegri and his African band sallied forth, and rode proudly through the Christian camp; nor could the Spanish cavaliers refrain from regarding with admiration that haughty warrior and his devoted and dauntless followers.

The capture of Coin was accompanied by that of Cartama: the fortifications of the latter were repaired and garrisoned; but Coin being too extensive to be defended by a moderate force, its walls were demolished. The siege of these places struck such terror into the surrounding country that the Moors of many of the neighboring towns abandoned their homes and fled with such of their effects as they could carry away; upon which the king gave orders to demolish their walls and towers.

King Ferdinand now left his camp and his heavy artillery near Cartama, and proceeded with his lighter troops to reconnoiter Malaga. By this time, the secret plan of attack, arranged in the council of war at Cordova, was known to all the world. The vigilant warrior El Zagal had thrown himself into the place; he had put all the fortifications, which were of vast strength, into a state of defense; and had sent orders to the alcaydes of the mountain towns, to hasten with their forces to his assistance.

*Pulgar, part 3, cap. 42.

The very day that Ferdinand appeared before the place, El Zagal sallied forth to receive him, at the head of a thousand cavalry, the choicest warriors of Granada. A hot skirmish took place among the gardens and olive trees near the city. Many were killed on both sides; and this gave the Christians a sharp foretaste of what they might expect if they attemped to besiege the place.

When the skirmish was over, the Marques of Cadiz had a private conference with the king. He represented the difficulty of besieging Malaga with their present force, especially as their plans had been discovered and anticipated, and the whole country was marching over the mountains to oppose them. The marques, who had secret intelligence from all quarters, had received a letter from Juceph Xerife, a Moor of Ronda, of Christian lineage, apprising him of the situation of that important place and its garrison, which at that moment laid it open to attack; and the marques was urgent with the king to seize upon this critical moment, and secure a place which was one of the most powerful Moorish fortresses on the frontiers, and in the hands of Hamet el Zegri had been the scourge of Andalusia. The good marques had another motive for his advice, becoming of a true and loyal knight. In the deep dungeons of Ronda languished several of his companions in arms, who had been captured in the defeat in the Axarquia. To break their chains, and restore them to liberty and light, he felt to be his peculiar duty, as one of those who had most promoted that disastrous enterprise.

King Ferdinand listened to the advice of the marques. He knew the importance of Ronda, which was considered one of the keys to the kingdom of Granada; and he was disposed to punish the inhabitants, for the aid they had rendered to the garrison of Coin. The siege of Malaga, therefore, was abandoned for the present, and preparations made for a rapid and secret move against the city of Ronda.

CHAPTER THIRTY

SIEGE OF RONDA

THE bold Hamet el Zegri, the alcayde of Ronda, had returned sullenly to his stronghold after the surrender of Coin. He had fleshed his sword in battle with the Christians, but his thirst for vengeance was still unsatisfied. Hamet gloried in the strength of his fortress and the valor of his people. A fierce and warlike populace was at his command; his signal-fires could summon all the warriors of the Serrania; his Comares almost subsisted on the spoils of Andalusia; and in the rock on which his fortress was built were hopeless dungeons, filled with Christian captives, who had been carried off by these war-hawks of the mountains.

Ronda was considered as impregnable. It was situated in the heart of wild and rugged mountains, and perched upon an isolated rock, crested by a strong citadel, with triple walls and towers. A deep ravine, or rather a perpendicular chasm of the rocks, of frightful depth, surrounded three parts of the city; through this flowed the Rio Verde, or Green River. There were two suburbs to the city, fortified by walls and towers, and almost inaccessible, from the natural asperity of the rocks. Around this rugged city were deep rich valleys, sheltered by the mountains, refreshed by constant streams, abounding with grain and the most delicious fruits, and yielding verdant meadows, in which was reared a renowned breed of horses, the best in the whole kingdom for a foray.

Hamet el Zegri had scarcely returned to Ronda, when he received intelligence that the Christian army was marching to the siege of Malaga, and orders from El Zagal to send troops to his assistance. Hamet sent a part of his garrison for that purpose; in the meantime, he meditated an expedition to which he was stimulated by pride and revenge. All Andalusia was now drained of its troops; there was an opportunity therefore for an inroad, by which he might wipe out the disgrace of his defeat at the battle of Lopera. Apprehending no danger to his mountain city, now that the storm of war had passed down into the vega of Malaga, he left but a remnant of his garrison to man its walls, and putting himself at the head of his band of Comares, swept down suddenly into the plains of Andalusia. He careered, almost without resistance, over those vast campinas or pasture lands which formed a part of the domains of the Duke of Medina Sidonia. In vain the bells were rung and the alarm-fires kindled—the band of Hamet had passed by, before any force could be assembled, and was only to be traced, like a hurricane, by the devastation it had made.

Hamet regained in safety the Serrania de Ronda, exulting in his successful inroad. The mountain glens were filled with long droves of cattle and flocks of sheep, from the campinas of Medina Sidonia. There were mules, too, laden with the plunder of the villages; and every warrior had some costly spoil of jewels, for his favorite mistress.

As the Zegri drew near to Ronda, he was roused from his dream of triumph by the sound of heavy ordnance bellowing through the mountain defiles. His heart misgave him—he put spurs to his horse and galloped in advance of his lagging cavalgada. As he proceeded, the noise of the ordnance increased, echoing from cliff to cliff. Spurring his horse up a craggy height which commanded an extensive view, he beheld, to his consternation, the country about Ronda white with the tents of a besieging army. The royal standard displayed before a proud encampment, showed that Ferdinand himself was present; while the incessant blaze and thunder of artillery and the volumes of overhanging smoke told the work of destruction that was going on.

The royal army had succeeded in coming upon Ronda by surprise, during the absence of its alcayde and most of its garrison; but its inhabitants were warlike, and defended themselves bravely, trusting that Hamet and his Comares would soon return to their assistance.

The fancied strength of their bulwarks had been of little avail against the batteries of the besiegers. In the space of four days, three towers, and great masses of the walls which defended the suburbs, were battered down, and the suburbs taken and plundered. Lombards and other heavy ordnance were now leveled at the walls of the city, and stones and missiles of all kinds hurled into the streets. The very rock on which the city stood shook with the thunder of the artillery; and the Christian captives, deep within its dungeons, hailed the sound as the promise of deliverance.

When Hamet el Zegri beheld his city thus surrounded and assailed, he called upon his men to follow him, and make a desperate attempt to cut their way through to its relief. They proceeded stealthily through the mountains, until they came to the nearest heights above the Christian camp. When night fell, and part of the army was sunk in sleep, they descended the rocks, and rushing suddenly upon the weakest part of the camp, endeavored to break their way through and gain the city. The camp was too strong to be forced; they were driven back to the crags of the mountains, from whence they defended themselves by showering down darts and stones upon their pursuers.

Hamet now lighted alarm-fires about the heights: his standard was joined by the neighboring mountaineers, and by troops from Malaga. Thus re-enforced, he made repeated assaults upon the Christians, cutting off all stragglers from the camp. All his attempts, however, to force his way into the city were fruitless; many of his bravest men were slain, and he was obliged to retreat into the fastnesses of the mountains.

In the meanwhile, the distress of Ronda was hourly increasing. The Marques of Cadiz, having possession of the suburbs, was enabled to approach to the very foot of the perpendicular precipice rising from the river, on the summit of which the city is built. At the foot of this rock is a living fountain of limpid water, gushing into a great natural basin. A secret mine led down from within the city to this fountain by several hundred steps cut in the solid rock. From hence the city obtained its chief supply of water; and these steps were deeply worn by the weary feet of Christian captives, employed in this painful labor. The Marques of Cadiz discovered this subterranean passage, and directed his pioneers to countermine in the side of the rock; they pierced to the shaft, and, stopping it up, deprived the city of the benefit of this precious fountain.

While the brave Marques of Cadiz was thus pressing the siege with zeal, and glowing with the generous thoughts of soon delivering his companions in arms from the Moorish dungeons, far other were the feelings of the alcayde Hamet el Zegri. He smote his breast and gnashed his teeth in impotent fury, as he beheld from the mountain cliffs the destruction of the city. Every thunder of the Christian ordnance seemed to batter against his heart. He saw tower after tower tumbling by day, and at night the city blazed like a volcano. "They fired not merely stones from their ordnance," says a chronicler of the times, "but likewise great balls of iron, cast in molds, which demolished everything they struck." They threw also balls of tow, steeped in pitch and oil and gunpowder, which, when once on fire, were not to be extinguished, and which set the houses in flames. Great was the horror of the inhabitants: they knew not where to fly for refuge: their houses were in a blaze, or shattered by the ordnance; the streets were perilous from the falling ruins and the bounding balls, which dashed to pieces everything they encountered. At night, the city looked like a fiery furnace; the cries and wailings of the women were heard between the thunders of the ordnance, and reached even to the Moors on the opposite mountains, who answered them by yells of fury and despair.

All hope of external succor being at an end, the inhabitants of Ronda were compelled to capitulate. Ferdinand was easily prevailed upon to grant them favorable terms. The place was capable of longer resistance; and he feared for the safety of his camp, as the forces were daily augmenting on the mountains, and making frequent assaults. The inhabitants were permitted to depart with their effects, either to Barbary or elsewhere; and those who chose to reside in Spain had lands assigned them, and were indulged in the practice of their religion.

No sooner did the place surrender than detachments were sent to attack the Moors who hovered about the neighboring mountains. Hamet el Zegri, however, did not remain to make a fruitless battle. He gave up the game as lost, and retreated with his Gomares, filled with grief and rage, but trusting to fortune to give him future vengeance.

The first care of the good Marques of Cadiz, on entering Ronda, was to deliver his unfortunate companions in arms from the dungeons of the fortress. What a difference in their looks from the time when, flushed with health and hope, and arrayed in military pomp, they had sallied forth upon the mountain foray! Many of them were almost naked, with irons at their ankles, and beards reaching to their waists. Their meeting with the marques was joyful; yet it had the look of grief, for their joy was mingled with many bitter recollections. There was an immense number of other captives, among whom were several young men of noble families, who, with filial piety, had surrendered themselves prisoners in place of their fathers.

The captives were all provided with mules and sent to the queen at Cordova. The humane heart of Isabella melted at the sight of the piteous cavalcade. They were all supplied by her with food and raiment, and money to pay their expenses to their homes. Their chains were hung as pious trophies against the exterior of the church of St. Juan de los Reyes, in Toledo, where the Christian traveler may regale his eyes with the sight of them at this very day.

Among the Moorish captives was a young Infidel maiden, of great beauty, who desired to become a Christian and to remain in Spain. She had been inspired with the light of the true faith, through the ministry of a young man who had been a captive in Ronda. He was anxious to complete

his good work by marrying her. The queen consented to
their pious wishes, having first taken care that the young
maiden should be properly purified by the holy sacrament of
baptism.

"Thus this pestilent nest of warfare and infidelity, the
city of Ronda," says the worthy Fray Antonio Agapida,
"was converted to the true faith by the thunder of our artillery—an example which was soon followed by Casanbonela,
Alarbella, and other towns in these parts, insomuch that in
the course of this expedition no less than seventy-two places
were rescued from the vile sect of Mahomet, and placed
under the benignant domination of the cross."

CHAPTER THIRTY-ONE

HOW THE PEOPLE OF GRANADA INVITED EL ZAGAL TO THE THRONE, AND HOW HE MARCHED TO THE CAPITAL

THE people of Granada were a versatile, unsteady race,
and exceedingly given to make and unmake kings. They
had, for a long time, vacillated between old Muley Aben
Hassan and his son Boabdil el Chico, sometimes setting up
the one, sometimes the other, and sometimes both at once,
according to the pinch and pressure of external evils. They
found, however, that the evils still went on increasing, in
defiance of every change, and were at their wits' end to
devise some new combination or arrangement, by which an
efficient government might be wrought out of two bad kings.
When the tidings arrived of the fall of Ronda, and the con-
sequent ruin of the frontier, a tumultuous assemblage took
place in one of the public squares. As usual, the people attributed the misfortunes of the country to the faults of their
rulers; for the populace never imagine that any part of their
miseries can originate with themselves. A crafty alfaqui,
named Alyme Mazer, who had watched the current of their
discontents, rose and harangued them: "You have been

choosing and changing," said he, "between two monarchs—
and who and what are they? Muley Aben Hassan, for one;
a man worn out by age and infirmities, unable to sally forth
against the foe, even when ravaging to the very gates of the
city: and Boabdil el Chico, for the other; an apostate, a
traitor, a deserter from his throne, a fugitive among the enemies of his nation, a man fated to misfortune, and proverbi-
ally named 'the unlucky.' In a time of overwhelming war,
like the present, he only is fit to sway a scepter who can
wield a sword. Would you seek such a man? You need
not look far. Allah has sent such a one, in this time of distress, to retrieve the fortunes of Granada. You already
know whom I mean. You know that it can be no other
than your general, the invincible Abdalla, whose surname of
El Zagal has become a watchword in battle, rousing the
courage of the faithful, and striking terror into the unbelievers."

The multitude received the words of the alfaqui with
acclamations; they were delighted with the idea of a third
king over Granada; and Abdalla el Zagal being of the royal
family, and already in the virtual exercise of royal power,
the measure had nothing in it that appeared either rash or
violent. A deputation was therefore sent to El Zagal at
Malaga, inviting him to repair to Granada to receive the
crown.

El Zagal expressed great surprise and repugnance, when
the mission was announced to him; and nothing but his
patriotic zeal for the public safety, and his fraternal eagerness to relieve the aged Aben Hassan from the cares of government, prevailed upon him to accept the offer. Leaving,
therefore, Rodovan Vanegas, one of the bravest Moorish
generals, in command of Malaga, he departed for Granada,
attended by three hundred trusty cavaliers.

Old Muley Aben Hassan did not wait for the arrival of
his brother. Unable any longer to buffet with the storms of
the times, his only solicitude was to seek some safe and quiet
harbor of repose. In one of the deep valleys which indent

the Mediterranean coast, and which are shut up on the land
side by stupendous mountains, stood the little city of Almunecar. The valley was watered by the limpid river Frio,
and abounded with fruits, with grain and pasturage. The
city was strongly fortified, and the garrison and alcayde were
devoted to the old monarch. This was the place chosen by
Muley Aben Hassan for his asylum. His first care was to
send thither all his treasures; his next care was to take
refuge there himself; his third, that his Sultana Zorayna,
and their two sons, should follow him.

In the meantime, Muley Abdalla el Zagal pursued his
journey toward the capital, attended by his three hundred
cavaliers. The road from Malaga to Granada winds close
by Alhama, and is dominated by that lofty fortress. This
had been a most perilous pass for the Moors, during the time
that Alhama was commanded by the Count de Tendilla: not
a traveler could escape his eagle eye, and his garrison was
ever ready for a sally. The Count de Tendilla, however,
had been relieved from this arduous post, and it had been
given in charge to Don Gutiere de Padilla, clavero or treasurer of the order of Calatrava; an easy, indulgent man,
who had with him three hundred gallant knights of his
order, besides other mercenary troops. The garrison had
fallen off in discipline; the cavaliers were hardy in fight and
daring in foray, but confident in themselves and negligent
of proper precautions. Just before the journey of El Zagal,
a number of these cavaliers, with several soldiers of fortune
of the garrison, in all about one hundred and seventy men,
had sallied forth to harass the Moorish country during its
present distracted state, and, having ravaged the valleys of
the Sierra Nevada, or Snowy Mountains, were returning to
Alhama in gay spirits and laden with booty.

As El Zagal passed through the neighborhood of Alhama,
he recollected the ancient perils of the road, and sent light
cerradors in advance, to inspect each rock and ravine where
a foe might lurk in ambush. One of these scouts, overlooking a narrow valley which opened upon the road, descried a

troop of horsemen on the banks of a little stream. They were dismounted, and had taken the bridles from their steeds, that they might crop the fresh grass on the banks of the river. The horsemen were scattered about, some reposing in the shade of rocks and trees, others gambling for the spoil they had taken: not a sentinel was posted to keep guard; everything showed the perfect security of men who consider themselves beyond the reach of danger.

These careless cavaliers were in fact the knights of Calatrava, with a part of their companions in arms, returning from their foray. A part of their force had passed on with the cavalgada; ninety of the principal cavaliers had halted to refresh themselves in this valley. El Zagal smiled with ferocious joy when he heard of their negligent security. "Here will be trophies," said he, "to grace our entrance into Granada."

Approaching the valley with cautious silence, he wheeled into it at full speed at the head of his troop, and attacked the Christians so suddenly and furiously that they had not time to put the bridles upon their horses, or even to leap into the saddles. They made a confused but valiant defense, fighting among the rocks and in the rugged bed of the river. Their defense was useless; seventy-nine were slain, and the remaining eleven were taken prisoners.

A party of the Moors galloped in pursuit of the cavalgada: they soon overtook it, winding slowly up a hill. The horsemen who conveyed it, perceiving the enemy at a distance, made their escape, and left the spoil to be retaken by the Moors. El Zagal gathered together his captives and his booty and proceeded, elated with success, to Granada.

He paused before the gate of Elvira, for as yet he had not been proclaimed king. This ceremony was immediately performed; for the fame of his recent exploit had preceded him, and had intoxicated the minds of the giddy populace. He entered Granada in a sort of triumph. The eleven captive knights of Calatrava walked in front; next were paraded the ninety captured steeds, bearing the armor and weapons

of their late owners, and led by as many mounted Moors:
then came seventy Moorish horsemen, with as many Christian heads hanging at their saddle-bows: Muley Abdalla el
Zagal followed, surrounded by a number of distinguished
cavaliers splendidly attired; and the pageant was closed by
a long cavalgada of the flocks and herds and other booty
recovered from the Christians.*

The populace gazed with almost savage triumph at these
captive cavaliers and the gory heads of their companions,
knowing them to have been part of the formidable garrison
of Alhama, so long the scourge of Granada and the terror
of the vega.   They hailed this petty triumph as an auspicious
opening of the reign of their new monarch; for several days
the names of Muley Aben Hassan and Boabdil el Chico were
never mentioned but with contempt, and the whole city resounded with the praises of El Zagal, or the valiant.

CHAPTER THIRTY-TWO

HOW THE COUNT DE CABRA ATTEMPTED TO CAPTURE AN-
OTHER KING, AND HOW HE FARED IN HIS ATTEMPT

THE elevation of a bold and active veteran to the throne
of Granada, in place of its late bedridden king, made an important difference in the aspect of the war, and called for
some blow that should dash the confidence of the Moors
in their new monarch, and animate the Christians to fresh
exertions.

Don Diego de Cordova, the brave Count de Cabra, was
at this time in his castle of Vaena, where he kept a wary eye
upon the frontier.   It was now the latter part of August,
and he grieved that the summer should pass away without
an inroad into the country of the foe.   He sent out his scouts
on the prowl, and they brought him word that the important

* Zurita, lib. 20, c. 62.   Mariana, Hist. de España.   Abarca, Annales
de Aragon.

post of Moclin was but weakly garrisoned. This was a cas-
tellated town, strongly situated upon a high mountain, partly
surrounded by thick forests, and partly girdled by a river.
It defended one of the rugged and solitary passes by which
the Christians were wont to make their inroads; insomuch
that the Moors, in their figurative way, denominated it the
shield of Granada.

The Count de Cabra sent word to the monarchs of the
feeble state of the garrison, and gave it as his opinion that,
by a secret and rapid expedition, the place might be surprised. King Ferdinand asked the advice of his counselors.
Some cautioned him against the sanguine temperament of
the count, and his heedlessness of danger; Moclin, they observed, was near to Granada, and might be promptly re-enforced. The opinion of the count, however, prevailed; the
king considering him almost infallible, in matters of border
warfare, since his capture of Boabdil el Chico.

The king departed, therefore, from Cordova, and took
post at Alcala la Real, for the purpose of being near to
Moclin. The queen, also, proceeded to Vaena, accompanied
by her children, Prince Juan and the Princess Isabella, and
her great counselor in all matters, public and private, spiritual and temporal, the venerable grand cardinal of Spain.

Nothing could exceed the pride and satisfaction of the
loyal Count de Cabra, when he saw this stately train winding along the dreary mountain roads and entering the gates
of Vaena. He received his royal guests with all due ceremony, and lodged them in the best apartments that the warrior castle afforded, being the same that had formerly been
occupied by the royal captive Boabdil.

King Ferdinand had concerted a wary plan to insure the
success of the enterprise. The Count de Cabra and Don
Martin Alonzo de Montemayor were to set forth with their
troops, so as to reach Moclin by a certain hour, and to intercept all who should attempt to enter or should sally from the
town. The Master of Calatrava, the troops of the grand
cardinal, commanded by the Count of Buendia, and the

forces of the bishop of Jaen, led by that belligerent prelate, amounting in all to four thousand horse and six thousand foot, were to set off in time to co-operate with the Count de Cabra, so as to surround the town. The king was to follow with his whole force, and encamp before the place.

And here the worthy padre Fray Antonio Agapida breaks forth into a triumphant eulogy of the pious prelates, who thus mingled personally in these scenes of warfare. As this was a holy crusade (says he), undertaken for the advancement of the faith and the glory of the church, so was it always countenanced and upheld by saintly men: for the victories of their most Catholic majesties were not followed, like those of mere worldly sovereigns, by erecting castles and towers, and appointing alcaydes and garrisons; but by the founding of convents and cathedrals, and the establishment of wealthy bishoprics. Wherefore their majesties were always surrounded, in court or camp, in the cabinet or in the field, by a crowd of ghostly advisers, inspiriting them to the prosecution of this most righteous war. Nay, the holy men of the church did not scruple, at times, to buckle on the cuirass over the cassock, to exchange the crosier for the lance, and thus, with corporal hands and temporal weapons, to fight the good fight of the faith.

But to return from this rhapsody of the worthy friar. The Count de Cabra, being instructed in the complicated arrangements of the king, marched forth at midnight to execute them punctually. He led his troops by the little river that winds below Vaena, and so up the wild defiles of the mountains, marching all night, and stopping only in the heat of the following day, to repose under the shadowy cliffs of a deep barranca, calculating to arrive at Moclin exactly in time to co-operate with the other forces.

The troops had scarcely stretched themselves on the earth to take repose, when a scout arrived, bringing word that El Zagal had suddenly sallied out of Granada with a strong force, and had encamped in the vicinity of Moclin. It was plain that the wary Moor had received information of the intended attack. This, however, was not the idea that presented itself to the mind of the Count de Cabra. He had captured one king—here was a fair opportunity to secure another. What a triumph to lodge another captive monarch in his castle of Vaena!—what a prisoner to deliver into the hands of his royal mistress! Fired with the thoughts, the good count forgot all the arrangements of the king; or, rather, blinded by former success, he trusted everything to courage and fortune, and thought that, by one bold swoop, he might again bear off the royal prize, and wear his laurels without competition.* His only fear was that the Master of Calatrava, and the belligerent bishop, might come up in time to share the glory of the victory; so, ordering every one to horse, this hot-spirited cavalier pushed on for Moclin, without allowing his troops the necessary time for repose.

The evening closed as the count arrived in the neighborhood of Moclin. It was the full of the moon, and a bright and cloudless night. The count was marching through one of those deep valleys or ravines, worn in the Spanish mountains by the brief but tremendous torrents which prevail during the autumnal rains. It was walled on each side by lofty and almost perpendicular cliffs, but great masses of moonlight were thrown into the bottom of the glen, glittering on the armor of the shining squadrons, as they silently passed through it. Suddenly the war-cry of the Moors rose in various parts of the valley: "El Zagal! El Zagal!" was shouted from every cliff, accompanied by showers of missiles that struck down several of the Christian warriors. The count lifted up his eyes, and beheld, by the light of the moon, every cliff glistening with Moorish soldiery. The deadly shower fell thickly round him, and the shining armor of his followers made them fair objects for the aim of the enemy. The count saw his brother Gonzalo struck dead by his side; his own horse sunk under him, pierced by four Moorish lances; and he received a wound in the hand from an arquebuse.

---

* Mariana, lib. 25, c. 17.   Abarca, Zurita, etc.

He remembered the horrible massacre of the mountains of Malaga, and feared a similar catastrophe. There was no time to pause. His brother's horse, freed from his slaughtered rider, was running at large; seizing the reins, he sprang into the saddle, called upon his men to follow him, and, wheeling round, retreated out of the fatal valley.

The Moors, rushing down from the heights, pursued the retreating Christians. The chase endured for a league, but it was a league of rough and broken road, where the Christians had to turn and fight at almost every step. In these short but fierce combats the enemy lost many cavaliers of note; but the loss of the Christians was infinitely more grievous, comprising numbers of the noblest warriors of Vaena and its vicinity. Many of the Christians, disabled by wounds or exhausted by fatigue, turned aside and endeavored to conceal themselves among rocks and thickets, but never more rejoined their companions, being slain or captured by the Moors, or perishing in their wretched retreats.

The arrival of the troops led by the Master of Calatrava and the bishop of Jaen put an end to the rout. El Zagal contented himself with the laurels he had gained, and, ordering the trumpets to call off his men from the pursuit, returned in great triumph to Moclin.*

Queen Isabella was at Vaena, awaiting with great anxiety the result of the expedition. She was in a stately apartment of the castle, looking toward the road that winds through the mountains from Moclin, and regarding the watch towers that crowned the neighboring heights, in hopes of favorable signals. The prince and princess, her children, were with her, and her venerable counselor, the grand cardinal. All shared in the anxiety of the moment. At length couriers were seen riding toward the town. They entered its gates, but before they reached the castle the nature of their tidings was known to the queen, by the shrieks and wailings that rose from the streets below. The messen-

---

* Zurita, lib. 20, c. 4. Pulgar, Cronica.

gers were soon followed by wounded fugitives, hastening home to be relieved or to die among their friends and families. The whole town resounded with lamentations; for it had lost the flower of its youth, and its bravest warriors. Isabella was a woman of courageous soul, but her feelings were overpowered by the spectacle of woe which presented itself on every side; her maternal heart mourned over the death of so many loyal subjects, who so shortly before had rallied round her with devoted affection; and, losing her usual self-command, she sunk into deep despondency.

In this gloomy state of mind a thousand apprehensions crowded upon her. She dreaded the confidence which this success would impart to the Moors; she feared also for the important fortress of Alhama, the garrison of which had not been re-euforced since its foraging party had been cut off by this same El Zagal. On every side the queen saw danger and disaster, and feared that a general reverse was about to attend the Castilian arms.

The grand cardinal comforted her with both spiritual and worldly counsel. He told her to recollect that no country was ever conquered without occasional reverses to the conquerors; that the Moors were a warlike people, fortified in a rough and mountainous country, where they never could be conquered by her ancestors—and that in fact her armies had already, in three years, taken more cities than those of any of her predecessors had been able to do in twelve. He concluded by offering himself to take the field, with three thousand cavalry, his own retainers, paid and maintained by himself, and either hasten to the relief of Alhama, or undertake any other expedition her majesty might command. The discreet words of the cardinal soothed the spirit of the queen, who always looked to him for consolation; and she soon recovered her usual equanimity.

Some of the counselors of Isabella, of that politic class who seek to rise by the faults of others, were loud in their censures of the rashness of the count. The queen defended him with prompt generosity. "The enterprise," said she, "was rash, but not more rash than that of Lucena, which was crowned with success, and which we have all applauded as the height of heroism. Had the Count de Cabra succeeded in capturing the uncle, as he did the nephew, who is there that would not have praised him to the skies?"

The magnanimous words of the queen put a stop to all invidious remarks in her presence; but certain of the courtiers, who had envied the count the glory gained by his former achievements, continued to magnify, among themselves, his present imprudence, and we are told by Fray Antonio Agapida that they sneeringly gave the worthy cavalier the appellation of Count de Cabra, the king-catcher.

Ferdinand had reached the place on the frontier called the Fountain of the King, within three leagues of Moclin, when he heard of the late disaster. He greatly lamented the precipitation of the count, but forbore to express himself with severity, for he knew the value of that loyal and valiant cavalier.[*] He held a council of war to determine what course was to be pursued. Some of his cavaliers advised him to abandon the attempt upon Moclin, the place being strongly re-enforced, and the enemy inspirited by his recent victory. Certain old Spanish hidalgos reminded him that he had but few Castilian troops in his army, without which stanch soldiery his predecessors never presumed to enter the Moorish territory; while others remonstrated that it would be beneath the dignity of a king to retire from an enterprise on account of the defeat of a single cavalier and his retainers. In this way the king was distracted by a multitude of counselors, when fortunately a letter from the queen put an end to his perplexities. Proceed we, in the next chapter, to relate what was the purport of that letter.

---

[*] Abarca, Annales de Aragon.

CHAPTER THIRTY-THREE

EXPEDITION AGAINST THE CASTLES OF CAMBIL AND ALBAHAR

"HAPPY are those princes," exclaims the worthy padre Fray Antonio Agapida, "who have women and priests to advise them, for in these dwelleth the spirit of counsel. While Ferdinand and his captains were confounding each other in their deliberations at the Fountain of the King, a quiet but deep little council of war was held in the state apartment of the old castle of Vaena, between Queen Isabella, the venerable Pedro Gonzalez de Mendoza, grand cardinal of Spain, and Don Garcia Osorio, the belligerent bishop of Jaen. This last worthy prelate, who had exchanged his miter for a helm, no sooner beheld the defeat of the enterprise against Moclin than he turned the reins of his sleek, stall-fed steed, and hastened back to Vaena, full of a project for the employment of the army, the advancement of the faith, and the benefit of his own diocese. He knew that the actions of the king were influenced by the opinions of the queen, and that the queen always inclined a listening ear to the counsels of saintly men: he laid his plans, therefore, with the customary wisdom of his cloth, to turn the ideas of the queen into the proper channel; and this was the purport of the worthy bishop's suggestions.

The bishopric of Jaen had for a long time been harassed by two Moorish castles, the scourge and terror of all that part of the country. They were situated on the frontiers of the kingdom of Granada, about four leagues from Jaen, in a deep, narrow, and rugged valley, surrounded by lofty mountains. Through this valley runs the Rio Frio (or Cold River), in a deep channel, worn between high precipitous banks. On each side of the stream rise two vast rocks, nearly perpendicular, within a stone's-throw of each other;

blocking up the gorge of the valley. On the summits of these rocks stood the two formidable castles, Cambil and Albahar, fortified with battlements and towers of great height and thickness. They were connected together by a bridge thrown from rock to rock across the river. The road, which passed through the valley, traversed this bridge, and was completely commanded by these castles. They stood like two giants of romance, guarding the pass and dominating the valley.

The kings of Granada, knowing the importance of these castles, kept them always well garrisoned, and victualed to stand a siege, with fleet steeds and hard riders, to forage the country of the Christians. The warlike race of the Abencerrages, the troops of the royal household, and others of the choicest chivalry of Granada, made them their strongholds or posts of arms, from whence to sally forth on those predatory and roving enterprises which were the delight of the Moorish cavaliers. As the wealthy bishopric of Jaen lay immediately at hand, it suffered more peculiarly from these marauders. They drove off the fat beeves and the flocks of sheep from the pastures, and swept the laborers from the field; they scoured the country to the very gates of Jaen, so that the citizens could not venture from their walls without the risk of being borne off captive to the dungeons of these castles.

The worthy bishop, like a good pastor, beheld with grief of heart his fat bishopric daily waxing leaner and leaner, and poorer and poorer; and his holy ire was kindled at the thoughts that the possessions of the church should thus be at the mercy of a crew of Infidels. It was the urgent counsel of the bishop, therefore, that the military force, thus providentially assembled in the neighborhood, since it was apparently foiled in its attempt upon Moclin, should be turned against these insolent castles, and the country delivered from their domination. The grand cardinal supported the suggestion of the bishop, and declared that he had long meditated the policy of a measure of the kind. Their united opinions

found favor with the queen, and she dispatched a letter on
the subject to the king. It came just in time to relieve him
from the distraction of a multitude of counselors, and he immediately undertook the reduction of those castles.

The Marques of Cadiz was accordingly sent in advance,
with two thousand horse, to keep a watch upon the garrisons,
and prevent all entrance or exit, until the king should arrive
with the main army and the battering artillery. The queen,
to be near at hand in case of need, moved her quarters to the
city of Jaen, where she was received with martial honors by
the belligerent bishop, who had buckled on his cuirass and
girded on his sword to fight in the cause of his diocese.

In the meantime, the Marques of Cadiz arrived in the
valley, and completely shut up the Moors within their walls.
The castles were under the command of Mahomet Lentin
Ben Usef, an Abencerrage, and one of the bravest cavaliers
of Granada. In his garrisons were many troops of the fierce
African tribe of Comares. Mahomet Lentin, confident in
the strength of his fortresses, smiled as he looked down from
his battlements upon the Christian cavalry, perplexed in the
rough and narrow valley. He sent forth skirmishing parties
to harass them, and there were many sharp combats between
small parties and single knights; but the Moors were driven
back to their castles, and all attempts to send intelligence of
their situation to Granada were frustrated by the vigilance
of the Marques of Cadiz.

At length the legions of the royal army came pouring,
with vaunting trumpet and fluttering banner, along the defiles of the mountains. They halted before the castles, but
the king could not find room in the narrow and rugged valley to form his camp: he had to divide it into three parts,
which were posted on different heights; and his tents whitened the sides of the neighboring hills. When the encampment was formed, the army remained gazing idly at the
castles. The artillery was upward of four leagues in the
rear, and without artillery all attack would be in vain.

The alcayde Mahomet Lentin knew the nature of the road

by which the artillery had to be brought. It was merely a narrow and rugged path, at times scaling almost perpendicular crags and precipices, up which it was utterly impossible for wheel carriages to pass; neither was it in the power of man or beast to draw up the lombards and other ponderous ordnance. He felt assured, therefore, that they never could be brought to the camp; and, without their aid, what could the Christians effect against his rock-built castles? He scoffed at them, therefore, as he saw their tents by day and their fires by night covering the surrounding heights. "Let them linger here a little while longer," said he, "and the autumnal torrents will wash them from the mountains."

While the alcayde was thus closely mewed up within his walls, and the Christians remained inactive in their camp, he noticed, one calm autumnal day, the sound of implements of labor echoing among the mountains, and now and then the crash of a falling tree, or a thundering report, as if some rock had been heaved from its bed and hurled into the valley. The alcayde was on the battlements of his castle, surrounded by his knights. "Methinks," said he, "these Christians are making war upon the rocks and trees of the mountains, since they find our castles unassailable."

The sounds did not cease even during the night: every now and then, the Moorish sentinel, as he paced the battlements, heard some crash echoing among the heights. The return of day explained the mystery. Scarcely did the sun shine against the summits of the mountains, than shouts burst from the cliffs opposite to the castles, and were answered from the camp, with joyful sound of kettle-drums and trumpets.

The astonished Moors lifted up their eyes, and beheld, as it were, a torrent of war breaking out of a narrow defile. There was a multitude of men, with pickaxes, spades, and bars of iron, clearing away every obstacle; while behind them slowly moved along great teams of oxen, dragging heavy ordnance, and all the munitions of battering artillery.

"What cannot women and priests effect when they unite

in council?" exclaims again the worthy Antonio Agapida. The queen had held another consultation with the grand cardinal and the belligerent bishop of Jaen. It was clear that the heavy ordnance could never be conveyed to the camp by the regular road of the country; and without battering artillery nothing could be effected. It was suggested, however, by the zealous bishop, that another road might be opened through a more practicable part of the mountains. It would be an undertaking extravagant and chimerical with ordinary means; and, therefore, unlooked for by the enemy; but what could not kings effect, who had treasures and armies at command?

The project struck the enterprising spirit of the queen. Six thousand men, with pickaxes, crowbars, and every other necessary implement, were set to work day and night to break a road through the very center of the mountains. No time was to be lost, for it was rumored that El Zagal was about to march with a mighty host to the relief of the castles. The bustling bishop of Jaen acted as pioneer to mark the route and superintend the laborers; and the grand cardinal took care that the work should never languish through lack of means.*

"When king's treasures," says Fray Antonio Agapida, "are dispensed by priestly hands there is no stint, as the glorious annals of Spain bear witness." Under the guidance of these ghostly men it seemed as if miracles were effected. Almost an entire mountain was leveled, valleys filled up, trees hewn down, rocks broken and overturned; in short, all the obstacles which nature had heaped around entirely and promptly vanished. In little more than twelve days this gigantic work was effected, and the ordnance dragged to the camp, to the great triumph of the Christians and confusion of the Moors.†

No sooner was the heavy artillery arrived than it was

---

* Zurita, Annales de Aragon, lib. 20, c. 64.   Pulgar part 3, cap. 51.
† Idem.

mounted, in all haste, upon the neighboring heights; Francisco Ramirez de Madrid, the first engineer in Spain, superintended the batteries, and soon opened a destructive fire upon the castles.

When the valiant alcayde, Mahomet Lentin, found his towers tumbling about him, and his bravest men dashed from the walls, without the power of inflicting a wound upon the foe, his haughty spirit was greatly exasperated. "Of what avail," said he, bitterly, "is all the prowess of knighthood against these cowardly engines that murder from afar."

For a whole day a tremendous fire kept thundering upon the castle of Albahar. The lombards discharged large stones, which demolished two of the towers, and all the battlements which guarded the portal. If any Moors attempted to defend the walls or repair the breaches, they were shot down by ribadoquines and other small pieces of artillery. The Christian soldiery issued forth from the camp under cover of this fire; and, approaching the castles, discharged flights of arrows and stones through the openings made by the ordnance.

At length, to bring the siege to a conculsion, Francisco Ramirez elevated some of the heaviest artillery on a mount that rose in form of a cone or pyramid, on the side of the river near to Albahar, and commanded both castles. This was an operation of great skill and excessive labor, but it was repaid by complete success; for the Moors did not dare to wait until this terrible battery should discharge its fury. Satisfied that all further resistance was vain, the valiant alcayde made signal for a parley. The articles of capitulation were soon arranged. The alcayde and his garrisons were permitted to return in safety to the city of Granada, and the castles were delivered into the possession of King Ferdinand, on the day of the festival of St. Matthew, in the month of September. They were immediately repaired, strongly garrisoned, and delivered in charge to the city of Jaen.

The effects of this triumph were immediately apparent.

Quiet and security once more settled upon the bishopric. The husbandmen tilled their fields in peace, the herds and flocks fattened unmolested in the pastures, and the vineyards yielded corpulent skinsful of rosy wine. The good bishop enjoyed, in the gratitude of his people, the approbation of his conscience, the increase of his revenues, and the abundance of his table, a reward for all his toils and perils. "This glorious victory," exclaims Fray Antonio Agapida, "achieved by such extraordinary management and infinite labor, is a shining example of what a bishop can effect, for the promotion of the faith and the good of his diocese."

CHAPTER THIRTY-FOUR

ENTERPRISE OF THE KNIGHTS OF CALATRAVA AGAINST ZALEA

WHILE these events were taking place on the northern frontier of the kingdom of Granada, the important fortress of Alhama was neglected, and its commander, Don Gutiere de Padilla, clavero of Calatrava, reduced to great perplexity. The remnant of the foraging party, which had been surprised and massacred by the fierce El Zagal when on his way to Granada to receive the crown, had returned in confusion and dismay to the fortress. They could only speak of their own disgrace, being obliged to abandon their cavalgada, and to fly, pursued by a superior force: of the flower of their party, the gallant knights of Calatrava, who had remained behind in the valley, they knew nothing. A few days cleared up all the mystery of their fate: tidings were brought that their bloody heads had been borne in triumph into Granada by the ferocious El Zagal. The surviving knights of Calatrava, who formed a part of the garrison, burned to revenge the death of their comrades, and to wipe out the stigma of this defeat; but the clavero had been rendered cautious by disaster—he resisted all their entreaties for a foray. His garrison was weakened by the loss of so many of its bravest men; the vega was patroled by numerous and powerful squadrons, sent forth by the warlike El Zagal; above all, the movements of the garrison were watched by the warriors of Zalea, a strong town, only two leagues distant, on the road toward Loxa. This place was a continual check upon Alhama when in its most powerful state, placing ambuscades to entrap the Christian cavaliers in the course of their sallies. Frequent and bloody skirmishes had taken place in consequence; and the troops of Alhama, when returning from their forays, had often to fight their way back through the squadrons of Zalea. Thus surrounded by dangers, Don Gutiere de Padilla restrained the eagerness of his troops for a sally, knowing that any additional disaster might be followed by the loss of Alhama.

In the meanwhile, provisions began to grow scarce; they were unable to forage the country as usual for supplies, and depended for relief upon the Castilian sovereigns. The defeat of the Count de Cabra filled the measure of their perplexities, as it interrupted the intended re-enforcements and supplies. To such extremity were they reduced that they were compelled to kill some of their horses for provisions.

The worthy clavero, Don Gutiere de Padilla, was pondering one day on this gloomy state of affairs, when a Moor was brought before him who had surrendered himself at the gate of Alhama, and claimed an audience. Don Gutiere was accustomed to visits of the kind from renegado Moors, who roamed the country as spies and adalides; but the countenance of this man was quite unknown to him. He had a box strapped to his shoulders, containing divers articles of traffic, and appeared to be one of those itinerant traders who often resorted to Alhama and the other garrison towns, under pretext of vending trivial merchandise, such as amulets, perfumes, and trinkets, but who often produced rich shawls, golden chains and necklaces, and valuable gems and jewels.

The Moor requested a private conference with the clavero: "I have a precious jewel," said he, "to dispose of."

"I want no jewels," replied Don Gutiere.

"For the sake of Him who died on the cross, the great Prophet of your faith," said the Moor, solemnly, "refuse not my request; the jewel I speak of you alone can purchase, but I can only treat about it in secret."

Don Gutiere perceived there was something hidden under these mystic and figurative terms in which the Moors were often accustomed to talk. He motioned to his attendants to retire. When they were alone, the Moor looked cautiously round the apartment, and then, approaching close to the knight, demanded in a low voice, "What will you give me if I deliver the fortress of Zalea into your hands?"

Don Gutiere looked with surprise at the humble individual that made such a suggestion.

"What means have you," said he, "of effecting such a proposition?"

"I have a brother in the garrison of Zalea," replied the Moor, "who, for a proper compensation, would admit a body of troops into the citadel."

Don Gutiere turned a scrutinizing eye upon the Moor. "What right have I to believe," said he, "that thou wilt be truer to me than to those of thy blood and thy religion?"

"I renounce all ties to them, either of blood or religion," replied the Moor; "my mother was a Christian captive; her country shall henceforth be my country, and her faith my faith." *

The doubts of Don Gutiere were not dispelled by this profession of mongrel Christianity. "Granting the sincerity of thy conversion," said he, "art thou under no obligations of gratitude or duty to the alcayde of the fortress thou wouldst betray?"

The eyes of the Moor flashed fire at the words; he gnashed his teeth with fury. "The alcayde," cried he, "is a dog! He has deprived my brother of his just share of booty; he has robbed me of my merchandise, treated me worse than a

---

* Cura de los Palacios,

Jew when I murmured at his injustice, and ordered me to be thrust forth ignominiously from his walls. May the curse of God fall upon my head if I rest content until I have full revenge!''

"Enough," said Don Gutiere: "I trust more to thy revenge than thy religion."

The good clavero called a council of his officers. The knights of Calatrava were unanimous for the enterprise—zealous to appease the manes of their slaughtered comrades. Don Gutiere reminded them of the state of the garrison, enfeebled by their late loss, and scarcely sufficient for the defense of the walls. The cavaliers replied that there was no achievement without risk, and that there would have been no great actions recorded in history had there not been daring spirits ready to peril life to gain renown.

Don Gutiere yielded to the wishes of his knights, for to have resisted any further might have drawn on him the imputation of timidity. He ascertained by trusty spies that everything in Zalea remained in the usual state, and he made all the requisite arrangements for the attack.

When the appointed night arrived all the cavaliers were anxious to engage in the enterprise; but the individuals were decided by lot. They set out under the guidance of the Moor; and when they had arrived in the vicinity of Zalea, they bound his hands behind his back, and their leader pledged his knightly word to strike him dead on the first sign of treachery. He then bade him to lead the way.

It was near midnight when they reached the walls of the fortress. They passed silently along until they found themselves below the citadel. Here their guide made a low and preconcerted signal: it was answered from above, and a cord let down from the wall. The knights attached to it a ladder, which was drawn up and fastened. Gutiere Munoz was the first that mounted, followed by Pedro de Alvanado, both brave and hardy soldiers. A handful succeeded; they were attacked by a party of guards, but held them at bay until more of their comrades ascended; with their assistance.

they gained possession of a tower and part of the wall. The garrison, by this time, was aroused; but before they could reach the scene of action most of the cavaliers were within the battlements. A bloody contest raged for about an hour —several of the Christians were slain, but many of the Moors; at length the whole citadel was carried, and the town submitted without resistance.

Thus did the gallant knights of Calatrava gain the strong town of Zalea with scarcely any loss, and atone for the inglorious defeat of their companions by El Zagal. They found the magazines of the place well stored with provisions, and were enabled to carry a seasonable supply to their own famishing garrison.

The tidings of this event reached the sovereigns, just after the surrender of Cambil and Albahar. They were greatly rejoiced at this additional success of their arms, and immediately sent strong re-enforcements and ample supplies for both Alhama and Zalea. They then dismissed the army for the winter, Ferdinand and Isabella retired to Alcala de Henares, where the queen, on the 16th of December, 1485, gave birth to the Princess Catharine, afterward wife of Henry VIII. of England. Thus prosperously terminated the checkered campaign of this important year.

CHAPTER THIRTY-FIVE

DEATH OF MULEY ABEN HASSAN

MULEY ABDALLA EL ZAGAL had been received with great acclamations at Granada, on his return from defeating the Count de Cabra. He had endeavored to turn his victory to the greatest advantage with his subjects; giving tilts and tournaments, and other public festivities, in which the Moors delighted. The loss of the castles of Cambil and Albahar, and of the fortress of Zalea, however, checked this sudden tide of popularity; and some of the fickle populace began to doubt whether they had not been rather precipitate in deposing his brother, Muley Aben Hassan.

That superannuated monarch remained in his faithful town of Almunecar, on the border of the Mediterranean, surrounded by a few adherents, together with his wife Zorayna and his children; and he had all his treasures safe in his possession. The fiery heart of the old king was almost burned out, and all his powers of doing either harm or good seemed at an end.

While in this passive and helpless state, his brother El Zagal manifested a sudden anxiety for his health. He had him removed, with all tenderness and care, to Salobrena, another fortress on the Mediterranean coast, famous for its pure and salubrious air; and the alcayde, who was a devoted adherent to El Zagal, was charged to have especial care that nothing was wanting to the comfort and solace of his brother.

Salobrena was a small town, situated on a lofty and rocky hill, in the midst of a beautiful and fertile vega, shut up on three sides by mountains, and opening on the fourth to the Mediterranean. It was protected by strong walls and a powerful castle, and, being deemed impregnable, was often used by the Moorish kings as a place of deposit for their treasures. They were accustomed also to assign it as a residence for such of their sons and brothers as might endanger the security of their reign. Here the princes lived, in luxurious repose: they had delicious gardens, perfumed baths, a harem of beauties at their command—nothing was denied them but the liberty to depart; that alone was wanting to render this abode an earthly paradise.

Such was the delightful place appointed by El Zagal for the residence of his brother; but, notwithstanding its wonderful salubrity, the old monarch had not been removed thither many days before he expired. There was nothing extraordinary in his death: life with him had long been glimmering in the socket, and for some time past he might rather have been numbered with the dead than with the living. The public, however, are fond of seeing things in a

sinister and mysterious point of view, and there were many
dark surmises as to the cause of this event. El Zagal acted
in a manner to heighten these suspicions: he caused the
treasures of his deceased brother to be packed on mules and
brought to Granada, where he took possession of them, to
the exclusion of the children of Aben Hassan. The Sultana
Zorayna and her two sons were lodged in the Alhambra, in
the tower of the Comares. This was a residence in a palace
—but it had proved a royal prison to the Sultana Ayax la
Horra, and her youthful son Boabdil. There the unhappy
Zorayna had time to meditate upon the disappointment of all
those ambitious schemes for herself and children, for which
she had stained her conscience with so many crimes, and induced her cruel husband to imbrue his hands in the blood of
his other offspring.

The corpse of old Muley Aben Hassan was also brought
to Granada, not in a state becoming the remains of a once-
powerful sovereign, but transported on a mule, like the corpse
of the poorest peasant. It received no honor or ceremonial
from El Zagal, and appears to have been interred obscurely,
to prevent any popular sensation; and it is recorded by an
ancient and faithful chronicler of the time that the body of
the old monarch was deposited by two Christian captives in
his osario or charnel-house.* Such was the end of the turbulent Muley Aben Hassan, who, after passing his life in constant contests for empire, could scarce gain quiet admission
into the corner of a sepulcher.

No sooner were the populace well assured that old Muley
Aben Hassan was dead, and beyond recovery, than they all
began to extol his memory and deplore his loss. They admitted that he had been fierce and cruel, but then he had
been brave; he had, to be sure, pulled this war upon their
heads, but he had likewise been crushed by it. In a word,
he was dead; and his death atoned for every fault; for a
king, recently dead, is generally either a hero or a saint.

---

* Cura de los Palacios. c. 77.

In proportion as they ceased to hate old Muley Aben Hassan, they began to hate his brother El Zagal. The circumstances of the old king's death, the eagerness to appropriate his treasures, the scandalous neglect of his corpse, and the imprisonment of his sultana and children, all filled the public mind with gloomy suspicions; and the epithet of Fratricide! was sometimes substituted for that of El Zagal, in the low murmurings of the people.

As the public must always have some object to like as well as to hate, there began once more to be an inquiry after their fugitive king, Boabdil el Chico. That unfortunate monarch was still at Cordova, existing on the cool courtesy and meager friendship of Ferdinand; which had waned exceedingly ever since Boabdil had ceased to have any influence in his late dominions. The reviving interest expressed in his fate by the Moorish public, and certain secret overtures made to him, once more aroused the sympathy of Ferdinand: he immediately advised Boabdil again to set up his standard within the frontiers of Granada, and furnished him with money and means for the purpose. Boabdil advanced but a little way into his late territories; he took up his post at Velez el Blanco, a strong town on the confines of Murcia; there he established the shadow of a court, and stood, as it were, with one foot over the border, and ready to draw that back upon the least alarm. His presence in the kingdom, however, and his assumption of royal state, gave life to his faction in Granada. The inhabitants of the Albaycin, the poorest but most warlike part of the populace, were generally in his favor: the more rich, courtly, and aristocratical inhabitants of the quarter of the Alhambra rallied round what appeared to be the most stable authority, and supported the throne of El Zagal. So it is in the admirable order of sublunary affairs: everything seeks its kind; the rich befriend the rich, the powerful stand by the powerful, the poor enjoy the patronage of the poor—and thus a universal harmony prevails.

CHAPTER THIRTY-SIX

OF THE CHRISTIAN ARMY WHICH ASSEMBLED AT THE CITY OF CORDOVA

GREAT and glorious was the style with which the Catholic sovereigns opened another year's campaign of this eventful war. It was like commencing another act of a stately and heroic drama, where the curtain rises to the inspiring sound of martial melody, and the whole stage glitters with the array of warriors and the pomp of arms. The ancient city of Cordova was the place appointed by the sovereigns for the assemblage of the troops; and early in the spring of 1486 the fair valley of the Guadalquivir resounded with the shrill blast of trumpet, and the impatient neighing of the war-horse. In this splendid era of Spanish chivalry, there was a rivalship among the nobles who most should distinguish him-self by the splendor of his appearance, and the number and equipments of his feudal followers. Every day beheld some cavalier of note, the representative of some proud and pow-erful house, entering the gates of Cordova with sound of trumpet, and displaying his banner and device, renowned in many a contest. He would appear in sumptuous array, sur-rounded by pages and lackeys no less gorgeously attired, and followed by a host of vassals and retainers, horse and foot, all admirably equipped in burnished armor.

Such was the state of Don Inigo Lopez de Mendoza, Duke of Infantado; who may be cited as a picture of a warlike noble of those times. He brought with him five hundred men-at-arms of his household, armed and mounted *à la gineta* and *à la guisa*. The cavaliers who attended him were magnifi-cently armed and dressed. The housings of fifty of his horses were of rich cloth, embroidered with gold; and others were of brocade. The sumpter mules had housings of the same, with halters of silk; while the bridles, head-pieces and all the harnessing glittered with silver.

The camp equipage of these noble and luxurious warriors was equally magnificent. Their tents were gay pavilions, of various colors, fitted up with silken hangings and decorated with fluttering pennons. They had vessels of gold and silver for the service of their tables, as if they were about to engage in a course of stately feasts and courtly revels, instead of the stern encounters of rugged and mountainous warfare. Sometimes they passed through the streets of Cordova at night, in splendid cavalcade, with great numbers of lighted torches, the rays of which falling upon polished armor and nodding plumes, and silken scarfs, and trappings of golden embroidery, filled all beholders with admiration.*

But it was not the chivalry of Spain alone which thronged the streets of Cordova. The fame of this war had spread throughout Christendom: it was considered a kind of crusade; and Catholic knights from all parts hastened to signalize themselves in so holy a cause. There were several valiant chevaliers from France, among whom the most distinguished was Gaston du Leon, Seneschal of Toulouse. With him came a gallant train, well armed and mounted, and decorated with rich surcoats and panaches of feathers. These cavaliers, it is said, eclipsed all others in the light festivities of the court: they were devoted to the fair, but not after the solemn and passionate manner of the Spanish lovers; they were gay, gallant and joyous in their amours and captivated by the vivacity of their attacks. They were at first held in light estimation by the grave and stately Spanish knights, until they made themselves to be respected by their wonderful prowess in the field.

The most conspicuous of the volunteers, however, who appeared in Cordova on this occasion, was an English knight of royal connection. This was the Lord Scales, Earl of Rivers, brother to the Queen of England, wife of Henry VII.

*Pulgar, part 3, cap. 41, 56.

He had distinguished himself in the preceding year, at the battle of Bosworth field, where Henry Tudor, then Earl of Richmond, overcame Richard III. That decisive battle having left the country at peace, the Earl of Rivers, having conceived a passion for warlike scenes, repaired to the Castilian court, to keep his arms in exercise, in a campaign against the Moors. He brought with him a hundred archers, all dexterous with the long-bow and the clothyard arrow; also two hundred yeomen, armed cap-a-pie, who fought with pike and battle-ax—men robust of frame and of prodigious strength. The worthy padre Fray Antonio Agapida describes this stranger knight and his followers with his accustomed accuracy and minuteness.

"This cavalier," he observes, "was from the far island of England, and brought with him a train of his vassals; men who had been hardened in certain civil wars which raged in their country. They were a comely race of men, but too fair and fresh for warriors, not having the sunburned warlike hue of our old Castilian soldiery. They were huge feeders also, and deep carousers, and could not accommodate themselves to the sober diet of our troops, but must fain eat and drink after the manner of their own country. They were often noisy and unruly, also, in their wassail; and their quarter of the camp was prone to be a scene of loud revel and sudden brawl. They were, withal, of great pride, yet it was not like our inflammable Spanish pride; they stood not much upon the *pundonor*, the high punctilio, and rarely drew the stiletto in their disputes; but their pride was silent and contumelious. Though from a remote and somewhat barbarous island, they believed themselves the most perfect men upon earth, and magnified their chieftain, the Lord Scales, beyond the greatest of their grandees. With all this, it must be said of them that they were marvelous good men in the field, dexterous archers, and powerful with the battle-ax. In their great pride and self-will, they always sought to press in the advance and take the post of danger, trying to outvie our Spanish chivalry. They did not rush on fiercely to the fight, nor make a brilliant onset like the Moorish and Spanish troops, but they went into the fight deliberately and persisted obstinately, and were slow to find out when they were beaten. Withal they were much esteemed, yet little liked by our soldiery, who considered them stanch companions in the field, yet coveted but little fellowship with them in the camp.

"Their commander, the Lord Scales, was an accomplished cavalier, of gracious and noble presence and fair speech; it was a marvel to see so much courtesy in a knight brought up so far from our Castilian court. He was much honored by the king and queen, and found great favor with the fair dames about the court, who indeed are rather prone to be pleased with foreign cavaliers. He went always in costly state, attended by pages and esquires, and accompanied by noble young cavaliers of his country, who had enrolled themselves under his banner to learn the gentle exercise of arms. In all pageants and festivals, the eyes of the populace were attracted by the singular bearing and rich array of the English earl and his train, who prided themselves in always appearing in the garb and manner of their country—and were indeed something very magnificent, delectable, and strange to behold."

The worthy chronicler is no less elaborate in his description of the Masters of Santiago, Calatrava, and Alcantara, and their valiant knights, armed at all points, and decorated with the badges of their orders. These, he affirms, were the flower of Christian chivalry: being constantly in service, they became more steadfast and accomplished in discipline than the irregular and temporary levies of the feudal nobles. Calm, solemn, and stately, they sat like towers upon their powerful chargers. On parades, they manifested none of the show and ostentation of the other troops; neither, in battle, did they endeavor to signalize themselves by any fiery vivacity or desperate and vainglorious exploit—everything, with them, was measured and sedate; yet it was observed that none were more warlike in their appearance in the camp, or more terrible for their achievements in the field.

The gorgeous magnificence of the Spanish nobles found but little favor in the eyes of the sovereigns. They saw that it caused a competition in expense, ruinous to cavaliers of moderate fortune; and they feared that a softness and effeminacy might thus be introduced, incompatible with the stern nature of the war. They signified their disapprobation to several of the principal noblemen, and recommended a more sober and soldierlike display while in actual service.

"These are rare troops for a tourney, my lord," said Ferdinand to the Duke of Infantado, as he beheld his retainers glittering in gold and embroidery; "but gold, though gorgeous, is soft and yielding: iron is the metal for the field."

"Sire," replied the duke, "if my men parade in gold, your majesty will find they fight with steel." The king smiled, but shook his head, and the duke treasured up his speech in his heart.

It remains now to reveal the immediate object of this mighty and chivalrous preparation; which had, in fact, the gratification of a royal pique at bottom. The severe lesson which Ferdinand had received from the veteran Ali Atar, before the walls of Loxa, though it had been of great service in rendering him wary in his attacks upon fortified places, yet rankled sorely in his mind; and he had ever since held Loxa in peculiar odium. It was, in truth, one of the most belligerent and troublesome cities on the borders; incessantly harassing Andalusia by its incursions. It also intervened between the Christian territories and Alhama, and other important places gained in the kingdom of Granada. For all these reasons, King Ferdinand had determined to make another grand attempt upon this warrior city; and for this purpose he had summoned to the field his most powerful chivalry.

It was in the month of May that the king sallied from Cordova at the head of his army. He had twelve thousand cavalry and forty thousand foot-soldiers, armed with crossbows, lances, and arquebuses. There were six thousand pioneers, with hatchets, pickaxes, and crowbars for leveling roads. He took with him, also, a great train of lombards and other heavy artillery, with a body of Germans skilled in the service of ordnance and the art of battering walls.

It was a glorious spectacle (says Fray Antonio Agapida) to behold this pompous pageant issuing forth from Cordova, the pennons and devices of the proudest houses of Spain, with those of gallant stranger knights, fluttering above a sea of crests and plumes; to see it slowly moving, with flash of helm, and cuirass, and buckler, across the ancient bridge, and reflected in the waters of the Guadalquivir, while the neigh of steed and blast of trumpet vibrated in the air, and resounded to the distant mountains. "But, above all," concludes the good father, with his accustomed zeal, "it was triumphant to behold the standard of the faith everywhere displayed, and to reflect that this was no worldly-minded army, intent upon some temporal scheme of ambition or revenge; but a Christian host, bound on a crusade to extirpate the vile seed of Mahomet from the land, and to extend the pure dominion of the church."

CHAPTER THIRTY–SEVEN

HOW FRESH COMMOTIONS BROKE OUT IN GRANADA, AND HOW THE PEOPLE UNDERTOOK TO ALLAY THEM

WHILE perfect unity of object and harmony of operation gave power to the Christian arms, the devoted kingdom of Granada continued a prey to internal feuds. The transient popularity of El Zagal had declined ever since the death of his brother, and the party of Boabdil el Chico was daily gaining strength: the Albaycin and the Alhambra were again arrayed against each other in deadly strife, and the streets of unhappy Granada were daily dyed in the blood of her children. In the midst of these dissensions, tidings arrived of the formidable army assembling at Cordova. The rival factions paused in their infatuated brawls, and were roused to a temporary sense of the common danger. They forthwith resorted to their old expedient of new-modeling their government, or rather of making and unmaking kings. The elevation of El Zagal to the throne had not produced the desired effect—what then was to be done? Recall Boabdil el Chico and acknowledge him again as sovereign? While they were in a popular tumult of deliberation, Hamet Aben Zarrax, surnamed El Santo, arose among them. This was the same wild, melancholy man who had predicted the woes of Granada. He issued from one of the caverns of the adjacent height which overhangs the Darro, and has since been called the Holy Mountain. His appearance was more haggard than ever; for the unheeded spirit of prophecy seemed to have turned inwardly and preyed upon his vitals. "Beware, oh Moslems," exclaimed he, "of men who are eager to govern, yet are unable to protect. Why slaughter each other for El Chico or El Zagal? Let your kings renounce their contests, unite for the salvation of Granada, or let them be deposed."

Hamet Aben Zarrax had long been revered as a saint—he was now considered an oracle. The old men and the nobles immediately consulted together how the two rival kings might be brought to accord. They had tried most expedients: it was now determined to divide the kingdom between them; giving Granada, Malaga, Velez Malaga, Almeria, Almunecar, and their dependencies, to El Zagal—and the residue to Boabdil el Chico. Among the cities granted to the latter, Loxa was particularly specified, with a condition that he should immediately take command of it in person; for the council thought the favor he enjoyed with the Castilian monarchs might avert the threatened attack.

El Zagal readily accorded to this arrangement; he had been hastily elevated to the throne by an ebullition of the people, and might be as hastily cast down again. It secured him one-half of a kingdom to which he had no hereditary right, and he trusted to force or fraud to gain the other half hereafter. The wily old monarch even sent a deputation to his nephew, making a merit of offering him cheerfully the half which he had thus been compelled to relinquish, and inviting him to enter into an amicable coalition for the good of the country.

The heart of Boabdil shrunk from all connection with a man who had sought his life, and whom he regarded as the murderer of his kindred. He accepted one-half of the kingdom as an offer from the nation, not to be rejected by a prince who scarcely held possession of the ground he stood on. He asserted, nevertheless, his absolute right to the whole, and only submitted to the partition out of anxiety for the present good of his people. He assembled his handful of adherents, and prepared to hasten to Loxa. As he mounted his horse to depart, Hamet Aben Zarrax stood suddenly before him. "Be true to thy country and thy faith," cried he: "hold no further communication with these Christian dogs. Trust not the hollow-hearted friendship of the Castilian king; he is mining the earth beneath thy feet. Choose one of two things; be a sovereign or a slave—thou canst not be both."

Boabdil ruminated on these words; he made many wise resolutions, but he was prone always to act from the impulse of the moment, and was unfortunately given to temporize in his policy. He wrote to Ferdinand, informing him that Loxa and certain other cities had returned to their allegiance, and that he held them as vassal to the Castilian crown, according to their convention. He conjured him, therefore, to refrain from any meditated attack, offering free passage to the Spanish army to Malaga, or any other place under the dominion of his uncle.*

Ferdinand turned a deaf ear to the entreaty and to all professions of friendship and vassalage. Boabdil was nothing to him, but as an instrument for stirring up the flames of civil war. He now insisted that he had entered into a hostile league with his uncle, and had consequently forfeited all claims to his indulgence; and he prosecuted, with the greater earnestness, his campaign against the city of Loxa.

* Zurita. lib. 20. c. 68.

"Thus," observes the worthy Fray Antonio Agapida, "thus did this most sagacious sovereign act upon the text in the eleventh chapter of the Evangelist St. Luke, that 'a kingdom divided against itself cannot stand.' He had induced these Infidels to waste and destroy themselves by internal dissensions, and finally cast forth the survivor; while the Moorish monarchs, by their ruinous contests, made good the old Castilian proverb in cases of civil war, 'El vencido vencido, y el vencidor perdido' (the conquered conquered, and the conqueror undone)."*

CHAPTER THIRTY-EIGHT

HOW KING FERDINAND HELD A COUNCIL OF WAR, AT THE ROCK OF THE LOVERS

THE royal army, on its march against Loxa, lay encamped, one pleasant evening in May, in a meadow on the banks of the river Yeguas, around the foot of a lofty cliff called the Rock of the Lovers. The quarters of each nobleman formed as it were a separate little encampment; his stately pavilion, surmounted by his fluttering pennon, rising above the surrounding tents of his vassals and retainers. A little apart from the others, as it were in proud reserve, was the encampment of the English earl. It was sumptuous in its furniture and complete in all its munitions. Archers, and soldiers armed with battle-axes, kept guard around it; while above, the standard of England rolled out its ample folds and flapped in the evening breeze.

The mingled sounds of various tongues and nations were heard from the soldiery, as they watered their horses in the stream, or busied themselves round the fires which began to glow, here and there, in the twilight: the gay chanson of the Frenchman, singing of his amours on the pleasant banks of the Loire, or the sunny regions of the Garonne; the broad

---

* Garibay, lib. 40, c. 33.

guttural tones of the German, chanting some doughty *krieger lied*, or extolling the vintage of the Rhine; the wild romance of the Spaniard, reciting the achievements of the Cid, and many a famous passage of the Moorish wars; and the long and melancholy ditty of the Englishman, treating of some feudal hero or redoubtable outlaw of his distant island.

On a rising ground, commanding a view of the whole encampment, stood the ample and magnificent pavilion of the king, with the banner of Castile and Aragon, and the holy standard of the cross, erected before it. In this tent were assembled the principal commanders of the army, having been summoned by Ferdinand to a council of war, on receiving tidings that Boabdil had thrown himself into Loxa with a considerable re-enforcement. After some consultation, it was determined to invest Loxa on both sides: one part of the army should seize upon the dangerous but commanding height of Santo Albohacen, in front of the city; while the remainder, making a circuit, should encamp on the opposite side.

No sooner was this resolved upon than the Marques of Cadiz stood forth and claimed the post of danger in behalf of himself and those cavaliers, his companions in arms, who had been compelled to relinquish it by the general retreat of the army on the former siege. The enemy had exulted over them, as if driven from it in disgrace. To regain that perilous height, to pitch their tents upon it, and to avenge the blood of their valiant compeer, the Master of Calatrava, who had fallen upon it, was due to their fame; the marques demanded therefore that they might lead the advance and secure that height, engaging to hold the enemy employed until the main army should take its position on the opposite side of the city.

King Ferdinand readily granted his permission, upon which the Count de Cabra entreated to be admitted to a share of the enterprise. He had always been accustomed to serve in the advance; and now that Boabdil was in the field, and a king was to be taken, he could not content himself with remaining in the rear. Ferdinand yielded his consent, for he was disposed to give the good count every opportunity to retrieve his late disaster.

The English earl, when he heard there was an enterprise of danger in question, was hot to be admitted to the party; but the king restrained his ardor. "These cavaliers," said he, "conceive that they have an account to settle with their pride; let them have the enterprise to themselves, my lord; if you follow these Moorish wars long, you will find no lack of perilous service."

The Marques of Cadiz, and his companions in arms, struck their tents before daybreak; they were five thousand horse and twelve thousand foot, and marched rapidly along the defiles of the mountains; the cavaliers being anxious to strike the blow, and get possession of the height of Albohacen, before the king with the main army should arrive to their assistance.

The city of Loxa stands on a high hill, between two mountains, on the banks of the Xenil. To attain the height of Albohacen, the troops had to pass over a tract of rugged and broken country, and a deep valley, intersected by those canals and water-courses with which the Moors irrigated their lands; they were extremely embarrassed in this part of their march, and in imminent risk of being cut up in detail before they could reach the height.

The Count de Cabra, with his usual eagerness, endeavored to push across this valley, in defiance of every obstacle: he, in consequence, soon became entangled with his cavalry among the canals; but his impatience would not permit him to retrace his steps and choose a more practicable but circuitous route. Others slowly crossed another part of the valley, by the aid of pontoons; while the Marques of Cadiz, Don Alonzo de Aguilar, and the Count de Urena, being more experienced in the ground from their former campaign, made a circuit round the bottom of the height, and, winding up it, began to display their squadrons and elevate their banners on the redoubtable post, which, in the former siege, they had been compelled so reluctantly to abandon.

CHAPTER THIRTY-NINE

HOW THE ROYAL ARMY APPEARED BEFORE THE CITY OF
LOXA, AND HOW IT WAS RECEIVED; AND OF THE
DOUGHTY ACHIEVEMENTS OF THE ENGLISH EARL

THE advance of the Christian army upon Loxa threw
the wavering Boabdil el Chico into one of his usual dilemmas;
and he was greatly perplexed between his oath of allegiance
to the Spanish sovereigns and his sense of duty to his subjects.   His doubts were determined by the sight of the enemy
glittering upon the height of Albohacen, and by the clamors
of the people to be led forth to battle.   "Allah!" exclaimed
he, "thou knowest my heart: thou knowest I have been true
in my faith to this Christian monarch.   I have offered to
hold Loxa as his vassal, but he has preferred to approach it
as an enemy—on his head be the infraction of our treaty!"

Boabdil was not wanting in courage; he only needed decision.   When he had once made up his mind, he acted
vigorously; the misfortune was, he either did not make it
up at all, or he made it up too late.   He who decides tardily
generally acts rashly, endeavoring to make up by hurry of
action for slowness of deliberation.   Boabdil hastily buckled
on his armor, and sallied forth, surrounded by his guards,
and at the head of five hundred horse and four thousand foot,
the flower of his army.   Some he detached to skirmish with
the Christians who were scattered and perplexed in the valley,
and to prevent their concentrating their forces; while, with
his main body, he pressed forward to drive the enemy from
the height of Albohacen, before they had time to collect there
in any number, or to fortify themselves in that important
position.

The worthy Count de Cabra was yet entangled with his
cavalry among the water-courses of the valley, when he

heard the war-cries of the Moors and saw their army rushing over the bridge. He recognized Boabdil himself, by his
splendid armor, the magnificent caparison of his steed, and
the brilliant guard which surrounded him. The royal host
swept on toward the height of Albohacen: an intervening
hill hid it from his sight; but loud shouts and cries, the din
of drums and trumpets, and the reports of arquebuses, gave
note that the battle had begun.

Here was a royal prize in the field, and the Count de
Cabra unable to get into the action! The good cavalier was
in an agony of impatience; every attempt to force his way
across the valley only plunged him into new difficulties.
At length, after many eager but ineffectual efforts, he was
obliged to order his troops to dismount, and slowly and carefully to lead their horses back, along slippery paths, and
amid plashes of mire and water, where often there was scarce
a foothold. The good count groaned in spirit, and sweat
with mere impatience as he went, fearing the battle might
be fought, and the prize won or lost, before he could reach
the field. Having at length toilfully unraveled the mazes
of the valley, and arrived at firmer ground, he ordered his
troops to mount, and led them full gallop to the height.
Part of the good count's wishes were satisfied, but the dearest were disappointed: he came in season to partake of the
very hottest of the fight, but the royal prize was no longer
in the field.

Boabdil had led on his men with impetuous valor, or
rather with hurried rashness. Heedlessly exposing himself
in the front of the battle, he received two wounds in the very
first encounter. His guards rallied round him, defended
him with matchless valor, and bore him, bleeding, out of the
action. The Count de Cabra arrived just in time to see the
loyal squadron crossing the bridge, and slowly conveying
their disabled monarch toward the gate of the city.

The departure of Boabdil made no difference in the fury
of the battle. A Moorish warrior, dark and terrible in
aspect, mounted on a black charger and followed by a band

of savage Comares, rushed forward to take the lead. It was Hamet el Zegri, the fierce alcayde of Ronda, with the remnant of his once redoubtable garrison. Animated by his example, the Moors renewed their assaults upon the height. It was bravely defended, on one side by the Marques of Cadiz, on another by Don Alonzo de Aguilar; and as fast as the Moors ascended, they were driven back and dashed down the declivities. The Count de Urena took his stand upon the fatal spot where his brother had fallen; his followers entered with zeal into the feelings of their commander, and heaps of the enemy sunk beneath their weapons—sacrifices to the manes of the lamented Master of Calatrava.

The battle continued with incredible obstinacy. The Moors knew the importance of the height to the safety of the city; the cavaliers felt their honors staked to maintain it. Fresh supplies of troops were poured out of the city; some battled on the height, while some attacked the Christians who were still in the valley and among the orchards and gardens, to prevent their uniting their forces. The troops in the valley were gradually driven back, and the whole host of the Moors swept around the height of Albohacen. The situation of the Marques de Cadiz and his companions was perilous in the extreme: they were a mere handful; and, while they were fighting hand to hand with the Moors who assailed the height, they were galled from a distance by the crossbows and arquebuses of a host that augmented each moment in number. At this critical juncture, King Ferdinand emerged from the mountains with the main body of the army, and advanced to an eminence commanding a full view of the field of action. By his side was the noble English cavalier, the Earl of Rivers. This was the first time he had witnessed a scene of Moorish warfare. He looked with eager interest at the chance-medley fight before him, where there was the wild career of cavalry, the irregular and tumultuous rush of infantry, and where Christian helm and Moorish turban were intermingled in deadly struggle. The high blood of the English knight mounted at the sight, and his soul was stirred within him, by the confused war-cries, the clangor of drums and trumpets, and the reports of arquebuses, that came echoing up the mountains. Seeing that the king was sending a re-enforcement to the field, he entreated permission to mingle in the affray, and fight according to the fashion of his country. His request being granted, he alighted from his steed: he was merely armed *en blanco*, that is to say, with morion, back-piece, and breast-plate; his sword was girded by his side, and in his hand he wielded a powerful battle-ax. He was followed by a body of his yeomen, armed in like manner, and by a band of archers with bows made of the tough English yew-tree. The earl turned to his troops, and addressed them briefly and bluntly, according to the manner of his country. "Remember, my merry men all," said he, "the eyes of strangers are upon you; you are in a foreign land, fighting for the glory of God, and the honor of merry old England!" A loud shout was the reply. The earl waved his battle-ax over his head: "St. George for England!" cried he; and to the inspiring sound of this old English war-cry, he and his followers rushed down to the battle with manly and courageous heart.* They soon made their way into the midst of the enemy; but when engaged in the hottest of the fight, they made no shouts or outcries. They pressed steadily forward, dealing their blows to right and left, hewing down the Moors, and cutting their way, with their battle-axes, like woodmen in a forest; while the archers, pressing into the opening they made, plied their bows vigorously, and spread death on every side.

When the Castilian mountaineers beheld the valor of the English yeomanry, they would not be outdone in hardihood. They could not vie with them in weight or bulk, but for vigor and activity they were surpassed by none. They kept pace with them, therefore, with equal heart and rival prowess, and gave a brave support to the stout Englishmen.

The Moors were confounded by the fury of these assaults,

---

* Cura de los Palacios.

and disheartened by the loss of Hamet el Zegri, who was carried wounded from the field. They gradually fell back upon the bridge; the Christians followed up their advantage, and drove them over it tumultuously. The Moors retreated into the suburb; and Lord Rivers and his troops entered with them pell-mell, fighting in the streets and in the houses. King Ferdinand came up to the scene of action with his royal guard, and the Infidels were driven within the city walls. Thus were the suburbs gained by the hardihood of the English lord, without such an event having been premeditated.*

The Earl of Rivers, notwithstanding he had received a wound, still urged forward in the attack. He penetrated almost to the city gate, in defiance of a shower of missiles that slew many of his followers. A stone, hurled from the battlements, checked his impetuous career: it struck him in the face, dashed out two of his front teeth, and laid him senseless on the earth. He was removed to a short distance by his men; but, recovering his senses, refused to permit himself to be taken from the suburb.

When the contest was over, the streets presented a piteous spectacle—so many of their inhabitants had died in the defense of their thresholds, or been slaughtered without resistance. Among the victims was a poor weaver, who had been at work in his dwelling at this turbulent moment. His wife urged him to fly into the city. "Why should I fly?" said the Moor—"to be reserved for hunger and slavery? I tell you, wife, I will await the foe here; for better is it to die quickly by the steel than to perish piecemeal in chains and dungeons." He said no more, but resumed his occupation of weaving; and, in the indiscriminate fury of the assault, was slaughtered at his loom.†

The Christians remained masters of the field, and proceeded to pitch three encampments for the prosecution of the siege. The king, with the great body of the army, took a position on the side of the city next to Granada: the Mar-

---

* Cura de los Palacios.   MS.   † Pulgar, part 3, c. 58.

ques of Cadiz and his brave companions once more pitched their tents upon the height of Sancto Albohacen: but the English earl planted his standard sturdily within the suburb he had taken.

CHAPTER FORTY

CONCLUSION OF THE SIEGE OF LOXA

HAVING possession of the heights of Albohacen and the suburb of the city, the Christians were enabled to choose the most favorable situations for their batteries. They immediately destroyed the stone bridge by which the garrison had made its sallies; and they threw two wooden bridges across the river, and others over the canals and streams, so as to establish an easy communication between the different camps.

When all was arranged, a heavy fire was opened upon the city from various points. They threw, not only balls of stone and iron, but great carcasses of fire, which burst like meteors on the houses, wrapping them instantly in a blaze. The walls were shattered, and the towers toppled down, by tremendous discharges from the lombards. Through the openings thus made, they could behold the interior of the city—houses tumbling or in flames—men, women, and children, flying in terror through the streets, and slaughtered by the shower of missiles sent through the openings from smaller artillery, and from crossbows and arquebuses.

The Moors attempted to repair the breaches, but fresh discharges from the lombards buried them beneath the ruins of the walls they were mending. In their despair, many of the inhabitants rushed forth into the narrow streets of the suburbs, and assailed the Christians with darts, scimiters, and poniards, seeking to destroy rather than defend, and heedless of death, in the confidence that to die fighting with an unbeliever was to be translated at once to paradise.

For two nights and a day this awful scene continued;

when certain of the principal inhabitants began to reflect upon the hopelessness of the conflict: their king was disabled, their principal captains were either killed or wounded, their fortifications little better than heaps of ruins. They had urged the unfortunate Boabdil to the conflict; they now clamored for a capitulation. A parley was procured from the Christian monarch, and the terms of surrender were soon adjusted. They were to yield up the city immediately, with all their Christian captives, and to sally forth with as much of their property as they could take with them. The Marques of Cadiz, on whose honor and humanity they had great reliance, was to escort them to Granada, to protect them from assault or robbery: such as chose to remain in Spain were to be permitted to reside in Castile, Aragon, or Valencia. As to Boabdil el Chico, he was to do homage as vassal to King Ferdinand, but no charge was to be urged against him of having violated his former pledge. If he should yield up all pretensions to Granada, the title of Duke of Guadix was to be assigned to him, and the territory thereto annexed, provided it should be recovered from El Zagal within six months.

The capitulation being arranged, they gave as hostages the alcayde of the city, and the principal officers, together with the sons of their late chieftain, the veteran Ali Atar. The warriors of Loxa then issued forth, humbled and dejected at having to surrender those walls which they had so long maintained with valor and renown; and the women and children filled the air with lamentations at being exiled from their native homes.

Last came forth Boabdil, most truly called El Zogoybi the unlucky. Accustomed, as he was, to be crowned and uncrowned, to be ransomed and treated as a matter of bargain, he had acceded of course to the capitulation. He was enfeebled by his wounds, and had an air of dejection; yet it is said his conscience acquitted him of a breach of faith toward the Castilian sovereigns, and the personal valor he had displayed had caused a sympathy for him among many of the Christian cavaliers.   He knelt to Ferdinand according to the forms of vassalage, and then departed, in melancholy mood, for Priego, a town about three leagues distant.

Ferdinand immediately ordered Loxa to be repaired, and strongly garrisoned.   He was greatly elated at the capture of this place, in consequence of his former defeat before its walls.   He passed great encomiums upon the commanders who had distinguished themselves; and historians dwell particularly upon his visit to the tent of the English earl.   His majesty consoled him for the loss of his teeth by the consideration that he might otherwise have lost them by natural decay; whereas the lack of them would now be esteemed a beauty rather than a defect, serving as a trophy of the glorious cause in which he had. been engaged.

The earl replied that he gave thanks to God and to the holy Virgin, for being thus honored by a visit from the most potent king in Christendom; that he accepted with all gratitude his gracious consolation for the loss of his teeth, though he held it little to lose two teeth in the service of God, who had given him all: "A speech," says Fray Antonio Agapida, "full of most courtly wit and Christian piety; and one only marvels that it should have been made by a native of an island so far distant from Castile."

CHAPTER FORTY-ONE

CAPTURE OF ILLORA

KING FERDINAND followed up his victory at Loxa by laying siege to the strong town of Illora.   This redoubtable fortress was perched upon a high rock, in the midst of a spacious valley.   It was within four leagues of the Moorish capital; and its lofty castle, keeping vigilant watch over a wide circuit of country, was termed the right eye of Granada.

The alcayde of Illora was one of the bravest of the Moorish commanders, and made every preparation to defend his fortress to the last extremity. He sent the women and children, the aged and infirm, to the metropolis. He placed barricadoes in the suburbs, opened doors of communication from house to house, and pierced their walls with loopholes for the discharge of crossbows, arquebuses, and other missiles.

King Ferdinand arrived before the place with all his forces; he stationed himself upon the hill of Encinilla, and distributed the other encampments in various situations, so as to invest the fortress. Knowing the valiant character of the alcayde, and the desperate courage of the Moors, he ordered the encampments to be fortified with trenches and pallisadoes, the guards to be doubled, and sentinels to be placed in all the watch-towers of the adjacent heights.

When all was ready, the Duke del Infantado demanded the attack; it was his first campaign, and he was anxious to disprove the royal insinuation made against the hardihood of his embroidered chivalry. King Ferdinand granted his demand with a becoming compliment to his spirit; he ordered the Count de Cabra to make a simultaneous attack upon a different quarter. Both chiefs led forth their troops—those of the duke in fresh and brilliant armor, richly ornamented, and as yet uninjured by the service of the field; those of the count were weatherbeaten veterans, whose armor was dented and hacked in many a hard-fought battle. The youthful duke blushed at the contrast. "Cavaliers," cried he, "we have been reproached with the finery of our array: let us prove that a trenchant blade may rest in a gilded sheath. Forward! to the foe! and I trust in God, that as we enter this affray knights well accoutered, so we shall leave it cavaliers well proved." His men responded by eager acclamations, and the duke led them forward to the assault. He advanced under a tremendous shower of stones, darts, balls, and arrows; but nothing could check his career; he entered the suburb sword in hand; his men fought furiously, though with great loss, for every dwelling had been turned into a fortress. After a severe conflict, they succeeded in driving the Moors into the town, about the same time that the other suburb was carried by the Count de Cabra and his veterans. The troops of the Duke del Infantado came out of the contest thinned in number, and covered with blood, and dust, and wounds: they received the highest encomiums of the king, and there was never afterward any sneer at their embroidery.

The suburbs being taken, three batteries, each furnished with eight huge lombards, were opened upon the fortress. The damage and havoc were tremendous, for the fortifications had not been constructed to withstand such engines. The towers were overthrown, the walls battered to pieces; the interior of the place was all exposed, houses demolished, and many people slain. The Moors were terrified by the tumbling ruins and the tremendous din. The alcayde had resolved to defend the place until the last extremity; he beheld it a heap of rubbish; there was no prospect of aid from Granada; his people had lost all spirit to fight, and were vociferous for a surrender; with a reluctant heart he capitulated. The inhabitants were permitted to depart with all their effects, excepting their arms; and were escorted in safety by the Duke del Infantado and the Count de Cabra to the bridge of Pinos, within two leagues of Granada.

King Ferdinand gave directions to repair the fortifications of Illora, and to place it in a strong state of defense. He left, as alcayde of the town and fortress, Gonsalvo de Cordova, younger brother of Don Alonzo de Aguilar. This gallant cavalier was captain of the royal guards of Ferdinand and Isabella, and gave already proofs of that prowess which afterward rendered him so renowned.

CHAPTER FORTY-TWO

OF THE ARRIVAL OF QUEEN ISABELLA AT THE CAMP BEFORE
MOCLIN; AND OF THE PLEASANT SAYINGS OF
THE ENGLISH EARL

THE war of Granada, however poets may embroider it with the flowers of their fancy, was certainly one of the sternest of those iron conflicts which have been celebrated under the name of holy wars. The worthy Fray Antonio Agapida dwells with unsated delight upon the succession of rugged mountain enterprises, bloody battles, and merciless sackings and ravages which characterized it; yet we find him on one occasion pausing in the full career of victory over the Infidels, to detail a stately pageant of the Catholic sovereigns.

Immediately on the capture of Loxa, Ferdinand had written to Isabella, soliciting her presence at the camp, that he might consult with her as to the disposition of their newly-acquired territories.

It was in the early part of June that the queen departed from Cordova with the Princess Isabella and numerous ladies of her court. She had a glorious attendance of cavaliers and pages, with many guards and domestics. There were forty mules, for the use of the queen, the princess, and their train.

As this courtly cavalcade approached the Rock of the Lovers, on the banks of the river Yeguas, they beheld a splendid train of knights advancing to meet them. It was headed by that accomplished cavalier the Marques, Duke de Cadiz, accompanied by the adelantado of Andalusia. He had left the camp the day after the capture of Illora, and advanced thus far to receive the queen and escort her over the borders. The queen received the marques with distinguished honor; for he was esteemed the mirror of chivalry. His actions in this war had become the theme of every tongue, and many hesitated not to compare him in prowess to the immortal Cid.*

Thus gallantly attended, the queen entered the vanquished frontier of Granada; journeying securely along the pleasant banks of the Xenil, so lately subject to the scourings of the Moors. She stopped at Loxa, where she administered aid and consolation to the wounded, distributing money among them for their support, according to their rank.

---

* Cura de los Palacios.

The king, after the capture of Illora, had removed his camp before the fortress of Moclin, with an intention of besieging it. Thither the queen proceeded, still escorted through the mountain roads by the Marques of Cadiz. As Isabella drew near to the camp the Duke del Infantado issued forth a league and a half to receive her, magnificently arrayed, and followed by all his chivalry in glorious attire. With him came the standard of Seville, borne by the men-at-arms of that renowned city; and the prior of St. Juan, with his followers. They arrayed themselves in order of battle, on the left of the road by which the queen was to pass.

The worthy Agapida is loyally minute in his description of the state and grandeur of the Catholic sovereigns. The queen rode a chestnut mule, seated in a magnificent saddle-chair decorated with silver gilt. The housings of the mule were of fine crimson cloth; the borders embroidered with gold; the reins and head-piece were of satin, curiously embossed with needlework of silk, and wrought with golden letters. The queen wore a brial or regal skirt of velvet, under which were others of brocade; a scarlet mantle, ornamented in the Morisco fashion; and a black hat, embroidered round the crown and brim.

The Infanta was likewise mounted on a chestnut mule, richly caparisoned: she wore a brial or skirt of black brocade, and a black mantle ornamented like that of the queen.

When the royal cavalcade passed by the chivalry of the Duke del Infantado, which was drawn out in battle array, the queen made a reverence to the standard of Seville, and ordered it to pass to the right hand. When she approached the camp, the multitude ran forth to meet her, with great demonstrations of joy; for she was universally beloved by her subjects. All the battalions sallied forth in military array, bearing the various standards and banners of the camp, which were lowered in salutation as she passed.

The king now came forth in royal state, mounted on a superb chestnut horse, and attended by many grandees of Castile. He wore a jubon or close vest of crimson cloth, with cuisses or short skirts of yellow satin, a loose cassock of brocade, a rich Moorish scimiter, and a hat with plumes. The grandees who attended him were arrayed with wonderful magnificence, each according to his taste and invention.

These high and mighty princes (says Antonio Agapida) regard each other with great deference, as allied sovereigns, rather than with connubial familiarity as mere husband and wife. When they approached each other, therefore, before embracing, they made three profound reverences; the queen taking off her hat, and remaining in a silk net or caul, with her face uncovered. The king then approached and embraced her, and kissed her respectfully on the cheek. He also embraced his daughter, the princess; and, making the sign of the cross, he blessed her, and kissed her on the lips.[*]

The good Agapida seems scarcely to have been more struck with the appearance of the sovereigns than with that of the English earl. He followed (says he) immediately after the king, with great pomp, and, in an extraordinary manner, taking precedence of all the rest. He was mounted "*a la guisa*," or with long stirrups, on a superb chestnut horse, with trappings of azure silk which reached to the ground. The housings were of mulberry, powdered with stars of gold. He was armed in proof, and wore over his armor a short French mantle of black brocade; he had a white French hat with plumes, and carried on his left arm a small round buckler, banded with gold. Five pages attended him, appareled in silk and brocade, and mounted on horses sumptuously caparisoned; he had also a train of followers, bravely attired after the fashion of his country.

He advanced in a chivalrous and courteous manner, making his reverences first to the queen and infanta, and afterward to the king. Queen Isabella received him graciously, complimenting him on his courageous conduct at Loxa, and condoling with him on the loss of his teeth. The earl, however, made light of his disfiguring wound; saying that "our

---

[*] Cura de los Palacios.

blessed Lord, who had built all that house, had opened a window there, that He might see more readily what passed within:" * whereupon the worthy Fray Antonio Agapida is more than ever astonished at the pregnant wit of this island cavalier. The earl continued some little distance by the side of the royal family, complimenting them all with courteous speeches, his horse curveting and caracoling, but being managed with great grace and dexterity; leaving the grandees and the people at large not more filled with admiration at the strangeness and magnificence of his state than at the excellence of his horsemanship.†

To testify her sense of the gallantry and services of this noble English knight, who had come from so far to assist in their wars, the queen sent him the next day presents of twelve horses, with stately tents, fine linen, two beds with coverings of gold brocade, and many other articles of great value.

Having refreshed himself, as it were, with the description of this progress of Queen Isabella to the camp, and the glorious pomp of the Catholic sovereigns, the worthy Antonio Agapida returns with renewed relish to his pious work of discomfiting the Moors.

The description of this royal pageant, and the particulars concerning the English earl, thus given from the manuscript of Fray Antonio Agapida, agree precisely with the chronicle of Andres Bernaldes, the curate of los Palacios. The English earl makes no further figure in this war. It appears from various histories that he returned in the course of the year to England. In the following year, his passion for fighting took him to the Continent at the head of four hundred adventurers, in aid of Francis, Duke of Brittany, against Louis XI. of France. He was killed in the same year (1488) in the battle of St. Alban's, between the Bretons and the French.

---

* Pietro Martyr, Epist. 61.   † Cura de los Palacios.

CHAPTER FORTY-THREE

"THE Catholic sovereigns," says Fray Antonio Agapida, "had by this time closely clipped the right wing of the Moorish vulture." In other words, most of the strong fortresses along the western frontier of Granada had fallen beneath the Christian artillery. The army now lay encamped before the town of Moclin, on the frontier of Jaen, one of the most stubborn fortresses of the border. It stood on a high rocky hill, the base of which was nearly girdled by a river: a thick forest protected the back part of the town, toward the mountain. Thus strongly situated, it domineered, with its frowning battlements and massive towers, all the mountain passes into that part of the country, and was called "the shield of Granada." It had a double arrear of blood to settle with the Christians; two hundred years before a Master of Santiago and all his cavaliers had been lanced by the Moors before its gates. It had recently made terrible slaughter among the troops of the good Count de Cabra, in his precipitate attempt to entrap the old Moorish monarch. The pride of Ferdinand had been piqued by being obliged on that occasion to recede from his plan, and abandon his concerted attack on the place; he was now prepared to take a full revenge.

El Zagal, the old warrior king of Granada, anticipating a second attempt, had provided the place with ample ammunitions and provisions; had ordered trenches to be digged, and additional bulwarks thrown up; and caused all the old men, the women, and the children, to be removed to the capital.

Such was the strength of the fortress, and the difficulties of its position, that Ferdinand anticipated much trouble in reducing it, and made every preparation for a regular siege. In the center of his camp were two great mounds, one of sacks of flour, the other of grain, which were called the royal granary. Three batteries of heavy ordnance were opened against the citadel and principal towers, while smaller artillery, engines for the discharge of missiles, arquebuses and crossbows, were distributed in various places, to keep up a fire into any breaches that might be made, and upon those of the garrison who should appear on the battlements.

The lombards soon made an impression on the works, demolishing a part of the wall, and tumbling down several of those haughty towers, which from their height had been impregnable before the invention of gunpowder. The Moors repaired their walls as well as they were able, and, still confiding in the strength of their situation, kept up a resolute defense, firing down from their lofty battlements and towers upon the Christian camp. For two nights and a day an incessant fire was kept up, so that there was not a moment in which the roaring of ordnance was not heard, or some damage sustained by the Christians or the Moors. It was a conflict, however, more of engineers and artillerists than of gallant cavaliers; there was no sally of troops, or shock of armed men, or rush and charge of cavalry. The knights stood looking on with idle weapons, waiting until they should have an opportunity of signalizing their prowess by scaling the walls or storming the breaches. As the place, however, was assailable only in one part, there was every prospect of a long and obstinate resistance.

The engineers, as usual, discharged not merely balls of stone and iron to demolish the walls, but flaming balls of inextinguishable combustibles, designed to set fire to the houses. One of these, which passed high through the air like a meteor, sending out sparks and crackling as it went, entered the window of a tower which was used as a magazine of gunpowder. The tower blew up with a tremendous explosion; the Moors who were upon its battlements were hurled into the air, and fell mangled in various parts of the town; and the houses in its vicinity were rent and over-thrown as with an earthquake.

The Moors, who had never witnessed an explosion of the kind, ascribed the destruction of the tower to a miracle. Some who had seen the descent of the flaming ball imagined that fire had fallen from heaven to punish them for their pertinacity. The pious Agapida, himself, believes that this fiery missive was conducted by divine agency to confound the Infidels; an opinion in which he is supported by other Catholic historians.*

Seeing heaven and earth, as it were, combined against them, the Moors lost all heart: they capitulated, and were permitted to depart with their effects, leaving behind all arms and munitions of war.

The Catholic army (says Antonio Agapida) entered Moclin in solemn state, not as a licentious host, intent upon plunder and desolation, but as a band of Christian warriors, coming to purify and regenerate the land. The standard of the cross, that ensign of this holy crusade, was borne in the advance, followed by the other banners of the army. Then came the king and queen, at the head of a vast number of armed cavaliers. They were accompanied by a band of priests and friars, with the choir of the royal chapel, chanting the canticle, "Te deum laudamus." As they were moving through the streets in this solemn manner, every sound hushed excepting the anthem of the choir, they suddenly heard, issuing, as it were, from under ground, a chorus of voices chanting the solemn response, "Benedictum qui venit in nomine domini." † The procession paused in wonder. The sounds arose from Christian captives, and among them several priests, who were confined in subterraneous dungeons.

The heart of Isabella was greatly touched. She ordered the captives to be drawn forth from their cells, and was still

* Pulgar, Garibay, Lucio Marino Siculo, Cosas Memoral. de Hispan, lib. 20.
† Marino Siculo.

more moved at beholding, by their wan, discolored, and emaciated appearance, how much they had suffered. Their hair
and beards were overgrown and shagged; they were wasted
by hunger, half naked, and in chains. She ordered that they
should be clothed and cherished, and money furnished them
to bear them to their homes.*

Several of the captives were brave cavaliers, who had
been wounded and made prisoners, in the defeat of the Count
de Cabra by El Zagal, in the preceding year. There were
also found other melancholy traces of that disastrous affair.
On visiting the narrow pass where the defeat had taken
place, the remains of several Christian warriors were found
in thickets, or hidden behind rocks, or in the clefts of the
mountains. These were some who had been struck from
their horses, and wounded too severely to fly. They had
crawled away from the scene of action, and concealed themselves to avoid falling into the hands of the enemy, and had
thus perished miserably and alone. The remains of those of
note were known by their armor and devices, and were
mourned over by their companions who had shared the disasters of that day.†

The queen had these remains piously collected, as the
relics of so many martyrs who had fallen in the cause of
the faith. They were interred with great solemnity in the
mosques of Moclin, which had been purified and consecrated
to Christian worship. "There," says Antonio Agapida,
"rest the bones of those truly Catholic knights, in the holy
ground which in a manner had been sanctified by their blood;
and all pilgrims passing through those mountains offer up
prayers and masses for the repose of their souls."

The queen remained for some time at Moclin, administering comfort to the wounded and the prisoners, bringing the
newly acquired territory into order, and founding churches
and monasteries and other pious institutions. "While the

---

* Illescas, Hist. Pontif, lib. 6, c. 20, § 1.

† Pulgar, part 3, cap. 61.

king marched in front, laying waste the land of the Philistines," says the figurative Antonio Agapida, "Queen Isabella followed his traces as the binder follows the reaper, gathering and garnering the rich harvest that has fallen beneath his sickle. In this she was greatly assisted by the counsels of that cloud of bishops, friars, and other saintly men, which continually surrounded her, garnering the first fruits of this Infidel land into the granaries of the church." Leaving her thus piously employed, the king pursued his career of conquest, determined to lay waste the vega, and carry fire and sword to the very gates of Granada.

CHAPTER FORTY-FOUR

HOW KING FERDINAND FORAGED THE VEGA; AND OF THE BATTLE OF THE BRIDGE OF PINOS, AND THE FATE OF THE TWO MOORISH BROTHERS

MULEY ABDALLA EL ZAGAL had been under a spell of ill fortune ever since the suspicious death of the old king, his brother. Success had deserted his standard; and, with his fickle subjects, want of success was one of the greatest crimes in a sovereign. He found his popularity declining, and he lost all confidence in his people. The Christian army marched in open defiance through his territories, and sat down deliberately before his fortresses; yet he dared not lead forth his legions to oppose them, lest the inhabitants of the Albaycin, ever ripe for a revolt, should rise and shut the gates of Granada against his return.

Every few days, some melancholy train entered the metropolis, the inhabitants of some captured town, bearing the few effects that had been spared them, and weeping and bewailing the desolation of their homes. When the tidings arrived that Illora and Moclin had fallen, the people were seized with consternation. "The right eye of Granada is extinguished," exclaimed they; "the shield of Granada is

broken: what shall protect us from the inroad of the foe?"
When the survivors of the garrisons of those towns arrived,
with downcast looks, bearing the marks of battle, and destitute of arms and standards, the populace reviled them in
their wrath; but they answered, "We fought as long as we
had force to fight, or walls to shelter us; but the Christians
laid our towns and battlements in ruins, and we looked in
vain for aid from Granada."

The alcaydes of Illora and Moclin were brothers; they
were alike in prowess, and the bravest among the Moorish
cavaliers. They had been the most distinguished in all tilts
and tourneys which graced the happier days of Granada,
and had distinguished themselves in the sterner conflicts of
the field. Acclamation had always followed their banners,
and they had long been the delight of the people. Yet now,
when they returned after the capture of their fortresses, they
were followed by the unsteady populace with execrations.
The hearts of the alcaydes swelled with indignation; they
found the ingratitude of their countrymen still more intolerable than the hostility of the Christians.

Tidings came that the enemy was advancing with his triumphant legions to lay waste the country about Granada.
Still El Zagal did not dare to take the field. The two
alcaydes of Illora and Moclin stood before him: "We have
defended your fortresses," said they, "until we were almost
buried under their ruins, and for our reward we receive
scoffings and revilings; give us, oh king, an opportunity
where knightly valor may signalize itself, not shut up behind stone walls, but in the open conflict of the field. The
enemy approaches to lay our country desolate: give us men
to meet him in the advance, and let shame light upon our
heads if we be found wanting in the battle!"

The two brothers were sent forth, with a large force of
horse and foot; El Zagal intended, should they be successful, to issue forth with his whole force, and by a decisive
victory repair the losses he had suffered. When the people
saw the well-known standards of the brothers going forth to

battle there was a feeble shout; but the alcaydes passed on
with stern countenances, for they knew the same voices
would curse them were they to return unfortunate. They
cast a farewell look upon fair Granada, and upon the beautiful fields of their infancy, as if for these they were willing to
lay down their lives, but not for an ungrateful people.

The army of Ferdinand had arrived within two leagues
of Granada, at the Bridge of Pinos, a pass famous in the
wars of the Moors and Christians for many a bloody conflict.
It was the pass by which the Castilian monarchs generally
made their inroads, and .was capable of great defense, from
the ruggedness of the country and the difficulty of the bridge.
The king, with the main body of the army, had attained the
brow of a hill, when they beheld the advance guard, under
the Marques of Cadiz and the Master of Santiago, furiously
attacked by the enemy, in the vicinity of the bridge. The
Moors rushed to the assault with their usual shouts, but with
more than usual ferocity. There was a hard struggle at the
bridge; both parties knew the importance of that pass.

The king particularly noted the prowess of two Moorish
cavaliers, alike in arms and devices, and whom by their
bearing and attendance he perceived to be commanders of
the enemy. They were the two brothers, the alcaydes of
Illora and Moclin. Wherever they turned, they carried confusion and death into the ranks of the Christians; but they
fought with desperation rather than valor. The Count de
Cabra, and his brother Don Martin de Cordova, pressed forward with eagerness against them; but having advanced too
precipitately, were surrounded by the foe, and in imminent
danger. A young Christian knight, seeing their peril, hastened with his followers to their relief. The king recognized
him for Don Juan de Aragon, Count of Ribargoza, his own
nephew; for he was illegitimate son of the Duke of Villahermosa, illegitimate brother of King Ferdinand. The splendid
armor of Don Juan, and the sumptuous caparison of his steed,
rendered him a brilliant object of attack. He was assailed
on all sides, and his superb steed slain under him; yet still he

fought valiantly, bearing for a time the brunt of the fight, and giving the exhausted forces of the Count de Cabra time to recover breath.

Seeing the peril of these troops and the general obstinacy of the fight, the king ordered the royal standard to be advanced, and hastened, with all his forces, to the relief of the Count de Cabra. At his approach, the enemy gave way, and retreated toward the bridge. The two Moorish commanders endeavored to rally their troops, and animate them to defend this pass to the utmost: they used prayers, remonstrances, menaces—but almost in vain. They could only collect a scanty handful of cavaliers; with these they planted themselves at the head of the bridge, and disputed it inch by inch. The fight was hot and obstinate, for but few could contend hand to hand, yet many discharged crossbows and arquebuses from the banks. The river was covered with the floating bodies of the slain. The Moorish band of cavaliers was almost entirely cut to pieces; the two brothers fell, covered with wounds, upon the bridge they had so resolutely defended. They had given up the battle for lost, but had determined not to return alive to ungrateful Granada.

When the people of the capital heard how devotedly they had fallen, they lamented greatly their deaths, and extolled their memory: a column was erected to their honor in the vicinity of the bridge, which long went by the name of "the Tomb of the Brothers."

The army of Ferdinand now marched on, and established its camp in the vicinity of Granada. The worthy Agapida gives many triumphant details of the ravages committed in the vega, which was again laid waste; the grain, fruits, and other productions of the earth, destroyed—and that earthly paradise rendered a dreary desert. He narrates several fierce but ineffectual sallies and skirmishes of the Moors, in defense of their favorite plain; among which one deserves to be mentioned, as it records the achievements of one of the saintly heroes of this war.

During one of the movements of the Christian army,

near the walls of Granada, a battalion of fifteen hundred cavalry, and a large force of foot, had sallied from the city, and posted themselves near some gardens, which were surrounded by a canal, and traversed by ditches, for the purpose of irrigation.

The Moors beheld the Duke del Infantado pass by, with his two splendid battalions; one of men-at-arms, the other of light cavalry, armed *a la gineta*. In company with him, but following as a rear-guard, was Don Garcia Osorio, the belligerent bishop of Jaen, attended by Francisco Bovadillo, the corregidor of his city, and followed by two squadrons of men-at-arms, from Jaen, Anduxar, Ubeda, and Baeza.* The success of last year's campaign had given the good bishop an inclination for warlike affairs, and he had once more buckled on his cuirass.

The Moors were much given to stratagem in warfare. They looked wistfully at the magnificent squadrons of the Duke del Infantado; but their martial discipline precluded all attack: the good bishop promised to be a more easy prey. Suffering the duke and his troops to pass unmolested, they approached the squadrons of the bishop, and, making a pretended attack, skirmished slightly, and fled in apparent confusion. The bishop considered the day his own, and, seconded by his corregidor Bovadillo, followed with valorous precipitation. The Moors fled into the *Huerta del Rey*, or orchard of the king; the troops of the bishop followed hotly after them.

When the Moors perceived their pursuers fairly embarrassed among the intricacies of the garden, they turned fiercely upon them, while some of their number threw open the sluices of the Xenil. In an instant, the canal which encircled and the ditches which traversed the garden, were filled with water, and the valiant bishop and his followers found themselves overwhelmed by a deluge.† A scene of great confusion succeeded. Some of the men of Jaen, stout-

---

* Pulgar, part 3, cap. 62.   † Pulgar.

est of heart and hand, fought with the Moors in the garden, while others struggled with the water, endeavoring to escape across the canal, in which attempt many horses were drowned.

Fortunately, the Duke del Infantado perceived the snare into which his companions had fallen, and dispatched his light cavalry to their assistance. The Moors were compelled to flight, and driven along the road of Elvira up to the gates of Granada.* Several Christian cavaliers perished in this affray; the bishop himself escaped with difficulty, having slipped from his saddle in crossing the canal, but saving himself by holding on to the tail of his charger. This perilous achievement seems to have satisfied the good bishop's belligerent propensities. He retired on his laurels (says Agapida) to his city of Jaen; where, in the fruition of all good things, he gradually waxed too corpulent for his corselet, which was hung up in the hall of his episcopal palace; and we hear no more of his military deeds throughout the residue of the holy war of Granada.†

King Ferdinand, having completed his ravage of the vega, and kept El Zagal shut up in his capital, conducted his army back through the pass of Lope to rejoin Queen Isabella at Moclin. The fortresses lately taken being well garrisoned and supplied, he gave the command of the frontier to his cousin, Don Fadrique de Toledo, afterward so famous in the Netherlands as the Duke of Alva. The campaign being thus completely crowned with success, the sovereigns returned in triumph to the city of Cordova.

---

* Pulgar.

† "Don Luis Osorio fue obispo de Jaen desde el año de 1483, y presidio in esta Iglesia hasta el de 1496 in que murio en Flandes, a donde fue acompañando a la princesa Doña Juana, esposa del archiduque Don Felipe."—" Espana Sagrada," por Fr. M. Bisco, tom. 41, trat. 77, cap. 4.

CHAPTER FORTY-FIVE

ATTEMPT OF EL ZAGAL UPON THE LIFE OF BOABDIL, AND HOW THE LATTER WAS ROUSED TO ACTION

No sooner did the last squadron of Christian cavalry disappear behind the mountain of Elvira, and the note of its trumpets die away upon the ear, than the long-suppressed wrath of old Muley el Zagal burst forth. He determined no longer to be half a king, reigning over a divided kingdom, in a divided capital; but to exterminate, by any means, fair or foul, his nephew Boabdil and his faction. He turned furiously upon those whose factious conduct had deterred him from sallying upon the foe; some he punished by confiscations, others by banishment, others by death. Once undisputed monarch of the entire kingdom, he trusted to his military skill to retrieve his fortunes, and drive the Christians over the frontier.

Boabdil, however, had again retired to Velez el Blanco, on the confines of Murcia, where he could avail himself, in case of emergency, of any assistance or protection afforded him by the policy of Ferdinand. His defeat had blighted his reviving fortunes, for the people considered him as inevitably doomed to misfortune. Still, while he lived, El Zagal knew he would be a rallying point for faction, and liable at any moment to be elevated into power by the capricious multitude. He had recourse, therefore, to the most perfidious means to compass his destruction. He sent embassadors to him, representing the necessity of concord for the salvation of the kingdom, and even offering to resign the title of king, and to become subject to his sway, on receiving some estate on which he could live in tranquil retirement. But while the embassadors bore these words of peace, they were furnished with poisoned herbs, which they were to administer secretly to Boabdil; and if they failed in this attempt, they had pledged themselves to dispatch him openly, while engaged in conversation. They were instigated to this treason by promises of great reward, and by assurances from the alfaquis that Boabdil was an apostate, whose death would be acceptable to Heaven.

The young monarch was secretly apprised of the concerted treason, and refused an audience to the embassadors. He denounced his uncle as the murderer of his father and his kindred, and the usurper of his throne; and vowed never to relent in hostility to him until he should place his head on the walls of the Alhambra.

Open war again broke out between the two monarchs, though feebly carried on, in consequence of their mutual embarrassments. Ferdinand again extended his assistance to Boabdil, ordering the commanders of his fortresses to aid him in all enterprises against his uncle, and against such places as refused to acknowledge him as king; and Don Juan de Bonavides, who commanded in Lorca, even made inroads in his name, into the territories of Almeria, Baza, and Guadix, which owned allegiance to El Zagal.

The unfortunate Boabdil had three great evils to contend with—the inconstancy of his subjects, the hostility of his uncle, and the friendship of Ferdinand. The last was by far the most baneful: his fortunes withered under it. He was looked upon as the enemy of his faith and of his country. The cities shut their gates against him; the people cursed him; even the scanty band of cavaliers, who had hitherto followed his ill-starred banner, began to desert him; for he had not wherewithal to reward or even to support them. His spirits sunk with his fortune, and he feared that in a little time he should not have a spot on earth whereon to plant his standard, nor an adherent to rally under it.

In the midst of his despondency, he received a message from his lion-hearted mother, the Sultana Ayxa la Horra. "For shame," said she, "to linger timorously about the borders of your kingdom, when a usurper is seated in your capital. Why look abroad for perfidious aid, when you have loyal hearts beating true to you in Granada? The Albaycin is ready to throw open its gates to receive you. Strike home vigorously—a sudden blow may mend all, or make an end. A throne or a grave!—for a king, there is no honorable medium.''

Boabdil was of an undecided character, but there are circumstances which bring the most wavering to a decision, and when once resolved they are apt to act with a daring impulse unknown to steadier judgments. The message of the sultana roused him from a dream. Granada, beautiful Granada, with its stately Alhambra, its delicious gardens, its gushing and limpid fountains sparkling among groves of orange, citron, and myrtle, rose before him. ''What have I done,'' exclaimed he, ''that I should be an exile from this paradise of my forefathers—a wanderer and fugitive in my own kingdom, while a murderous usurper sits proudly upon my throne? Surely Allah will befriend the righteous cause; one blow, and all may be my own.''

He summoned his scanty band of cavaliers. ''Who is ready to follow his monarch unto the death?'' said he: and every one laid his hand upon his scimiter. ''Enough!'' said he; ''let each man arm himself and prepare his steed in secret, for an enterprise of toil and peril: if we succeed, our reward is empire.''

[END OF VOLUME ONE]

VOLUME TWO

CHAPTER ONE

HOW BOABDIL RETURNED SECRETLY TO GRANADA, AND HOW HE WAS RECEIVED.

"IN the hand of God," exclaims an old Arabian chronicler, "is the destiny of princes; He alone giveth empire. A single Moorish horseman, mounted on a fleet Arabian steed, was one day traversing the mountains which extend between Granada and the frontier of Murcia. He galloped swiftly through the valleys, but paused and looked out cautiously from the summit of every height. A squadron of cavaliers followed warily at a distance. There were fifty lances. The richness of their armor and attire showed them to be warriors of noble rank, and their leader had a lofty and prince-like demeanor." The squadron thus described by the Arabian chronicler was the Moorish king Boabdil and his devoted followers.

For two nights and a day they pursued their adventurous journey, avoiding all populous parts of the country, and choosing the most solitary passes of the mountains. They suffered severe hardships and fatigues, but they suffered without a murmur: they were accustomed to rugged campaigning, and their steeds were of generous and unyielding spirit. It was midnight, and all was dark and silent as they descended from the mountains and approached the city of Granada. They passed along quietly under the shadow of its walls, until they arrived near the gate of the Albaycin. Here Boabdil ordered his followers to halt and remain concealed. Taking but four or five with him, he advanced resolutely to the gate and knocked with the hilt of his scimiter. The guards demanded who sought to enter at that unseasonable hour. "Your king!" exclaimed Boabdil, "open the gate and admit him!"

The guards held forth a light, and recognized the person of the youthful monarch. They were struck with sudden awe, and threw open the gates; and Boabdil and his followers entered unmolested. They galloped to the dwellings of the principal inhabitants of the Albaycin, thundering at their portals and summoning them to rise and take arms for their rightful sovereign. The summons was instantly obeyed: trumpets resounded throughout the streets—the gleam of torches and the flash of arms showed the Moors hurrying to their gathering-places—and by daybreak the whole force of the Albaycin was rallied under the standard of Boabdil. Such was the success of this sudden and desperate act of the young monarch; for we are assured by contemporary historians that there had been no previous concert or arrangement. "As the guards opened the gates of the city to admit him," observes a pious chronicler, "so God opened the hearts of the Moors to receive him as their king." *

In the morning early, the tidings of this event roused El Zagal from his slumbers in the Alhambra. The fiery old warrior assembled his guard in haste, and made his way sword in hand to the Albaycin, hoping to come upon his nephew by surprise. He was vigorously met by Boabdil and his adherents, and driven back into the quarter of the Alhambra. An encounter took place between the two kings, in the square before the principal mosque; here they fought hand to hand with implacable fury, as though it had been agreed to decide their competition for the crown by single combat. In the tumult of this chance-medley affray, however, they were separated, and the party of El Zagal was ultimately driven from the square.

The battle raged for some time in the streets and places

---

* Pulgar.

of the city, but finding their powers of mischief cramped within such narrow limits, both parties sallied forth into the fields, and fought beneath the walls until evening. Many fell on both sides, and at night each party withdrew into its quarter, until the morning gave them light to renew the unnatural conflict. For several days, the two grand divisions of the city remained like hostile powers arrayed against each other. The party of the Alhambra was more numerous than that of the Albaycin, and contained most of the nobility and chivalry; but the adherents of Boabdil were men hardened and strengthened by labor and habitually skilled in the exercise of arms.

The Albaycin underwent a kind of siege by the forces of El Zagal; they effected breaches in the walls, and made repeated attempts to carry it sword in hand, but were as often repulsed. The troops of Boabdil, on the other hand, made frequent sallies; and in the conflicts which took place the hatred of the combatants arose to such a pitch of fury that no quarter was given on either side.

Boabdil perceived the inferiority of his force; he dreaded also that his adherents, being for the most part tradesmen and artisans, would become impatient of this interruption of their gainful occupations, and disheartened by these continual scenes of carnage. He sent missives, therefore, in all haste, to Don Fadrique de Toledo, who commanded the Christian forces on the frontier, entreating his assistance.

Don Fadrique had received instructions from the politic Ferdinand, to aid the youthful monarch in all his contests with his uncle. He advanced, therefore, with a body of troops near to Granada, but, wary lest some treachery might be intended, he stood for some time aloof, watching the movements of the parties. The furious and sanguinary nature of the conflicts which distracted unhappy Granada soon convinced him that there was no collusion between the monarchs. He sent Boabdil, therefore, a re-enforcement of Christian foot-soldiers and arquebusiers, under Fernan Alvarez de Sotomayer, alcayde of Colomera. This was as a firebrand thrown in to light up anew the flames of war in the city, which remained raging between the Moorish inhabitants for the space of fifty days.

CHAPTER TWO

HOW KING FERDINAND LAID SIEGE TO VELEZ MALAGA

HITHERTO the events of this renowned war have been little else than a succession of brilliant but brief exploits, such as sudden forays and wild skirmishes among the mountains, or the surprisals of castles, fortresses, and frontier towns. We approach now to more important and prolonged operations, in which ancient and mighty cities, the bulwarks of Granada, were invested by powerful armies, subdued by slow and regular sieges, and thus the capital left naked and alone.

The glorious triumphs of the Catholic sovereigns (says Fray Antonio Agapida) had resounded throughout the east, and filled all heathenesse with alarm. The Grand-Turk Bajazet II. and his deadly foe, the Grand Soldan of Egypt, suspending for a time their bloody feuds, entered into a league to protect the religion of Mahomet and the kingdom of Granada from the hostilities of the Christians. It was concerted between them that Bajazet should send a powerful armada against the island of Sicily, then appertaining to the Spanish crown, for the purpose of distracting the attention of the Castilian sovereigns; while, at the same time, great bodies of troops should be poured into Granada, from the opposite coast of Africa.

Ferdinand and Isabella received timely intelligence of these designs. They resolved at once to carry the war into the seaboard of Granada, to possess themselves of its ports, and thus, as it were, to bar the gates of the kingdom against all external aid. Malaga was to be the main object of attack: it was the principal seaport of the kingdom, and

almost necessary to its existence. It had long been the seat
of opulent commerce, sending many ships to the coasts of
Syria and Egypt. It was also the great channel of communication with Africa, through which were introduced
supplies of money, troops, arms, and steeds from Tunis,
Tripoli, Fez, Tremezan, and other Barbary powers. It was
emphatically called, therefore, "the hand and mouth of
Granada." Before laying siege to this redoubtable city,
however, it was deemed necessary to secure the neighboring
city of Velez Malaga and its dependent places, which might
otherwise harass the besieging army.

For this important campaign, the nobles of the kingdom
were again summoned to take the field with their forces in
the spring of 1487. The menaced invasion of the Infidel
powers of the east had awakened new ardor in the bosoms of
all true Christian knights; and so zealously did they respond
to the summons of the sovereigns, that an army of twenty
thousand cavalry and fifty thousand foot, the flower of
Spanish warriors, led by the bravest of Spanish cavaliers,
thronged the renowned city of Cordova, at the appointed
time.

On the night before this mighty host set forth upon its
march an earthquake shook the city. The inhabitants,
awakened by the shaking of the walls and rocking of the
towers, fled to the courts and squares, fearing to be overwhelmed by the ruins of their dwellings. The earthquake
was most violent in the quarter of the royal residence, the
site of the ancient palace of the Moorish kings. Many looked
upon this as an omen of some impending evil; but Fray
Antonio Agapida, in that infallible spirit of divination which
succeeds an event, plainly reads in it a presage that the empire of the Moors was about to be shaken to its center.

It was on Saturday, the eve of the Sunday of Palms (says
a worthy and loyal chronicler of the time), that the most
Catholic monarch departed with his army, to render service
to Heaven, and make war upon the Moors.* Heavy rains

* Pulgar. Cronica de los Reyes Catholicos.

had swelled all the streams and rendered the roads deep and difficult. The king, therefore, divided his host into two bodies. In one he put all the artillery, guarded by a strong body of horse, and commanded by the Master of Alcantara and Martin Alonzo, Senior of Montemayor. This division was to proceed by the road through the valleys, where pasturage abounded for the oxen which drew the ordnance.

The main body of the army was led by the king in person. It was divided into numerous battalions, each commanded by some distinguished cavalier. The king took the rough and perilous road of the mountains, and few mountains are more rugged and difficult than those of Andalusia. The roads are mere mule-paths, straggling amid rocks and along the verge of precipices, clambering vast craggy heights, or descending into frightful chasms and ravines, with scanty and uncertain foothold for either man or steed. Four thousand pioneers were sent in advance, under the alcayde de los Donzeles, to conquer, in some degree, the asperities of the road. Some had pickaxes and crowbars to break the rocks, others had implements to construct bridges over the mountain torrents, while it was the duty of others to lay stepping stones in the smaller streams. As the country was inhabited by fierce Moorish mountaineers, Don Diego de Castrillo was dispatched, with a body of horse and foot, to take possession of the heights and passes. Notwithstanding every precaution, the royal army suffered excessively on its march. At one time, there was no place to encamp, for five leagues of the most toilsome and mountainous country; and many of the beasts of burden sunk down and perished on the road.

It was with the greatest joy, therefore, that the royal army emerged from these stern and frightful defiles, and came to where they looked down upon the vega of Velez Malaga. The region before them was one of the most delectable to the eye that ever was ravaged by an army. Sheltered from every rude blast by a screen of mountains, and sloping and expanding to the south, this lovely valley was quickened by the most generous sunshine, watered by the silver meanderings of the Velez, and refreshed by cooling breezes from the Mediterranean. The sloping hills were covered with vineyards and olive-trees; the distant fields waved with grain, or were verdant with pasturage; while around the city were delightful gardens, the favorite retreats of the Moors, where their white pavilions gleamed among groves of oranges, citrons, and pomegranates, and were surmounted by stately palms—those plants of southern growth, bespeaking a generous climate and a cloudless sky.

In the upper part of this delightful valley the city of Velez Malaga reared its warrior battlements in stern contrast to the landscape. It was built on the declivity of a steep and isolated hill, and strongly fortified by walls and towers. The crest of the hill rose high above the town, into a mere crag, inaccessible on every other side, and crowned by a powerful castle, which domineered over the surrounding country. Two suburbs swept down into the valley, from the skirts of the town, and were defended by bulwarks and deep ditches. The vast ranges of gray mountains, often capped with clouds, which rose to the north, were inhabited by a hardy and warlike race, whose strong fortresses of Comares, Camillas, Competa, and Benemarhorga, frowned down from cragged heights.

At the time that the Christian host arrived in sight of this valley, a squadron was hovering on the smooth sea before it, displaying the banner of Castile. This was commanded by the Count of Trevento, and consisted of four armed galleys, conveying a number of caravels laden with supplies for the army.

After surveying the ground, King Ferdinand encamped on the side of a mountain which advanced close to the city, and which was the last of a rugged sierra, or chain of heights, that extended quite to Granada. On the summit of this mountain, and overlooking the camp, was a Moorish town, powerfully fortified, called Bentomiz, and which, from its vicinity, had been considered capable of yielding great assistance to Velez Malaga. Several of the generals remonstrated with the king for choosing a post so exposed to asaults from the mountaineers. Ferdinand replied that he should thus cut off all communication between the town and the city; and that as to the danger, his soldiers must keep the more vigilant guard against surprise.

King Ferdinand rode forth, attended by several cavaliers and a small number of cuirassiers, appointing the various stations of the camp. While a body of foot-soldiers were taking possession, as an advanced guard, of an important height which overlooked the city, the king retired to a tent to take refreshment. While at table, he was startled by a sudden uproar, and, looking forth, beheld his soldiers flying before a superior force of the enemy. The king had on no other armor but a cuirass; seizing a lance, however, he sprang upon his horse and galloped to protect the fugitives, followed by his handful of knights and cuirassiers. When the Spaniards saw the king hastening to their aid, they turned upon their pursuers. Ferdinand, in his eagerness, threw himself into the midst of the foe. One of his grooms was killed beside him; but, before the Moor who slew him could escape, the king transfixed him with his lance. He then sought to draw his sword, which hung at his saddle-bow—but in vain. Never had he been exposed to such peril—he was surrounded by the enemy, without a weapon wherewith to defend himself.

In this moment of awful jeopardy, the Marques of Cadiz, the Count de Cabra, the adelantado of Murcia, with two other cavaliers, named Garcilasso de la Vega and Diego de Atayde, came galloping to the scene of action, and, surrounding the king, made a loyal rampart of their bodies against the assaults of the Moors. The horse of the marques was pierced by an arrow, and that worthy cavalier exposed to imminent danger; but, with the aid of his valorous companions, he quickly put the enemy to flight, and pursued them, with slaughter, to the very gates of the city.

When those loyal warriors returned from the pursuit, they remonstrated with the king for exposing his life in personal conflict, seeing that he had so many valiant captains whose business it was to fight. They reminded him that the life of a prince was the life of his people, and that many a brave army was lost by the loss of its commander. They entreated him, therefore, in future, to protect them with the force of his mind in the cabinet, rather than of his arm in the field.

Ferdinand acknowledged the wisdom of their advice, but declared that he could not see his people in peril without venturing his person to assist them: a reply (says the old chroniclers) which delighted the whole army, inasmuch as they saw that he not only governed them as a good king, but protected them as a valiant captain. Ferdinand, however, was conscious of the extreme peril to which he had been exposed, and made a vow never again to venture into battle without having his sword girt to his side.*

When this achievement of the king was related to Isabella, she trembled amid her joy at his safety; and afterward, in memorial of the event, she granted to Velez Malaga, as the arms of the city, the figure of the king on horseback, with a groom lying dead at his feet and the Moors flying.†

The camp was formed, but the artillery was yet on the road, advancing with infinite labor, at the rate of merely a league a day; for heavy rains had converted the streams of the valleys into raging torrents, and completely broken up the roads. In the meantime, King Ferdinand ordered an assault on the suburbs of the city. They were carried, after a sanguinary conflict of six hours, in which many Christian cavaliers were killed and wounded, and, among the latter, Don Alvaro of Portugal, son of the Duke of Braganza. The suburbs were then fortified toward the city, with trenches and palisadoes, and garrisoned by a chosen force, under Don Fadrique de Toledo. Other trenches were dug round the city, and from the suburbs to the royal camp, so as to cut off all communication with the surrounding country.

---

* Illescas, Hist. Pontif., lib. 6, c. 20.   Wedmar, Hist. Velez Malaga.
† Idem.

Bodies of troops were also sent to take possession of the mountain passes, by which the supplies for the army had to be brought. The mountains, however, were so steep and rugged, and so full of defiles and lurking-places, that the Moors could sally forth and retreat in perfect security; frequently swooping down upon Christian convoys, and bearing off both booty and prisoners to their strongholds. Sometimes the Moors would light fires at night, on the sides of the mountains, which would be answered by fires from the watch-towers and fortresses. By these signals, they would concert assaults upon the Christian camp, which, in consequence, was obliged to be continually on the alert, and ready to fly to arms.

King Ferdinand flattered himself that the manifestation of his force had struck sufficient terror into the city, and that by offers of clemency it might be induced to capitulate. He wrote a letter, therefore, to the commanders, promising, in case of immediate surrender, that all the inhabitants should be permitted to depart with their effects; but threatening them with fire and sword if they persisted in defense. This letter was dispatched by a cavalier named Carvajal, who, putting it on the end of a lance, gave it to the Moors who were on the walls of the city. The commanders replied that the king was too noble and magnanimous to put such a threat in execution, and that they should not surrender, as they knew the artillery could not be brought to the camp, and they were promised succor by the King of Granada.

At the same time that he received this reply, the king learned that at the strong town of Comares, upon a height about two leagues distant from the camp, a large number of warriors had assembled from the Axarquia, the same mountains in which the Christian cavaliers had been massacred in the beginning of the war; others were daily expected, for this rugged sierra was capable of furnishing fifteen thousand fighting men.

King Ferdinand felt that his army, thus disjointed, and inclosed in an enemy's country, was in a perilous situation, and that the utmost discipline and vigilance were necessary. He put the camp under the strictest regulations, forbidding all gambling, blasphemy, or brawl, and expelling all loose women and their attendant bully ruffians, the usual fomenters of riot and contention among soldiery. He ordered that none should sally forth to skirmish, without permission from their commanders; that none should set fire to the woods on the neighboring mountains; and that all word of security given to Moorish places or individuals should be inviolably observed. These regulations were enforced by severe penalties, and had such salutary effect, that, though a vast host of various people was collected together, not an opprobrious epithet was heard, nor a weapon drawn in quarrel.

In the meantime, the cloud of war went on, gathering about the summits of the mountains; multitudes of the fierce warriors of the sierra descended to the lower heights of Bentomiz, which overhung the camp, intending to force their way to the city. A detachment was sent against them, which, after sharp fighting, drove them to the higher cliffs of the mountain, where it was impossible to pursue them.

Ten days had elapsed since the encampment of the army, yet still the artillery had not arrived. The lombards and other heavy ordnance were left in despair at Antiquera; the rest came groaning slowly through the narrow valleys, which were filled with long trains of artillery and cars laden with munitions. At length part of the smaller ordnance arrived within half a league of the camp, and the Christians were animated with the hopes of soon being able to make a regular attack upon the fortifications of the city.

CHAPTER THREE

HOW KING FERDINAND AND HIS ARMY WERE EXPOSED TO IMMINENT PERIL BEFORE VELEZ MALAGA

WHILE the standard of the cross waved on the hills before Velez Malaga, and every height and cliff bristled with hostile arms, the civil war between the factions of the Alhambra and the Albaycin, or rather between El Zagal and El Chico, continued to convulse the city of Granada. The tidings of the investment of Velez Malaga at length roused the attention of the old men and the alfaquis, whose heads were not heated by the daily broils. They spread themselves through the city, and endeavored to arouse the people to a sense of their common danger.

"Why," said they, "continue these brawls between brethren and kindred? what battles are these, where even triumph is ignominious and the victor blushes and conceals his scars? Behold the Christians ravaging the land won by the valor and blood of your forefathers; dwelling in the houses they have built, sitting under the trees they have planted, while your brethren wander about, houseless and desolate. Do you wish to seek your real foe?—he is encamped on the mountain of Bentomiz. Do you want a field for the display of your valor?—you will find it before the walls of Velez Malaga."

When they had roused the spirit of the people they made their way to the rival kings and addressed them with like remonstrances. Hamet Aben Zarrax, the inspired santon, reproached El Zagal with his blind and senseless ambition: "You are striving to be king," said he, bitterly, "yet suffer the kingdom to be lost!"

El Zagal found himself in a perplexing dilemma. He had a double war to wage—with the enemy without and the enemy within. Should the Christians gain possession of the seacoast, it would be ruinous to the kingdom; should he leave Granada to oppose them, his vacant throne might be seized on by his nephew. He made a merit of necessity, and, pretending to yield to the remonstrances of the alfaquis, endeavored to compromise with Boabdil. He expressed deep concern at the daily losses of the country, caused by the dissensions of the capital; an opportunity now presented to retrieve all by a blow. The Christians had in a manner put themselves in a tomb between the mountains—nothing remained but to throw the earth upon them. He offered to resign the title of king, to submit to the government of his nephew, and fight under his standard; all he desired was to hasten to the relief of Velez Malaga and to take full vengeance on the Christians.

Boabdil spurned his proposition as the artifice of a hypocrite and a traitor. "How shall I trust a man," said he, "who has murdered my father and my kindred by treachery, and has repeatedly sought my own life, both by violence and stratagem?"

El Zagal boiled with rage and vexation—but there was no time to be lost. He was beset by the alfaquis and the nobles of his court; the youthful cavaliers were hot for action, the common people loud in their complaints that the richest cities were abandoned to the mercy of the enemy. The old warrior was naturally fond of fighting; he saw also that to remain inactive would endanger both crown and kingdom, whereas a successful blow would secure his popularity in Granada. He had a much more powerful force than his nephew, having lately received re-enforcements from Baza, Guadix and Almeria; he could march with a large force, therefore, to the relief of Velez Malaga, and yet leave a strong garrison in the Alhambra. He took his measures accordingly, and departed suddenly in the night, at the head of one thousand horse and twenty thousand foot. He took the most unfrequented roads, along the chain of mountains extending from Granada to the height of Bentomiz, and proceeded with such rapidity as to arrive there before King Ferdinand had notice of his approach.

The Christians were alarmed one evening by the sudden blazing of great fires on the mountains about the fortress of Bentomiz. By the ruddy light, they beheld the flash of weapons and the array of troops, and they heard the distant sound of Moorish drums and trumpets. The fires of Bentomiz were answered by fires on the towers of Velez Malaga. The shouts of "El Zagal! El Zagal!" echoed along the cliffs and resounded from the city; and the Christians found that the old warrior king of Granada was on the mountain above their camp.

The spirits of the Moors were suddenly raised to a pitch of the greatest exultation, while the Christians were astonished to see this storm of war ready to burst upon their heads. The Count de Cabra, with his accustomed eagerness when there was a king in the field, would fain have scaled the heights, and attacked El Zagal before he had time to form his camp; but Ferdinand, who was more cool and wary, restrained him. To attack the height would be to abandon the siege. He ordered every one, therefore, to keep vigilant watch at his post, and to stand ready to defend it to the utmost, but on no account to sally forth and attack the enemy.

All night the signal-fires kept blazing along the mountains, rousing and animating the whole country. The morning sun rose over the lofty summit of Bentomiz on a scene of martial splendor. As its rays glanced down the mountain, they lighted up the white tents of the Christian cavaliers, cresting its lower prominences, their pennons and ensigns fluttering in the morning breeze. The sumptuous pavilions of the king, with the holy standard of the cross and the royal banners of Castile and Aragon, dominated the encampment. Beyond lay the city, its lofty castle and numerous towers glistening with arms; while above all, and just on the profile of the height, in the full blaze of the rising sun, were descried the tents of the Moor, his turbaned troops clustering about them, and his Infidel banners floating against the sky. Columns of smoke rose where the night-fires had blazed, and the clash of the Moorish cymbal, the bray of trumpet, and the neigh of steed, were faintly heard from the airy heights. So pure and transparent is the atmosphere in this region that every object can be distinctly seen at a great distance; and the Christians were able to behold the formidable hosts of foes that were gathering on the summits of the surrounding mountains.

One of the first measures of the Moorish king was to detach a large force, under Rodovan de Vanegas, alcayde of

Granada, to fall upon the convoy of ordnance, which stretched, for a great distance, through the mountain defiles. Ferdinand had anticipated this attempt, and sent the commander of Leon, with a body of horse and foot, to re-enforce the Master of Alcantara. El Zagal, from his mountain height, beheld the detachment issue from the camp, and immediately recalled Rodovan de Vanegas. The armies now remained quiet for a time, the Moor looking grimly down upon the Christian camp, like a tiger meditating a bound upon his prey. The Christians were in fearful jeopardy—a hostile city below them, a powerful army above them, and on every side mountains filled with implacable foes.

After El Zagal had maturely considered the situation of the Christian camp, and informed himself of all the passes of the mountain, he conceived a plan to surprise the enemy, which he flattered himself would insure their ruin, and perhaps the capture of King Ferdinand. He wrote a letter to the alcayde of the city, commanding him, in the dead of the night, on a signal-fire being made from the mountain, to sally forth with all his troops and fall furiously upon the Christian camp. The king would, at the same time, rush down with his army from the mountain and assail it on the opposite side; thus overwhelming it, at the hour of deep repose. This letter he dispatched by a renegado Christian, who knew all the secret roads of the country, and, if taken, could pass himself for a Christian who had escaped from captivity.

The fierce El Zagal, confident in his stratagem, looked down upon the Christians as his devoted victims. As the sun went down, and the long shadows of the mountain stretched across the vega, he pointed with exultation to the camp below, apparently unconscious of the impending danger. "Allah Achbar!" exclaimed he, "God is great! Behold the unbelievers are delivered into our hands; their king and choicest chivalry will soon be at our mercy. Now is the time to show the courage of men, and, by one glorious victory, retrieve all that we have lost. Happy he who falls

fighting in the cause of the Prophet! he will at once be transported to the paradise of the faithful, and surrounded by
immortal houris. Happy he who shall survive victorious!
he will behold Granada—an earthly paradise!—once more
delivered from its foes, and restored to all its glory." The
words of El Zagal were received with acclamations by his
troops, who waited impatiently for the appointed hour, to
pour down from their mountain-hold upon the Christians.

CHAPTER FOUR

RESULT OF THE STRATAGEM OF EL ZAGAL TO SURPRISE KING FERDINAND

QUEEN ISABELLA and her court had remained at Cordova, in great anxiety for the result of the royal expedition.
Every day brought tidings of the difficulties which attended
the transportation of the ordnance and munitions, and of the
critical state of the army.

While in this state of anxious suspense, couriers arrived
with all speed from the frontiers, bringing tidings of the sudden sally of El Zagal from Granada, to surprise the camp.
All Cordova was in consternation. The destruction of the
Andalusian chivalry, among the mountains of this very
neighborhood, was called to mind; it was feared that similar
ruin was about to burst forth, from rocks and precipices,
upon Ferdinand and his army.

Queen Isabella shared in the public alarm, but it served
to rouse all the energies of her heroic mind. Instead of
uttering idle apprehensions, she sought only how to avert
the danger. She called upon all the men of Andalusia, under
the age of seventy, to arm and hasten to the relief of their
sovereign; and she prepared to set out with the first levies.
The grand cardinal of Spain, old Pedro Gonzalez de Mendoza, in whom the piety of the saint and the wisdom of the
counselor were mingled with the fire of the cavalier, offered

high pay to all horsemen who would follow him to aid their king and the Christian cause; and, buckling on armor, prepared to lead them to the scene of danger.

The summons of the queen roused the quick Andalusian spirit. Warriors who had long since given up fighting, and had sent their sons to battle, now seized the sword and lance that were rusting on the wall, and marshaled forth their gray-headed domestics and their grandchildren for the field. The great dread was, that all aid would arrive too late; El Zagal and his host had passed like a storm through the mountains, and it was feared the tempest had already burst upon the Christian camp.

In the meantime, the night had closed which had been appointed by El Zagal for the execution of his plan. He had watched the last light of day expire, and all the Spanish camp remained tranquil. As the hours wore away, the camp-fires were gradually extinguished. No drum or trumpet sounded from below. Nothing was heard, but now and then the dull heavy tread of troops, or the echoing tramp of horses—the usual patrols of the camp and the changes of the guards. El Zagal restrained his own impatience, and that of his troops, until the night should be advanced, and the camp sunk in that heavy sleep from which men are with difficulty awakened; and, when awakened, so prone to be bewildered and dismayed.

At length the appointed hour arrived. By order of the Moorish king, a bright flame sprung up from the height of Bentomiz; but El Zagal looked in vain for the responding light from the city. His impatience would brook no longer delay; he ordered the advance of the army, to descend the mountain defile and attack the camp. The defile was narrow and overhung by rocks: as the troops proceeded, they came suddenly, in a shadowy hollow, upon a dark mass of Christian warriors. A loud shout burst forth, and the Christians rushed to assail them; the Moors, surprised and disconcerted, retreated in confusion to the height. When El Zagal heard there was a Christian force posted in the defile, he doubted some counter-plan of the enemy. He gave orders to light the mountain fires. On a signal given, bright flames sprung out on every height, from great pyres of wood, prepared for the purpose: cliff blazed out after cliff, until the whole atmosphere was in a glow of furnace light. The ruddy glare lighted up the glens and passes of the mountain, and fell strongly upon the Christian camp, revealing all its tents and every post and bulwark. Wherever El Zagal turned his eyes, he beheld the light of his fires flashed back from cuirass, and helm, and sparkling lance; he beheld a grove of spears planted in every pass, every assailable point bristling with arms, and squadrons of horse and foot in battle array, awaiting his attack.

In fact, the letter of El Zagal to the alcayde of Velez Malaga had been intercepted by the vigilant Ferdinand; the renegado messenger hanged; and secret measures taken, after the night had closed in, to give the enemy a warm reception. El Zagal saw that his plan of surprise was discovered and foiled; furious with disappointment, he ordered his troops forward to the attack. They rushed down the defile, but were again encountered by the mass of Christian warriors, being the advance guard of the army, commanded by Don Hurtado de Mendoza, brother of the grand cardinal. The Moors were again repulsed and retreated up the height. Don Hurtado would have followed them, but the ascent was steep and rugged, and easily defended by the Moors. A sharp action was kept up through the night with crossbows, darts, and arquebuses. The cliffs echoed with deafening uproar, while the fires blazing upon the mountains threw a lurid and uncertain light upon the scene.

When the day dawned, and the Moors saw that there was no co-operation from the city, they began to slacken in their ardor: they beheld also every pass of the mountain filled with Christian troops, and began to apprehend an assault in return. Just then King Ferdinand sent the Marques of Cadiz, with horse and foot, to seize upon a height occupied by a battalion of the enemy. The marques assailed the

Moors with his usual intrepidity and soon put them to flight. The others, who were above, seeing their comrades flying, were seized with a sudden alarm: they threw down their arms and retreated. One of those unaccountable panics, which now and then seize upon great bodies of people, and to which the light-spirited Moors were very prone, now spread throughout the camp. They were terrified, they knew not why, or at what. They threw away swords, lances, breast-plates, crossbows, everything that could burden or impede their flight; and, spreading themselves wildly over the moun-tains, fled headlong down the defiles. They fled without pur-suers—from the glimpse of each other's arms, from the sound of each other's footsteps. Rodovan de Vanegas, the brave alcayde of Granada, alone succeeded in collecting a body of the fugitives; he made a circuit with them through the passes of the mountain, and forcing his way across a weak part of the Christian lines, galloped toward Velez Malaga. The rest of the Moorish host was completely scattered. In vain did El Zagal and his knights attempt to rally them; they were left almost alone, and had to consult their own security by flight.

The Marques of Cadiz, finding no opposition, ascended from height to height, cautiously reconnoitering, and fearful of some stratagem or ambush. All, however, was quiet. He reached with his men the place which the Moorish army had occupied: the heights were abandoned, and strewed with cuirasses, scimiters, crossbows, and other weapons. His force was too small to pursue the enemy, but returned to the royal camp laden with the spoils.

King Ferdinand, at first, could not credit so signal and miraculous· a defeat; he suspected some lurking stratagem. He ordered, therefore, that a strict watch should be main-tained throughout the camp, and every one be ready for in-stant action. The following night, a thousand cavaliers and hidalgos kept guard about the royal tent, as they had done for several preceding nights; nor did the king relax this vigilance, until he received certain intelligence that the enemy was completely scattered and El Zagal flying in confusion.

The tidings of this rout, and of the safety of the Christian army, arrived at Cordova just as re-enforcements were on the point of setting out. The anxiety and alarm of the queen and the public were turned to transports of joy and gratitude. The forces were disbanded, solemn processions were made, and *Te Deums* chanted in the churches, for so signal a victory.

CHAPTER FIVE

HOW THE PEOPLE OF GRANADA REWARDED THE VALOR OF EL ZAGAL

THE daring spirit of the old warrior, Muley Abdalla el Zagal, in sallying forth to defend his territories, while he left an armed rival in his capital, had struck the people of Granada with admiration. They recalled his former exploits, and again anticipated some hardy achievement from his furious valor. Couriers from the army reported its formidable position on the height of Bentomiz. For a time, there was a pause in the bloody commotions of the city; all attention was turned to the blow about to be struck at the Christian camp. The same considerations which diffused anxiety and terror through Cordova, swelled every bosom with exulting confidence in Granada. The Moors expected to hear of another massacre like that in the mountains of Malaga. "El Zagal has again entrapped the enemy!" was the cry. "The power of the unbelievers is about to be struck to the heart. We shall soon see the Christian king led captive to the capital." Thus the name of El Zagal was on every tongue. He was extolled as the savior of the country; the only one worthy of wearing the Moorish crown. Boabdil was reviled as basely remaining passive while his country was invaded; and so violent became the clamor of the populace that his adherents trembled for his safety.

While the people of Granada were impatiently looking out
for tidings of the anticipated victory, scattered horsemen
came spurring across the vega. They were fugitives from
the Moorish army, and brought the first incoherent account
of its defeat. Every one who attempted to tell the tale of
this unaccountable panic and dispersion was as if bewildered
by the broken recollection of some frightful dream. He knew
not how or why it came to pass. He talked of a battle in the
night, among rocks and precipices, by the glare of bale-fires;
of multitudes of armed foes in every pass, seen by gleams
and flashes; of the sudden horror that seized upon the army
at daybreak; its headlong flight, and total dispersion. Hour
after hour, the arrival of other fugitives confirmed the story
of ruin and disgrace.

In proportion to their recent vaunting was the humiliation that now fell upon the people of Granada. There was
a universal burst, not of grief, but indignation. They confounded the leader with the army—the deserted, with those
who had abandoned him; and El Zagal, from being their
idol, became suddenly the object of their execration. He
had sacrificed the army; he had disgraced the nation; he
had betrayed the country. He was a dastard, a traitor;
he was unworthy to reign!

On a sudden, one among the multitude shouted, "Long
live Boabdil el Chico!" the cry was echoed on all sides, and
every one shouted, "Long live Boabdil el Chico! long live
the legitimate king of Granada: and death to all usurpers!"
In the excitement of the moment they thronged to the Albaycin; and those who had lately besieged Boabdil with
arms now surrounded his palace with acclamations. The
keys of the city, and of all the fortresses, were laid at
his feet; he was borne in state to the Alhambra, and once
more seated, with all due ceremony, on the throne of his
ancestors.

Boabdil had by this time become so accustomed to be
crowned and uncrowned by the multitude that he put no
great faith in the duration of their loyalty. He knew that

he was surrounded by hollow hearts, and that most of the courtiers of the Alhambra were secretly devoted to his uncle. He ascended the throne as the rightful sovereign, who had been dispossessed of it by usurpation; and he ordered the heads of four of the principal nobles to be struck off, who had been most zealous in support of the usurper. Executions of the kind were matters of course, on any change in Moorish government; and Boabdil was lauded for his moderation and humanity, in being content with so small a sacrifice. The factions were awed into obedience; the populace, delighted with any change, extolled Boabdil to the skies; and the name of Muley Abdalla el Zagal was for a time a byword of scorn and opprobrium throughout the city.

Never was any commander more astonished and confounded by a sudden reverse of fortune than El Zagal. The evening had seen him with a powerful army at his command, his enemy within his grasp, and victory about to cover him with glory, and to consolidate his power—the morning beheld him a fugitive among the mountains, his army, his prosperity, his power, all dispelled, he knew not how—gone like a dream of the night. In vain had he tried to stem the headlong flight of the army. He saw his squadrons breaking and dispersing among the cliffs of the mountains, until, of all his host, only a handful of cavaliers remained faithful to him. With these he made a gloomy retreat toward Granada, but with a heart full of foreboding. When he drew near to the city, he paused on the banks of the Xenil, and sent forth scouts to collect intelligence. They returned with dejected countenances: "The gates of Granada," said they, "are closed against you. The banner of Boabdil floats on the tower of the Alhambra."

El Zagal turned his steed and departed in silence. He retreated to the town of Almunecar, and from thence to Almeria, which places still remained faithful to him. Restless and uneasy at being so distant from the capital, he again changed his abode, and repaired to the city of Guadix, within a few leagues of Granada. Here he remained, endeavoring to rally his forces, and preparing to avail himself of any sudden change in the fluctuating politics of the metropolis.

CHAPTER SIX

SURRENDER OF VELEZ MALAGA AND OTHER PLACES

THE people of Velez Malaga had beheld the camp of Muley Abdalla el Zagal, covering the summit of Bentomiz, and glittering in the last rays of the setting sun. During the night, they had been alarmed and perplexed by signal-fires on the mountain, and by the sound of distant battle. When the morning broke, the Moorish army had vanished as if by enchantment. While the inhabitants were lost in wonder and conjecture, a body of cavalry, the fragment of the army saved by Rodovan de Vanegas, the brave alcayde of Granada, came galloping to the gates. The tidings of the strange discomfiture of the host filled the city with con-sternation; but Rodovan exhorted the people to continue their resistance. He was devoted to El Zagal, and confi-dent in his skill and prowess; and felt assured that he would soon collect his scattered forces and return with fresh troops from Granada. The people were comforted by the words, and encouraged by the presence of Rodovan; and they had still a lingering hope that the heavy artillery of the Chris-tians might be locked up in the impassable defiles of the mountains. This hope was soon at an end. The very next day they beheld long laborious lines of ordnance slowly mov-ing into the Spanish camp, lombards, ribadoquines, cata-pultas, and cars laden with munitions—while the escort, under the brave Master of Alcantara, wheeled in great bat-talions into the camp, to augment the force of the besiegers.

The intelligence that Granada had shut its gates against El Zagal, and that no re-enforcements were to be expected, completed the despair of the inhabitants; even Rodovan him-self lost confidence, and advised capitulation.

The terms were arranged between the alcayde and the noble Count de Cifuentes; the latter had been prisoner of Rodovan at Granada, who had treated him with chivalrous courtesy. They had conceived a mutual esteem for each other, and met as ancient friends.

Ferdinand granted favorable conditions, for he was eager to proceed against Malaga. The inhabitants were permitted to depart with their effects, except their arms, and to reside, if they chose it, in Spain, in any place distant from the sea. One hundred and twenty Christians, of both sexes, were rescued from captivity by the surrender of Velez Malaga, and were sent to Cordova, where they were received with great tenderness by the queen and her daughter the Infanta Isabella, in the famous cathedral, in the midst of public rejoicings for the victory.

The capture of Velez Malaga was followed by the surrender of Bentomiz, Comares, and all the towns and fortresses of the Axarquia, which were strongly garrisoned, and discreet and valiant cavaliers appointed as their alcaydes. The inhabitants of nearly forty towns of the Alpuxarra mountains, also, sent deputations to the Castilian sovereigns, taking the oath of allegiance as Mudehares or Moslem vassals.

About the same time came letters from Boabdil el Chico, announcing to the sovereigns the revolution of Granada in his favor. He solicited kindness and protection for the inhabitants who had returned to their allegiance, and for those of all other places which should renounce adherence to his uncle. By this means (he observed) the whole kingdom of Granada would soon be induced to acknowledge his sway, and would be held by him in faithful vassalage to the Castilian crown.

The Catholic sovereigns complied with his request. Protection was immediately extended to the inhabitants of Granada, permitting them to cultivate their fields in peace, and to trade with the Christian territories in all articles excepting arms; being provided with letters of surety from some Christian captain or alcayde. The same favor was promised to all other places, which, within six months, should renounce El Zagal and come under 'allegiance to the younger king. Should they not do so within that time, the sovereigns threatened to make war upon them, and conquer them for themselves. This measure had a great effect in inducing many to return to the standard of Boabdil.

Having made every necessary arrangement for the government and security of the newly conquered territory, Ferdinand turned his attention to the great object of his campaign, the reduction of Malaga.

CHAPTER SEVEN

OF THE CITY OF MALAGA AND ITS INHABITANTS

THE city of Malaga lies in the lap of a fertile valley, surrounded by mountains, excepting on the part which lies open to the sea. As it was one of the most important, so it was one of the strongest, cities of the Moorish kingdom. It was fortified by walls of prodigious strength, studded with a great number of huge towers. On the land side, it was protected by a natural barrier of mountains; and on the other, the waves of the Mediterranean beat against the foundations of its massive bulwarks.

At one end of the city, near the sea, on a high mound, stood the Alcazaba or citadel—a fortress of great strength. Immediately above this rose a steep and rocky mount, on the top of which, in old times, had been a Pharo or lighthouse, from which the height derived its name of Gibralfaro.* It was at present crowned by an immense castle, which, from its lofty and cragged situation, its vast walls and mighty towers, was deemed impregnable. It communicated with the Alcazaba by a covered way, six paces broad, leading down between two walls, along the profile or ridge of the

---

* A corruption of *Gibel-faro;* the hill of the lighthouse.

rock. The castle of Gibralfaro commanded both citadel and city, and was capable, if both were taken, of maintaining a siege. Two large suburbs adjoined the city: in the one toward the sea were the dwelling-houses of the most opulent inhabitants, adorned with hanging gardens; the other, on the land side, was thickly peopled, and surrounded by strong walls and towers.

Malaga possessed a brave and numerous garrison, and the common people were active, hardy, and resolute; but the city was rich and commercial, and under the habitual control of numerous opulent merchants, who dreaded the ruinous consequences of a siege. They were little zealous for the warlike renown of their city, and longed rather to participate in the enviable security of property, and the lucrative privileges of safe traffic with the Christian territories, granted to all places which declared for Boabdil. At the head of these gainful citizens was Ali Dordux, a mighty merchant of uncounted wealth, whose ships traded to every part of the Levant, and whose word was as a law in Malaga. Ali Dordux assembled the most opulent and important of his commercial brethren, and they repaired in a body to the Alcazaba, where they were received by the alcayde, Albozen Connixa, with that deference generally shown to men of their great local dignity and power of purse. Ali Dordux was ample and stately in his form, and fluent and emphatic in his discourse; his eloquence had an effect therefore upon the alcayde, as he represented the hopelessness of a defense of Malaga, the misery that must attend a siege, and the ruin that must follow a capture by force of arms. On the other hand, he set forth the grace that might be obtained from the Castilian sovereigns, by an early and voluntary acknowledgment of Boabdil as king; the peaceful possession of their property, and the profitable commerce with the Christian ports that would be allowed them. He was seconded by his weighty and important coadjutors; and the alcayde, accustomed to regard them as the arbiters of the affairs of the place, yielded to their united counsels. He departed, therefore, with all speed to the Christian camp, empowered to arrange a capitulation with the Castilian monarch; and in the meantime, his brother remained in command of the Alcazaba.

There was at this time, as alcayde, in the old crag-built castle of Gibralfaro, a warlike and fiery Moor, an implacable enemy of the Christians. This was no other than Hamet Zeli, surnamed El Zegri, the once formidable alcayde of Ronda, and the terror of its mountains. He had never for-given the capture of his favorite fortress, and panted for ven-geance on the Christians. Notwithstanding his reverses, he had retained the favor of El Zagal, who knew how to ap-preciate a bold warrior of the kind, and had placed him in command of this important fortress of Gibralfaro.

Hamet el Zegri had gathered round him the remnant of his band of Comares, with others of the same tribe. These fierce warriors were nestled, like so many war-hawks, about their lofty cliff. They looked down with martial contempt upon the commercial city of Malaga, which they were placed to protect; or, rather, they esteemed it only for its military importance, and its capability of defense. They held no communion with its trading, gainful inhabitants, and even considered the garrison of the Alcazaba as their inferiors. War was their pursuit and passion; they rejoiced in its tur-bulent and perilous scenes; and, confident in the strength of the city, and, above all, of their castle, they set at defiance the menace of Christian invasion. There were among them, also, many apostate Moors, who had once embraced Christian-ity, but had since recanted, and had fled from the vengeance of the Inquisition. These were desperadoes, who had no mercy to expect, should they again fall into the hands of the enemy.

Such were the fierce elements of the garrison of Gibral-faro; and its rage may easily be conceived at hearing that Malaga was to be given up without a blow; that they were to sink into Christian vassals, under the intermediate sway of Boabdil el Chico; and that the alcayde of the Alcazaba had departed to arrange the terms of capitulation.

Hamet el Zegri determined to avert, by desperate means, the threatened degradation. He knew that there was a large party in the city faithful to El Zagal, being composed of warlike men, who had taken refuge from the various mountain towns which had been captured: their feelings were desperate as their fortunes, and, like Hamet, they panted for revenge upon the Christians. With these he had a secret conference, and received assurances of their adherence to him in any measures of defense. As to the counsel of the peaceful inhabitants, he considered it unworthy the consideration of a soldier; and he spurned at the interference of the wealthy merchant Ali Dordux, in matters of warfare.

"Still," said Hamet el Zegri, "let us proceed regularly." So he descended with his Comares to the citadel, entered it suddenly, put to death the brother of the alcayde, and such of the garrison as made any demur, and then summoned the principal inhabitants of Malaga, to deliberate on measures for the welfare of the city.* The wealthy merchants again mounted to the citadel, excepting Ali Dordux, who refused to obey the summons. They entered with hearts filled with awe, for they found Hamet surrounded by his grim African guard, and all the stern array of military power, and they beheld the bloody traces of the recent massacre.

Hamet el Zegri rolled a dark and searching eye upon the assembly. "Who," said he, "is loyal and devoted to Muley Abdalla el Zagal?" Every one present asserted his loyalty. "Good!" said Hamet; "and who is ready to prove his devotion to his sovereign, by defending this his important city to the last extremity?" Every one present declared his readiness. "Enough!" observed Hamet; "the alcayde Albozen Connixa has proved himself a traitor to his sovereign, and to you all; for he has conspired to deliver the place to the Christians. It behooves you to choose some other commander capable of defending your city against the approaching enemy." The assembly declared unanimously that there

---

* Cura de los Palacios. c. 82.

was no one so worthy of the command as himself. So Hamet el Zegri was appointed alcayde of Malaga, and immediately proceeded to man the forts and towers with his partisans, and to make every preparation for a desperate resistance.

Intelligence of these occurrences put an end to the negotiations between King Ferdinand and the superseded alcayde Albozen Connixa, and it was supposed there was no alternative but to lay siege to the place. The Marques of Cadiz, however, found at Velez a Moorish cavalier of some note, a native of Malaga, who offered to tamper with Hamet el Zegri for the surrender of the city, or at least of the castle of Gibralfaro. The marques communicated this to the king: "I put this business, and the key of my treasury, into your hands," said Ferdinand; "act, stipulate, and disburse, in my name, as you think proper."

The marques armed the Moor with his own lance, cuirass, and target, and mounted him on one of his own horses. He equipped in similar style, also, another Moor, his companion and relation. They bore secret letters to Hamet from the marques, offering him the town of Coin in perpetual inheritance, and four thousand doblas in gold, if he would deliver up Gibralfaro; together with large sums to be distributed among his officers and soldiers: and he offered unlimited rewards for the surrender of the city.*

Hamet had a warrior's admiration of the Marques of Cadiz, and received his messengers with courtesy in his fortress of Gibralfaro. He even listened to their propositions with patience, and dismissed them in safety, though with an absolute refusal. The marques thought his reply was not so peremptory as to discourage another effort. The emissaries were dispatched, therefore, a second time, with further propositions. They approached Malaga in the night, but found the guards doubled, patrols abroad, and the whole place on the alert. They were discovered, pursued, and only saved

* Cura de los Palacios. c. 82.

themselves by the fleetness of their steeds, and their knowledge of the passes of the mountains.

Finding all attempts to tamper with the faith of Hamet el Zegri utterly futile, King Ferdinand publicly summoned the city to surrender, offering the most favorable terms in case of immediate compliance; but threatening captivity to all the inhabitants in case of resistance.

The message was delivered in presence of the principal inhabitants, who, however, were too much in awe of the stern alcayde to utter a word. Hamet el Zegri then rose haughtily, and replied that the city of Malaga had not been confided to him to be surrendered, but defended; and the king should witness how he acquitted himself of his charge.*

The messengers returned with formidable accounts of the force of the garrison, the strength of the fortifications, and the determined spirit of the commander and his men. The king immediately sent orders to have the heavy artillery forwarded from Antiquera; and, on the 7th of May, marched with his army toward Malaga.

CHAPTER EIGHT

ADVANCE OF KING FERDINAND AGAINST MALAGA

The army of Ferdinand advanced in lengthened line, glittering along the foot of the mountains which border the Mediterranean; while a fleet of vessels, freighted with heavy artillery and warlike munitions, kept pace with it at a short distance from the land, covering the sea with a thousand gleaming sails. When Hamet el Zegri saw this force approaching, he set fire to the houses of the suburbs which adjoined the walls, and sent forth three battalions to encounter the advance guard of the enemy.

The Christian army drew near to the city, at that end

* Pulgar, part 3, cap. 74.

where the castle and rocky height of Gibralfaro defend the seaboard. Immediately opposite, at about two bow-shots' distance, stood the castle; and between it and the high chain of mountains was a steep and rocky hill, commanding a pass through which the Christians must march to penetrate to the vega and surround the city. Hamet el Zegri ordered the three battalions to take their stations, one on this hill, another in the pass near the castle, and a third on the side of the mountain near the sea.

A body of Spanish foot-soldiers of the advance guard, sturdy mountaineers of Gallicia, sprang forward to climb the side of the height next the sea; at the same time a number of cavaliers and hidalgos of the royal household attacked the Moors who guarded the pass below. The Moors defended their posts with obstinate valor. The Gallicians were repeatedly overpowered and driven down the hill, but as often rallied, and being re-enforced by the hidalgos and cavaliers, returned to the assault. This obstinate struggle lasted for six hours: the strife was of a deadly kind, not merely with crossbows and arquebuses, but hand to hand, with swords and daggers; no quarter was claimed or given on either side —they fought not to make captives, but to slay. It was but the advance of the Christian army that was engaged; so narrow was the pass along the coast that the army could proceed only in file: horse and foot, and beasts of burden, were crowded one upon another, impeding each other, and blocking up the narrow and rugged defile. The soldiers heard the uproar of the battle, the sound of trumpets, and the war-cries of the Moors—but tried in vain to press forward to the assistance of their companions.

At length a body of foot-soldiers of the Holy Brotherhood climbed, with great difficulty, the steep side of the mountain which overhung the pass, and advanced with seven banners displayed. The Moors, seeing this force above them, abandoned the pass in despair. The battle was still raging on the height; the Gallicians, though supported by Castilian troops under Don Hurtado de Mendoza and Garcilasso de la

Vega, were severely pressed and roughly handled by the
Moors; at length a brave standard-bearer, Luys Mazedo by
name, threw himself into the midst of the enemy, and planted
his banner on the summit. The Gallicians and Castilians,
stimulated by this noble self-devotion, followed him fighting
desperately, and the Moors were at length driven to their
castle of Gibralfaro.*

This important height being taken, the pass lay open to
the army; but by this time evening was advancing, and the
host was too weary and exhausted to seek proper situations
for the encampment. The king, attended by several grandees and cavaliers, went the rounds at night, stationing outposts toward the city, and guards and patrols to give the
alarm on the least movement of the enemy. All night the
Christians lay upon their arms, lest there should be some
attempt to sally forth and attack them.

When the morning dawned, the king gazed with admiration at this city, which he hoped soon to add to his dominions. It was surrounded on one side by vineyards, gardens,
and orchards, which covered the hills with verdure; on the
other side, its walls were bathed by the smooth and tranquil
sea. Its vast and lofty towers and prodigious castles, hoary
with age, yet unimpaired in strength, showed the labors of
magnanimous men in former times to protect their favorite
abode. Hanging gardens, groves of oranges, citrons, and
pomegranates, with tall cedars and stately palms, were mingled with the stern battlements and towers—bespeaking the
opulence and luxury that reigned within.

In the meantime, the Christian army poured through the
pass, and, throwing out its columns and extending its lines,
took possession of every vantage-ground around the city.
King Ferdinand surveyed the ground, and appointed the
stations of the different commanders.

The important mount which had cost so violent a struggle, and faced the powerful fortress of Gibralfaro, was given

* Pulgar. Cronica.

in charge to Roderigo Ponce de Leon, Marques of Cadiz, who, in all sieges, claimed the post of danger. He had several noble cavaliers with their retainers in his encampment, which consisted of fifteen hundred horse and fourteen thousand foot; and extended from the summit of the mount to the margin of the sea, completely blocking up the approach to the city on that side. From this post, a line of encampments extended quite round the city to the seaboard, fortified by bulwarks and deep ditches; while a fleet of armed ships and galleys stretched before the harbor; so that the place was completely invested by sea and land. The various parts of the valley now resounded with the din of preparation, and were filled with artificers preparing warlike engines and munitions: armorers and smiths, with glowing forges and deafening hammers; carpenters and engineers, constructing machines wherewith to assail the walls; stone-cutters, shaping stone balls for the ordnance; and burners of charcoal, preparing fuel for the furnaces and forges.

When the encampment was formed, the heavy ordnance was landed from the ships and mounted in various parts of the camp. Five huge lombards were placed on the mount commanded by the Marques of Cadiz, so as to bear upon the castle of Gibralfaro.

The Moors made strenuous efforts to impede these preparations. They kept up a heavy fire from their ordnance upon the men employed in digging trenches or constructing batteries, so that the latter had to work principally in the night. The royal tents had been stationed conspicuously, and within reach of the Moorish batteries; but were so warmly assailed that they had to be removed behind a hill.

When the works were completed, the Christian batteries opened in return, and kept up a tremendous cannonade; while the fleet, approaching the land, assailed the city vigorously on the opposite side.

"It was a glorious and delectable sight," observes Fray Antonio Agapida, "to behold this Infidel city thus surrounded, by sea and land, by a mighty Christian force.

Every mound in its circuit was, as it were, a little city of tents, bearing the standard of some renowned Catholic warrior. Beside the warlike ships and galleys which lay before the place, the sea was covered with innumerable sails, passing and repassing, appearing and disappearing, being engaged in bringing supplies for the subsistence of the army. It seemed a vast spectacle contrived to recreate the eye, did not the volleying bursts of flame and smoke from the ships, which seemed to lie asleep on the quiet sea, and the thunder of ordnance from camp and city, from tower and battlement, tell the deadly warfare that was raging.

"At night, the scene was far more direful than in the day. The cheerful light of the sun was gone; there was nothing but the flashes of artillery, or the baleful gleams of combustibles thrown into the city and the conflagration of the houses. The fire kept up from the Christian batteries was incessant; there were seven great lombards in particular, called The Seven Sisters of Ximenes, which did tremendous execution. The Moorish ordnance replied in thunder from the walls; Gibralfaro was wrapped in volumes of smoke, rolling about its base; and Hamet el Zegri and his Comares looked out with triumph upon the tempest of war they had awakened. Truly they were so many demons incarnate," concludes the pious Fray Antonio Agapida, "who were permitted by Heaven to enter into and possess this Infidel city, for its perdition."

CHAPTER NINE

SIEGE OF MALAGA

THE attack on Malaga, by sea and land, was kept up for several days with tremendous violence, but without producing any great impression, so strong were the ancient bulwarks of the city. The Count de Cifuentes was the first to signalize himself by any noted achievement. A main tower of the suburb had been shattered by the ordnance, and the

battlements demolished, so as to yield no shelter to its defenders. Seeing this, the count assembled a gallant band of
cavaliers of the royal household, and advanced to take it by
storm. They applied scaling-ladders, and mounted, sword
in hand. The Moors, having no longer battlements to protect them, descended to a lower floor, and made furious resistance from the windows and loopholes. They poured
down boiling pitch and resin, and hurled stones and darts
and arrows on the assailants. Many of the Christians were
slain, their ladders were destroyed by flaming combustibles,
and the count was obliged to retreat from before the tower.
On the following day he renewed the attack with superior
force, and, after a severe combat, succeeded in planting his
victorious banner on the tower.

The Moors now assailed the tower in their turn. They
undermined the part toward the city, placed props of wood
under the foundation, and, setting fire to them, drew off to a
distance. In a little while the props gave way, the foundation sunk, and the tower was rent; part of its wall fell with
a tremendous noise; many of the Christians were thrown out
headlong, and the rest were laid open to the missiles of the
enemy.

By this time, however, a breach had been made in the
wall adjoining the tower, and troops poured in to the assistance of their comrades. A continued battle was kept up, for
two days and a night, by re-enforcements from camp and city.
The parties fought backward and forward through the breach
of the wall, with alternate success; and the vicinity of the
tower was strewn with the dead and wounded. At length
the Moors gradually gave way, disputing every inch of
ground, until they were driven into the city; and the Christians remained masters of the greater part of the suburb.

This partial success, though gained with great toil and
bloodshed, gave temporary animation to the Christians; they
soon found, however, that the attack on the main works of
the city was a much more arduous task. The garrison contained veterans who had served in many of the towns cap-

tured by the Christians. They were no longer confounded and dismayed by the battering ordnance and other strange engines of foreign invention, and had become expert in parrying their effects, in repairing breaches, and erecting counterworks.

The Christians, accustomed of late to speedy conquests of Moorish fortresses, became impatient of the slow progress of the siege. Many were apprehensive of a scarcity of provisions, from the difficulty of subsisting so numerous a host in the heart of the enemy's country, where it was necessary to transport supplies across rugged and hostile mountains, or subjected to the uncertainties of the sea. Many also were alarmed at a pestilence which broke out in the neighboring villages; and some were so overcome by these apprehensions as to abandon the camp and return to their homes.

Several of the loose and worthless hangers-on that infest all great armies, hearing these murmurs, thought that the siege would soon be raised, and deserted to the enemy, hoping to make their fortunes. They gave exaggerated accounts of the alarms and discontents of the army, and represented the troops as daily returning home in bands. Above all, they declared that the gunpowder was nearly exhausted, so that the artillery would soon be useless. They assured the Moors, therefore, that if they persisted a little longer in their defense, the king would be obliged to draw off his forces and abandon the siege.

The reports of these renegadoes gave fresh courage to the garrison; they made vigorous sallies upon the camp, harassing it by night and day, and obliging every part to be guarded with the most painful vigilance. They fortified the weak parts of their walls with ditches and palisadoes, and gave every manifestation of a determined and unyielding spirit.

Ferdinand soon received intelligence of the reports which had been carried to the Moors; he understood that they had been informed, likewise, that the queen was alarmed for the safety of the camp, and had written repeatedly urging him to abandon the siege. As the best means of disproving all these falsehoods, and of destroying the vain hopes of the enemy, Ferdinand wrote to the queen, entreating her to come and take up her residence in the camp.

CHAPTER TEN

SIEGE OF MALAGA CONTINUED—OBSTINACY OF HAMET EL ZEGRI

GREAT was the enthusiasm of the army, when they beheld their patriot queen advancing in state, to share the toils and dangers of her people. Isabella entered the camp, attended by the dignitaries and the whole retinue of her court, to manifest that this was no temporary visit. On one side of her was her daughter, the Infanta; on the other, the grand cardinal of Spain, Hernando de Talavera, the prior of Prado, confessor to the queen, followed, with a great train of prelates, courtiers, cavaliers, and ladies of distinction. The cavalcade moved in calm and stately order through the camp, softening the iron aspect of war by this array of courtly grace and female beauty.

Isabella had commanded that, on her coming to the camp, the horrors of war should be suspended, and fresh offers of peace made to the enemy. On her arrival, therefore, there had been a general cessation of firing throughout the camp. A messenger was, at the same time, dispatched to the besieged, informing them of her being in the camp, and of the determination of the sovereigns to make it their settled residence until the city should be taken. The same terms were offered, in case of immediate surrender, that had been granted to Velez Malaga; but the inhabitants were threatened with captivity and the sword should they persist in their defense.

Hamet el Zegri received this message with haughty contempt, and dismissed the messenger without deigning a reply. "The Christian sovereigns," said he, "have made this offer in consequence of their despair. The silence of their batteries proves the truth of what has been told us, that their powder is exhausted. They have no longer the means of demolishing our walls; and if they remain much longer, the autumnal rains will interrupt their convoys, and fill their camp with famine and disease. The first storm will disperse their fleet, which has no neighboring port of shelter: Africa will then be open to us, to procure re-enforcements and supplies.''

The words of Hamet el Zegri were hailed as oracular by his adherents. Many of the peaceful part of the community, however, ventured to remonstrate, and to implore him to accept the proffered mercy. The stern Hamet silenced them with a terrific threat: he declared that whoever should talk of capitulating, or should hold any communication with the Christians, should be put to death. The fierce Comares, like true men of the sword, acted upon the menace of their chieftain as upon a written law, and having detected several of the inhabitants in secret correspondence with the enemy, they set upon and slew them, and then confiscated their effects. This struck such terror into the citizens that those who had been loudest in their murmurs became suddenly mute, and were remarked as evincing the greatest bustle and alacrity in the defense of the city.

When the messenger returned to the camp and reported the contemptuous reception of the royal message, King Ferdinand was exceedingly indignant. Finding the cessation of firing, on the queen's arrival, had encouraged a belief among the enemy that there was a scarcity of powder in the camp, he ordered a general discharge from all the batteries. The sudden burst of war from every quarter soon convinced the Moors of their error, and completed the confusion of the citizens, who knew not which most to dread, their assailants or their defenders, the Christians or the Comares.

That evening the sovereigns visited the encampment of the Marques of Cadiz, which commanded a view over a great part of the city and the camp. The tent of the marques was of great magnitude, furnished with hangings of rich brocade and French cloth of the rarest texture. It was in the Oriental style; and, as it crowned the height, with the surrounding tents of other cavaliers, all sumptuously furnished, presented a gay and silken contrast to the opposite towers of Gibralfaro. Here a splendid collation was served up to the sovereigns; and the courtly revel that prevailed in this chivalrous encampment, the glitter of pageantry, and the bursts of festive music, made more striking the gloom and silence that reigned over the Moorish castle.

The Marques of Cadiz, while it was yet light, conducted his royal visitors to every point that commanded a view of the warlike scene below. He caused the heavy lombards also to be discharged, that the queen and ladies of the court might witness the effect of those tremendous engines. The fair dames were filled with awe and admiration, as the mountain shook beneath their feet with the thunder of the artillery, and they beheld great fragments of the Moorish walls tumbling down the rocks and precipices.

While the good marques was displaying these things to his royal guests, he lifted up his eyes, and to his astonishment beheld his own banner hanging out from the nearest tower of Gibralfaro. The blood mantled in his cheek, for it was a banner which he had lost at the time of the memorable massacre of the heights of Malaga.* To make this taunt more evident, several of the Comares displayed themselves upon the battlements, arrayed in the helmets and cuirasses of some of the cavaliers slain or captured on that occasion. The Marques of Cadiz restrained his indignation, and held his peace; but several of his cavaliers vowed loudly to revenge this cruel bravado on the ferocious garrison of Gibralfaro.

---

* Diego de Valera.   Cronica, MS.

CHAPTER ELEVEN

ATTACK OF THE MARQUES OF CADIZ UPON GIBRALFARO

THE Marques of Cadiz was not a cavalier that readily forgave an injury or an insult. On the morning after the royal banquet, his batteries opened a tremendous fire upon Gibralfaro. All day, the encampment was wrapped in wreaths of smoke; nor did the assault cease with the day—but, throughout the night, there was an incessant flashing and thundering of the lombards, and, the following morning, the assault rather increased than slackened in fury. The Moorish bulwarks were no proof against those formidable engines. In a few days, the lofty tower on which the taunting banner had been displayed was shattered, a smaller tower in its vicinity reduced to ruins, and a great breach made in the intervening walls.

Several of the hot-spirited cavaliers were eager for storming the breach, sword in hand; others, more cool and wary, pointed out the rashness of such an attempt; for the Moors had worked indefatigably in the night; they had dug a deep ditch within the breach, and had fortified it with palisadoes and a high breastwork. All, however, agreed that the camp might safely be advanced near to the ruined walls, and that it ought to be done in return for the insolent defiance of the enemy.

The Marques of Cadiz felt the temerity of the measure, but he was unwilling to dampen the zeal of these high-spirited cavaliers; and having chosen the post of danger in the camp, it did not become him to decline any service, merely because it might appear perilous. He ordered his outposts, therefore, to be advanced within a stone's-throw of the breach, but exhorted the soldiers to maintain the utmost vigilance.

The thunder of the batteries had ceased; the troops, exhausted by two nights' fatigue and watchfulness, and apprehending no danger from the dismantled walls, were half of them asleep; the rest were scattered about in negligent security. On a sudden, upward of two thousand Moors sallied forth from the castle, led on by Alrahan Zenete, the principal captain under Hamet. They fell with fearful havoc upon the advance guard, slaying many of them in their sleep, and putting the rest to headlong flight.

The marques was in his tent, about a bow-shot distance, when he heard the tumult of the onset, and beheld his men flying in confusion. He rushed forth, followed by his standard-bearer. "Turn again, cavaliers!" exclaimed he; "I am here, Ponce de Leon! to the foe! to the foe!" The flying troops stopped at hearing his well-known voice, rallied under his banner and turned upon the enemy. The encampment by this time was roused; several cavaliers from the adjoining stations had hastened to the scene of action, with a number of Gallicians and soldiers of the Holy Brotherhood. An obstinate and bloody contest ensued; the ruggedness of the place, the rocks, chasms, and declivities broke it into numerous combats; Christian and Moor fought hand to hand, with swords and daggers; and often, grappling and struggling, rolled together down the precipices.

The banner of the marques was in danger of being taken: he hastened to its rescue, followed by some of his bravest cavaliers. They were surrounded by the enemy, and several of them cut down. Don Diego Ponce de Leon, brother to the marques, was wounded by an arrow; and his son-in-law, Luis Ponce, was likewise wounded: they succeeded, however, in rescuing the banner, and bearing it off in safety. The battle lasted for an hour; the height was covered with killed and wounded, and the blood flowed in streams down the rocks; at length, Alrahan Zenete being disabled by the thrust of a lance, the Moors gave way and retreated to the castle.

They now opened a galling fire from their battlements

and towers, approaching the breaches so as to discharge their crossbows and arquebuses into the advance guard of the encampment. The marques was singled out; the shot fell thick about him, and one passed through his buckler, and struck upon his cuirass, but without doing him any injury. Every one now saw the danger and inutility of approaching the camp thus near to the castle; and those who had counseled it were now urgent that it should be withdrawn. It was accordingly moved back to its original ground, from which the marques had most reluctantly advanced it. Nothing but his valor and timely aid had prevented this attack on his outpost from ending in a total rout of all that part of the army.

Many cavaliers of distinction fell in this contest; but the loss of none was felt more deeply than that of Ortega de Prado, captain of escaladors. He was one of the bravest men in the service; the same who had devised the first successful blow of the war, the storming of Alhama, where he was the first to plant and mount the scaling-ladders. He had always been high in the favor and confidence of the noble Ponce de Leon, who knew how to appreciate and avail himself of the merits of all able and valiant men.*

CHAPTER TWELVE

SIEGE OF MALAGA CONTINUED—STRATAGEMS OF VARIOUS KINDS

GREAT were the exertions now made, both by the besiegers and the besieged, to carry on this contest with the utmost vigor. Hamet el Zegri went the rounds of the walls and towers, doubling the guards, and putting everything in the best posture of defense. The garrison was divided into parties of a hundred, to each of which a captain was ap-

* Zurita. Mariana. Abarca.

pointed. Some were to patrol, others to sally forth and skirmish with the enemy, and others to hold themselves armed and in reserve. Six albatozas, or floating batteries, were manned and armed with pieces of artillery, to attack the fleet.

On the other hand the Castilian sovereigns kept open a communication by sea with various parts of Spain, from which they received provisions of all kinds; they ordered supplies of powder also from Valencia, Barcelona, Sicily, and Portugal. They made great preparations also for storming the city. Towers of wood were constructed, to move on wheels, each capable of holding one hundred men; they were furnished with ladders, to be thrown from their summits to the tops of the walls; and within those ladders, others were incased, to be let down for the descent of the troops into the city. There were gallipagos or tortoises, also, being great wooden shields, covered with hides, to protect the assailants, and those who undermined the walls.

Secret mines were commenced in various places; some were intended to reach to the foundations of the walls, which were to be propped up with wood, ready to be set on fire; others were to pass under the walls, and remain ready to be broken open so as to give entrance to the besiegers. At these mines the army worked day and night; and during these secret preparations, the ordnance kept up a fire upon the city, to divert the attention of the besieged.

In the meantime, Hamet el Zegri displayed wonderful vigor and ingenuity in defending the city, and in repairing or fortifying, by deep ditches, the breaches made by the enemy. He noted, also, every place where the camp might be assailed with advantage, and gave the besieging army no repose night or day. While his troops sallied on the land, his floating batteries attacked the besiegers on the sea; so that there was incessant skirmishing. The tents called the Queen's Hospital were crowded with wounded, and the whole army suffered from constant watchfulness and fatigue. To guard against the sudden assaults of the Moors, the trenches were deepened and palisadoes erected in front of the camp; and in that part facing Gibralfaro, where the rocky heights did not admit of such defenses, a high rampart of earth was thrown up. The cavaliers Garcilasso de la Vega, Juan de Zuniga, and Diego de Atayde, were appointed to go the rounds, and keep vigilant watch that these fortifications were maintained in good order.

In a little while, Hamet discovered the mines secretly commenced by the Christians: he immediately ordered counter-mines. The soldiers mutually worked until they met, and fought hand to hand in these subterranean passages. The Christians were driven out of one of their mines; fire was set to the wooden framework and the mine destroyed. Encouraged by this success, the Moors attempted a general attack upon the camp, the mines, and the besieging fleet. The battle lasted for six hours, on land and water, above and below ground, on bulwark, and in trench and mine; the Moors displayed wonderful intrepidity, but were finally repulsed at all points, and obliged to retire into the city, where they were closely invested, without the means of receiving any assistance from abroad.

The horrors of famine were now added to the other miseries of Malaga. Hamet el Zegri, with the spirit of a man bred up to war, considered everything as subservient to the wants of the soldier, and ordered all the grain in the city to be gathered and garnered up for the sole use of those who fought. Even this was dealt out sparingly, and each soldier received four ounces of bread in the morning, and two in the evening, for his daily allowance.

The wealthy inhabitants, and all those peacefully inclined, mourned over a resistance which brought destruction upon their houses, death into their families, and which they saw must end in their ruin and captivity: still none of them dared to speak openly of capitulation, or even to manifest their grief, lest they should awaken the wrath of their fierce defenders. They surrounded their civic champion, Ali Dordux, the great and opulent merchant, who had buckled on shield and cuirass, and taken spear in hand, for the defense of his native city, and, with a large body of the braver citizens, had charge of one of the gates and a considerable portion of the walls. Drawing Ali Dordux aside, they poured forth their griefs to him in secret. "Why," said they, "should we suffer our native city to be made a mere bulwark and fighting-place for foreign barbarians and desperate men? They have no families to care for, no property to lose, no love for the soil, and no value for their lives. They fight to gratify a thirst for blood or a desire for revenge, and will fight on until Malaga become a ruin and its people slaves. Let us think and act for ourselves, our wives, and our children. Let us make private terms with the Christians before it is too late, and save ourselves from destruction."

The bowels of Ali Dordux yearned toward his fellow-citizens; he bethought him also of the sweet security of peace, and the bloodless yet gratifying triumphs of gainful traffic. The idea also of a secret negotiation or bargain with the Castilian sovereigns, for the redemption of his native city, was more conformable to his accustomed habits than this violent appeal to arms; for though he had for a time assumed the warrior, he had not forgotten the merchant. Ali Dordux communed, therefore, with the citizen-soldiers under his command, and they readily conformed to his opinion. Concerting together, they wrote a proposition to the Castilian sovereigns, offering to admit the army into the part of the city intrusted to their care, on receiving assurance of protection for the lives and properties of the inhabitants. This writing they delivered to a trusty emissary to take to the Christian camp, appointing the hour and place of his return, that they might be ready to admit him unperceived.

The Moor made his way in safety to the camp, and was admitted to the presence of the sovereigns. Eager to gain the city without further cost of blood or treasure, they gave a written promise to grant the conditions; and the Moor set out joyfully on his return. As he approached the walls where Ali Dordux and his confederates were waiting to receive him, he was descried by a patroling band of Comares, and considered a spy coming from the camp of the besiegers. They issued forth and seized him, in sight of his employers, who gave themselves up for lost. The Comares had conducted him nearly to the gate, when he escaped from their grasp and fled. They endeavored to overtake him, but were encumbered with armor; he was lightly clad, and he fled for his life. One of the Comares paused, and, leveling his crossbow, let fly a bolt, which pierced the fugitive between the shoulders; he fell, and was nearly within their grasp, but rose again, and with a desperate effort attained the Christian camp. The Comares gave over the pursuit, and the citizens returned thanks to Allah for their deliverance from this fearful peril. As to the faithful messenger, he died of his wound shortly after reaching the camp, consoled with the idea that he had preserved the secret and the lives of his employers.

CHAPTER THIRTEEN

SUFFERINGS OF THE PEOPLE OF MALAGA

THE sufferings of Malaga spread sorrow and anxiety among the Moors; and they dreaded lest this beautiful city, once the bulwark of the kingdom, should fall into the hands of the unbelievers. The old warrior king, Abdalla el Zagal, was still sheltered in Guadix, where he was slowly gathering together his shattered forces. When the people of Guadix heard of the danger and distress of Malaga, they urged to be led to its relief; and the alfaquis admonished El Zagal not to desert so righteous and loyal a city, in its extremity. His own warlike nature made him feel a sympathy for a place that made so gallant a resistance; and he dispatched as powerful a re-enforcement as he could spare, under conduct of a chosen captain, with orders to throw themselves into the city.

Intelligence of this re-enforcement reached Boabdil el Chico in his royal palace of the Alhambra. Filled with hostility against his uncle, and desirous of proving his loyalty to the Castilian sovereigns, he immediately sent forth a superior force of horse and foot, under an able commander, to intercept the detachment. A sharp conflict ensued; the troops of El Zagal were routed with great loss, and fled back in confusion to Guadix.

Boabdil, not being accustomed to victories, was flushed with his melancholy triumph. He sent tidings of it to the Castilian sovereigns, accompanied with rich silks, boxes of Arabian perfume, a cup of gold, richly wrought, and a female captive of Ubeda, as presents to the queen; and four Arabian steeds magnificently caparisoned, a sword and dagger richly mounted, and several albornozes and other robes sumptuously embroidered, for the king. He entreated them, at the same time, always to look upon him with favor as their devoted vassal.

Boabdil was fated to be unfortunate even in his victories. His defeat of the forces of his uncle, destined to the relief of unhappy Malaga, shocked the feelings and cooled the loyalty of many of his best adherents. The mere men of traffic might rejoice in their golden interval of peace; but the chivalrous spirits of Granada spurned a security purchased by such sacrifices of pride and affection. The people at large, having gratified their love of change, began to question whether they had acted generously by their old fighting monarch. "El Zagal," said they, "was fierce and bloody, but then he was true to his country; he was a usurper, it is true, but then he maintained the glory of the crown which he usurped. If his scepter was a rod of iron to his subjects, it was a sword of steel against their enemies. This Boabdil sacrifices religion, friends, country, everything, to a mere shadow of royalty, and is content to hold a rush for a scepter."

These factious murmurs soon reached the ears of Boabdil and he apprehended another of his customary reverses. He sent in all haste to the Castilian sovereigns, beseeching military aid to keep him on his throne. Ferdinand graciously complied with a request so much in unison with his policy. A detachment of one thousand cavalry and two thousand infantry was sent, under the command of Don Fernandez Gonsalvo of Cordova, subsequently renowned as the great captain. With this succor, Boabdil expelled from the city all those who were hostile to him and in favor of his uncle. He felt secure in these troops, from their being distinct in manners, language, and religion, from his subjects; and compromised with his pride, in thus exhibiting that most unnatural and humiliating of all regal spectacles, a monarch supported on his throne by foreign weapons, and by soldiers hostile to his people.

Nor was Boabdil el Chico the only Moorish sovereign that sought protection from Ferdinand and Isabella. A splendid galley, with latine sails, and several banks of oars, displaying the standard of the crescent, but likewise a white flag in sign of amity, came one day into the harbor. An embassador landed from it within the Christian lines. He came from the King of Tremezan, and brought presents similar to those of Boabdil, consisting of Arabian coursers, with bits, stirrups, and other furniture of gold, together with costly Moorish mantles; for the queen, there were sumptuous shawls, robes, and silken stuffs, ornaments of gold, and exquisite Oriental perfumes.

The King of Tremezan had been alarmed at the rapid conquests of the Spanish arms, and startled by the descent of several Spanish cruisers on the coast of Africa. He craved to be considered a vassal to the Castilian sovereigns, and that they would extend such favor and security to his ships and subjects as had been shown to other Moors who had submitted to their sway. He requested a painting of their arms, that he and his subjects might recognize and respect their standard, whenever they encountered it. At the same time he implored their clemency toward unhappy Malaga, and that its inhabitants might experience the same favor that had been shown toward the Moors of other captured cities.

The embassy was graciously received by the Christian sovereigns. They granted the protection required; ordering their commanders to respect the flag of Tremezan, unless it should be found rendering assistance to the enemy. They sent also to the Barbary monarch their royal arms, molded in escutcheons of gold, a hand's-breadth in size.*

While thus the chances of assistance from without daily decreased, famine raged in the city. The inhabitants were compelled to eat the flesh of horses, and many died of hunger. What made the sufferings of the citizens the more intolerable, was to behold the sea covered with ships, daily arriving with provisions for the besiegers. Day after day, also, they saw herds of fat cattle, and flocks of sheep, driven into the camp. Wheat and flour were piled in huge mounds in the center of the encampments, glaring in the sunshine, and tantalizing the wretched citizens, who, while they and their children were perishing with hunger, beheld prodigal abundance reigning within a bow-shot of their walls.

CHAPTER FOURTEEN

HOW A MOORISH SANTON UNDERTOOK TO DELIVER THE CITY
OF MALAGA FROM THE POWER OF ITS ENEMIES

THERE lived at this time, in a hamlet in the neighborhood of Guadix, an ancient Moor of the name of Abrahin Algerbi. He was a native of Guerba, in the kingdom of Tunis, and had for several years led the life of a santon or hermit. The hot sun of Africa had dried his blood and rendered him of an exalted yet melancholy temperament. He passed most of his time in meditation, prayer, and rigorous abstinence, until his body was wasted and his mind bewil-

---

* Cura de los Palacios, c. 84   Pulgar, part 3, c. 86.

dered, and he fancied himself favored with divine revelations. The Moors, who have a great reverence for all enthusiasts of the kind, looked upon him as inspired, listened to all his ravings as veritable prophecies, and denominated him *el santo*, or the saint.

The woes of the kingdom of Granada had long exasperated the gloomy spirit of this man, and he had beheld with indignation this beautiful country wrested from the dominion of the faithful and becoming a prey to the unbelievers. He had implored the blessings of Allah on the troops which issued forth from Guadix for the relief of Malaga; but when he saw them return, routed and scattered by their own countrymen, he retired to his cell, shut himself up from the world, and was plunged for a time in the blackest melancholy.

On a sudden, he made his appearance again in the streets of Guadix, his face haggard, his form emaciated, but his eye beaming with fire. He said that Allah had sent an angel to him in the solitude of his cell, revealing to him a mode of delivering Malaga from its perils, and striking horror and confusion into the camp of the unbelievers. The Moors listened with eager credulity to his words: four hundred of them offered to follow him even to the death, and to obey implicitly his commands. Of this number many were Comares, anxious to relieve their countrymen, who formed part of the garrison of Malaga.

They traversed the kingdom by the wild and lonely passes of the mountains, concealing themselves in the day and traveling only in the night, to elude the Christian scouts. At length they arrived at the mountains which tower above Malaga, and, looking down, beheld the city completely invested; a chain of encampments extending round it from shore to shore, and a line of ships blockading it by sea; while the continual thunder of artillery, and the smoke rising in various parts, showed that the siege was pressed with great activity. The hermit scanned the encampments warily from his lofty height. He saw that the part of the encampment of the Marques of Cadiz which was at the foot of the height, and on the margin of the sea, was most assailable, the rocky soil not admitting of ditches or palisadoes. Remaining concealed all day, he descended with his followers at night to the seacoast, and approached silently to the outworks. He had given them their instructions; they were to rush suddenly upon the camp, fight their way through, and throw themselves into the city.

It was just at the gray of the dawning, when objects are obscurely visible, that they made this desperate attempt. Some sprang suddenly upon the sentinels, others rushed into the sea and got round the works, others clambered over the breastworks. There was sharp skirmishing; a great part of the Moors were cut to pieces, but about two hundred succeeded in getting into the gates of Malaga.

The santon took no part in the conflict, nor did he endeavor to enter the city. His plans were of a different nature. Drawing apart from the battle, he threw himself on his knees on a rising ground, and, lifting his hands to heaven, appeared to be absorbed in prayer. The Christians, as they were searching for fugitives in the clefts of the rocks, found him at his devotions. He stirred not at their approach, but remained fixed as a statue, without changing color or moving a muscle. Filled with surprise not unmingled with awe, they took him to the Marques of Cadiz. He was wrapped in a coarse albornoz or Moorish mantle; his beard was long and grizzled, and there was something wild and melancholy in his look that inspired curiosity. On being examined, he gave himself out as a saint to whom Allah had revealed the events that were to take place in that siege. The marques demanded when and how Malaga was to be taken. He replied that he knew full well, but he was forbidden to reveal those important secrets except to the king and queen. The good marques was not more given to superstitious fancies than other commanders of his time, yet there seemed something singular and mysterious about this man; he might have some important intelligence to communicate; so he was persuaded to send him to the king and queen. He was conducted to the royal tent, surrounded by a curious multitude, exclaiming, "El Moro Santo!" for the news had spread through the camp that they had taken a Moorish prophet.

The king, having dined, was taking his siesta or afternoon's sleep in his tent; and the queen, though curious to see this singular man, yet, from a natural delicacy and reserve, delayed until the king should be present. He was taken therefore to an adjoining tent, in which were Dona Beatrix de Bovadilla, Marchioness of Moya, and Don Alvaro of Portugal, son of the Duke of Braganza, with two or three attendants. The Moor, ignorant of the Spanish tongue, had not understood the conversation of the guards, and supposed from the magnificence of the furniture and the silken hangings that this was the royal tent. From the respect paid by the attendants to Don Alvaro and the marchioness, he concluded that they were the king and queen.

He now asked for a draught of water; a jar was brought to him, and the guard released his arm to enable him to drink. The marchioness perceived a sudden change in his countenance, and something sinister in the expression of his eye, and shifted her position to a more remote part of the tent. Pretending to raise the water to his lips, the Moor unfolded his albornoz, so as to grasp a scimiter which he wore concealed beneath; then, dashing down the jar, he drew his weapon, and gave Don Alvaro a blow on the head that struck him to the earth and nearly deprived him of life. Turning then upon the marchioness, he made a violent blow at her; but in his eagerness and agitation his scimiter caught in the drapery of the tent; the force of the blow was broken, and the weapon struck harmless upon some golden ornaments of her head-dress *

Ruy Lopez de Toledo, treasurer to the queen, and Juan de Belalcazar, a sturdy friar, who were present, grappled and struggled with the desperado; and immediately the guards, who had conducted him from the Marques de Cadiz, fell upon him and cut him to pieces.†

* Pietro Martyr, Epist. 62.   † Cura de los Palacios.

The king and queen, brought out of their tents by the noise, were filled with horror when they learned the imminent peril from which they had escaped. The mangled body of the Moor was taken by the people to the camp and thrown into the city from a catapult. The Comares gathered up the body with deep reverence, as the remains of a saint; they washed and perfumed it, and buried it with great honor and loud lamentations. In revenge of his death, they slew one of their principal Christian captives, and, having tied his body upon an ass, they drove the animal forth into the camp.

From this time, there was appointed an additional guard around the tents of the king and queen, composed of twelve hundred cavaliers of rank, of the kingdoms of Castile and Aragon. No person was admitted to the royal presence armed; no Moor was allowed to enter the camp without a previous knowledge of his character and business; and on no account was any Moor to be introduced into the presence of the sovereigns.

An act of treachery of such ferocious nature gave rise to a train of gloomy apprehensions. There were many cabins and sheds about the camp, constructed of branches of trees which had become dry and combustible; and fears were entertained that they might be set on fire by the Mudexares or Moorish vassals, who visited the army. Some even dreaded that attempts might be made to poison the wells and fountains. To quiet these dismal alarms, all Mudexares were ordered to leave the camp; and all loose, idle loiterers, who could not give a good account of themselves, were taken into custody.

CHAPTER FIFTEEN

HOW HAMET EL ZEGRI WAS HARDENED IN HIS OBSTINACY BY THE ARTS OF A MOORISH ASTROLOGER

AMONG those followers of the santon that had effected their entrance into the city was a dark African of the tribe of the Comares, who was likewise a hermit or dervise, and passed among the Moors for a holy and inspired man. No sooner were the mangled remains of his predecessor buried with the honors of martyrdom than this dervise elevated himself in his place, and professed to be gifted with the spirit of prophecy. He displayed a white banner, which, he assured the Moors, was sacred; that he had retained it for twenty years for some signal purpose, and that Allah had revealed to him that under that banner the inhabitants of Malaga should sally forth upon the camp of the unbelievers, put it to utter rout, and banquet upon the provisions in which it abounded.* The hungry and credulous Moors were elated at this prediction, and cried out to be led forth at once to the attack; but the dervise told them the time was not yet arrived, for every event had its allotted day in the decrees of fate; they must wait patiently, therefore, until the appointed time should be revealed to him by Heaven. Hamet el Zegri listened to the dervise with profound reverence, and his example had great effect in increasing the awe and deference of his followers. He took the holy man up into his stronghold of Gibralfaro, consulted him on all occasions and hung out his white banner on the loftiest tower, as a signal of encouragement to the people of the city.

In the meantime, the prime chivalry of Spain was gradually assembling before the walls of Malaga. The army which had commenced the siege had been worn out by extreme hardships, having had to construct immense works, to dig trenches and mines, to mount guard by sea and land, to patrol the mountains, and to sustain incessant conflicts. The sovereigns were obliged, therefore, to call upon various distant cities for re-enforcements of horse and foot. Many nobles, also, assembled their vassals, and repaired, of their own accord, to the royal camp.

Every little while, some stately galley or gallant caravel would stand into the harbor, displaying the well-known banner of some Spanish cavalier, and thundering from its artil

---

* Cura de los Palacios.

lery a salutation to the sovereigns and a defiance to the Moors. On the land side, also, re-enforcements would be seen, winding down from the mountains to the sound of drum and trumpet, and marching into the camp with glistening arms, as yet unsullied by the toils of war.

One morning, the whole sea was whitened by the sails and vexed by the oars of ships and galleys bearing toward the port. One hundred vessels of various kinds and sizes arrived, some armed for warlike service, others deep freighted with provisions. At the same time, the clangor of drum and trumpet bespoke the arrival of a powerful force by land, which came pouring in lengthening columns into the camp. This mighty re-enforcement was furnished by the Duke of Medina Sidonia, who reigned like a petty monarch over his vast possessions. He came with this princely force, a volunteer to the royal standard, not having been summoned by the sovereigns; and he brought, moreover, a loan of twenty thousand doblas of gold.

When the camp was thus powerfully re-enforced, Isabella advised that new offers of an indulgent kind should be made to the inhabitants; for she was anxious to prevent the miseries of a protracted siege, or the effusion of blood that must attend a general attack. A fresh summons was, therefore, sent for the city to surrender, with a promise of life, liberty, and property, in case of immediate compliance; but denouncing all the horrors of war if the defense were obstinately continued.

Hamet el Zegri again rejected the offer with scorn. His main fortifications as yet were but little impaired, and were capable of holding out much longer; he trusted to the thousand evils and accidents that beset a besieging army, and to the inclemencies of the approaching season; and it is said that he, as well as his followers, had an infatuated belief in the predictions of the dervise.

The worthy Fray Antonio Agapida does not scruple to affirm that the pretended prophet of the city was an arch necromancer or Moorish magician, ''of which there be countless many," says he, "in the filthy sect of Mahomet"; and that he was leagued with the prince of the powers of the air to endeavor to work the confusion and defeat of the Christian army. The worthy father asserts, also, that Hamet employed him in a high tower of the Gibralfaro, which commanded a wide view over sea and land, where he wrought spells and incantations with astrolabes and other diabolical instruments, to defeat the Christian ships and forces, whenever they were engaged with the Moors.

To the potent spells of this sorcerer, he ascribes the perils and losses sustained by a party of cavaliers of the royal household, in a desperate combat to gain two towers of the suburb, near the gate of the city called la Puerto de Granada. The Christians, led on by Ruy Lopez de Toledo, the valiant treasurer of the queen, took, and lost, and retook the towers, which were finally set on fire by the Moors, and abandoned to the flames by both parties. To the same malignant influence he attributes the damage done to the Christian fleet, which was so vigorously assailed by the albatozas or floating batteries of the Moors, that one ship, belonging to the Duke of Medina Sidonia, was sunk, and the rest were obliged to retire.

"Hamet el Zegri," says Fray Antonio Agapida, "stood on the top of the high tower of Gibralfaro, and beheld this injury wrought upon the Christian force, and his proud heart was puffed up. And the Moorish necromancer stood beside him. And he pointed out to him the Christian host below, encamped on every eminence around the city, and covering its fertile valley, and the many ships floating upon the tranquil sea; and he bade him be strong of heart, for that in a few days all this mighty fleet would be scattered by the winds of heaven; and that he should sally forth, under guidance of the sacred banner, and attack this host and utterly defeat it, and make spoil of those sumptuous tents; and Malaga should be triumphantly revenged upon her assailants. So the heart of Hamet was hardened like that of Pharaoh, and he persisted in setting at defiance the Catholic sovereigns and their army of saintly warriors."

CHAPTER SIXTEEN

SIEGE OF MALAGA CONTINUED—DESTRUCTION OF A TOWER
BY FRANCISCO RAMIREZ DE MADRID

SEEING the infatuated obstinacy of the besieged, the Christians now approached their works to the walls, gaining one position after another, preparatory to a general assault. Near the barrier of the city was a bridge with four arches, defended at each end by a strong and lofty tower, by which a part of the army would have to pass in making an attack. The commander-in-chief of the artillery, Francisco Ramirez de Madrid, was ordered to take possession of this bridge. The approach to it was perilous in the extreme, from the exposed situation of the assailants, and the number of Moors that garrisoned the towers. Francisco Ramirez, therefore, secretly excavated a mine leading beneath the first tower, and placed a piece of ordnance with its mouth upward, immediately under the foundation, with a train of powder to produce an explosion at the necessary moment.

When this was arranged, he advanced slowly with his forces in face of the towers, erecting bulwarks at every step, and gradually gaining ground, until he arrived near to the bridge. He then planted several pieces of artillery in his works, and began to batter the tower. The Moors replied bravely from their battlements; but in the heat of the combat, the piece of ordnance under the foundation was discharged. The earth was rent open, a part of the tower overthrown, and several of the Moors torn to pieces; the rest took to flight, overwhelmed with terror at this thundering explosion bursting beneath their feet, and at beholding the earth vomiting flames and smoke; for never before had they witnessed such a stratagem in warfare. The Christians rushed forward and took possession of the abandoned post, and immediately commenced an attack upon the other tower at the opposite end of the bridge, to which the Moors had retired. An incessant fire of crossbows and arquebuses was kept up between the rival towers, volleys of stones were discharged, and no one dared to venture upon the intermediate bridge.

Francisco de Ramirez at length renewed his former mode of approach, making bulwarks step by step, while the Moors, stationed at the other end, swept the bridge with their artillery. The combat was long and bloody—furious on the part of the Moors, patient and persevering on the part of the Christians. By slow degrees, they accomplished their advance across the bridge, drove the enemy before them, and remained masters of this important pass.

For this valiant and skillful achievement, King Ferdinand, after the surrender of the city, conferred the dignity of knighthood upon Francisco Ramirez, in the tower which he had so gloriously gained.* The worthy padre Fray Antonio Agapida indulges in more than a page of extravagant eulogy upon this invention of blowing up the foundation of the tower by a piece of ordnance, which he affirms to be the first instance on record of gunpowder being used in a mine.

CHAPTER SEVENTEEN

HOW THE PEOPLE OF MALAGA EXPOSTULATED WITH HAMET EL ZEGRI

WHILE the dervise was deluding the garrison of Malaga with vain hopes, the famine increased to a terrible degree. The Comares ranged about the city as though it had been a conquered place, taking by force whatever they found eatable in the houses of the peaceful citizens; and breaking open vaults and cellars, and demolishing walls, wherever they thought provisions might be concealed.

---

* Pulgar, part 3, c. 91.

The wretched inhabitants had no longer bread to eat; the horse-flesh also now failed them, and they were fain to devour skins and hides toasted at the fire, and to assuage the hunger of their children with vine-leaves cut up and fried in oil. Many perished of famine, or of the unwholesome food with which they endeavored to relieve it; and many took refuge in the Christian camp, preferring captivity to the horrors which surrounded them.

At length the sufferings of the inhabitants became so great as to conquer even their fears of Hamet and his Comares. They assembled before the house of Ali Dordux, the wealthy merchant, whose stately mansion was at the foot of the hill of the Alcazaba, and they urged him to stand forth as their leader, and to intercede with Hamet el Zegri for a surrender. Ali Dordux was a man of courage as well as policy; he perceived also that hunger was giving boldness to the citizens, while he trusted it was subduing the fierceness of the soldiery. He armed himself, therefore, cap-a-pie, and undertook this dangerous parley with the alcayde. He associated with him an alfaqui named Abrahen Alharis, and an important inhabitant named Amar ben Amar; and they ascended to the fortress of Gibralfaro, followed by several of the trembling merchants.

They found Hamet el Zegri, not, as before, surrounded by ferocious guards and all the implements of war, but in a chamber of one of the lofty towers, at a table of stone, covered with scrolls traced with strange characters and mystic diagrams; while instruments of singular and unknown form lay about the room. Beside Hamet el Zegri stood the prophetic dervise, who appeared to have been explaining to him the mysterious inscriptions of the scrolls. His presence filled the citizens with awe, for even Ali Dordux considered him a man inspired.

The alfaqui Abrahen Alharis, whose sacred character gave him boldness to speak, now lifted up his voice and addressed Hamet el Zegri. "We implore you," said he, solemnly, "in the name of the most powerful God, no longer to persist in a vain resistance, which must end in our destruction, but deliver up the city while clemency is yet to be obtained. Think how many of our warriors have fallen by the sword; do not suffer those who survive to perish by famine. Our wives and children cry to us for bread, and we have none to give them. We see them expire in lingering agony before our eyes, while the enemy mocks our misery by displaying the abundance of his camp. Of what avail is our defense? Are our walls peradventure more strong than the walls of Ronda? Are our warriors more brave than the defenders of Loxa? The walls of Ronda were thrown down, and the warriors of Loxa had to surrender. Do we hope for succor? —from whence are we to receive it? The time for hope is gone by. Granada has lost its power; it no longer possesses chivalry, commanders, or a king. Boabdil sits a vassal in the degraded halls of the Alhambra; El Zagal is a fugitive, shut up within the walls of Guadix. The kingdom is divided against itself—its strength is gone, its pride fallen, its very existence at an end. In the name of Allah, we conjure thee, who art our captain, be not our direst enemy; but surrender these ruins of our once happy Malaga, and deliver us from these overwhelming horrors."

Such was the supplication forced from the inhabitants by the extremity of their sufferings. Hamet el Zegri listened to the alfaqui without anger, for he respected the sanctity of his office. His heart, too, was at that moment lifted up with a vain confidence. "Yet a few days of patience," said he, "and all these evils will suddenly have an end. I have been conferring with this holy man, and find that the time of our deliverance is at hand. The decrees of fate are inevitable; it is written in the book of destiny that we shall sally forth and destroy the camp of the unbelievers, and banquet upon those mountains of grain which are piled up in the midst of it. So Allah hath promised, by the mouth of this His prophet. Allah Achbar! God is great. Let no man oppose the decrees of Heaven!"

The citizens bowed with profound reverence, for no true

Moslem pretends to struggle against whatever is written in the book of fate. Ali Dordux, who had come prepared to champion the city and to brave the ire of Hamet, humbled himself before this holy man, and gave faith to his prophecies as the revelations of Allah. So the deputies returned to the citizens, and exhorted them to be of good cheer: "A few days longer," said they, "and our sufferings are to terminate. When the white banner is removed from the tower, then look out for deliverance; for the hour of sallying forth will have arrived." The people retired to their homes with sorrowful hearts; they tried in vain to quiet the cries of their famishing children; and day by day, and hour by hour, their anxious eyes were turned to the sacred banner, which still continued to wave on the tower of Gibralfaro.

CHAPTER EIGHTEEN

HOW HAMET EL ZEGRI SALLIED FORTH WITH THE SACRED BANNER TO ATTACK THE CHRISTIAN CAMP

"THE Moorish necromancer," observes the worthy Fray Antonio Agapida, "remained shut up in a tower of the Gibralfaro, devising devilish means to work mischief and discomfiture upon the Christians. He was daily consulted by Hamet el Zegri, who had great faith in those black and magic arts, which he had brought with him from the bosom of heathen Africa."

From the account given of this dervise and his incantations by the worthy father, it would appear that he was an astrologer, and was studying the stars, and endeavoring to calculate the day and hour when a successful attack might be made upon the Christian camp.

Famine had now increased to such a degree as to distress even the garrison of Gibralfaro, although the Comares had seized upon all the provisions they could find in the city.

Their passions were sharpened by hunger, and they became restless and turbulent, and impatient for action.

Hamet el Zegri was one day in council with his captains, perplexed by the pressure of events, when the dervise entered among them. "The hour of victory," exclaimed he, "is at hand. Allah has commanded that to-morrow morning ye shall sally forth to the fight. I will bear before you the sacred banner, and deliver your enemies into your hands. Remember, however, that ye are but instruments in the hands of Allah, to take vengeance on the enemies of the faith. Go into battle, therefore, with pure hearts, forgiving each other all past offenses; for those who are charitable toward each other will be victorious over the foe." The words of the dervise were received with rapture: all Gibralfaro and the Alcazaba resounded immediately with the din of arms; and Hamet sent throughout the towers and fortifications of the city, and selected the choicest troops and most distinguished captains for this eventual combat.

In the morning early, the rumor went throughout the city that the sacred banner had disappeared from the tower of Gibralfaro, and all Malaga was roused to witness the sally that was to destroy the unbelievers. Hamet descended from his stronghold, accompanied by his principal captain, Alrahan Zenete, and followed by his Comares. The dervise led the way, displaying the white banner, the sacred pledge of victory. The multitude shouted "Allah Achbar!" and prostrated themselves before the banner as it passed. Even the dreaded Hamet was hailed with praises; for in their hopes of speedy relief through the prowess of his arm the populace forgot everything but his bravery. Every bosom in Malaga was agitated by hope and fear—the old men, the women and children, and all who went not forth to battle, mounted on tower and battlement and roof to watch a combat that was to decide their fate.

Before sallying forth from the city, the dervise addressed the troops, reminding them of the holy nature of this enterprise, and warning them not to forfeit the protection of the sacred banner by any unworthy act. They were not to pause to make spoil nor to take prisoners; they were to press forward, fighting valiantly, and granting no quarter. The gate was then thrown open, and the dervise issued forth, followed by the army. They directed their assaults upon the encampments of the Master of Santiago and the Master of Alcantara, and came upon them so suddenly that they killed and wounded several of the guards. Alrahan Zenete made his way into one of the tents, where he beheld several Christian striplings just starting from their slumber. The heart of the Moor was suddenly touched with pity for their youth, or perhaps he scorned the weakness of the foe. He smote them with the flat instead of the edge of the sword. "Away, imps," cried he, "away to your mothers." The fanatic dervise reproached him with his clemency—"I did not kill them," replied Zenete, "because I saw no beards!" *

The alarm was given in the camp, and the Christians rushed from all quarters to defend the gates of the bulwarks. Don Pedro Puerto Carrero, Senior of Moguer, and his brother Don Alonzo Pacheco, planted themselves, with their followers, in the gateway of the encampment of the Master of Santiago, and bore the whole brunt of battle until they were reenforced. The gate of the encampment of the Master of Calatrava was in like manner defended by Lorenzo Saurez de Mendoza. Hamet el Zegri was furious at being thus checked, where he had expected a miraculous victory. He led his troops repeatedly to the attack, hoping to force the gates before succor should arrive: they fought with vehement ardor, but were as often repulsed; and every time they returned to the assault, they found their enemies doubled in number. The Christians opened a cross-fire of all kinds of missiles, from their bulwarks; the Moors could effect but little damage upon a foe thus protected behind their works, while they themselves were exposed from head to foot. The Christians singled out the most conspicuous cavaliers, the

---

* Cura de los Palacios, c. 84.

greater part of whom were either slain or wounded. Still the Moors, infatuated by the predictions of the prophet, fought desperately and devotedly, and they were furious to revenge the slaughter of their leaders. They rushed upon certain death, endeavoring madly to scale the bulwarks, or force the gates, and fell amid showers of darts and lances, filling the ditches with their mangled bodies.

Hamet el Zegri raged along the front of the bulwarks, seeking an opening for attack. He gnashed his teeth with fury, as he saw so many of his chosen warriors slain around him. He seemed to have a charmed life; for, though constantly in the hottest of the fight, amid showers of missiles, he still escaped uninjured. Blindly confiding in the prophecy of victory, he continued to urge on his devoted troops. The dervise, too, ran like a maniac through the ranks, waving his white banner, and inciting the Moors by howlings rather than by shouts. In the midst of his frenzy, a stone from a catapult struck him on the head and dashed out his bewildered brains.*

When the Moors beheld their prophet slain, and his banner in the dust, they were seized with despair, and fled in confusion to the city. Hamet el Zegri made some effort to rally them, but was himself confounded by the fall of the dervise. He covered the flight of his broken forces, turning repeatedly upon their pursuers, and slowly making his retreat into the city.

The inhabitants of Malaga witnessed from their walls, with trembling anxiety, the whole of this disastrous conflict. At the first onset, when they beheld the guards of the camp put to flight, they exclaimed, "Allah has given us the victory!" and they sent up shouts of triumph. Their exultation, however, was soon turned into doubt, when they beheld their troops repulsed in repeated attacks. They could see, from time to time, some distinguished warrior laid low, and others brought back bleeding to the city. When at length

* Garibay, lib. 18, c. 33.

the sacred banner fell, and the routed troops came flying to the gates, pursued and cut down by the foe, horror and despair seized upon the populace.

As Hamet el Zegri entered the gates, he heard nothing but loud lamentations: mothers, whose sons had been slain, shrieked curses after him as he passed; some, in the anguish of their hearts, threw down their famishing babes before him, exclaiming, "Trample on them with thy horse's feet; for we have no food to give them, and we cannot endure their cries." All heaped execrations on his head, as the cause of the woes of Malaga.

The warlike part of the citizens also, and many warriors, who, with their wives and children, had taken refuge in Malaga from the mountain fortresses, now joined in the popular clamor, for their hearts were overcome by the sufferings of their families.

Hamet el Zegri found it impossible to withstand this torrent of lamentations, curses, and reproaches. His military ascendency was at an end; for most of his officers, and the prime warriors of his African band, had fallen in this disastrous sally. Turning his back, therefore, upon the city, and abandoning it to its own counsels, he retired with the remnant of his Comares to his stronghold in the Gibralfaro.

CHAPTER NINETEEN

HOW THE CITY OF MALAGA CAPITULATED

THE people of Malaga, being no longer overawed by Hamet el Zegri and his Comares, turned to Ali Dordux, the magnanimous merchant, and put the fate of the city into his hands. He had already gained the alcaydes of the castle of the Genoese, and of the citadel, into his party, and in the late confusion had gained the sway over those important fortresses. He now associated himself with the alfaqui, Abrahen Alharis and four of the principal inhabitants, and, forming a provisional junta, they sent heralds to the Christian sovereigns, offering to surrender the city on certain terms, protecting the persons and property of the inhabitants, permitting them to reside as Mudexares or tributary vassals, either in Malaga or elsewhere.

When the heralds arrived at the camp, and made known their mission to King Ferdinand, his anger was kindled. "Return to your fellow-citizens," said he, "and tell them that the day of grace is gone by. They have persisted in a fruitless defense, until they are driven by necessity to capitulate; they must surrender unconditionally, and abide the fate of the vanquished. Those who merit death shall suffer death: those who merit captivity shall be made captives."

This stern reply spread consternation among the people of Malaga; but Ali Dordux comforted them, and undertook to go in person and pray for favorable terms. When the people beheld this great and wealthy merchant, who was so eminent in their city, departing with his associates on this mission, they plucked up heart; for they said, "Surely the Christian king will not turn a deaf ear to such a man as Ali Dordux!"

Ferdinand, however, would not even admit the embassadors to his presence. "Send them to the devil!" said he, in a great passion, to the commander of Leon; "I'll not see them. Let them get back to their city. They shall all surrender to my mercy, as vanquished enemies." *

To give emphasis to this reply, he ordered a general discharge from all the artillery and batteries; and there was a great shout throughout the camp, and all the lombards and catapults, and other engines of war, thundered furiously upon the city, doing great damage.

Ali Dordux and his companions returned to the city with downcast countenances, and could scarce make the reply of the Christian sovereign be heard, for the roaring of the artillery, the tumbling of the walls, and the cries of women and

---

* Cura de los Palacios, cap. 84.

children. The citizens were greatly astonished and dismayed, when they found the little respect paid to their most eminent man; but the warriors who were in the city exclaimed, "What has this merchant to do with questions between men of battle? Let us not address the enemy as abject suppliants who have no power to injure, but as valiant men, who have weapons in their hands."

So they dispatched another message to the Christian sovereigns, offering to yield up the city and all their effects, on condition of being secured in their personal liberty. Should this be denied, they declared they would hang from the battlements fifteen hundred Christian captives, male and female; that they would put all their old men, their women and children into the citadel, set fire to the city, and sally forth sword in hand, to fight until the last gasp. "In this way," said they, "the Spanish sovereigns shall gain a bloody victory, and the fall of Malaga be renowned while the world endures."

To this fierce and swelling message, Ferdinand replied that if a single Christian captive were injured not a Moor in Malaga but should be put to the edge of the sword.

A great conflict of counsels now arose in Malaga. The warriors were for following up their menace by some desperate act of vengeance or of self-devotion. Those who had families looked with anguish upon their wives and daughters, and thought it better to die than live to see them captives. By degrees, however, the transports of passion and despair subsided, the love of life resumed its sway, and they turned once more to Ali Dordux, as the man most prudent in council and able in negotiation. By his advice, fourteen of the principal inhabitants were chosen from the fourteen districts of the city, and sent to the camp, bearing a long letter, couched in terms of the most humble supplication.

Various debates now took place in the Christian camp. Many of the cavaliers were exasperated against Malaga for its long resistance, which had caused the death of many of their relations and favorite companions. It had long been a stronghold also for Moorish depredators, and the mart where most of the warriors captured in the Axarquia had been exposed in triumph and sold to slavery. They represented, moreover, that there were many Moorish cities yet to be besieged; and that an example ought to be made of Malaga, to prevent all obstinate resistance thereafter. They advised, therefore, that all the inhabitants should be put to the sword!*

The humane heart of Isabella revolted at such sanguinary counsels: she insisted that their triumph should not be disgraced by cruelty. Ferdinand, however, was inflexible in refusing to grant any preliminary terms, insisting on an unconditional surrender.

The people of Malaga now abandoned themselves to paroxysms of despair; on the one side they saw famine and death, on the other slavery and chains. The mere men of the sword, who had no families to protect, were loud for signalizing their fall by some illustrious action. "Let us sacrifice our Christian captives, and then destroy ourselves," cried some. "Let us put all the women and children to death, set fire to the city, fall on the Christian camp, and die sword in hand," cried others.

Ali Dordux gradually made his voice be heard amid the general clamor. He addressed himself to the principal inhabitants, and to those who had children. "Let those who live by the sword, die by the sword," cried he; "but let us not follow their desperate counsels. Who knows what sparks of pity may be awakened in the bosoms of the Christian sovereigns when they behold our unoffending wives and daughters, and our helpless little ones! The Christian queen, they say, is full of mercy."

At these words, the hearts of the unhappy people of Malaga yearned over their families, and they empowered Ali Dordux to deliver up their city to the mercy of the Castilian sovereigns.

The merchant now went to and fro, and had several communications with Ferdinand and Isabella, and interested

* Pulgar.

several principal cavaliers in his cause; and he sent rich presents to the king and queen, of Oriental merchandise, and silks and stuffs of gold, and jewels and precious stones, and spices and perfumes, and many other sumptuous things which he had accumulated in his great tradings with the east; and he gradually found favor in the eyes of the sovereigns.* Finding that there was nothing to be obtained for the city, he now, like a prudent man and able merchant, began to negotiate for himself and his immediate friends. He represented that from the first they had been desirous of yielding up the city, but had been prevented by warlike and high-handed men, who had threatened their lives: he entreated, therefore, that mercy might be extended to them, and that they might not be confounded with the guilty.

The sovereigns had accepted the presents of Ali Dordux— how could they then turn a deaf ear to his petition? So they granted a pardon to him, and to forty families which he named; and it was agreed that they should be protected in their liberties and property, and permitted to reside in Malaga as Mudexares or Moslem vassals, and to follow their customary pursuits.† All this being arranged, Ali Dordux delivered up twenty of the principal inhabitants, to remain as hostages, until the whole city should be placed in the possession of the Christians.

Don Gutierre de Cardenas, senior commander of Leon, now entered the city, armed cap-a-pie, on horseback, and took possession in the name of the Castilian sovereigns. He was followed by his retainers, and by the captains and cavaliers of the army; and in a little while the standards of the cross, and of the blessed Santiago, and of the Catholic sovereigns, were elevated on the principal tower of the Alcazaba. When these standards were beheld from the camp, the queen and the princess and the ladies of the court, and all the royal retinue, knelt down and gave thanks and praises to the Holy Virgin and to Santiago, for this great triumph of the faith;

---

* MS. Chron. of Valera.   † Cura de los Palacios.

and the bishops and other clergy who were present, and the choristers of the royal chapel, chanted "*Te Deum Lauda-mus*," and "*Gloria in Excelsis*."

CHAPTER TWENTY

FULFILLMENT OF THE PROPHECY OF THE DERVISE—FATE OF HAMET EL ZEGRI

No sooner was the city delivered up than the wretched inhabitants implored permission to purchase bread for themselves and their children, from the heaps of grain which they had so often gazed at wistfully from their walls. Their prayer was granted, and they issued forth with the famished eagerness of starving men. It was piteous to behold the struggles of those unhappy people, as they contended who first should have their necessities relieved.

"Thus," says the pious Fray Antonio Agapida, "thus are the predictions of false prophets sometimes permitted to be verified, but always to the confusion of those who trust in them; for the words of the Moorish necromancer came to pass, that the people of Malaga should eat of those heaps of bread; but they ate in humiliation and defeat, and with sorrow and bitterness of heart."

Dark and fierce were the feelings of Hamet el Zegri, as he looked down from the castle of Gibralfaro and beheld the Christian legions pouring into the city, and the standard of the cross supplanting the crescent on the citadel. "The people of Malaga," said he, "have trusted to a man of trade, and he has trafficked them away; but let us not suffer ourselves to be bound hand and foot, and delivered up as part of his bargain. We have yet strong walls around us and trusty weapons in our hands. Let us fight until buried beneath the last tumbling tower of Gibralfaro, or, rushing down from among its ruins, carry havoc among the unbelievers, as they throng the streets of Malaga!"

The fierceness of the Comares, however, was broken. They could have died in the breach, had their castle been assailed; but the slow advances of famine subdued their strength without rousing their passions, and sapped the force both of soul and body.   They were almost unanimous for a surrender.

It was a hard struggle for the proud spirit of Hamet to bow itself to ask for terms.   Still he trusted that the valor of his defense would gain him respect in the eyes of a chivalrous foe.   "Ali," said he. "has negotiated like a merchant; I will capitulate as a soldier."   He sent a herald, therefore, to Ferdinand, offering to yield up his castle, but demanding a separate treaty.*   The Castilian sovereign made a laconic and stern reply: "He shall receive no terms but such as have been granted to the community of Malaga."

For two days Hamet el Zegri remained brooding in his castle, after the city was in possession of the Christians; at length, the clamors of his followers compelled him to surrender.   When the broken remnant of this fierce African garrison descended from their cragged fortress, they were so worn by watchfulness, famine and battle, yet carried such a lurking fury in their eyes, that they looked more like fiends than men.   They were all condemned to slavery, excepting Alrahan Zenete.   The instance of clemency which he had shown in refraining to harm the Spanish striplings, on the last sally from Malaga, won him favorable terms.   It was cited as a magnanimous act by the Spanish cavaliers, and all admitted, that, though a Moor in blood, he possessed the Christian heart of a Castilian hidalgo.†

As to Hamet el Zegri, on being asked what moved him to such hardened obstinacy, he replied: "When I undertook my command, I pledged myself to fight in defense of my faith, my city, and my sovereign, until slain or made prisoner; and, depend upon it, had I had men to stand by me, I

---

* Cura de los Palacios.   † Cura de los Palacios, cap. 84.

should have died fighting, instead of thus tamely surrendering myself without a weapon in my hand."

"Such," says the pious Fray Antonio Agapida, "was the diabolical hatred and stiff-necked opposition of this Infidel to our holy cause. But he was justly served by our most Catholic and high-minded sovereign for his pertinacious defense of the city; for Ferdinand ordered that he should be loaded with chains and thrown into a dungeon."*

CHAPTER TWENTY-ONE

HOW THE CASTILIAN SOVEREIGNS TOOK POSSESSION OF THE CITY OF MALAGA, AND HOW KING FERDINAND SIGNALIZED HIMSELF BY HIS SKILL IN BARGAINING WITH THE INHABITANTS FOR THEIR RANSOM

One of the first cares of the conquerors, on entering Malaga, was to search for Christian captives. Nearly sixteen hundred men and women were found, and among them were persons of distinction. Some of them had been ten, fifteen, and twenty years in captivity. Many had been servants to the Moors, or laborers on public works, and some had passed their time in chains and dungeons. Preparations were made to celebrate their deliverance as a Christian triumph. A tent was erected not far from the city, and furnished with an altar and all the solemn decorations of a chapel. Here the king and queen waited to receive the Christian captives. They were assembled in the city and marshaled forth in piteous procession. Many of them had still the chains and shackles on their legs; they were wasted with famine, their hair and beards overgrown and matted, and their faces pale and haggard from long confinement. When they beheld themselves restored to liberty, and sur-

---

* Pulgar. Cronica.

rounded by their countrymen, some stared wildly about as if in a dream, others gave way to frantic transports, but most of them wept for joy. All present were moved to tears by so touching a spectacle. When the procession arrived at what is called the Gate of Granada, it was met by a great concourse from the camp, with crosses and pennons, who turned and followed the captives, singing hymns of praise and thanksgiving. When they came in presence of the king and queen, they threw themselves on their knees and would have kissed their feet, as their saviors and deliverers; but the sovereigns prevented such humiliation, and graciously extended to them their hands. They then prostrated themselves before the altar, and all present joined them in giving thanks to God for their liberation from this cruel bondage. By orders of the king and queen, their chains were then taken off, and they were clad in decent raiment, and food was set before them. After they had eat and drank, and were refreshed and invigorated, they were provided with money and all things necessary for their journey, and were sent joyfully to their homes.

While the old chroniclers dwell with becoming enthusiasm on this pure and affecting triumph of humanity, they go on, in a strain of equal eulogy, to describe a spectacle of a far different nature. It so happened, that there were found in the city twelve of those renegado Christians who had deserted to the Moors and conveyed false intelligence during the siege: a barbarous species of punishment was inflicted upon them, borrowed, it is said, from the Moors, and peculiar to these wars. They were tied to stakes in a public place, and horsemen exercised their skill in transpiercing them with pointed reeds, hurled at them while careering at full speed, until the miserable victims expired beneath their wounds. Several apostate Moors, also, who, having embraced Christianity, had afterward relapsed into their early faith and had taken refuge in Malaga from the vengeance of the Inquisition, were publicly burned. "These," says an old Jesuit historian, exultingly, "these were the tilts of reeds and the illuminations most pleasing for this victorious festival, and for the Catholic piety of our sovereigns!"*

When the city was cleansed from the impurities and offensive odors which had collected during the siege, the bishops and other clergy who accompanied the court, and the choir of the royal chapel, walked in procession to the principal mosque, which was consecrated, and entitled Santa Maria de la Incarnacion. This done, the king and queen entered the city, accompanied by the grand cardinal of Spain, and the principal nobles and cavaliers of the army, and heard a solemn mass. The church was then elevated into a cathedral, and Malaga was made a bishopric, and many of the neighboring towns were comprehended in its diocese. The queen took up her residence in the Alcazaba, in the apartments of her valiant treasurer, Ruy Lopez, from whence she had a view of the whole city; but the king established his quarters in the warrior castle of Gibralfaro.

And now came to be considered the disposition of the Moorish prisoners. All those who were strangers in the city, and had either taken refuge there, or had entered to defend it, were at once considered slaves. They were divided into three lots: one was set apart for the service of God, in redeeming Christian captives from bondage, either in the kingdom of Granada or in Africa; the second lot was divided among those who had aided either in field or cabinet, in the present siege, according to their rank; the third was appropriated to defray, by their sale, the great expenses incurred in the reduction of the place. A hundred of the Comares were sent as presents to Pope Innocent VIII., and were led in triumph through the streets of Rome, and afterward converted to Christianity. Fifty Moorish maidens were sent to the Queen Joanna of Naples, sister to King Ferdinand, and thirty to the Queen of Portugal. Isabella made presents of

---

* "Los renegados fueron acañavareados; y los conversos quemados; y estos fueron las cañas, y luminarias mas alegres, por la fiesta de la vitoria, para la piedad Catholica de nuestros Reyes."—"Abarca, Annales de Aragon," tom. 2, Rey xxx., c. 3.

others to the ladies of her household, and of the noble families of Spain.

Among the inhabitants of Malaga were four hundred and fifty Moorish Jews, for the most part women, speaking the Arabic language and dressed in the Morisco fashion. These were ransomed by a wealthy Jew of Castile, farmer-general of the royal revenues derived from the Jews of Spain. He agreed to make up, within a certain time, the sum of twenty thousand doblas, or pistoles of gold; all the money and jewels of the captives being taken in part payment. They were sent to Castile, in two armed galleys.

As to the great mass of Moorish inhabitants, they implored that they might not be scattered and sold into captivity, but might be permitted to ransom themselves by an amount paid within a certain time. Upon this King Ferdinand took the advice of certain of his ablest counselors: they said to him, "If you hold out a prospect of hopeless captivity, the Infidels will throw all their gold and jewels into wells and pits, and you will lose the greater part of the spoil; but if you fix a general rate of ransom, and receive their money and jewels in part payment, nothing will be destroyed." The king relished greatly this advice; and it was arranged that all the inhabitants should be ransomed at the general rate of thirty doblas or pistoles in gold for each individual, male or female, large or small; that all their gold, jewels, and other valuables should be received immediately in part payment of the general amount, and that the residue should be paid within eight months; that if any of the number, actually living, should die in the interim, their ransom should nevertheless be paid. If, however, the whole of the amount were not paid at the expiration of the eight months, they should all be considered and treated as slaves.

The unfortunate Moors were eager to catch at the least hope of future liberty, and consented to these hard conditions. The most rigorous precautions were taken to exact them to the uttermost. The inhabitants were numbered by houses and families, and their names taken down; their most precious effects were made up into parcels, and sealed and inscribed with their names; and they were ordered to repair with them to certain large corrales or inclosures adjoining the Alcazaba, which were surrounded by high walls and overlooked by watch-towers, to which places the cavalgadas of Christian captives had usually been driven, to be confined, until the time of sale, like cattle in a market. The Moors were obliged to leave their houses one by one; all their money, necklaces, bracelets and anklets of gold, pearl, coral, and precious stones, were taken from them at the threshold, and their persons so rigorously searched that they carried off nothing concealed.

Then might be seen old men and helpless women, and tender maidens, some of high birth and gentle condition, passing through the streets, heavily burdened, toward the Alcazaba. As they left their homes, they smote their breasts, and wrung their hands, and raised their weeping eyes to heaven in anguish; and this is recorded as their plaint: "O Malaga! city so renowned and beautiful! where now is the strength of thy castles, where the grandeur of thy towers? Of what avail have been thy mighty walls, for the protection of thy children? Behold them driven from thy pleasant abodes, doomed to drag out a life of bondage in a foreign land, and to die far from the home of their infancy! What will become of thy old men and matrons when their gray hairs shall be no longer reverenced? What will become of thy maidens, so delicately reared and tenderly cherished, when reduced to hard and menial servitude? Behold, thy once happy families are scattered asunder, never again to be united; sons are separated from their fathers, husbands from their wives, and tender children from their mothers: they will bewail each other in foreign lands, but their lamentations will be the scoff of the stranger. O Malaga! city of our birth! who can behold thy desolation and not shed tears of bitterness?" *

---

* Pulgar.

When Malaga was completely secured, a detachment was sent against two fortresses near the sea, called Mixas and Osuna, which had frequently harassed the Christian camp. The inhabitants were threatened with the sword unless they instantly surrendered. They claimed the same terms that had been granted to Malaga, imagining them to be freedom of person and security of property. Their claim was granted; they were transported to Malaga with all their riches, and, on arriving there, were overwhelmed with consternation at finding themselves captives. "Ferdinand," observes Fray Antonio Agapida, "was a man of his word; they were shut up in the inclosure at the Alcazaba with the people of Malaga, and shared their fate."

The unhappy captives remained thus crowded in the courtyards of the Alcazaba, like sheep in a fold, until they could be sent by sea and land to Seville. They were then distributed about in city and country, each Christian family having one or more to feed and maintain as servants, until the term fixed for the payment of the residue of the ransom should expire. The captives had obtained permission that several of their number should go about among the Moorish towns of the kingdom of Granada, collecting contributions to aid in the purchase of their liberties; but these towns were too much impoverished by the war, and engrossed by their own distresses, to lend a listening ear: so the time expired without the residue of the ransom being paid, and all the captives of Malaga, to the number, as some say, of eleven, and others of fifteen thousand, became slaves! "Never," exclaims the worthy Fray Antonio Agapida, in one of his usual bursts of zeal and loyalty, "never has there been recorded a more adroit and sagacious arrangement than this made by the Catholic monarch, by which he not only secured all the property and half of the ransom of these Infidels, but finally got possession of their persons into the bargain. This truly may be considered one of the greatest triumphs of the pious and politic Ferdinand, and as raising him above the generality of conquerors, who have merely the valor to gain victories, but lack the prudence and management necessary to turn them to account.''

CHAPTER TWENTY-TWO

HOW KING FERDINAND PREPARED TO CARRY THE WAR INTO A DIFFERENT PART OF THE TERRITORIES OF THE MOORS

THE western part of the kingdom of Granada had now been conquered by the Christian arms. The seaport of Malaga was captured: the fierce and warlike inhabitants of the Serrania de Ronda, and the other mountain holds of the frontier, were all disarmed and reduced to peaceful and laborious vassalage; their haughty fortresses, which had so long overawed the valleys of Andalusia, now displayed the standard of Castile and Aragon; the watch-towers, which crowned every height, and from whence the Infidels had kept a vulture eye over the Christian territories, were now either dismantled or garrisoned with Catholic troops. ''What signalized and sanctified this great triumph,'' adds the worthy Fray Antonio Agapida, ''were the emblems of ecclesiastical domination which everywhere appeared. In every direction arose stately convents and monasteries, those fortresses of the faith, garrisoned by its spiritual soldiery of monks and friars. The sacred melody of Christian bells was again heard among the mountains, calling to early matins, or sounding the Angeles at the solemn hour of evening.''

While this part of the kingdom was thus reduced by the Christian sword, the central part, round the city of Granada, forming the heart of the Moorish territory, was held in vassalage of the Castilian monarch, by Boabdil surnamed el Chico. That unfortunate prince lost no occasion to propitiate the conquerors of his country by acts of homage, and by professions that must have been foreign to his heart. No sooner had he heard of the capture of Malaga than he sent congratulations to the Catholic sovereigns, accompanied with presents of horses richly caparisoned for the king, and precious cloth of gold and Oriental perfumes for the queen. His congratulations and his presents were received with the utmost graciousness; and the shortsighted prince, lulled by the temporary and politic forbearance of Ferdinand, flattered himself that he was securing the lasting friendship of that monarch.

The policy of Boabdil had its transient and superficial advantages. The portion of Moorish territory under his immediate sway had a respite from the calamities of war: the husbandmen cultivated their luxuriant fields in security, and the vega of Granada once more blossomed like the rose. The merchants again carried on a gainful traffic; the gates of the city were thronged with beasts of burden, bringing the rich products of every clime. Yet, while the people of Granada rejoiced in their teeming fields and crowded marts, they secretly despised the policy which had procured them these advantages, and held Boabdil for little better than an apostate and an unbeliever. Muley Abdalla el Zagal was now the hope of the unconquered part of the kingdom; and every Moor, whose spirit was not quite subdued with his fortunes, lauded the valor of the old monarch and his fidelity to the faith, and wished success to his standard.

El Zagal, though he no longer sat enthroned in the Alhambra, yet reigned over more considerable domains than his nephew. His territories extended from the frontier of Jaen along the borders of Murcia to the Mediterranean, and reached into the center of the kingdom. On the northeast, he held the cities of Baza and Guadix, situated in the midst of fertile regions. He had the important seaport of Almeria, also, which at one time rivaled Granada itself in wealth and population. Besides these, his territories included a great part of the Alpuxarra mountains, which extend across the kingdom and shoot out branches toward the seacoast. This mountainous region was a stronghold of wealth and power. Its stern and rocky heights, rising to the clouds, seemed to set invasion at defiance; yet within their rugged embraces were sheltered delightful valleys, of the happiest temperature and richest fertility. The cool springs and limpid rills which gushed out in all parts of the mountains, and the abundant streams which, for a great part of the year, were supplied by the Sierra Nevada, spread a perpetual verdure over the skirts and slopes of the hills, and, collecting in silver rivers in the valleys, wound along among plantations of mulberry trees, and groves of oranges and citrons, of almonds, figs, and pomegranates. Here was produced the finest silk of Spain, which gave employment to thousands of manufacturers. The sunburned sides of the hills, also, were covered with vineyards; the abundant herbage of the mountain ravines, and the rich pasturage of the valleys, fed vast flocks and herds; and even the arid and rocky bosoms of the heights teemed with wealth, from the mines of various metals with which they were impregnated. In a word, the Alpuxarra mountains had ever been the great source of revenue to the monarchs of Granada. Their inhabitants, also, were hardy and warlike, and a sudden summons from the Moorish king could at any time call forth fifty thousand fighting men from their rocky fastnesses.

Such was the rich but rugged fragment of an empire which remained under the sway of the old warrior monarch El Zagal. The mountain barriers by which it was locked up had protected it from most of the ravages of the present war. El Zagal prepared himself, by strengthening every fortress, to battle fiercely for its maintenance.

The Catholic sovereigns saw that fresh troubles and toils awaited them. The war had to be carried into a new quarter, demanding immense expenditures; and new ways and means must be devised to replenish their exhausted coffers. "As this was a holy war, however," says Fray Antonio Agapida, "and peculiarly redounded to the prosperity of the church, the clergy were full of zeal, and contributed vast sums of money and large bodies of troops. A pious fund was also produced, from the first fruits of that glorious institution, the Inquisition."

It so happened that about this time there were many families of wealth and dignity in the kingdoms of Aragon and Valencia, and the principality of Catalonia, whose forefathers had been Jews, but had been converted to Christianity. Notwithstanding the outward piety of these families, it was surmised, and soon came to be strongly suspected, that many of them had a secret hankering after Judaism; and it was even whispered that some of them practiced Jewish rites in private.

The Catholic monarch (continues Agapida) had a righteous abhorrence of all kinds of heresy, and a fervent zeal for the faith; he ordered, therefore, a strict investigation of the conduct of these pseudo-Christians. Inquisitors were sent into these provinces for the purpose, who proceeded with their accustomed zeal. The consequence was that many families were convicted of apostasy from the Christian faith, and of the private practice of Judaism. Some, who had grace and policy sufficient to reform in time, were again received into the Christian fold, after being severely mulcted and condemned to heavy penance; others were burned at *auto da fés*, for the edification of the public, and their property was confiscated for the good of the state.

As these Hebrews were of great wealth, and had a hereditary passion for jewelry, there was found abundant store in their possession of gold and silver, of rings and necklaces, and strings of pearl and coral, and precious stones; treasures easy of transportation and wonderfully adapted for the emergencies of war. "In this way," concludes the pious Agapida, "these backsliders, by the all-seeing contrivances of Providence, were made to serve the righteous cause which they had so treacherously deserted; and their apostate wealth was sanctified by being devoted to the service of Heaven and the crown, in this holy crusade against the Infidels."

It must be added, however, that these pious financial expedients received some check from the interference of Queen Isabella. Her penetrating eyes discovered that many enormities had been committed under color of religious zeal, and many innocent persons accused by false witnesses of apostasy, either through malice or a hope of obtaining their wealth; she caused strict investigation, therefore, into the proceedings which had been held; many of which were reversed, and suborners punished in proportion to their guilt. *

CHAPTER TWENTY-THREE

HOW KING FERDINAND INVADED THE EASTERN SIDE OF THE KINGDOM OF GRANADA, AND HOW HE WAS RE- CEIVED BY EL ZAGAL

"MULEY ABDALLA EL ZAGAL," says the venerable Jesuit father, Pedro Abarca, "was the most venomous Mahometan in all Morisma:" and the worthy Fray Antonio Agapida most devoutly echoes his opinion: "Certainly," adds the latter, "none ever opposed a more heathenish and diabolical ob- stinacy to the holy inroads of the cross and sword."

El Zagal felt that it was necessary to do something to quicken his popularity with the people, and that nothing was more effectual than a successful inroad. The Moors loved the stirring call to arms, and a wild foray among the moun- tains; and delighted more in a hasty spoil, wrested with hard fighting from the Christians, than in all the steady and certain gains secured by peaceful traffic.

There reigned at this time a careless security along the frontier of Jaen. The alcaydes of the Christian fortresses were confident of the friendship of Boabdil el Chico, and they fancied his uncle too distant and too much engrossed by his own perplexities to think of molesting them. On a sud- den, El Zagal issued out of Guadix with a chosen band, passed rapidly through the mountains which extend behind Granada, and fell like a thunderbolt upon the territories in the neighborhood of Alcala la Real. Before the alarm could

* Pulgar, part 3, c. 100.

be spread and the frontier roused, he had made a wide career of destruction through the country, sacking and burning villages, sweeping off flocks and herds, and carrying away captives. The warriors of the frontier assembled; but El Zagal was already far on his return through the mountains; and he re-entered the gates of Guadix in triumph, his army laden with Christian spoil, and conducting an immense cavalgada. Such was one of the fierce El Zagal's preparatives for the expected invasion of the Christian king, exciting the warlike spirit of his people, and gaining for himself a transient popularity.

King Ferdinand assembled his army at Murcia in the spring of 1488. He left that city on the fifth of June, with a flying camp of four thousand horse and fourteen thousand foot. The Marques of Cadiz led the van, followed by the adelantado of Murcia. The army entered the Moorish frontier by the seacoast, spreading terror through the land; wherever it appeared, the towns surrendered without a blow, so great was the dread of experiencing the woes which had desolated the opposite frontier. In this way, Vera, Velez el Rubio, Velez el Blanco, and many towns of inferior note, to the number of sixty, yielded at the first summons.

It was not until it approached Almeria that the army met with resistance. This important city was commanded by the Prince Zelim, a relation of El Zagal. He led forth his Moors bravely to the encounter, and skirmished fiercely with the advance guard in the gardens near the city. King Ferdinand came up with the main body of the army, and called off his troops from the skirmish. He saw that to attack the place with his present force was fruitless. Having reconnoitered the city and its environs, therefore, against a future campaign, he retired with his army and marched toward Baza.

The old warrior El Zagal was himself drawn up in the city of Baza, with a powerful garrison. He felt confidence in the strength of the place, and rejoiced when he heard that the Christian king was approaching. In the valley in front of Baza there extended a great tract of gardens, like a continued grove, and intersected by canals and watercourses. In this he stationed a powerful ambuscade of arquebusiers and crossbowmen. The vanguard of the Christian army came marching gayly up the valley, with great sound of drum and trumpet, and led on by the Marques of Cadiz and the adelantado of Murcia. As they drew near, El Zagal sallied forth with horse and foot, and attacked them for a time with great spirit. Gradually falling back, as if pressed by their superior valor, he drew the exulting Christians among the gardens. Suddenly the Moors in ambuscade burst from their concealment, and opened such a terrible fire in flank and rear that many of the Christians were slain, and the rest thrown into confusion. King Ferdinand arrived in time to see the disastrous situation of his troops, and gave signal for the vanguard to retire.

El Zagal did not permit the foe to draw off unmolested. Ordering out fresh squadrons, he fell upon the rear of the retreating troops with loud and triumphant shouts, driving them before him with dreadful havoc. The old war-cry of "El Zagal! El Zagal!" was again put up by the Moors, and was echoed with transport from the walls of the city. The Christians were for a time in imminent peril of a complete rout, when fortunately the adelantado of Murcia threw himself with a large body of horse and foot between the pursuers and the pursued, covering the retreat of the latter, and giving them time to rally. The Moors were now attacked so vigorously in turn that they gave over the unequal contest, and drew back slowly into the city. Many valiant cavaliers were slain in this skirmish, among the number of whom was Don Philip of Aragon, Master of the chivalry of St. George of Montesor; he was illegitimate son of the king's illegitimate brother Don Carlos, and his death was greatly bewailed by Ferdinand. He had formerly been archbishop of Palermo, but had doffed the cassock for the cuirass, and had thus, according to Fray Antonio Agapida, gained a glorious crown of martyrdom by falling in this holy war.

The warm reception of his advance guard by the old warrior El Zagal brought King Ferdinand to a pause: he encamped on the banks of the neighboring river Guadalquiton, and began to consider whether he had acted wisely in undertaking this campaign with his present force. His late successes had probably rendered him overconfident: El Zagal had again schooled him into his characteristic caution. He saw that the old warrior was too formidably ensconced in Baza to be dislodged by anything except a powerful army and battering artillery; and he feared that, should he persist in his invasion, some disaster might befall his army, either from the enterprise of the foe or from a pestilence which prevailed in various parts of the country.

Ferdinand retired, therefore, from before Baza, as he had on a former occasion from before Loxa, all the wiser for a wholesome lesson in warfare, but by no means grateful to those who had given it, and with a solemn determination to have his revenge upon his teachers.

He now took measures for the security of the places gained in this campaign; placing in them strong garrisons, well armed and supplied, charging their alcaydes to be vigilant on their posts and to give no rest to the enemy. The whole of the frontier was placed under the command of the brave Luis Fernandez Puerto Carrero. As it was evident, from the warlike character of El Zagal, that there would be abundance of active service and hard fighting, many hidalgos and young cavaliers, eager for distinction, remained with Puerto Carrero.

All these dispositions being made, King Ferdinand closed the dubious campaign of this year, not, as usual, by returning in triumph at the head of his army to some important city of his dominions, but by disbanding the troops, and repairing to pray at the cross of Caravaca.

CHAPTER TWENTY-FOUR

HOW THE MOORS MADE VARIOUS ENTERPRISES AGAINST THE CHRISTIANS

"While the pious King Ferdinand," observes Fray Antonio Agapida, "was humbling himself before the cross, and devoutly praying for the destruction of his enemies, that fierce pagan El Zagal, depending merely on his arm of flesh and sword of steel, pursued his diabolical outrages upon the Christians." No sooner was the invading army disbanded than El Zagal sallied forth from his stronghold, and carried fire and sword into all those parts that had submitted to the Spanish yoke. The castle of Nixar, being carelessly guarded, was taken by surprise, and its garrison put to the sword. The old warrior raged with sanguinary fury about the whole frontier, attacking convoys, slaying, wounding, and making prisoners, and coming by surprise upon the Christians wherever they were off their guard.

The alcayde of the fortress of Cullar, confiding in the strength of its walls and towers, and in its difficult situation, being built on the summit of a lofty hill, and surrounded by precipices, ventured to absent himself from his post. The vigilant El Zagal was suddenly before it, with a powerful force: he stormed the town sword in hand, fought the Christians from street to street, and drove them with great slaughter to the citadel. Here a veteran captain by the name of Juan de Avalos, a gray-headed warrior scarred in many a battle, assumed the command and made an obstinate defense. Neither the multitude of the enemy, nor the vehemence of their attacks, though led on by the terrible El Zagal himself, had power to shake the fortitude of this doughty old soldier.

The Moors undermined the outer walls and one of the towers of the fortress, and made their way into the exterior court. The alcayde manned the tops of his towers, pouring down melted pitch, and showering darts, arrows, stones, and all kinds of missiles, upon the assailants. The Moors were driven out of the court; but, being re-enforced with fresh troops, returned repeatedly to the assault. For five days the combat was kept up: the Christians were nearly exhausted, but they were sustained by the cheerings of their stanch old alcayde; and they feared death from the cruel El Zagal should they surrender. At length the approach of a powerful force under Puerto Carrero relieved them from this fearful peril. El Zagal abandoned the assault, but set fire to the town in his rage and disappointment, and retired to his stronghold of Guadix.

The example of El Zagal roused his adherents to action. Two bold Moorish alcaydes, Ali Altar and Yza Altar, commanding the fortresses of Alhenden and Salobrena, laid waste the country of the subjects of Boabdil, and the places which had recently submitted to the Christians: they swept off the cattle, carried off captives, and harassed the whole of the newly conquered frontier.

The Moors also of Almeria, and Tavernas, and Purchena, made inroads into Murcia, and carried fire and sword into its most fertile regions. On the opposite frontier, also, among the wild valleys and rugged recesses of the Sierra Bormeja, or Red Mountains, many of the Moors who had lately submitted again flew to arms. The Marques of Cadiz suppressed by timely vigilance the rebellion of the mountain town of Gausin, situated on a high peak, almost among the clouds; but others of the Moors fortified themselves in rock-built towers and castles, inhabited solely by warriors, from whence they carried on a continual war of forage and depredation; sweeping suddenly down into the valleys, and carrying off flocks and herds and all kinds of booty to these eagle-nests, to which it was perilous and fruitless to pursue them.

The worthy Fray Antonio Agapida closes his history of this checkered year in quite a different strain from those triumphant periods with which he is accustomed to wind up the victorious campaigns of the sovereigns. "Great and mighty," says this venerable chronicler, "were the floods and tempests which prevailed throughout the kingdoms of Castile and Aragon, about this time. It seemed as though the windows of Heaven were again opened, and a second deluge overwhelming the face of nature. The clouds burst as it were in cataracts upon the earth; torrents rushed down from the mountains, overflowing the valleys; brooks were swelled into raging rivers; houses were undermined; mills were swept away by their own streams; the affrighted shepherds saw their flocks drowned in the midst of the pasture, and were fain to take refuge for their lives in towers and high places. The Guadalquivir for a time became a roaring and tumultuous sea, inundating the immense plain of the Zablada, and filling the fair city of Seville with affright.

"A vast black cloud moved over the land, accompanied by a hurricane and a trembling of the earth. Houses were unroofed, the walls and battlements of fortresses shaken, and lofty towers rocked to their foundations. Ships, riding at anchor, were either stranded or swallowed up; others, under sail, were tossed to and fro upon mountain waves, and cast upon the land, where the whirlwind rent them in pieces and scattered them in fragments in the air. Doleful was the ruin and great the terror, where this baleful cloud passed by; and it left a long track of desolation over sea and land. Some of the faint-hearted," adds Antonio Agapida, "looked upon this torment of the elements as a prodigious event, out of the course of nature. In the weakness of their fears, they connected it with those troubles which occurred in various places, considering it a portent of some great calamity, about to be wrought by the violence of the bloody-handed El Zagal and his fierce adherents."

CHAPTER TWENTY-FIVE

HOW KING FERDINAND PREPARED TO BESIEGE THE CITY OF BAZA, AND HOW THE CITY PREPARED FOR DEFENSE

THE stormy winter had passed away, and the spring of 1489 was advancing; yet the heavy rains had broken up the roads, the mountain brooks were swollen to raging torrents, and the late shallow and peaceful rivers were deep, turbulent and dangerous. The Christian troops had been summoned to assemble in early spring on the frontiers of Jaen, but were slow in arriving at the appointed place. They were entangled in the miry defiles of the mountains, or fretted impatiently on the banks of impassable floods. It was late in the month of May before they assembled in sufficient force to attempt the proposed invasion; when, at length, a valiant army, of thirteen thousand horse and forty thousand foot, marched merrily over the border. The queen remained at the city of Jaen, with the prince-royal and the princesses her children, accompanied and supported by the venerable cardinal of Spain, and those reverend prelates who assisted in her councils throughout this holy war.

The plan of King Ferdinand was to lay siege to the city of Baza, the key of the remaining possessions of the Moor. That important fortress taken, Guadix and Almeria must soon follow, and then the power of El Zagal would be at an end. As the Catholic king advanced, he had first to secure various castles and strongholds in the vicinity of Baza, which might otherwise harass his army. Some of these made obstinate resistance, especially the town of Cuxar. The Christians assailed the walls with various machines, to sap them and batter them down. The brave alcayde, Hubec Adalgan, opposed force to force and engine to engine. He manned his towers with his bravest warriors, who rained

down an iron snower upon the enemy; and he linked cal-
drons together by strong chains, and cast fire from them,
consuming the wooden engines of their assailants, and those
who managed them.

The siege was protracted for several days: the bravery of
the alcayde could not save his fortress from an overwhelming
foe, but it gained him honorable terms. Ferdinand permitted
the garrison and the inhabitants to repair with their effects
to Baza; and the valiant Hubec Adalgan marched forth with
the remnant of his force, and took the way to that devoted
city.

The delays which had been caused to the invading army
by these various circumstances, had been diligently improved
by the old Moorish monarch El Zagal; who felt that he was
now making his last stand for empire, and that this campaign would decide whether he should continue a king, or
sink into a vassal. El Zagal was but a few leagues from
Baza, at the city of Guadix. This last was the most important point of his remaining territories, being a kind of
bulwark between them and the hostile city of Granada, the
seat of his nephew's power. Though he heard of the tide of
war, therefore, that was collecting and rolling toward the
city of Baza, he dared not go in person to its assistance. He
dreaded that, should he leave Guadix, Boabdil would attack
him in rear while the Christian army was battling with
him in front. El Zagal trusted in the great strength of Baza
to defy any violent assault; and he profited by the delays of
the Christian army to supply it with all possible means of
defense. He sent thither all the troops he could spare from
his garrison of Guadix, and dispatched missives throughout
his territories, calling upon true Moslems to hasten to Baza,
to make a devoted stand in defense of their homes, their
liberties, and their religion. The cities of Tavernas and
Purchena, and the surrounding heights and valleys, responded to his orders, and sent forth their fighting men to
the field. The rocky fastnesses of the Alpuxarras resounded
with the din of arms: troops of horse and bodies of foot-

soldiers were seen winding down the rugged cliffs and defiles of those marble mountains, and hastening toward Baza. Many brave cavaliers of Granada also, spurning the quiet and security of Christian vassalage, secretly left the city and hastened to join their fighting countrymen. The great dependence of El Zagal, however, was upon the valor and loyalty of his cousin and brother-in law, Cidi Yahye Alnayar Aben Zelim, who was alcayde of Almeria—a cavalier experienced in warfare and redoubtable in the field. He wrote to him to leave Almeria and repair, with all speed, at the head of his troops, to Baza. Cidi Yahye departed immediately, with ten thousand of the bravest Moors in the kingdom. These were for the most part hardy mountaineers, tempered to sun and storm, and tried in many a combat. None equaled them for a sally or a skirmish. They were adroit in executing a thousand stratagems, ambuscadoes, and evolutions. Impetuous in their assaults, yet governed in their utmost fury by a word or sign from their commander, at the sound of a trumpet they would check themselves in the midst of their career, wheel off and disperse; and at another sound of a trumpet, they would as suddenly re-assemble and return to the attack. They were upon the enemy when least expected, coming like a rushing blast, spreading havoc and consternation, and then passing away in an instant; so that when one recovered from the shock and looked around, behold nothing was to be seen or heard of this tempest of war, but a cloud of dust and the clatter of retreating hoofs.

When Cidi Yahye led his train of ten thousand valiant warriors into the gates of Baza, the city rang with acclamations, and for a time the inhabitants thought themselves secure. El Zagal, also, felt a glow of confidence notwithstanding his own absence from the city. "Cidi Yahye," said he, "is my cousin and my brother-in-law; related to me by blood and marriage, he is a second self: happy is that monarch who has his kindred to command his armies."

With all these re-enforcements, the garrison of Baza amounted to above twenty thousand men. There were at this time three principal leaders in the city—Mohammed ben Hassan, surnamed the veteran, who was military governor or alcayde, an old Moor of great experience and discretion; the second was Hamet Abu Zali, who was captain of the troops stationed in the place; and the third was Hubec Adalgan, the valiant alcayde of Cuxar, who had repaired hither with the remains of his garrison. Over all these Cidi Yahye exercised a supreme command, in consequence of his being of the blood-royal, and in the especial confidence of Muley Abdalla el Zagal. He was eloquent and ardent in council, and fond of striking and splendid achievements; but he was a little prone to be carried away by the excitement of the moment and the warmth of his imagination. The councils of war of these commanders, therefore, were more frequently controlled by the opinions of the old alcayde Mohammed ben Hassan, for whose shrewdness, caution and experience Cidi Yahye himself felt the greatest deference.

The city of Baza was situated in a great valley, eight leagues in length and three in breadth, called the Hoya, or basin of Baza. It was surrounded by a range of mountains called the Sierra of Xabalcohol, the streams of which, collecting themselves into two rivers, watered and fertilized the country. The city was built in the plain; but one part of it was protected by the rocky precipices of the mountain, and by a powerful citadel; the other part was defended by massive walls, studded with immense towers. It had suburbs toward the plain, imperfectly fortified by earthen walls. In front of these suburbs extended a tract of orchards and gardens, nearly a league in length, so thickly planted as to resemble a continued forest. Here, every citizen who could afford it had his little plantation, and his garden of fruits and flowers and vegetables, watered by canals and rivulets, and dominated by a small tower to serve for recreation or defense. This wilderness of groves and gardens, intersected in all parts by canals and runs of water, and studded by above a thousand small towers, formed a kind of protection to this side of the city, rendering all approach extremely

difficult and perplexed, and affording covert to the defenders.

While the Christian army had been detained before the
frontier posts, the city of Baza had been a scene of hurried
and unremitting preparation. All the grain of the surrounding valley, though yet unripe, was hastily reaped and borne
into the city, to prevent it yielding sustenance to the enemy.
The country was drained of all its supplies; flocks and herds
were driven, bleating and bellowing, into the gates; long
trains of beasts of burden, some laden with food, others with
lances, darts, and arms of all kinds, kept pouring into the
place. Already there were munitions collected sufficient for
a siege of fifteen months; yet still the eager and hasty preparation was going on, when the army of Ferdinand came
in sight.

On one side might be seen scattered parties of foot and
horse spurring to the gates, and muleteers hurrying forward
their burdened animals, all anxious to get under shelter
before the gathering storm; on the other side, the cloud of
war came sweeping down the valley, the roll of drum or
clang of trumpet resounding occasionally from its deep bosom,
or the bright glance of arms flashing forth, like vivid lightning, from its columns. King Ferdinand pitched his tents in
the valley, beyond the green labyrinth of gardens. He sent
his heralds to summon the city to surrender, promising the
most favorable terms in case of immediate compliance, and
avowing in the most solemn terms his resolution never to
abandon the siege until he had possession of the place.

Upon receiving this summons, the Moorish commanders
held a council of war. The Prince Cidi Yahye, indignant
at the menace of the king, was for retorting by a declaration
that the garrison never would surrender, but would fight
until buried under the ruins of the walls. "Of what avail,"
said the veteran Mohammed, "is a declaration of the kind,
which we may falsify by our deeds? Let us threaten what
we know we can perform, and let us endeavor to perform
more than we threaten."

In conformity to the advice of Mohammed ben Hassan, therefore, a laconic reply was sent to the Christian monarch, thanking him for his offer of favorable terms, but informing him that they were placed in the city to defend, not to surrender it.

CHAPTER TWENTY-SIX

THE BATTLE OF THE GARDENS BEFORE BAZA

When the reply of the Moorish commanders was brought to King Ferdinand, he prepared to press the siege with the utmost rigor. Finding the camp too far from the city, and that the intervening orchards afforded shelter for the sallies of the Moors, he determined to advance it beyond the gardens, in the space between them and the suburbs, where his batteries would have full play upon the city walls. A detachment was sent in advance, to take possession of the gardens, and to keep a check upon the suburbs, opposing any sally, while the encampment should be formed and fortified. The various commanders entered the orchards at different points. The young cavaliers marched fearlessly forward, but the experienced veterans foresaw infinite peril in the mazes of this verdant labyrinth. The Master of St. Jago, as he led his troops into the center of the gardens, exhorted them to keep by one another, and to press forward in defiance of all difficulty or danger; assuring them that God would give them the victory if they attacked hardily and persisted resolutely.

Scarce had they entered the verge of the orchards, when a din of drums and trumpets, mingled with war-cries, was heard from the suburbs, and a legion of Moorish warriors on foot poured forth. They were led on by the Prince Cidi Yahye. He saw the imminent danger of the city should the Christians gain possession of the orchards. "Soldiers," he cried, "we fight for life and liberty, for our families, our country, our religion; * nothing is left for us to depend upon but the strength of our hands, the courage of our hearts, and the almighty protection of Allah.'' The Moors answered him with shouts of war, and rushed to the encounter. The two hosts met in the midst of the gardens. A chance-medley combat ensued, with lances, arquebuses, crossbows, and scimiters; the perplexed nature of the ground, cut up and intersected by canals and streams, the closeness of the trees, the multiplicity of towers and petty edifices, gave greater advantages to the Moors, who were on foot, than to the Christians, who were on horseback. The Moors, too, knew the ground, with all its alleys and passes; and were thus enabled to lurk, to sally forth, to attack, and to retreat, almost without injury.

The Christian commanders, seeing this, ordered many of the horsemen to dismount and fight on foot. The battle then became fierce and deadly, each disregarding his own life, provided he could slay his enemy. It was not so much a general battle as a multitude of petty actions; for every orchard and garden had its distinct contest. No one could see further than the little scene of fury and bloodshed around him, nor know how the general battle fared. In vain the captains exerted their voices, in vain the trumpets brayed forth signals and commands—all was confounded and unheard, in the universal din and uproar. No one kept to his standard, but fought as his own fury or fear dictated. In some places the Christians had the advantage, in others the Moors; often, a victorious party, pursuing the vanquished, came upon a superior and triumphant force of the enemy, and the fugitives turned back upon them in an overwhelming wave. Some broken remnants, in their terror and confusion, fled from their own countrymen and sought refuge among their enemies, not knowing friend from foe, in the obscurity of the groves. The Moors were more adroit in

---

* "Illi (Mauri) pro fortunis, pro libertate, pro laribus patriis, pro vita dorique certabant."—" Pietro Martyr," Epist. 70.

these wild skirmishings, from their flexibility, lightness, and agility, and the rapidity with which they would disperse, rally, and return again to the charge.*

The hardest fighting was about the small garden towers and pavilions, which served as so many petty fortresses. Each party by turns gained them, defended them fiercely, and were driven out; many of the towers were set on fire, and increased the horrors of the fight by the wreaths of smoke and flame in which they wrapped the groves, and by the shrieks of those who were burning.

Several of the Christian cavaliers, bewildered by the up-roar and confusion, and shocked at the carnage which pre-vailed, would have led their men out of the action, but they were entangled in a labyrinth, and knew not which way to retreat. While in this perplexity, the standard-bearer of one of the squadrons of the grand cardinal had his arm carried off by a cannon-ball; the standard was wellnigh falling into the hands of the enemy, when Roderigo de Mendoza, an in-trepid youth, natural son of the grand cardinal, rushed to its rescue, through a shower of balls, lances, and arrows, and, bearing it aloft, dashed forward with it into the hottest of the combat, followed by his shouting soldiery.

King Ferdinand, who remained in the skirts of the or-chard, was in extreme anxiety. It was impossible to see much of the action, for the multiplicity of trees and towers and the wreaths of smoke; and those who were driven out defeated, or came out wounded and exhausted, gave differ-ent accounts, according to the fate of the partial conflicts in which they had been engaged. Ferdinand exerted himself to the utmost to animate and encourage his troops to this blind encounter, sending re-enforcements of horse and foot to those points where the battle was most sanguinary and doubtful.

Among those who were brought forth mortally wounded was Don Juan de Luna, a youth of uncommon merit, greatly

* Mariana, lib. 25, cap. 13.

prized by the king, beloved by the army, and recently married to Donna Catalina de Urrea, a young lady of distinguished beauty.* They laid him at the foot of a tree, and endeavored to stanch and bind up his wounds with a scarf which his bride had wrought for him; but his life-blood flowed too profusely; and while a holy friar was yet administering to him the last sacred offices of the church, he expired, almost at the feet of his sovereign.

On the other hand, the veteran alcayde Mohammed ben Hassan, surrounded by a little band of chieftains, kept an anxious eye upon the scene of combat from the walls of the city. For nearly twelve hours the battle had raged without intermission. The thickness of the foliage hid all the particulars from their sight; but they could see the flash of swords and glance of helmets among the trees. Columns of smoke rose in every direction, while the clash of arms, the thundering of ribadoquines and arquebuses, the shouts and cries of the combatants, and the groans and supplications of the wounded, bespoke the deadly conflict that was waging in the bosom of the groves. They were harassed, too, by the shrieks and lamentations of the Moorish women and children, as their wounded relations were brought bleeding from the scene of action; and were stunned by a general outcry of woe on the part of the inhabitants, as the body of Redoan Zalfarga, a renegado Christian, and one of the bravest of their generals, was borne breathless into the city.

At length, the din of battle approached nearer to the skirts of the orchards. They beheld their warriors driven out from among the groves by fresh squadrons of the enemy, and, after disputing the ground inch by inch, obliged to retire to a place between the orchards and the suburbs, which was fortified with palisadoes.

The Christians immediately planted opposing palisadoes, and established strong outposts near to this retreat of the Moors; while, at the same time, King Ferdinand ordered

---

* Mariana.   P. Martyr.   Zurita.

that his encampment should be pitched within the hard-won orchards.

Hohammed ben Hassan sallied forth to the aid of the Prince Cidi Yahye, and made a desperate attempt to dislodge the enemy from this formidable position: but the night had closed, and the darkness rendered it impossible to make any impression. The Moors, however, kept up constant assaults and alarms throughout the night; and the weary Christians, exhausted by the toils and sufferings of the day, were not allowed a moment of repose.*

CHAPTER TWENTY-SEVEN

SIEGE OF BAZA—EMBARRASSMENTS OF THE ARMY

THE morning sun rose upon a piteous scene before the walls of Baza. The Christian outposts, harassed throughout the night, were pale and haggard; while the multitudes of slain which lay before their palisadoes showed the fierce attacks they had sustained, and the bravery of their defense.

Beyond them lay the groves and gardens of Baza; once the favorite resorts for recreation and delight—now a scene of horror and desolation. The towers and pavilions were smoking ruins; the canals and watercourses were discolored with blood and choked with the bodies of the slain. Here and there, the ground, deep dinted with the tramp of man and steed, and plashed and slippery with gore, showed where there had been some fierce and mortal conflict; while the bodies of Moors and Christians, ghastly in death, lay half concealed among the matted and trampled shrubs, and flowers, and herbage.

Amid these sanguinary scenes arose the Christian tents, which had been hastily pitched among the gardens in the

* Pulgar, part 3, cap. 106, 107. Cura de los Palacios, cap. 92. Zurita, lib. 20, cap. 81.

preceding evening. The experience of the night, however, and the forlorn aspect of everything in the morning, convinced King Ferdinand of the perils and hardships to which his camp must be exposed in its present situation; and, after a consultation with his principal cavaliers, he resolved to abandon the orchards.

It was a dangerous movement to extricate his army from so entangled a situation, in the face of so alert and daring an enemy. A bold front was therefore kept up toward the city; additional troops were ordered to the advanced posts, and works begun as if for a settled encampment. Not a tent was struck in the gardens; but in the meantime, the most active and unremitting exertions were made to remove all the baggage and furniture of the camp back to the original station.

All day, the Moors beheld a formidable show of war maintained in front of the gardens; while in the rear, the tops of the Christian tents, and the pennons of the different commanders, were seen rising above the groves. Suddenly, toward evening, the tents sunk and disappeared; the outposts broke up their stations and withdrew and the whole shadow of an encampment was fast vanishing from their eyes.

The Moors saw too late the subtle maneuver of King Ferdinand. Cidi Yahye again sallied forth with a large force of horse and foot, and pressed furiously upon the Christians. The latter, however, experienced in Moorish attack, retired in close order, sometimes turning upon the enemy and driving them to their barricadoes, and then pursuing their retreat. In this way the army was extricated, without much further loss, from the perilous labyrinths of the gardens.

The camp was now out of danger; but it was also too distant from the city to do mischief, while the Moors could sally forth and return without hinderance. The king called a council of war to consider in what manner to proceed. The Marques of Cadiz was for abandoning the siege for the present, the place being too strong, too well garrisoned and provided, and too extensive, to be either carried by assault or invested and reduced by famine, with their limited forces;

while, in lingering before it, the army would be exposed to the usual maladies and sufferings of besieging armies, and, when the rainy season came on, would be shut up by the swelling of the rivers. He recommended, instead, that the king should throw garrisons of horse and foot into all the towns captured in the neighborhood, and leave them to keep up a predatory war upon Baza, while he should overrun and ravage all the country; so that, in the following year, Almeria and Guadix, having all their subject towns and territories taken from them, might be starved into submission.

Don Gutierre de Cardenas, senior commander of Leon, on the other hand, maintained that to abandon the siege would be construed by the enemy into a sign of weakness and irresolution. It would give new spirits to the partisans of El Zagal, and would gain to his standard many of the wavering subjects of Boabdil, if it did not encourage the fickle populace of Granada to open rebellion. He advised therefore that the siege should be prosecuted with vigor.

The pride of Ferdinand pleaded in favor of the last opinion; for it would be doubly humiliating again to return from a campaign in this part of the Moorish kingdom without effecting a blow. But when he reflected on all that his army had suffered, and on all that they must suffer should the siege continue—especially from the difficulty of obtaining a regular supply of provisions for so numerous a host, across a great extent of rugged and mountainous country—he determined to consult the safety of his people, and to adopt the advice of the Marques of Cadiz.

When the soldiery heard that the king was about to raise the siege in mere consideration of their sufferings, they were filled with generous enthusiasm, and entreated, as with one voice, that the siege might never be abandoned until the city surrendered.

Perplexed by conflicting counsels, the king dispatched messengers to the queen at Jaen, requesting her advice. Posts had been stationed between them, in such manner that missives from the camp could reach the queen within ten hours. Isabella sent instantly her reply. She left the policy of raising or continuing the siege to the decision of the king and his captains; but should they determine to persevere, she pledged herself, with the aid of God, to forward them men, money, provisions, and all other supplies, until the city should be taken.

The reply of the queen determined Ferdinand to persevere; and when his determination was made known to the army, it was hailed with as much joy as if it had been tidings of a victory.

CHAPTER TWENTY-EIGHT

SIEGE OF BAZA CONTINUED—HOW KING FERDINAND COMPLETELY INVESTED THE CITY

THE Moorish Prince Cidi Yahye had received tidings of the doubts and discussions in the Christian camp, and flattered himself with hopes that the besieging army would soon retire in despair, though the veteran alcayde Mohammed shook his head with incredulity at the suggestion. A sudden movement, one morning, in the Christian camp, seemed to confirm the sanguine hopes of the prince. The tents were struck, the artillery and baggage were conveyed away, and bodies of soldiers began to march along the valley. The momentary gleam of triumph was soon dispelled. The Catholic king had merely divided his host into two camps, the more effectually to distress the city. One, consisting of four thousand horse and eight thousand foot, with all the artillery and battering engines, took post on the side of the city toward the mountain. This was commanded by the valiant Marques of Cadiz, with whom were Don Alonzo de Aguilar, Luis Fernandez Puerto Carrero, and many other distinguished cavaliers.

The other camp was commanded by the king, having six

thousand horse and a great host of foot-soldiers, the hardy mountaineers of Biscay, Guipuscon, Gallicia, and the Asturias. Among the cavaliers who were with the king were the brave Count de Tendilla, Don Roderigo de Mendoza, and Don Alonzo de Cardenas, Master of Santiago. The two camps were wide asunder, on opposite sides of the city, and between them lay the thick wilderness of orchards. Both camps were therefore fortified by great trenches, breast-works, and palisadoes. The veteran Mohammed, as he saw these two formidable camps glittering on each side of the city, and noted the well-known pennons of renowned commanders fluttering above them, still comforted his companions: "These camps," said he, "are too far removed from each other for mutual succor and co-operation; and the forest of orchards is as a gulf between them." This consolation was but of short continuance. Scarcely were the Christian camps fortified, when the ears of the Moorish garrison were startled by the sound of innumerable axes and the crash of falling trees. They looked with anxiety from their highest towers, and behold, their favorite groves were sinking beneath the blows of the Christian pioneers. The Moors sallied forth with fiery zeal to protect their beloved gardens, and the orchards in which they so much delighted. The Christians, however, were too well supported to be driven from their work. Day after day, the gardens became the scene of incessant and bloody skirmishings; yet still the devastation of the groves went on, for King Ferdinand was too well aware of the necessity of clearing away this screen of woods not to bend all his forces to the undertaking. It was a work, however, of gigantic toil and patience. The trees were of such magnitude, and so closely set together, and spread over so wide an extent, that notwithstanding four thousand men were employed, they could scarcely clear a strip of land ten paces broad within a day; and such were the interruptions from the incessant assaults of the Moors that it was full forty days before the orchards were completely leveled.

The devoted city of Baza now lay stripped of its beautiful covering of groves and gardens, at once its ornament, its delight, and its protection.   The besiegers went on slowly and surely, with almost incredible labors, to invest and isolate the city.   They connected their camps by a deep trench across the plain, a league in length, into which they diverted the waters of the mountain streams.   They protected this trench by palisadoes, fortified by fifteen castles, at regular distances. They dug a deep trench, also, two leagues in length, across the mountain in the rear of the city, reaching from camp to camp, and fortified it on each side with walls of earth, and stone, and wood.   Thus the Moors were inclosed on all sides by trenches, palisadoes, walls, and castles; so that it was impossible for them to sally beyond this great line of circumvallation—nor could any force enter to their succor.   Ferdinand made an attempt, likewise, to cut off the supply of water from the city: ''For water,'' observes the worthy Agapida, ''is more necessary to these Infidels than bread, making use of it in repeated daily ablutions enjoined by their damnable religion, and employing it in baths and in a thousand other idle and extravagant modes, of which we Spaniards and Christians make but little account.''

There was a noble fountain of pure water, which gushed out at the foot of the hill Albohacen, just behind the city. The Moors had almost a superstitious fondness for this fountain, and chiefly depended upon it for their supplies.   Receiving intimation from some deserters of the plan of King Ferdinand to get possession of this precious fountain, they sallied forth at night, and threw up such powerful works upon the impending hill as to set all attempts of the Christian assailants at defiance.

CHAPTER TWENTY-NINE

EXPLOIT OF HERNANDO PEREZ DEL PULGAR AND OTHER CAVALIERS

THE siege of Baza, while it displayed the skill and science of the Christian commanders, gave but little scope for the adventurous spirit and fiery valor of the young Spanish cavaliers. They repined at the tedious monotony and dull security of their fortified camp, and longed for some soul-stirring exploit of difficulty and danger. Two of the most spirited of these youthful cavaliers were Francisco de Bazan and Antonio de Cueva, the latter of whom was son to the Duke of Albuquerque. As they were one day seated on the ramparts of the camp, and venting their impatience at this life of inaction, they were overheard by a veteran adalide, one of those scouts or guides who are acquainted with all parts of the country. "Senors," said he, "if you wish for a service of peril and profit, if you are willing to pluck the fiery old Moor by the beard, I can lead you to where you may put your mettle to the proof. Hard by the city of Guadix are certain hamlets rich in booty. I can conduct you by a way in which you may come upon them by surprise; and if you are as cool in the head as you are hot in the spur, you may bear off your spoils from under the very eyes of old El Zagal."

The idea of thus making booty at the very gates of Guadix pleased the hot-spirited youths. These predatory excursions were frequent about this time; and the Moors of Padul, Alhenden, and other towns of the Alpuxarras, had recently harassed the Christian territories by expeditions of the kind. Francisco de Bazan and Antonio de Cueva soon found other young cavaliers of their age eager to join in the adventure; and in a little while they had nearly three hundred horse and two hundred foot ready equipped and eager for the foray.

Keeping their destination secret, they sallied out of the camp on the edge of an evening, and, guided by the adalide, made their way by starlight through the most secret roads of the mountains. In this way they pressed on rapidly day and night, until early one morning, before cock-crowing, they fell suddenly upon the hamlets, made prisoners of the inhabitants, sacked the houses, ravaged the fields, and, sweeping through the meadows, gathered together all the flocks and herds. Without giving themselves time to rest, they set out upon their return, making with all speed for the mountains, before the alarm should be given and the country roused.

Several of the herdsmen, however, had fled to Guadix, and carried tidings of the ravage to El Zagal. The beard of old Muley trembled with rage; he immediately sent out six hundred of his choicest horse and foot, with orders to recover the booty, and to bring those insolent marauders captive to Guadix.

The Christian cavaliers were urging their cavalgada of cattle and sheep up a mountain, as fast as their own weariness would permit, when, looking back, they beheld a great cloud of dust, and presently descried the turbaned host hot upon their traces.

They saw that the Moors were superior in number; they were fresh also, both man and steed, whereas both they and their horses were fatigued by two days and two nights of hard marching. Several of the horsemen therefore gathered round the commanders, and proposed that they should relinquish their spoil and save themselves by flight. The captains, Francisco de Bazan and Antonio de Cueva, spurned at such craven counsel. "What!" cried they, "abandon our prey without striking a blow? Leave our foot-soldiers too in the lurch, to be overwhelmed by the enemy? If any one gives such counsel through fear, he mistakes the course of safety; for there is less danger in presenting a bold front to the foe than in turning a dastard back; and fewer men are killed in a brave advance than in a cowardly retreat."

Some of the cavaliers were touched by these words, and declared that they would stand by the foot-soldiers like true companions in arms: the great mass of the party, however, were volunteers, brought together by chance, who received no pay, nor had any common tie to keep them together in time of danger. The pleasure of the expedition being over, each thought but of his own safety, regardless of his companions. As the enemy approached, the tumult of opinions increased, and everything was in confusion. The captains, to put an end to the dispute, ordered the standard-bearer to advance against the Moors, well knowing that no true cavalier would hesitate to follow and defend his banner. The standard-bearer hesitated—the troops were on the point of taking to flight.

Upon this, a cavalier of the royal guards named Hernanado Perez del Pulgar, alcayde of the fortress of Salar, rode to the front. He took off a handkerchief which he wore round his head, after the Andalusian fashion, and, tying it to the end of his lance, elevated it in the air. "Cavaliers," cried he, "why do ye take weapons in your hands if you depend upon your feet for safety? This day will determine who is the brave man and who the coward. He who is disposed to fight shall not want a standard: let him follow this handkerchief." So saying, he waved his banner and spurred bravely against the Moors. His example shamed some and filled others with generous emulation: all turned with one accord, and, following the valiant Pulgar, rushed with shouts upon the enemy. The Moors scarcely waited to receive the shock of their encounter. Seized with a sudden panic, they took to flight, and were pursued for a considerable distance, with great slaughter. Three hundred of their dead strewed the road, and were stripped and despoiled by the conquerors; many were taken prisoners, and the Christian cavaliers returned in triumph to the camp, with a long cavalgada of sheep and cattle, and mules laden with booty, and bearing before them the singular standard which had conducted them to victory.

When King Ferdinand was informed of the gallant action of Hernando Perez del Pulgar, he immediately conferred on him the honor of knighthood, and ordered that, in memory of his achievement, he should bear for arms a lance with a handkerchief at the end of it, together with a castle and twelve lions. This is but one of many hardy and heroic deeds done by this brave cavalier in the wars against the Moors; by which he gained great renown, and the distinguished appellation of "El de las hazanas," or "He of the exploits." *

CHAPTER THIRTY

CONTINUATION OF THE SIEGE OF BAZA

THE old Moorish king El Zagal mounted a tower and looked out eagerly to enjoy the sight of the Christian marauders brought captive into the gates of Guadix; but his spirits fell when he beheld his own troops stealing back in the dusk of the evening in broken and dejected parties.

The fortune of war bore hard against the old monarch; his mind was harassed by the disastrous tidings brought each day from Baza, of the sufferings of the inhabitants, and the numbers of the garrison slain in the frequent skirmishes. He dared not go in person to the relief of the place, for his presence was necessary in Guadix to keep a check upon his nephew in Granada. He made efforts to send re-enforcements and supplies; but they were intercepted, and either captured or driven back. Still his situation was in some respects preferable to that of his nephew Boabdil. The old monarch was battling like a warrior, on the last step of his throne; El Chico remained a kind of pensioned vassal, in

* Hernando del Pulgar, the historian, secretary to Queen Isabella, is confounded with this cavalier, by some writers. He was also present at the siege of Baza, and has recounted this transaction in his chronicle of the Catholic sovereigns Ferdinand and Isabella.

the luxurious abode of the Alhambra. The chivalrous part of the inhabitants of Granada could not but compare the generous stand made by the warriors of Baza for their country and their faith, with their own time-serving submission to the yoke of an unbeliever. Every account they received of the woes of Baza wrung their hearts with agony; every account of the exploits of its devoted defenders brought blushes to their cheeks. Many stole forth secretly with their weapons, and hastened to join the besieged; and the partisans of El Zagal wrought upon the patriotism and passions of the remainder, until another of those conspiracies was formed that were continually menacing the unsteady throne of Granada. It was concerted by the conspirators to assail the Alhambra on a sudden; to slay Boabdil; to assemble all the troops, and march to Guadix; where, being re-enforced by the garrison of that place, and led on by the old warrior monarch, they might fall with overwhelming power upon the Christian army before Baza.

Fortunately for Boabdil, he discovered the conspiracy in time, and had the heads of the leaders struck off and placed upon the walls of the Alhambra—an act of severity unusual with this mild and wavering monarch, which struck terror into the disaffected, and produced a kind of mute tranquillity throughout the city.

King Ferdinand had full information of all these movements and measures for the relief of Baza, and took timely precautions to prevent them. Bodies of horsemen held watch in the mountain passes to prevent all supplies, and to intercept any generous volunteers from Granada; and watchtowers were erected, or scouts were placed on every commanding height, to give the alarm at the least sign of a hostile turban.

The Prince Cidi Yahye and his brave companions in arms were thus gradually walled up, as it were, from the rest of the world. A line of towers, the battlements of which bristled with troops, girdled their city; and behind the intervening bulwarks and palisadoes passed and repassed continual squadrons of troops. Week after week, and month after month, passed away, but Ferdinand waited in vain for the garrison to be either terrified or starved into surrender. Every day they sallied forth with the spirit and alacrity of troops high fed and flushed with confidence. "The Christian monarch," said the veteran Mohammed ben Hassan, "builds his hopes upon our growing faint and desponding— we must manifest unusual cheerfulness and vigor. What would be rashness in other service becomes prudence with us." The Prince Cidi Yahye agreed with him in opinion, and sallied forth with his troops upon all kinds of hare-brained exploits. They laid ambushes, concerted surprises, and made the most desperate assaults. The great extent of the Christian works rendered them weak in many parts: against these the Moors directed their attacks, suddenly breaking into them, making a hasty ravage, and bearing off their booty in triumph to the city. Sometimes they would sally forth by the passes and clefts of the mountain in the rear of the city, which it was difficult to guard, and, hurrying down into the plain, would sweep off all cattle and sheep that were grazing near the suburbs, and all stragglers from the camp.

These partisan sallies brought on many sharp and bloody encounters, in some of which Don Alonzo de Aguilar and the alcayde de los Donzeles distinguished themselves greatly. During one of these hot skirmishes, which happened on the skirts of the mountain, about twilight, a valiant cavalier, named Martin Galindo, beheld a powerful Moor dealing deadly blows about him, and making great havoc among the Christians. Galindo pressed forward and challenged him to single combat. The Moor, who was of the valiant tribe of the Abencerrages, was not slow in answering the call. Couching their lances, they rushed furiously upon each other. At the first shock the Moor was wounded in the face, and borne out of his saddle. Before Galindo could check his steed, and turn from his career, the Moor sprang upon his feet, recovered his lance, and, rushing upon him, wounded him in the head and the arm. Though Galindo was on horseback and the Moor on foot, yet such was the prowess and address of the latter that the Christian knight, being disabled in the arm, was in the utmost peril, when his comrades hastened to his assistance. At their approach, the valiant pagan retreated slowly up the rocks, keeping them at bay until he found himself among his companions.

Several of the young Spanish cavaliers, stung by the triumph of this Moslem knight, would have challenged others of the Moors to single combat; but King Ferdinand prohibited all vaunting encounters of the kind. He forbade his troops, also, to provoke skirmishes, well knowing that the Moors were more dexterous than most people in this irregular mode of fighting, and were better acquainted with the ground.

CHAPTER THIRTY-ONE

HOW TWO FRIARS ARRIVED AT THE CAMP, AND HOW THEY CAME FROM THE HOLY LAND

WHILE the holy Christian army (says Fray Antonio Agapida) was thus beleaguering this Infidel city of Baza, there rode into the camp, one day, two reverend friars of the order of Saint Francis. One was of portly person and authoritative air: he bestrode a goodly steed, well conditioned and well caparisoned; while his companion rode beside him, upon a humble hack, poorly accoutered, and, as he rode, he scarcely raised his eyes from the ground, but maintained a meek and lowly air.

The arrival of two friars in the camp was not a matter of much note, for in these holy wars the church militant continually mingled in the affray, and helmet and cowl were always seen together; but it was soon discovered that these worthy saints-errant were from a far country, and on a mission of great import.

They were, in truth, just arrived from the Holy Land, being two of the saintly men who kept vigil over the sepulcher of our blessed Lord at Jerusalem. He of the tall and portly form and commanding presence was Fray Antonio Millan, prior of the Franciscan convent in the holy city. He had a full and florid countenance, a sonorous voice, and was round, and swelling, and copious in his periods, like one accustomed to harangue, and to be listened to with deference. His companion was small and spare in form, pale of visage, and soft and silken and almost whispering in speech. "He had a humble and lowly way," says Agapida, "evermore bowing the head, as became one of his calling." Yet he was one of the most active, zealous, and effective brothers of the convent; and when he raised his small black eye from the earth, there was a keen glance out of the corner which showed that, though harmless as a dove, he was nevertheless as wise as a serpent.

These holy men had come on a momentous embassy from the grand soldan of Egypt; or, as Agapida terms him in the language of the day, the soldan of Babylon. The league which had been made between that potentate and his archfoe the Grand-Turk Bajazet II., to unite in arms for the salvation of Granada, as has been mentioned in a previous chapter of this chronicle, had come to naught. The Infidel princes had again taken up arms against each other, and had relapsed into their ancient hostility. Still the grand soldan, as head of the whole Moslem sect, considered himself bound to preserve the kingdom of Granada from the grasp of unbelievers. He dispatched, therefore, these two holy friars with letters to the Castilian sovereigns, as well as to the pope and to the king of Naples, remonstrating against the evils done to the Moors of the kingdom of Granada, who were of his faith and kindred; whereas it was well known that great numbers of Christians were indulged and protected in the full enjoyment of their property, their liberty, and their faith, in his dominions. He insisted, therefore, that this war should cease: that the Moors of Granada should be reinstated in the territory of which they had been dispossessed; otherwise he threatened to put to death all the Christians beneath his sway, to demolish their convents and temples, and to destroy the holy sepulcher.

This fearful menace had spread consternation among the Christians of Palestine; and when the intrepid Fray Antonio Millan and his lowly companion departed on their mission, they were accompanied far from the gates of Jerusalem by an anxious throng of brethren and disciples, who remained watching them with tearful eyes as they journeyed over the plains of Judea.

These holy embassadors were received with great distinction by King Ferdinand; for men of their cloth had ever high honor and consideration in his court. He had long and frequent conversations with them about the Holy Land; the state of the Christian church in the dominions of the grand soldan, and of the policy and conduct of that arch-Infidel toward it. The portly prior of the Franciscan convent was full, and round, and oratorical, in his replies; and the king expressed himself much pleased with the eloquence of his periods; but the politic monarch was observed to lend a close and attentive ear to the whispering voice of the lowly companion, "Whose discourse," adds Agapida, "though modest and low, was clear and fluent, and full of subtle wisdom." These holy friars had visited Rome in their journeying, where they had delivered the letter of the soldan to the sovereign pontiff. His holiness had written by them to the Castilian sovereigns, requesting to know what reply they had to offer to this demand of the Oriental potentate.

The king of Naples also wrote to them on the subject, but in wary terms. He inquired into the cause of this war with the Moors of Granada, and expressed great marvel at its events, as if (says Agapida) both were not notorious throughout all the Christian world. "Nay," adds the worthy friar with becoming indignation, "he uttered opinions savoring of little better than damnable heresy; for he observed that, although the Moors were of a different sect, they ought not to be maltreated without just cause; and hinted that if the Castilian sovereigns did not suffer any crying injury from the Moors, it would be improper to do anything which might draw great damage upon the Christians: as if, when once the sword of the faith was drawn, it ought ever to be sheathed until this scum of heathendom were utterly destroyed or driven from the land. But this monarch," he continues, "was more kindly disposed toward the Infidels than was honest and lawful in a Christian prince, and was at that very time in league with the soldan against their common enemy the Grand-Turk."

These pious sentiments of the truly Catholic Agapida are echoed by Padre Mariana in his history;* but the worthy chronicler Pedro Abarca attributes the interference of the king of Naples, not to lack of orthodoxy in religion, but to an excess of worldly policy; he being apprehensive that, should Ferdinand conquer the Moors of Granada, he might have time and means to assert a claim of the house of Aragon to the crown of Naples.

"King Ferdinand," continues the worthy father Pedro Abarca, "was no less master of dissimulation than his cousin of Naples; so he replied to him with the utmost suavity of manner, going into a minute and patient vindication of the war, and taking great apparent pains to inform him of those things which all the world knew, but of which the other pretended to be ignorant." † At the same time he soothed his solicitude about the fate of the Christians in the empire of the grand soldan, assuring him that the great revenue extorted from them in rents and tributes would be a certain protection against the threatened violence.

To the pope he made the usual vindication of the war; that it was for the recovery of ancient territory usurped by the Moors; for the punishment of wars and violences inflicted upon the Christians; and, finally, that it was a holy crusade for the glory and advancement of the church.

---

* Mariana, lib. 25, cap. 15.
† Abarca, Annales de Aragon, Rey xxx., cap. 3.

"It was a truly edifying sight," says Agapida, "to behold these friars, after they had had their audience of the king, moving about the camp always surrounded by nobles and cavaliers of high and martial renown. These were insatiable in their questions about the Holy Land, the state of the sepulcher of our Lord, and the sufferings of the devoted brethren who guarded it, and the pious pilgrims who resorted there to pay their vows. The portly prior of the convent would stand with lofty and shining countenance in the midst of these iron warriors, and declaim with resounding eloquence on the history of the sepulcher; but the humbler brother would ever and anon sigh deeply, and in low tones utter some tale of suffering and outrage, at which his steel-clad hearers would grasp the hilts of their swords, and mutter between their clinched teeth prayers for another crusade."

The pious friars, having finished their mission to the king, and been treated with all due distinction, took their leave and wended their way to Jaen, to visit the most Catholic of queens. Isabella, whose heart was the seat of piety, received them as sacred men, invested with more than human dignity. During their residence at Jaen, they were continually in the royal presence; the respectable prior of the convent moved and melted the ladies of the court by his florid rhetoric, but his lowly companion was observed to have continual access to the royal ear. That saintly and soft-spoken messenger (says Agapida) received the reward of his humility; for the queen, moved by his frequent representations, made in all modesty and lowliness of spirit, granted a yearly sum in perpetuity, of one thousand ducats in gold, for the support of the monks of the convent of the holy sepulcher.*

Moreover, on the departure of these holy embassadors,

---

* "La Reyna dio a los Frayles mil ducados de renta cado año para el sustanto de los religiosos del santo sepulcro, que es la mejor limosna y sustanto que hasta nuestros dias ha quedado a estos religiosas de Gerusalem: para donde les dio la Reyna un velo labrado por sus manos, para poner encima de la santa sepultura del Señor."—Garibay "Compend. Hist.," lib. 18, cap. 36.

the excellent and most Catholic queen delivered to them a veil devoutly embroidered with her own royal hands, to be placed over the holy sepulcher—a precious and inestimable present, which called forth a most eloquent tribute of thanks from the portly prior, but which brought tears into the eyes of his lowly companion.*

CHAPTER THIRTY-TWO

HOW QUEEN ISABELLA DEVISED MEANS TO SUPPLY THE ARMY WITH PROVISIONS

IT has been the custom to laud the conduct and address of King Ferdinand, in this most arduous and protracted war; but the sage Agapida is more disposed to give credit to the counsels and measures of the queen, who, he observes, though less ostensible in action, was in truth the very soul, the vital principle, of this great enterprise. While King Ferdinand was bustling in his camp and making a glittering display with his gallant chivalry, she, surrounded by her saintly counselors, in the episcopal palace of Jaen, was devising ways and means to keep the king and his army in existence. She had pledged herself to keep up a supply of men, and money, and provisions, until the city should be taken. The hardships of the siege caused a fearful waste of life, but the supply of

---

* It is proper to mention the result of this mission of the two friars, and which the worthy Agapida has neglected to record. At a subsequent period, the Catholic sovereigns sent the distinguished historian, Pietro Martyr, of Angleria, as embassador to the grand soldan. That able man made such representations as were perfectly satisfactory to the Oriental potentate. He also obtained from him the remission of many exactions and extortions heretofore practiced upon Christian pilgrims visiting the holy sepulcher; which, it is presumed, had been gently but cogently detailed to the monarch by the lowly friar. Pietro Martyr wrote an account of his embassy to the grand soldan—a work greatly esteemed by the learned, and containing much curious information. It is entitled "De Legatione Babylonica."

men was the least difficult part of her undertaking. So beloved was the queen by the chivalry of Spain, that, on her
calling on them for assistance, not a grandee or cavalier that
yet lingered at home, but either repaired in person or sent
forces to the camp; the ancient and warlike families vied
with each other in marshaling forth their vassals, and thus
the besieged Moors beheld each day fresh troops arriving
before their city, and new ensigns and pennons displayed,
emblazoned with arms well known to the veteran warriors.

But the most arduous task was to keep up a regular
supply of provisions. It was not the army alone that had to
be supported, but also the captured towns and their garrisons;
for the whole country around them had been ravaged, and
the conquerors were in danger of starving in the midst of the
land they had desolated. To transport the daily supplies for
such immense numbers was a gigantic undertaking, in a
country where there was neither water conveyance nor roads
for carriages. Everything had to be borne by beasts of
burden over rugged and broken paths of the mountains, and
through dangerous defiles, exposed to the attacks and plun-
derings of the Moors.

The wary and calculating merchants, accustomed to supply the army, shrunk from engaging, at their own risk, in so
hazardous an undertaking. The queen therefore hired fourteen thousand beasts of burden, and ordered all the wheat
and barley to be bought up in Andalusia, and in the domains
of the knights of Santiago and Calatrava. She distributed
the administration of these supplies among able and confi-
dential persons. Some were employed to collect the grain;
others, to take it to the mills; others, to superintend the
grinding and delivery; and others, to convey it to the camp.
To every two hundred animals a muleteer was allotted, to
take charge of them on the route. Thus, great lines of convoys were in constant movement, traversing to and fro,
guarded by large bodies of troops, to defend them from hovering parties of the Moors. Not a single day's intermission
was allowed, for the army depended upon the constant

arrival of these supplies for daily food. The grain, when brought into the camp, was deposited in an immense granary and sold to the army at a fixed price, which was never either raised or lowered.

Incredible were the expenses incurred in these supplies; but the queen had ghostly advisers, thoroughly versed in the art of getting at the resources of the country. Many worthy prelates opened the deep purses of the church and furnished loans from the revenues of their dioceses and convents; and their pious contributions were eventually rewarded by Providence a hundred-fold. Merchants and other wealthy individuals, confident of the punctual faith of the queen, advanced large sums on the security of her word; many noble families lent their plate, without waiting to be asked. The queen also sold certain annual rents in inheritance at great sacrifices, assigning the revenues of towns and cities for the payment. Finding all this insufficient to satisfy the enormous expenditure, she sent her gold and plate and all her jewels to the cities of Valencia and Barcelona, where they were pledged for a great amount of money, which was immediately appropriated to keep up the supplies of the army.

Thus, through the wonderful activity, judgment, and enterprise of this heroic and magnanimous woman, a great host, encamped in the heart of a warlike country, accessible only over mountain roads, was maintained in continual abundance. Nor was it supplied merely with the necessaries and comforts of life. The powerful escorts drew merchants and artificers from all parts, to repair, as if in caravans, to this great military market. In a little while, the camp abounded with tradesmen and artists of all kinds, to administer to the luxury and ostentation of the youthful chivalry. Here might be seen cunning artificers in steel, and accomplished armorers, achieving those rare and sumptuous helmets and cuirasses, richly gilt, inlaid, and embossed, in which the Spanish cavaliers delighted. Saddlers and harness-makers and horse-milliners, also, were there, whose tents glittered with gorgeous housings and caparisons. The merchants

spread forth their sumptuous silks, cloths, brocades, fine linen
and tapestry. The tents of the nobility were prodigally
decorated with all kinds of the richest stuffs, and dazzled the
eye with their magnificence; nor could the grave looks and
grave speeches of King Ferdinand prevent his youthful cavaliers from vying with each other in the splendor of their
dresses and caparisons, on all occasions of parade and ceremony.

CHAPTER THIRTY-THREE

OF THE DISASTERS WHICH BEFELL THE CAMP

WHILE the Christian camp, thus gay and gorgeous, spread
itself out like a holyday pageant before the walls of Baza—
while a long line of beasts of burden, laden with provisions
and luxuries, were seen descending the valley from morning
till night, and pouring into the camp a continued stream of
abundance—the unfortunate garrison found their resources
rapidly wasting away, and famine already began to pinch
the peaceful part of the community.

Cidi Yahye had acted with great spirit and valor as long
as there was any prospect of success; but he began to lose
his usual fire and animation, and was observed to pace the
walls of Baza with a pensive air, casting many a wistful look
toward the Christian camp, and sinking into profound reveries
and cogitations. The veteran alcayde, Mohammed ben Hassan, noticed these desponding moods, and endeavored to rally
the spirits of the prince. "The rainy season is at hand,"
would he cry; "the floods will soon pour down from the
mountains; the rivers will overflow their banks and inundate
the valleys. The Christian king already begins to waver;
he dare not linger and encounter such a season in a plain cut
up by canals and rivulets. A single wintry storm from our
mountains would wash away his canvas city, and sweep off
those gay pavilions like wreaths of snow before the blast."

The Prince Cidi Yahye took heart at these words, and

counted the days as they passed until the stormy season should commence. As he watched the Christian camp, he beheld it one morning in universal commotion: there was an unusual sound of hammers in every part, as if some new engines of war were constructing. At length, to his astonishment, the walls and roofs of houses began to appear above the bulwarks. In a little while there were above a thousand edifices of wood and plaster erected, covered with tiles taken from the demolished towers of the orchards, and bearing the pennons of various commanders and cavaliers; while the common soldiery constructed huts of clay and branches of trees, thatched with straw. Thus, to the dismay of the Moors, within four days the light tents and gay pavilions which had whitened their hills and plains passed away like summer clouds; and the unsubstantial camp assumed the solid appearance of a city, laid out into streets and squares. In the center rose a large edifice which overlooked the whole; and the royal standard of Aragon and Castile proudly floating above it showed it to be the palace of the king.*

Ferdinand had taken the sudden resolution thus to turn his camp into a city, partly to provide against the approaching season, and partly to convince the Moors of his fixed determination to continue the siege. In their haste to erect their dwellings, however, the Spanish cavaliers had not properly considered the nature of the climate. For the greater part of the year there scarcely falls a drop of rain on the thirsty soil of Andalusia. The ramblas, or dry channels of the torrents, remain deep and arid gashes and clefts in the sides of the mountains; the perennial streams shrink up to mere threads of water, which, tinkling down the bottoms of the deep barrancas or ravines, scarce feed and keep alive the rivers of the valleys. The rivers, almost lost in their wide and naked beds, seem like thirsty rills, winding in serpentine mazes through deserts of sand and stones; and so shallow and tranquil in their course as to be forded in safety in almost every part. One autumnal tempest of rain, however,

---

* Cura de los Palacios, Pulgar, etc.

changes the whole face of nature:—the clouds break in deluges among the vast congregation of mountains; the ramblas are suddenly filled with raging floods; the tinkling rivulets swell to thundering torrents, that come roaring down from the mountains, tumbling great masses of rocks in their career. The late meandering river spreads over its once naked bed, lashes its surges against the banks, and rushes like a wide and foaming inundation through the valley.

Scarcely had the Christians finished their slightly built edifices, when an autumnal tempest of the kind came scouring from the mountains. The camp was immediately overflowed. Many of the houses, undermined by the floods or beaten by the rain, crumbled away and fell to the earth, burying man and beast beneath their ruins. Several valuable lives were lost, and great numbers of horses and other animals perished. To add to the distress and confusion of the camp, the daily supply of provisions suddenly ceased; for the rain had broken up the roads and rendered the rivers impassable. A panic seized upon the army, for the cessation of a single day's supply produced a scarcity of bread and provender. Fortunately, the rain was but transient: the torrents rushed by and ceased; the rivers shrunk back again to their narrow channels, and the convoys that had been detained upon their banks arrived safely in the camp.

No sooner did Queen Isabella hear of this interruption of her supplies, than, with her usual vigilance and activity, she provided against its recurrence. She dispatched six thousand foot-soldiers, under the command of experienced officers, to repair the roads and to make causeways and bridges for the distance of seven Spanish leagues. The troops, also, who had been stationed in the mountains by the king to guard the defiles, made two paths—one for the convoys going to the camp, and the other for those returning, that they might not meet and impede each other. The edifices which had been demolished by the late floods were rebuilt in a firmer manner, and precautions were taken to protect the camp from future inundations.

CHAPTER THIRTY-FOUR

ENCOUNTERS BETWEEN THE CHRISTIANS AND MOORS BEFORE BAZA; AND THE DEVOTION OF THE INHABITANTS TO THE DEFENSE OF THEIR CITY

WHEN King Ferdinand beheld the ravage and confusion produced by a single autumnal storm, and bethought him of all the maladies to which a besieging camp is exposed in inclement seasons, he began to feel his compassion kindling for the suffering people of Baza, and an inclination to grant them more favorable terms. He sent, therefore, several messages to the alcayde Mohammed ben Hassan, offering liberty of person and security of property for the inhabitants, and large rewards for himself, if he would surrender the city.

The veteran Mohammed was not to be dazzled by the splendid offers of the monarch; he had received exaggerated accounts of the damage done to the Christian camp by the late storm, and of the sufferings and discontents of the army in consequence of the transient interruption of supplies: he considered the overtures of Ferdinand as proofs of the desperate state of his affairs. "A little more patience, a little more patience," said the shrewd old warrior, "and we shall see this cloud of Christian locusts driven away before the winter storms. When they once turn their backs, it will be our turn to strike; and with the help of Allah, the blow shall be decisive." He sent a firm though courteous refusal to the Castilian monarch, and in the meantime animated his companions to sally forth with more spirit than ever, to attack the Spanish outposts and those laboring in the trenches. The consequence was a daily occurrence of the most daring and bloody skirmishes, that cost the lives of many of the bravest and most adventurous cavaliers of either army.

In one of these sallies, nearly three hundred horse and

VOL. III.   * * *15

two thousand foot mounted the heights behind the city, to capture the Christians who were employed upon the works. They came by surprise upon a body of guards, esquires of the Count de Urena, killed some, put the rest to flight, and pursued them down the mountain, until they came in sight of a small force under the Count de Tendilla and Gonsalvo of Cordova. The Moors came rushing down with such fury that many of the men of the Count de Tendilla betook themselves to flight. The brave count considered it less dangerous to fight than to fly. Bracing his buckler, therefore, and grasping his trusty weapon, he stood his ground with his accustomed prowess. Gonsalvo of Cordova ranged himself by his side, and, marshaling the troops which remained with them, they made a valiant front to the Moors.

The Infidels pressed them hard, and were gaining the advantage, when Alonzo de Aguilar, hearing of the danger of his brother Gonsalvo, flew to his assistance, accompanied by the Count of Urena and a body of their troops. A hot fight ensued, from cliff to cliff and glen to glen. The Moors were fewer in number, but they excelled in the dexterity and lightness requisite for their scrambling skirmishes. They were at length driven from their vantage-ground, and pursued by Alonzo de Aguilar and his brother Gonsalvo to the very suburbs of the city, leaving many of the bravest of their men upon the field.

Such was one of innumerable rough encounters which were daily taking place, in which many brave cavaliers were slain, without any apparent benefit to either party. The Moors, notwithstanding repeated defeats and losses, continued to sally forth daily with astonishing spirit and vigor, and the obstinacy of their defense seemed to increase with their sufferings.

The Prince Cidi Yahye was ever foremost in these sallies, but he grew daily more despairing of success. All the money in the military chest was expended, and there was no longer wherewithal to pay the hired troops. Still the veteran Mohammed ben Hassan undertook to provide for this emergency. Summoning the principal inhabitants, he represented the necessity of some exertion and sacrifice on their part to maintain the defense of the city. "The enemy," said he, "dreads the approach of winter, and our perseverance drives him to despair. A little longer, and he will leave you in quiet enjoyment of your homes and families. But our troops must be paid to keep them in good heart. Our money is exhausted, and all our supplies are cut off. It is impossible to continue our defense without your aid."

Upon this the citizens consulted together, and they collected all their vessels of gold and silver, and brought them to Mohammed ben Hassan: "Take these," said they, "and coin them, or sell them, or pledge them, for money wherewith to pay the troops." The women of Baza also were seized with generous emulation: "Shall we deck ourselves with gorgeous apparel," said they, "when our country is desolate, and its defenders in want of bread?" So they took their collars, and bracelets and anklets, and other ornaments of gold, and all their jewels, and put them in the hands of the veteran alcayde: "Take these spoils of our vanity," said they, "and let them contribute to the defense of our homes and families. If Baza be delivered, we need no jewels to grace our rejoicing; and if Baza fall, of what avail are ornaments to the captive?"

By these contributions was Mohammed enabled to pay the soldiery, and to carry on the defense of the city with unabated spirit.

Tidings were speedily conveyed to King Ferdinand of this generous devotion on the part of the people of Baza, and the hopes which the Moorish commanders gave them that the Christian army would soon abandon the siege in despair. "They shall have a convincing proof of the fallacy of such hopes," said the politic monarch: so he wrote forthwith to Queen Isabella, praying her to come to the camp in state, with all her train and retinue, and publicly to take up her residence there for the winter. By this means, the Moors would be convinced of the settled determination of the sovereigns to persist in the siege until the city should surrender, and he trusted they would be brought to speedy capitulation.

CHAPTER THIRTY-FIVE

HOW QUEEN ISABELLA ARRIVED AT THE CAMP, AND THE CONSEQUENCES OF HER ARRIVAL

MOHAMMED BEN HASSAN still encouraged his companions with hopes that the royal army would soon relinquish the siege; when they heard, one day, shouts of joy from the Christian camp, and thundering salvos of artillery. Word was brought, at the same time, from the sentinels on the watch-towers, that a Christian army was approaching down the valley. Mohammed and his fellow-commanders ascended one of the highest towers of the walls, and beheld in truth a numerous force, in shining array, descending the hills, and heard the distant clangor of the trumpet and the faint swell of triumphant music.

As the host drew nearer, they descried a stately dame magnificently attired, whom they soon discovered to be the queen. She was riding on a mule, the sumptuous trappings of which were resplendent with gold, and reached to the ground. On her right hand rode her daughter, the Princess Isabella, equally splendid in her array; and on her left, the venerable grand cardinal of Spain. A noble train of ladies and cavaliers followed her, together with pages and esquires, and a numerous guard of hidalgos of high rank, arrayed in superb armor. When the veteran Mohammed ben Hassan beheld that this was the Queen Isabella, arriving in state to take up her residence in the camp, his heart failed him; he shook his head mournfully, and, turning to his captains, "Cavaliers," said he, "the fate of Baza is decided!"

The Moorish commanders remained gazing with a mingled feeling of grief and admiration at this magnificent pageant, which foreboded the fall of their city. Some of the troops would have sallied forth on one of their desperate skirmishes, to attack the royal guard; but the Prince Cidi Yahye forbade them; nor would he allow any artillery to be discharged, or any molestation or insult to be offered; for the character of Isabella was venerated even by the Moors; and most of the commanders possessed that high and chivalrous courtesy which belongs to heroic spirits—for they were among the noblest and bravest cavaliers of the Moorish nation.

The inhabitants of Baza, when they learned that the Christian queen was approaching the camp, eagerly sought every eminence that could command a view of the plain; and every battlement, and tower, and mosque, was covered with turbaned heads gazing at the glorious spectacle. They beheld King Ferdinand issue forth in royal state, attended by the Marques of Cadiz, the Master of Santiago, the Duke of Alva, the admiral of Castile, and many other nobles of renown; while the whole chivalry of the camp, sumptuously arrayed, followed in his train, and the populace rent the air with acclamations at the sight of the patriot queen.

When the sovereigns had met and embraced each other, the two hosts mingled together and entered the camp in martial pomp; and the eyes of the Infidel beholders were dazzled by the flash of armor, the splendor of golden caparisons, the gorgeous display of silks and brocades and velvets, of tossing plumes and fluttering banners. There was at the same time a triumphant sound of drums and trumpets, clarions and sackbuts, mingled with the sweet melody of the dulcimer, which came swelling in bursts of harmony that seemed to rise up to the heavens.*

On the arrival of the queen (says the historian Hernando del Pulgar, who was present at the time) it was marvelous to behold how all at once the rigor and turbulence of war were softened, and the storm of passion sunk into a calm. The sword was sheathed; the crossbow no longer lanched its deadly shafts; and the artillery, which had hitherto kept

---

* Cura de los Palacios.

up an incessant uproar, now ceased its thundering. On both sides, there was still a vigilant guard kept up; the sentinels bristled the walls of Baza with their lances, and the guards patroled the Christian camp, but there was no sallying forth to skirmish, nor any wanton violence or carnage.

Prince Cidi Yahye saw, by the arrival of the queen, that the Christians were determined to continue the siege, and he knew that the city would have to capitulate. He had been prodigal of the lives of his soldiers, as long as he thought a military good was to be gained by the sacrifice; but he was sparing of their blood in a hopeless cause, and weary of exasperating the enemy by an obstinate yet hopeless defense.

At the request of Prince Cidi Yahye, a parley was granted, and the Master commander of Leon, Don Gutierre de Cardenas, was appointed to confer with the veteran alcayde Mohammed. They met at an appointed place, within view of both camp and city, honorably attended by cavaliers of either army. Their meeting was highly courteous, for they had learned, from rough encounters in the field, to admire each other's prowess. The commander of Leon, in an earnest speech, pointed out the hopelessness of any further defense, and warned Mohammed of the ills which Malaga had incurred by its obstinacy. "I promise, in the name of my sovereigns," said he, "that if you surrender immediately, the inhabitants shall be treated as subjects, and protected in property, liberty and religion. If you refuse, you, who are now renowned as an able and judicious commander, will be chargeable with the confiscations, captivities and deaths which may be suffered by the people of Baza."

The commander ceased, and Mohammed returned to the city to consult with his companions. It was evident that all further resistance was hopeless; but the Moorish commanders felt that a cloud might rest upon their names, should they, of their own discretion, surrender so important a place without its having sustained an assault. Prince Cidi Yahye requested permission, therefore, to send an envoy to Guadix with a letter to the old monarch El Zagal, treating of the surrender; the request was granted, a safe conduct assured to the envoy, and the veteran alcayde Mohammed ben Hassan departed upon this momentous mission.

CHAPTER THIRTY-SIX

SURRENDER OF BAZA

THE old warrior king was seated in an inner chamber of the castle of Guadix, much cast down in spirit, and ruminating on his gloomy fortunes, when an envoy from Baza was announced, and the veteran alcayde Mohammed stood before him. El Zagal saw disastrous tidings written in his countenance: "How fares it with Baza?" said he, summoning up his spirits to the question. "Let this inform thee," replied Mohammed; and he delivered into his hands the letter from the Prince Cidi Yahye.

This letter spoke of the desperate situation of Baza; the impossibility of holding out longer, without assistance from El Zagal; and the favorable terms held out by the Castilian sovereigns. Had it been written by any other person, El Zagal might have received it with distrust and indignation; but he confided in Cidi Yahye as in a second self, and the words of his letter sunk deep in his heart. When he had finished reading it, he sighed deeply, and remained for some time lost in thought, with his head drooping upon his bosom. Recovering himself, at length, he called together the alfaquis and the old men of Guadix, and, communicating the tidings from Baza, solicited their advice. It was a sign of sore trouble of mind and dejection of heart, when El Zagal sought the advice of others; but his fierce courage was tamed, for he saw the end of his power approaching. The alfaquis and the old men did but increase the distraction of his mind by a variety of counsel, none of which appeared of any avail; for unless Baza were succored, it was impossible that it should hold out: and every attempt to succor it had proved ineffectual.

El Zagal dismissed his council in despair, and summoned the veteran Mohammed before him. "Allah Achbar!" exclaimed he, "God is great; there is but one God, and Mahomet is His prophet. Return to my cousin, Cidi Yahye; tell him it is out of my power to aid him; he must do as seems to him for the best. The people of Baza have performed deeds worthy of immortal fame; I cannot ask them to encounter further ills and perils in maintaining a hopeless defense."

The reply of El Zagal determined the fate of the city. Cidi Yahye and his fellow commanders immediately capitulated, and were granted the most favorable terms. The cavaliers and soldiers who had come from other parts to the defense of the place were permitted to depart freely with their arms, horses and effects. The inhabitants had their choice, either to depart with their property, or to dwell in the suburbs, in the enjoyment of their religion and laws, taking an oath of fealty to the sovereigns, and paying the same tribute they had paid to the Moorish kings. The city and citadel were to be delivered up in six days, within which period the inhabitants were to remove all their effects; and in the meantime, they were to place, as hostages, fifteen Moorish youths, sons of the principal inhabitants, in the hands of the commander of Leon. When Cidi Yahye and the alcayde Mohammed came to deliver up the hostages, among whom were the sons of the latter, they paid homage to the king and queen, who received them with the utmost courtesy and kindness, and ordered magnificent presents to be given to them, and likewise to the other Moorish cavaliers, consisting of money, robes, horses, and other things of great value.

The Prince Cidi Yahye was so captivated by the grace, the dignity, and generosity of Isabella, and the princely courtesy of Ferdinand, that he vowed never again to draw his sword against such magnanimous sovereigns. The queen, charmed with his gallant bearing and his animated professions of devotion, assured him that, having him on her side,

she already considered the war terminated which had desolated the kingdom of Granada.

Mighty and irresistible are words of praise from the lips
of sovereigns. Cidi Yahye was entirely subdued by this fair
speech from the illustrious Isabella. His heart burned with
a sudden flame of loyalty toward the sovereigns. He begged
to be enrolled among the most devoted of their subjects; and,
in the fervor of his sudden zeal, engaged not merely to dedi-
cate his sword to their service, but to exert all his influence,
which was great, in persuading his cousin, Muley Abdalla el
Zagal, to surrender the cities of Guadix and Almeria, and to
give up all further hostilities. Nay, so powerful was the
effect produced upon his mind by his conversation with the
sovereigns, that it extended even to his religion; for he became immediately enlightened as to the heathenish abomina-
tions of the vile sect of Mahomet, and struck with the truths
of Christianity, as illustrated by such powerful monarchs.
He consented, therefore, to be baptized, and to be gathered
into the fold of the church. The pious Agapida indulges in
a triumphant strain of exultation, on the sudden and surprising conversion of this princely Infidel: he considers it one of
the greatest achievements of the Catholic sovereigns, and
indeed one of the marvelous occurrences of this holy war:
"But it is given to saints and pious monarchs," says he, "to
work miracles in the cause of the faith; and such did the
most Catholic Ferdinand, in the conversion of the Prince
Cidi Yahye."

Some of the Arabian writers have sought to lessen the
wonder of this miracle, by alluding to great revenues granted
to the prince and his heirs by the Castilian monarchs, together with a territory in Marchena, with towns, lands, and
vassals; but in this (says Agapida) we only see a wise precaution of King Ferdinand, to clinch and secure the conversion of his proselyte. The policy of the Catholic monarch
was at all times equal to his piety. Instead also of vaunting
of this great conversion, and making a public parade of the
entry of the prince into the church, King Ferdinand ordered

that the baptism should be performed in private, and kept a profound secret. He feared that Cidi Yahye might otherwise be denounced as an apostate, and abhorred and abandoned by the Moors, and thus his influence destroyed in bringing the war to a speedy termination.*

The veteran Mohammed ben Hassan was likewise won by the magnanimity and munificence of the Castilian sovereigns, and entreated to be received into their service; and his example was followed by many other Moorish cavaliers, whose services were generously accepted and magnificently rewarded.

Thus, after a siege of six months and twenty days, the city of Baza surrendered on the 4th of December, 1489; the festival of the glorious Santa Barbara, who is said, in the Catholic calendar, to preside over thunder and lightning, fire and gunpowder, and all kinds of combustious explosions. The king and queen made their solemn and triumphant entry on the following day; and the public joy was heightened by the sight of upward of five hundred Christian captives, men, women, and children, delivered from the Moorish dungeons.

The loss of the Christians in this siege amounted to twenty thousand men, of whom seventeen thousand died of disease, and not a few of mere cold—a kind of death (says the historian Mariana) peculiarly uncomfortable; but (adds the venerable Jesuit) as these latter were chiefly people of ig- noble rank, baggage-carriers and such like, the loss was not of great importance.

The surrender of Baza was followed by that of Almunecar, Tavernas, and most of the fortresses of the Alpuxarra mountains; the inhabitants hoped, by prompt and voluntary sub- mission, to secure equally favorable terms with those granted to the captured city, and the alcaydes to receive similar re- wards to those lavished on its commanders; nor were either of them disappointed. The inhabitants were permitted to remain as Mudexares, in the quiet enjoyment of their prop-

---

* Conde, tom. 3, cap. 40.

erty and religion; and as to the alcaydes, when they came
to the camp to render up their charges, they were received
by Ferdinand with distinguished favor, and rewarded with
presents of money in proportion to the importance of the
places they had commanded.   Care was taken by the politic
monarch, however, not to wound their pride or shock their
delicacy; so these sums were paid under color of arrears due
to them for their services to the former government.   Ferdinand had conquered by dint of sword in the earlier part of
the war; but he found gold as potent as steel in this campaign of Baza.

With several of these mercenary chieftains came one
named Ali Aben Fahar, a seasoned warrior, who had held
many important commands.   He was a Moor of a lofty,
stern, and melancholy aspect, and stood silent and apart,
while his companions surrendered their several fortresses and
retired laden with treasure.   When it came to his turn to
speak, he addressed the sovereigns with the frankness of a
soldier, but with a tone of dejection and despair.

"I am a Moor," said he, "and of Moorish lineage, and
am alcayde of the fair towns and castles of Purchena and
Paterna.   These were intrusted to me to defend; but those
who should have stood by me have lost all strength and courage, and seek only for security.   These fortresses, therefore,
most potent sovereigns, are yours, whenever you will send to
take possession of them."

Large sums of gold were immediately ordered by Ferdinand to be delivered to the alcayde, as a recompense for so
important a surrender.   The Moor, however, put back the
gift with a firm and haughty demeanor: "I came not," said
he, "to sell what is not mine, but to yield what fortune has
made yours; and your majesties may rest assured that, had
I been properly seconded, death would have been the price
at which I would have sold my fortresses, and not the gold
you offer me."

The Castilian monarchs were struck with the lofty and
loyal spirit of the Moor, and desired to engage a man of such

fidelity in their service; but the proud Moslem could not be induced to serve the enemies of his nation and his faith.

"Is there nothing then," said Queen Isabella, "that we can do to gratify thee, and to prove to thee our regard?"

"Yes," replied the Moor; "I have left behind me, in the towns and valleys which I have surrendered, many of my unhappy countrymen, with their wives and children, who cannot tear themselves from their native abodes. Give me your royal word that they shall be protected in the peaceable enjoyment of their religion and their homes."

"We promise it," said Isabella; "they shall dwell in peace and security. But for thyself—what dost thou ask for thyself?"

"Nothing," replied Ali, "but permission to pass unmolested, with my horses and effects, into Africa."

The Castilian monarchs would fain have forced upon him gold and silver, and superb horses richly caparisoned, not as rewards, but as marks of personal esteem; but Ali Aben Fahar declined all presents and distinctions, as if he thought it criminal to flourish individually during a time of public distress; and disdained all prosperity that seemed to grow out of the ruins of his country.

Having received a royal passport, he gathered together his horses and servants, his armor and weapons, and all his warlike effects; bade adieu to his weeping countrymen with a brow stamped with anguish, but without shedding a tear; and, mounting his Barbary steed, turned his back upon the delightful valleys of his conquered country, departing on his lonely way, to seek a soldier's fortune amid the burning sands of Africa.*

---

* Pulgar. Garibay, lib. 40, cap. 40. Cura de los Palacios.

CHAPTER THIRTY-SEVEN

SUBMISSION OF EL ZAGAL TO THE CASTILIAN SOVEREIGNS

EVIL tidings never fail by the way through lack of messengers; they are wafted on the wings of the wind, and it is as if the very birds of the air would bear them to the ear of the unfortunate. The old king El Zagal buried himself in the recesses of his castle to hide himself from the light of day, which no longer shone prosperously upon him; but every hour brought missives, thundering at the gate, with the tale of some new disaster. Fortress after fortress had laid its keys at the feet of the Christian sovereigns: strip by strip of warrior mountain and green fruitful valley was torn from his domains and added to the territories of the conquerors. Scarcely a remnant remained to him, except a tract of the Alpuxarras, and the noble cities of Guadix and Almeria. No one any longer stood in awe of the fierce old monarch; the terror of his frown had declined with his power. He had arrived at that stage of adversity when a man's friends feel emboldened to tell him hard truths, and to give him unpalatable advice; and when his spirit is bowed down to listen quietly, if not meekly.

El Zagal was seated on his divan, his whole spirit absorbed in rumination on the transitory nature of human glory, when his kinsman and brother-in-law, the Prince Cidi Yahye, was announced. That illustrious convert to the true faith and the interests of the conquerors of his country had hastened to Guadix with all the fervor of a new proselyte, eager to prove his zeal in the service of Heaven and the Castilian sovereigns, by persuading the old monarch to abjure his faith and surrender his possessions.

Cidi Yahye still bore the guise of a Moslem, for his conversion was as yet a secret. The stern heart of El Zagal softened at beholding the face of a kinsman in this hour of adversity. He folded his cousin to his bosom, and gave thanks to Allah that amid all his troubles he had still a friend and counselor on whom he might rely.

Cidi Yahye soon entered upon the real purpose of his mission. He represented to El Zagal the desperate state of affairs, and the irretrievable decline of Moorish power in the kingdom of Granada. "Fate," said he, "is against our arms; our ruin is written in the heavens. Remember the prediction of the astrologers at the birth of your nephew Boabdil. We had hoped that their prediction was accomplished by his capture at Lucena; but it is now evident that the stars portended not a temporary and passing reverse of the kingdom, but a final overthrow. The constant succession of disasters which have attended our efforts show that the scepter of Granada is doomed to pass into the hands of the Christian monarchs. Such," concluded the prince emphatically, and with a profound and pious reverence, "such is the almighty will of God!"

El Zagal listened to these words in mute attention, without so much as moving a muscle of his face or winking an eyelid. When the prince had concluded he remained for a long time silent and pensive; at length, heaving a profound sigh from the very bottom of his heart, "Alahuma subahana hu!" exclaimed he, "the will of God be done! Yes, my cousin, it is but too evident that such is the will of Allah; and what He wills He fails not to accomplish. Had He not decreed the fall of Granada, this arm and this scimiter would have maintained it." *

"What then remains," said Cidi Yahye, "but to draw the most advantage from the wreck of empire that is left you? To persist in a war is to bring complete desolation upon the land, and ruin and death upon its faithful inhabitants. Are you disposed to yield up your remaining towns to your nephew El Chico, that they may augment his power,

---

* Conde. tom. 3. c. 40.

and derive protection from his alliance with the Christian sovereigns?"

The eye of El Zagal flashed fire at this suggestion. He grasped the hilt of his scimiter, and gnashed his teeth in fury. "Never," cried he, "will I make terms with that recreant and slave! Sooner would I see the banners of the Christian monarchs floating above my walls than they should add to the possessions of the vassal Boabdil!"

Cidi Yahye immediately seized upon this idea, and urged El Zagal to make a frank and entire surrender: "Trust," said he, "to the magnanimity of the Castilian sovereigns; they will doubtless grant you high and honorable terms. It is better to yield to them as friends what they must infallibly and before long wrest from you as enemies; for such, my cousin, is the almighty will of God!"

"Alahuma subahana hu!" repeated El Zagal, "the will of God be done!" So the old monarch bowed his haughty neck, and agreed to surrender his territories to the enemies of his faith, rather than suffer them to augment the Moslem power under the sway of his nephew.

Cidi Yahye now returned to Baza, empowered by El Zagal to treat on his behalf with the Christian sovereigns. The prince felt a species of exultation as he expatiated on the rich relics of empire which he was authorized to cede. There was a great part of that line of mountains which extends from the metropolis to the Mediterranean sea, with their series of beautiful green valleys, like precious emeralds set in a golden chain. Above all, there were Guadix and Almeria, two of the most inestimable jewels in the crown of Granada.

In return for these possessions, and for the claim of El Zagal to the rest of the kingdom, the sovereigns received him into their friendship and alliance, and gave him in perpetual inheritance the territory of Andarax and the valley of Alhaurin in the Alpuxarras, with half of the salinas or salt-pits of Maleha. He was to enjoy the title of king of Andarax, with two thousand Mudexares or conquered Moors for subjects; and his revenues were to be made up to the sum of

four millions of marevedies.*   All these he was to hold as a
vassal of the Castilian crown.

These arrangements being made, Cidi Yahye returned
with them to Muley Abdalla, and it was concerted that the
ceremony of surrender and homage should take place at the
city of Almeria.

On the 17th of December, King Ferdinand departed from
Baza with a part of his army, and the queen soon followed
with the remainder.   Ferdinand passed in triumph by several of the newly-acquired towns, exulting in these trophies
of his policy rather than his valor.   As he drew near to Almeria, the Moorish king came forth to meet him, accompanied
by the Prince Cidi Yahye and a number of the principal inhabitants on horseback.   The fierce brow of El Zagal was
clouded with a kind of forced humility; but there was an
impatient curl of the lip, with now and then a swelling of
the bosom and an indignant breathing from the distended
nostril.   It was evident he considered himself conquered, not
by the power of man, but by the hand of Heaven; and, while
he bowed to the decrees of fate, it galled his proud spirit to
have to humble himself before its mortal agent.   As he approached the Christian king, he alighted from his horse and
advanced to kiss his hand in token of homage.   Ferdinand,
however, respected the royal title which the Moor had held,
and would not permit the ceremony; but, bending from his
saddle, graciously embraced him, and requested him to re-
mount his steed.†   Several courteous speeches passed between them; and the fortress and city of Almeria, and all
the remaining territories of El Zagal, were delivered up in
form.   When all was accomplished, the old warrior Moor
retired to the mountains with a handful of adherents, to seek
his petty territory of Andarax, to bury his humiliation from
the world, and to console himself with the shadowy title of
a king.‡

---

*Cura de los Palacios, cap. 94.   †Cura de los Palacios, cap. 93.
‡ Pulgar, Garibay, etc.

CHAPTER THIRTY-EIGHT

EVENTS AT GRANADA SUBSEQUENT TO THE SUBMISSION OF EL ZAGAL

WHO can tell when to rejoice in this fluctuating world? Every wave of prosperity has its reacting surge, and we are often overwhelmed by the very billow on which we thought to be wafted into the haven of our hopes. When Yusef Aben Comixa, the vizier of Boabdil, surnamed El Chico, entered the royal saloon of the Alhambra and announced the capitulation of El Zagal, the heart of the youthful monarch leaped for joy. His great wish was accomplished; his uncle was defeated and dethroned, and he reigned without a rival, sole monarch of Granada. At length he was about to enjoy the fruits of his humiliation and vassalage. He beheld his throne fortified by the friendship and alliance of the Castilian monarchs; there could be no question, therefore, of its stability. "Allah Achbar!" exclaimed he, "God is great! Rejoice with me, oh Yusef; the stars have ceased their persecution. Henceforth let no man call me El Zogoybi."

In the first moment of his exultation, Boabdil would have ordered public rejoicings; but the shrewd Yusef shook his head. "The tempest has ceased," said he, "from one point of the heavens, but it may begin to rage from another. A troubled sea is beneath us, and we are surrounded by rocks and quicksands: let my lord the king defer rejoicings until all has settled into a calm." El Chico, however, could not remain tranquil, in this day of exultation; he ordered his steed to be sumptuously caparisoned, and, issuing out of the gate of the Alhambra, descended, with a glittering retinue, along the avenue of trees and fountains, into the city, to receive the acclamations of the populace. As he entered the great square of the Vivarambla, he beheld crowds of people in violent agitation; but, as he approached, what was his surprise to hear groans and murmurs and bursts of execration! The tidings had spread through Granada that Muley Abdalla el Zagal had been driven to capitulate, and that all his territories had fallen into the hands of the Christians. No one had inquired into the particulars, but all Granada had been thrown into a ferment of grief and indignation. In the heat of the moment, old Muley was extolled to the skies as a patriot prince, who had fought to the last for the salvation of his country—as a mirror of monarchs, scorning to compromise the dignity of his crown by any act of vassalage. Boabdil, on the contrary, had looked on exultingly at the hopeless yet heroic struggle of his uncle; he had rejoiced in the defeat of the faithful and the triumph of unbelievers; he had aided in the dismemberment and downfall of the empire. When they beheld him riding forth in gorgeous state, on what they considered a day of humiliation for all true Moslems, they could not contain their rage; and amid the clamors that met his ears, Boabdil more than once heard his name coupled with the epithets of traitor and renegado.

Shocked and discomfited, the youthful monarch returned in confusion to the Alhambra. He shut himself up within its innermost courts, and remained a kind of voluntary prisoner until the first burst of popular feeling should subside. He trusted that it would soon pass away; that the people would be too sensible of the sweets of peace to repine at the price at which it was obtained; at any rate, he trusted to the strong friendship of the Christian sovereigns to secure him even against the factions of his subjects.

The first missives from the politic Ferdinand showed Boabdil the value of his friendship. The Catholic monarch reminded him of a treaty which he had made when captured in the city of Loxa. By this, he had engaged that, in case the Catholic sovereigns should capture the cities of Guadix, Baza, and Almeria, he would surrender Granada into their hands within a limited time, and accept in exchange certain Moorish towns, to be held by him as their vassal.

Ferdinand now informed him that Guadix, Baza, and Almeria had fallen; he called upon him, therefore, to fulfill his
engagement.

If the unfortunate Boabdil had possessed the will he had
not the power to comply with this demand.   He was shut up
in the Alhambra, while a tempest of popular fury raged without.   Granada was thronged by refugees from the captured
towns, many of them disbanded soldiers, and others, broken-
down citizens, rendered fierce and desperate by ruin.   All
railed at Boabdil as the real cause of their misfortunes.   How
was he to venture forth in such a storm?—above all, how was
he to talk to such men of surrender?   In his reply to Ferdinand he represented the difficulties of his situation, and that,
so far from having control over his subjects, his very life
was in danger from their turbulence.   He entreated the
king, therefore, to rest satisfied for the present with his recent conquests, promising him that should he be able to
regain full empire over his capital and its inhabitants, it
would but be to rule over them as vassal to the Castilian
crown.

Ferdinand was not to be satisfied with such a reply.   The
time was come to bring his game of policy to a close, and to
consummate his conquest by seating himself on the throne
of the Alhambra.   Professing to consider Boabdil as a faith-
less ally, who had broken his plighted word, he discarded
him from his friendship, and addressed a second letter, not
to that monarch, but to the commanders and council of the
city.   He demanded a complete surrender of the place, with
all the arms in the possession either of the citizens or of others
who had recently taken refuge within its walls.   If the inhabitants should comply with this summons, he promised
them the indulgent terms which had been granted to Baza,
Guadix and Almeria; if they should refuse, he threatened
them with the fate of Malaga.*

The message of the Catholic monarch produced the great-

* Cura de los Palacios, cap. 96.

est commotion in the city. The inhabitants of the Alcaiceria, that busy hive of traffic, and all others who had tasted the sweets of gainful commerce during the late cessation of hostilities, were for securing their golden advantages by timely submission; others, who had wives and children, looked on them with tenderness and solicitude, and dreaded, by resistance, to bring upon them the horrors of slavery.

But, on the other hand, Granada was crowded with men from all parts, ruined by the war, exasperated by their sufferings, and eager only for revenge; with others, who had been reared amid hostilities, who had lived by the sword, and whom a return of peace would leave without home or hope. Besides these, there were others no less fiery and warlike in disposition, but animated by a loftier spirit. These were valiant and haughty cavaliers of the old chivalrous lineages, who had inherited a deadly hatred to the Christians from a long line of warrior ancestors, and to whom the idea was worse than death, that Granada, illustrious Granada! for ages the seat of Moorish grandeur and delight, should become the abode of unbelievers.

Among these cavaliers the most eminent was Muza ben Abil Gazan. He was of royal lineage, of a proud and generous nature, and a form combining manly strength and beauty. None could excel him in the management of the horse and dexterous use of all kinds of weapons: his gracefulness and skill in the tourney were the theme of praise among the Moorish dames, and his prowess in the field had made him the terror of the enemy. He had long repined at the timid policy of Boabdil, and had endeavored to counteract its enervating effects, and to keep alive the martial spirit of Granada. For this reason, he had promoted jousts and tiltings with the reed, and all those other public games which bear the semblance of war. He endeavored also to inculcate into his companions in arms those high chivalrous sentiments which lead to valiant and magnanimous deeds, but which are apt to decline with the independence of a nation. The generous efforts of Muza had been in a great measure successful: he was the idol of the youthful cavaliers; they regarded him as a mirror of chivalry, and endeavored to imitate his lofty and heroic virtues.

When Muza heard the demand of Ferdinand, that they should deliver up their arms, his eye flashed fire: "Does the Christian king think that we are old men," said he, "and that staffs will suffice us?—or that we are women, and can be contented with distaffs? Let him know that a Moor is born to the spear and scimiter; to career the steed, bend the bow, and lanch the javelin: deprive him of these, and you deprive him of his nature. If the Christian king desires our arms, let him come and win them; but let him win them dearly. For my part, sweeter were a grave beneath the walls of Granada, on the spot I had died to defend, than the richest couch within her palaces, earned by submission to the unbeliever."

The words of Muza were received with enthusiastic shouts by the warlike part of the populace. Granada once more awoke, as a warrior shaking off a disgraceful lethargy. The commanders and council partook of the public excitement, and dispatched a reply to the Christian sovereigns, declaring that they would suffer death rather than surrender their city.

CHAPTER THIRTY-NINE

HOW KING FERDINAND TURNED HIS HOSTILITIES AGAINST THE CITY OF GRANADA

WHEN King Ferdinand received the defiance of the Moors he made preparations for bitter hostilities. The winter season did not admit of an immediate campaign; he contented himself, therefore, with throwing strong garrisons into all his towns and fortresses in the neighborhood of Granada, and gave the command of all the frontier of Jaen to Inigo Lopez de Mendoza, Count of Tendilla, who had shown such consummate vigilance and address in maintaining the dangerous post of Alhama. This renowned veteran established his headquarters in the mountain city of Alcala la Real, within eight leagues of the city of Granada, and commanding the most important passes of that rugged frontier.

In the meantime, the city of Granada resounded with the stir of war. The chivalry of the nation had again control of its councils; and the populace, having once more resumed their weapons, were anxious to wipe out the disgrace of their late passive submission, by signal and daring exploits.

Muza ben Abil Gazan was the soul of action. He commanded the cavalry, which he had disciplined with uncommon skill: he was surrounded by the noblest youth of Granada, who had caught his own generous and martial fire, and panted for the field; while the common soldiers, devoted to his person, were ready to follow him in the most desperate enterprises. He did not allow their courage to cool for want of action. The gates of Granada once more poured forth legions of light scouring cavalry, which skirred the country up to the very gates of the Christian fortresses, sweeping off flocks and herds. The name of Muza became formidable throughout the frontier; he had many encounters with the enemy in the rough passes of the mountains, in which the superior lightness and dexterity of his cavalry gave him the advantage. The sight of his glistening legion, returning across the vega with long cavalgadas of booty, was hailed by the Moors as a revival of their ancient triumphs; but when they beheld Christian banners borne into their gates as trophies, the exultation of the light-minded populace was beyond all bounds.

The winter passed away; the spring advanced; yet Ferdinand delayed to take the field. He knew the city of Granada to be too strong and populous to be taken by assault, and too full of provisions to be speedily reduced by siege. "We must have patience and perseverance," said the politic monarch; "by ravaging the country this year we shall produce a scarcity the next, and then the city may be invested with effect."

An interval of peace, aided by the quick vegetation of a

prolific soil and happy climate, had restored the vega to all
its luxuriance and beauty; the green pastures on the borders
of the Xenil were covered with flocks and herds; the blooming orchards gave promise of abundant fruit, and the open
plain was waving with ripening corn.   The time was at hand
to put in the sickle and reap the golden harvest, when suddenly a torrent of war came sweeping down from the mountains; and Ferdinand, with an army of five thousand horse
and twenty thousand foot, appeared before the walls of Granada.   He had left the queen and princess at the fortress of
Moclin, and came attended by the Duke of Medina Sidonia,
the Marques of Cadiz, the Marques de Villena, the Counts
of Urena and Cabra, Don Alonzo de Aguilar, and other renowned cavaliers.   On this occasion, King Ferdinand for
the first time led his son Prince Juan into the field, and bestowed upon him the dignity of knighthood.   As if to stimu-
late him to grand achievements, the ceremony took place on
the banks of the grand canal, almost beneath the embattled
walls of that warlike city, the object of such daring enterprises,
and in the midst of that famous vega which had been the
field of so many chivalrous exploits.   Above them shone resplendent the red towers of the Alhambra, rising from amid
delicious groves, with the standard of Mahomet waving defiance to the Christian arms.

The Duke of Medina Sidonia, and the valiant Roderigo
Ponce de Leon, Marques of Cadiz, were sponsors; and all
the chivalry of the camp was assembled on the occasion.
The prince, after he was knighted, bestowed the same honor
on several youthful cavaliers of high rank, just entering, like
himself, on the career of arms.

Ferdinand did not loiter in carrying his desolating plans
into execution.   He detached parties in every direction to lay
waste the country; villages were sacked, burned, and destroyed, and the lovely vega once more laid waste with fire
and sword.   The ravage was carried so close to Granada
that the city was wrapped in the smoke of its gardens and
hamlets.   The dismal cloud rolled up the hill and hung about

the towers of the Alhambra, where the unfortunate Boabdil still remained shut up from the indignation of his subjects. The hapless monarch smote his breast, as he looked down from his mountain palace on the desolation effected by his late ally. He dared not even show himself in arms among the populace, for they cursed him as the cause of the miseries once more brought to their doors.

The Moors, however, did not suffer the Christians to carry on their ravages as unmolested as in former years. Muza incited them to incessant sallies. He divided his cavalry into small squadrons, each led by a daring commander. They were taught to hover round the Christian camp; to harass it from various and opposite quarters, cutting off convoys and straggling detachments; to waylay the army in its ravaging expeditions, lurking among rocks and passes of the mountains, or in hollows and thickets of the plain, and practicing a thousand stratagems and surprises.

The Christian army had one day spread itself out rather unguardedly in its foraging about the vega. As the troops commanded by the Marques of Villena approached the skirts of the mountains, they beheld a number of Moorish peasants hastily driving a herd of cattle into a narrow glen. The soldiers, eager for booty, pressed in pursuit of them. Scarcely had they entered the glen, when shouts arose from every side, and they were furiously attacked by an ambuscade of horse and foot. Some of the Christians took to flight; others stood their ground, and fought valiantly. The Moors had the vantage-ground; some showered darts and arrows from the cliffs of the rocks, others fought hand to hand on the plain; while their cavalry, rapid as lightning in their movements, carried havoc and confusion into the midst of the Christian forces.

The Marques de Villena, with his brother Don Alonzo de Pacheco, at the first onset of the Moors, spurred into the hottest of the fight. They had scarce entered, when Don Alonzo was struck lifeless from his horse, before the eyes of his brother. Estevan de Luzon, a gallant captain, fell fighting bravely by the side of the marques, who remained, with his chamberlain Solier and a handful of knights, surrounded by the enemy. Several cavaliers from other parts of the army hastened to their assistance, when King Ferdinand, seeing that the Moors had the vantage-ground and that the Christians were suffering severely, gave signal for retreat. The marques obeyed slowly and reluctantly, for his heart was full of grief and rage at the death of his brother. As he was retiring, he beheld his faithful chamberlain Solier defending himself valiantly against six Moors. The marques turned, and rushed to his rescue; he killed two of the enemy with his own hand, and put the rest to flight. One of the Moors, however, in retreating, rose in his stirrups, and, hurling his lance at the marques, wounded him in the right arm and crippled him for life.*

Such was one of the many ambuscadoes concerted by Muza; nor did he hesitate at times to present a bold front to the Christian forces, and to defy them in the open field. King Ferdinand soon perceived, however, that the Moors seldom provoked a battle without having the advantage of the ground; and that though the Christians generally appeared to have the victory, they suffered the greatest loss; for retreating was a part of the Moorish system, by which they would draw their pursuers into confusion, and then turn upon them with a more violent and fatal attack. He commanded his captains, therefore, to decline all challenges to skirmish, and to pursue a secure system of destruction, ravaging the country, and doing all possible injury to the enemy, with slight risk to themselves.

---

* In consequence of this wound, the marques was ever after obliged to write his signature with his left hand, though capable of managing his lance with his right. The queen one day demanded of him, why he had adventured his life for that of a domestic? "Does not your majesty think," replied he, "that I ought to risk one life for him who would have.adventured three for me had he possessed them?" The queen was charmed with the magnanimity of the reply, and often quoted the marques as setting an heroic example to the chivalry of the age.— Mariana, lib. 25, c. 15.

CHAPTER FORTY

THE FATE OF THE CASTLE OF ROMA

ABOUT two leagues from Granada, on an eminence commanding an extensive view of the vega, stood the strong Moorish castle of Roma, a great place of refuge and security. Hither the neighboring peasantry drove their flocks and herds, and hurried with their most precious effects, on the irruption of a Christian force; and any foraging or skirmishing party from Granada, on being intercepted in their return, threw themselves into Roma, manned its embattled towers, and set the enemy at defiance. The garrison were accustomed to these sudden claims upon their protection; to have parties of Moors clattering up to their gates, so hotly pursued that there was barely time to throw open the portal, receive them within, and shut out their pursuers; while the Christian cavaliers had many a time reined in their panting steeds, at the very entrance of the barbacan, and retired, cursing the strong walls of Roma, that robbed them of their prey.

The late ravages of Ferdinand, and the continual skirmishings in the vega, had roused the vigilance of the castle. One morning early, as the sentinels kept watch upon the battlements, they beheld a cloud of dust advancing rapidly from a distance: turbans and Moorish weapons soon caught their eyes; and as the whole approached, they descried a drove of cattle, urged on in great haste, and convoyed by one hundred and fifty Moors, who led with them two Christian captives in chains.

When the cavalgada had arrived near to the castle, a Moorish cavalier, of noble and commanding mien and splendid attire, rode up to the foot of the tower, and entreated admittance. He stated that they were returning with rich booty from a foray into the lands of the Christians, but that the enemy was on their traces, and they feared to be overtaken before they could reach Granada. The sentinels descended in all haste, and flung open the gates. The long cavalgada defiled into the courts of the castle, which were soon filled with lowing and bleating flocks and herds, with neighing and stamping steeds, and with fierce-looking Moors from the mountains. The cavalier who had asked admission was the chief of the party; he was somewhat advanced in life, of a lofty and gallant bearing, and had with him a son, a young man of great fire and spirit. Close by them followed the two Christian captives, with looks cast down and disconsolate.

The soldiers of the garrison had roused themselves from their sleep, and were busily occupied attending to the cattle which crowded the courts; while the foraging party distributed themselves about the castle to seek refreshment or repose. Suddenly a shout arose that was echoed from courtyard, and hall, and battlement. The garrison, astonished and bewildered, would have rushed to their arms, but found themselves, almost before they could make resistance, completely in the power of an enemy.

The pretended foraging party consisted of Mudexares or Moors tributary to the Christians; and the commanders were the Prince Cidi Yahye and his son Alnayer. They had hastened from the mountains with this small force to aid the Catholic sovereigns during the summer's campaign; and they had concerted to surprise this important castle, and present it to King Ferdinand, as a gage of their faith, and the first fruits of their devotion.

The polite monarch overwhelmed his new converts and allies with favors and distinctions, in return for this important acquisition; but he took care to dispatch a strong force of veteran and genuine Christian troops to man the fortress.

As to the Moors who had composed the garrison, Cidi Yahye remembered that they were his countrymen, and could not prevail upon himself to deliver them into Christian bondage. He set them at liberty, and permitted them to repair to Granada—"A proof," says the pious Agapida, "that his conversion was not entirely consummated, but that there were still some lingerings of the Infidel in his heart." His lenity was far from procuring him indulgence in the opinions of his countrymen; on the contrary, the inhabitants of Granada, when they learned from the liberated garrison the stratagem by which Roma had been captured, cursed Cidi Yahye for a traitor; and the garrison joined in the malediction.

But the indignation of the people of Granada was destined to be aroused to tenfold violence. The old warrior Muley Abdalla el Zagal had retired to his little mountain territory, and for a short time endeavored to console himself with his petty title of king of Andarax. He soon grew impatient, however, of the quiet and inaction of his mimic kingdom. His fierce spirit was exasperated by being shut up within such narrow limits, and his hatred rose to downright fury against Boabdil, whom he considered as the cause of his downfall. When tidings were brought him that King Ferdinand was laying waste the vega, he took a sudden resolution. Assembling the whole disposable force of his kingdom, which amounted to but two hundred men, he descended from the Alpuxarras and sought the Christian camp, content to serve as a vassal the enemy of his faith and his nation, so that he might see Granada wrested from the sway of his nephew.

In his blind passion, the old wrathful monarch injured his cause, and strengthened the cause of his adversary. The Moors of Granada had been clamorous in his praise, extolling him as a victim to his patriotism, and had refused to believe all reports of his treaty with the Christians; but when they beheld, from the walls of the city, his banner mingling with the banners of the unbelievers, and arrayed against his late people, and the capital he had commanded, they broke forth into curses and revilings, and heaped all kind of stigmas upon his name.

Their next emotion, of course, was in favor of Boabdil. They gathered under the walls of the Alhambra, and hailed

him as their only hope, as the sole dependence of the country. Boabdil could scarcely believe his senses when he heard
his name mingled with praises and greeted with acclamations.
Encouraged by this unexpected gleam of popularity, he ventured forth from his retreat, and was received with rapture.
All his past errors were attributed to the hardships of his
fortune, and the usurpation of his tyrant uncle; and whatever breath the populace could spare from uttering curses on
El Zagal was expended in shouts in honor of El Chico.

CHAPTER FORTY-ONE

HOW BOABDIL EL CHICO TOOK THE FIELD; AND HIS EXPEDITION AGAINST ALHENDIN

For thirty days had the vega been overrun by the Christian forces; and that vast plain, late so luxuriant and beautiful, was one wide scene of desolation. The destroying army,
having accomplished its task, passed over the bridge of Pinos
and wound up into the mountains, on the way to Cordova,
bearing away the spoils of towns and villages, and driving
off flocks and herds in long dusty columns. The sound of
the last Christian trumpet died away along the side of the
mountain of Elvira, and not a hostile squadron was seen
glistening on the mournful fields of the vega.

The eyes of Boabdil el Chico were at length opened to the
real policy of King Ferdinand, and he saw that he had no
longer anything to depend upon but the valor of his aım.
No time was to be lost in hastening to counteract the effect
of the late Christian ravage, and in opening the channel for
distant supplies to Granada.

Scarcely had the retiring squadrons of Ferdinand disappeared among the mountains, when Boabdil buckled on his
armor, sallied forth from the Alhambra, and prepared to
take the field. When the populace beheld him actually in
arms against his late ally, both parties thronged with zeal

to his standard. The hardy inhabitants also of the Sierra Nevada, or chain of snow-capped mountains which rise above Granada, descended from their heights, and hastened into the city gates, to proffer their devotion to their youthful king. The great square of the Vivarambla shone with the proud array of legions of cavalry, decked with the colors and devices of the most ancient Moorish families, and marshaled forth by the patriot Muza to follow the king to battle.

It was on the 15th of June that Boabdil once more issued forth from the gates of Granada on martial enterprise. A few leagues from the city, within full view of it, and at the entrance of the Alpuxarra mountains, stood the powerful castle of Alhendin. It was built on an eminence, rising from the midst of a small town, and commanding a great part of the vega, and the main road to the rich valleys of the Alpuxarras. The castle was commanded by a valiant Christian cavalier named Mendo de Quexada, and garrisoned by two hundred and fifty men, all seasoned and experienced warriors. It was a continual thorn in the side of Granada: the laborers of the vega were swept off from their fields by its hardy soldiers; convoys were cut off in the passes of the mountains; and as the garrison commanded a full view of the gates of the city, no band of merchants could venture forth on their needful journeys, without being swooped up by the war-hawks of Alhendin.

It was against this important fortress that Boabdil first led his troops. For six days and nights the fortress was closely besieged. The alcayde and his veteran garrison defended themselves valiantly, but they were exhausted by fatigue and constant watchfulness; for the Moors, being continually relieved by fresh troops from Granada, kept up an unremitted and vigorous attack. Twice the barbacan was forced, and twice the assailants were driven forth headlong with excessive loss. The garrison, however, was diminished in number by the killed and wounded; there were no longer soldiers sufficient to man the walls and gateway; and the brave alcayde was compelled to retire, with his surviving force, to the keep of the castle, in which he continued to make desperate resistance.

The Moors now approached the foot of the tower, under shelter of wooden screens covered with wet hides to ward off missiles and combustibles. They went to work vigorously to undermine the tower, placing props of wood under the foundations, to be afterward set on fire, so as to give the besiegers time to escape before the edifice should fall. Some of the Moors plied their crossbows and arquebuses to defend the workmen, and to drive the Christians from the wall; while the latter showered down stones, and darts, and melted pitch, and flaming combustibles, on the miners.

The brave Mendo de Quexada had cast many an anxious eye across the vega, in hopes of seeing some Christian force hastening to his assistance. Not a gleam of spear or helm was to be descried, for no one had dreamed of this sudden irruption of the Moors. The alcayde beheld his bravest men dead or wounded around him, while the remainder were sinking with watchfulness and fatigue. In defiance of all opposition, the Moors had accomplished their mine; the fire was brought before the walls that was to be applied to the stanchions in case the garrison persisted in defense. In a little while, the tower would crumble beneath him, and be rent and hurled a ruin to the plain. At the very last moment the brave alcayde made the signal of surrender. He marched forth with the remnant of his veteran garrison, who were all made prisoners. Boabdil immediately ordered the walls of the fortress to be razed, and fire to be applied to the stanchions, that the place might never again become a stronghold to the Christians and a scourge to Granada. The alcayde and his fellow-captives were led in dejected convoy across the vega, when they heard a tremendous crash behind them. They turned to look upon their late fortress, but beheld nothing but a heap of tumbling ruins, and a vast column of smoke and dust, where once had stood the lofty tower of Alhendin.

CHAPTER FORTY-TWO

EXPLOIT OF THE COUNT DE TENDILLA

BOABDIL EL CHICO followed up his success by capturing the two fortresses of Marchena and Buldy; he sent his alfaquis in every direction, to proclaim a holy war, and to summon all true Moslems of town or castle, mountain or valley, to saddle steed and buckle on armor, and hasten to the standard of the faith. The tidings spread far and wide, that Boabdil el Chico was once more in the field, and was victorious. The Moors of various places, dazzled by this gleam of success, hastened to throw off their sworn allegiance to the Castilian crown, and to elevate the standard of Boabdil; and the youthful monarch flattered himself that the whole kingdom was on the point of returning to its allegiance.

The fiery cavaliers of Granada were eager to renew those forays into the Christian lands in which they had formerly delighted. A number of them therefore concerted an irruption to the north, into the territory of Jaen, to harass the country about Quezada. They had heard of a rich convoy of merchants and wealthy travelers, on the way to the city of Baza; and they anticipated a glorious conclusion to their foray, in capturing this convoy.

Assembling a number of horsemen, lightly armed and fleetly mounted, and one hundred foot-soldiers, these hardy cavaliers issued forth by night from Granada, made their way in silence through the defiles of the mountains, crossed the frontier without opposition, and suddenly appeared, as if fallen from the clouds, in the very heart of the Christian country.

The mountainous frontier which separates Granada from Jaen was at this time under the command of the Count de Tendilla, the same veteran who had distinguished himself by his vigilance and sagacity when commanding the fortress of Alhama. He held his headquarters at the city of Alcala la Real, in its impregnable fortress, perched high among the mountains, about six leagues from Granada, and dominating all the frontier. From this cloud-capped hold among the rocks he kept an eagle eye upon Granada, and had his scouts and spies in all directions, so that a crow could not fly over the border without his knowledge. His fortress was a place of refuge for the Christian captives who escaped by night from the Moorish dungeons of Granada. Often, however, they missed their way in the defiles of the mountains, and, wandering about bewildered, either repaired by mistake to some Moorish town, or were discovered and retaken at daylight by the enemy. To prevent these accidents, the count had a tower built at his own expense, on the top of one of the heights near Alcala, which commanded a view of the vega and the surrounding country. Here he kept a light blazing throughout the night, as a beacon for all Christian fugitives, to guide them to a place of safety.

The count was aroused one night from his repose, by shouts and cries, which came up from the town and approached the castle walls. "To arms! to arms! the Moor is over the border!" was the cry. A Christian soldier, pale and emaciated, and who still bore traces of the Moorish chains, was brought before the count. He had been taken as guide by the Moorish cavaliers who had sallied from Granada, but had escaped from them among the mountains, and, after much wandering, had found his way to Alcala by the signal-fire.

Notwithstanding the bustle and agitation of the moment, the Count de Tendilla listened calmly and attentively to the account of the fugitive, and questioned him minutely as to the time of departure of the Moors, and the rapidity and direction of their march. He saw that it was too late to prevent their incursion and ravage; but he determined to await them, and give them a warm reception on their return. His soldiers were always on the alert and ready to take the field at a moment's warning.   Choosing a hundred and fifty lances, hardy and valiant men, well disciplined and well seasoned, as indeed were all his troops, he issued forth quietly before break of day, and, descending through the defiles of the mountains, stationed his little force in ambush, in a deep barranca, or dry channel of a torrent, near Barzina, but three leagues from Granada, on the road by which the marauders would have to return.   In the meantime, he sent out scouts to post themselves upon different heights, and look out for the approach of the enemy.

All day they remained concealed in the ravine, and for a great part of the following night; not a turban, however, was to be seen, excepting now and then a peasant returning from his labor, or a solitary muleteer hastening toward Granada.   The cavaliers of the count began to grow restless and impatient; they feared that the enemy might have taken some other route, or might have received intelligence of their ambuscade.   They urged the count to abandon the enterprise and return to Alcala.   "We are here," said they, "almost at the gates of the Moorish capital; our movements may have been descried, and, before we are aware, Granada may pour forth its legions of swift cavalry, and crush us with an overwhelming force."   The Count de Tendilla, however, persisted in remaining until his scouts should come in.   About two hours before daybreak, there were signal-fires on certain Moorish watch-towers of the mountains.   While they were regarding these with anxiety, the scouts came hurrying into the ravine: "The Moors are approaching," said they; "we have reconnoitered them near at hand.   They are between one and two hundred strong, but encumbered with many prisoners and much booty."   The Christian cavaliers laid their ears to the ground, and heard the distant tramp of horses and the tread of foot-soldiers.   They mounted their horses, braced their shields, couched their lances, and drew near to the entrance of the ravine where it opened upon the road.

The Moors had succeeded in waylaying and surprising the

Christian convoy on its way to Baza. They had captured a great number of prisoners, male and female, with great store of gold and jewels, and sumpter mules laden with rich merchandise. With these they had made a forced march over the dangerous parts of the mountains; but now, finding themselves so near to Granada, they fancied themselves in perfect security. They loitered along the road, therefore, irregularly and slowly, some singing, others laughing and exulting at having eluded the boasted vigilance of the Count de Tendilla; while ever and anon were heard the plaint of some female captive, bewailing the jeopardy of her honor, and the heavy sighing of `the merchant at beholding his property in the grasp of ruthless spoilers.

The Count de Tendilla waited until some of the escort had passed the ravine; then, giving the signal for assault, his cavaliers set up great shouts and cries, and charged furiously into the center of the foe. The obscurity of the place and the hour added to the terrors of the surprise. The Moors were thrown into confusion; some rallied, fought desperately, and fell covered with wounds. Thirty-six were killed and fifty-five were made prisoners; the rest, under cover of the darkness, made their escape to the rocks and defiles of the mountains.

The good count unbound the prisoners, gladdening the hearts of the merchants by restoring to them their merchandise. To the female captives also he restored·the jewels of which they had been despoiled, excepting such as had been lost beyond recovery. Forty-five saddle horses, of the choice Barbary breed, remained as captured spoils of the Moors, together with costly armor and booty of various kinds. Having collected everything in haste and arranged his cavalgada, the count urged his way with all speed for Alcala la Real, lest he should be pursued and overtaken by the Moors of Granada. As he wound up the steep ascent to his mountain city, the inhabitants poured forth to meet him with shouts of joy. His triumph was doubly enhanced by being received at the gates of the city by his wife, the daughter of

the Marques of Villena, a lady of distinguished merit, whom
he had not seen for the two years that he had been separated
from his home by the arduous duties of these iron wars.

CHAPTER FORTY-THREE

EXPEDITION OF BOABDIL EL CHICO AGAINST SALOBRENA— EXPLOIT OF HERNANDO PEREZ DEL PULGAR

KING BOABDIL found that his diminished territory was
too closely dominated by Christian fortresses like Alcala la
Real, and too strictly watched by vigilant alcaydes like the
Count of Tendilla, to be able to maintain itself by internal
resources. His foraging expeditions were liable to be intercepted and defeated, while the ravage of the vega had swept
off everything on which the city depended for future sustenance. He felt the want of a seaport, through which, as
formerly, he might keep open a communication with Africa,
and obtain re-enforcements and supplies from beyond the
sea. All the ports and harbors were in the hands of the
Christians, and Granada and its remnant of dependent terri
tory were completely landlocked.

In this emergency, the attention of Boabdil was called by
circumstances to the seaport of Salobrena. This redoubtable
town has already been mentioned in this chronicle as a place
deemed impregnable by the Moors; insomuch that their
kings were accustomed, in time of peril, to keep their treasures in its citadel. It was situated on a high rocky hill,
dividing one of those rich little vegas or plains which lie
open to the Mediterranean, but run like deep green bays into
the stern bosoms of the mountains. The vega was covered
with beautiful vegetation, with rice and cotton, with groves
of oranges, citrons, figs and mulberries, and with gardens
inclosed by hedges of reeds, of aloes, and the Indian fig.
Running streams of cool water from the springs and snows
of the Sierra Nevada kept this delightful valley continually

fresh and verdant; while it was almost locked up by mountain barriers, and lofty promontories that stretched far into
the sea.

Through the center of this rich vega, the rock of Salobrena
reared its rugged back, nearly dividing the plain, and advancing to the margin of the sea, with just a strip of sandy
beach at its foot, laved by the blue waves of the Mediterranean.

The town covered the ridge and sides of the rocky hill,
and was fortified by strong walls and towers; while on the
highest and most precipitous part stood the citadel, a huge
castle that seemed to form a part of the living rock; the
massive ruins of which, at the present day, attract the gaze
of the traveler, as he winds his way far below, along the
road which passes through the vega.

This important fortress had been intrusted to the command of Don Francisco Ramirez de Madrid, captain-general
of the artillery, and the most scientific of all the Spanish
leaders. That experienced veteran, however, was with the
king at Cordova, having left a valiant cavalier as alcayde
of the place.

Boabdil el Chico had full information of the state of the
garrison and the absence of its commander. Putting himself
at the head of a powerful force, therefore, he departed from
Granada, and made a rapid march through the mountains;
hoping, by this sudden move, to seize upon Salobrena before
King Ferdinand could come to its assistance.

The inhabitants of Salobrena were Mudexares, or Moors
who had sworn allegiance to the Christians. Still, when
they heard the sound of the Moorish drums and trumpets,
and beheld the squadrons of their countrymen advancing
across the vega, their hearts yearned toward the standard of
their nation and their faith. A tumult arose in the place;
the populace shouted the name of Boabdil el Chico, and,
throwing open the gates, admitted him within the walls.

The Christian garrison was too few in number to contend
for the possession of the town: they retreated to the citadel,
and shut themselves within its massive walls, which were

considered impregnable. Here they maintained a desperate defense, hoping to hold out until succor should arrive from the neighboring fortresses.

The tidings that Salobrena was invested by the Moorish king spread along the seacoast and filled the Christians with alarm. Don Francisco Enriquez, uncle of the king, commanded the city of Velez Malaga, about twelve leagues distant, but separated by ranges of those vast rocky mountains which are piled along the Mediterranean, and tower in steep promontories and precipices above its waves.

Don Francisco summoned the alcaydes of his district to hasten with him to the relief of this important fortress. A number of cavaliers and their retainers answered to his call, among whom was Hernando Perez del Pulgar, surnamed "El de las Hazanas" (he of the exploits)—the same who had signalized himself in a foray, by elevating a handkerchief on a lance for a banner and leading on his disheartened comrades to victory. As soon as Don Francisco beheld a little band collected round him, he set out with all speed for Salobrena. The march was rugged and severe, climbing and descending immense mountains, and sometimes winding along the edge of giddy precipices, with the surges of the sea raging far below. When Don Francisco arrived with his followers at the lofty promontory that stretches along one side of the little vega of Salobrena, he looked down with sorrow and anxiety upon a Moorish army of great force encamped at the foot of the fortress, while Moorish banners, on various parts of the walls, showed that the town was already in possession of the Infidels. A solitary Christian standard alone floated on the top of the castle-keep, showing that the brave garrison were hemmed up in their rock-built citadel.

Don Francisco found it impossible, with his small force, to make any impression on the camp of the Moors, or to get to the relief of the castle. He stationed his little band upon a rocky height near the sea, where they were safe from the assaults of the enemy. The sight of his friendly banner waving in their neighborhood cheered the heart of the garrison, and conveyed to them assurance of speedy succor from the king.

In the meantime, Hernando Perez del Pulgar, who always burned to distinguish himself by bold and striking exploits, in the course of a prowling expedition along the borders of the Moorish camp, remarked a postern-gate of the castle, opening upon the steep part of the rocky hill which looked toward the mountains.

A sudden thought flashed upon the daring mind of Pulgar: "Who will follow my banner," said he, "and make a dash for yonder postern?" A bold proposition, in time of warfare, never wants for bold spirits to accept it. Seventy resolute men immediately stepped forward. Pulgar put himself at their head; they cut their way suddenly through a weak part of the camp, fought their way up to the gate, which was eagerly thrown open to receive them; and succeeded in making their way into the fortress, before the alarm of their attempt had spread through the Moorish army.

The garrison was roused to new spirit by this unlooked-for re-enforcement, and were enabled to make a more vigorous resistance. The Moors had intelligence, however, that there was a great scarcity of water in the castle; and they exulted in the idea that this additional number of warriors would soon exhaust the cisterns and compel them to surrender. When Pulgar heard of this hope entertained by the enemy, he caused a bucket of water to be lowered from the battlements and threw a silver cup in bravado to the Moors.

The situation of the garrison, however, was daily growing more and more critical; they suffered greatly from thirst, while, to tantalize them in their sufferings, they beheld limpid streams winding in abundance through the green plain below them. They began to fear that all succor would arrive too late, when one day they beheld a little squadron of vessels far at sea, but standing toward the shore. There was some doubt at first whether it might not be a hostile armament from Africa; but as it approached, they descried, to their great joy, the banner of Castile.

It was a re-enforcement, brought in all haste by the governor of the fortress, Don Francisco Ramirez. The squadron anchored at a steep rocky island, which rises from the very margin of the smooth sandy beach, directly in front of the rock of Salobrena, and stretches out into the sea. On this island Ramirez landed his men, and was as strongly posted as if in a fortress. His force was too scanty to attempt a battle, but he assisted to harass and distract the besiegers. Whenever King Boabdil made an attack upon the fortress, his camp was assailed on one side by the troops of Ramirez, who landed from their island, and on another by those of Don Francisco Enriquez, who swept down from their rock, while Hernando del Pulgar kept up a fierce defense, from every tower and battlement of the castle.

The attention of the Moorish king was diverted also, for a time, by an ineffectual attempt to relieve the little port of Adra, which had recently declared in his favor, but which had been recaptured for the Christians by Cidi Yahye and his son Alnayar. Thus the unlucky Boabdil, bewildered on every hand, lost all the advantage that he had gained by his rapid march from Granada. While he was yet besieging the obstinate citadel, tidings were brought him that King Ferdinand was in full march, with a powerful host, to its assistance. There was no time for further delay: he made a furious attack with all his forces upon the castle, but was again repulsed by Pulgar and his coadjutors; when, abandoning the siege in despair, he retreated with his army, lest King Ferdinand should get between him and his capital. On his way back to Granada, however, he in some sort consoled himself for his late disappointment, by overrunning a part of the territories and possessions lately assigned to his uncle El Zagal and to Cidi Yahye. He defeated their alcaydes, destroyed several of their fortresses, burned their villages, and, leaving the country behind him reeking and smoking with his vengeance, returned with considerable booty, to repose himself within the walls of the Alhambra.

CHAPTER FORTY-FOUR

HOW KING FERDINAND TREATED THE PEOPLE OF GUADIX—
AND HOW EL ZAGAL FINISHED HIS REGAL CAREER

SCARCELY had Boabdil ensconced himself in his capital, when King Ferdinand, at the head of seven thousand horse and twenty thousand foot, again appeared in the vega. He had set out in all haste from Cordova to the relief of Salobrena; but, hearing on his march that the siege was raised, he turned with his army to make a second ravage round the walls of devoted Granada. His present forage lasted fifteen days, in the course of which everything that had escaped his former desolating visit was destroyed, and scarce a green thing or a living animal was left on the face of the land. The Moors sallied frequently and fought desperately, in defense of their fields, but the work of destruction was accomplished—and Granada, once the queen of gardens, was left surrounded by a desert.

From hence Ferdinand marched to crush a conspiracy which had lately manifested itself in the cities of Guadix, Baza and Almeria. These recently conquered places had entered into secret correspondence with King Boabdil, inviting him to march to their gates, promising to rise upon the Christian garrisons, seize upon the citadels, and surrender themselves into his power. The Marques of Villena had received notice of the conspiracy, and had suddenly thrown himself, with a large force, into Guadix. Under pretense of making a review of the inhabitants, he made them sally forth into the fields before the city. When the whole Moorish population capable of bearing arms was thus without the walls, he ordered the gates to be closed. He then permitted them to enter, two by two and three by three, and to take forth their wives, children and effects. The houseless Moors were fain to make themselves temporary hovels, in the gardens and orchards about the city; they were clamorous in their complaints at being thus excluded from their homes, but were told they must wait with patience until the charges against them could be investigated, and the pleasure of the king be known.*

When Ferdinand arrived at Guadix, he found the unhappy Moors in their cabins among the orchards. They complained bitterly of the deception that had been practiced upon them, and implored permission to return into the city, and live peaceably in their dwellings, as had been promised them in their articles of capitulation.

King Ferdinand listened graciously to their complaints: "My friends," said he in reply, "I am informed that there has been a conspiracy among you to kill my alcayde and garrison, and to take part with my enemy the king of Granada. I shall make a thorough investigation of this conspiracy. Those among you who shall be proved innocent shall be restored to their dwellings, but the guilty shall incur the penalty of their offenses. As I wish, however, to proceed with mercy as well as justice, I now give you your choice, either to depart at once without further question, going wherever you please, and taking with you your families and effects, under an assurance of safety; or to deliver up those who are guilty, not one of whom, I give you my royal word, shall escape punishment."

When the people of Guadix heard these words, they communed among themselves; and as most of them (says the worthy Agapida) were either culpable or feared to be considered so, they accepted the alternative, and departed sorrowfully, they and their wives and their little ones. "Thus," in the words of that excellent and contemporary historian, Andres Bernaldez, commonly called the curate of Los Palacios—"thus did the king deliver Guadix from the hands of the enemies of our holy faith, after seven hundred and

---

* Zurita, lib. 20, c. 85.   Cura de los Palacios, c. 97.

seventy years that it had been in their possession, ever since the time of Roderick the Goth; and this was one of the mysteries of our Lord, who would not consent that the city should remain longer in the power of the Moors:" a pious and sage remark, which is quoted with peculiar approbation by the worthy Agapida.

King Ferdinand offered similar alternatives to the Moors of Baza, Almeria, and other cities accused of participation in this conspiracy; who generally preferred to abandon their homes, rather than incur the risk of an investigation. Most of them relinquished Spain, as a country where they could no longer live in security and independence, and departed with their families for Africa; such as remained were suffered to live in villages and hamlets, and other unwalled places.*

While Ferdinand was thus occupied at Guadix, dispensing justice and mercy, and receiving cities in exchange, the old monarch Muley Abdalla, surnamed El Zagal, appeared before him. He was haggard with care and almost crazed with passion. He had found his little territory of Andarax, and his two thousand subjects, as difficult to govern as had been the distracted kingdom of Granada. The charm, which had bound the Moors to him, was broken when he appeared in arms under the banner of Ferdinand. He had returned from his inglorious campaign with his petty army of two hundred men, followed by the execrations of the people of Granada, and the secret repining of those he had led into the field. No sooner had his subjects heard of the successes of Boabdil el Chico, than they had seized their arms, assembled tumultuously, declared for the young monarch, and threatened the life of El Zagal.† The unfortunate old king had with difficulty evaded their fury; and this last lesson seemed entirely to have cured him of his passion for sovereignty. He now entreated Ferdinand to purchase the towns

---

* Garibay, lib. 13, cap. 39.   Pulgar, part 3, cap. 132.
† Cura de los Palacios, cap. 97.

and castles and other possessions which had been granted to
him; offering them at a low rate, and begging safe passage
for himself and his followers to Africa. King Ferdinand
graciously complied with his wishes. He purchased of him
three-and-twenty towns and villages in the valleys of Andarax
and Alhaurin, for which he gave him five millions of mara-
vedies. El Zagal relinquished his right to one-half of the
salinas or salt-pits of Maleha, in favor of his brother-in-law
Cidi Yahye. Having thus disposed of his petty empire and
possessions, he packed up all his treasure, of which he had
a great amount, and, followed by many Moorish families,
passed over to Africa.*

And here let us cast an eye beyond the present period of
our chronicle, and trace the remaining career of El Zagal.
His short and turbulent reign, and disastrous end, would
afford a wholesome lesson to unprincipled ambition, were not
all ambition of the kind fated to be blind to precept and
example. When he arrived in Africa, instead of meeting
with kindness and sympathy, he was seized and thrown into
prison by the king of Fez, as though he had been his vassal. He was accused of being the cause of the dissensions
and downfall of the kingdom of Granada; and the accusation
being proved to the satisfaction of the king of Fez, he condemned the unhappy El Zagal to perpetual darkness. A
basin of glowing copper was passed before his eyes, which
effectually destroyed his sight. His wealth, which had
probably been the secret cause of these cruel measures, was
confiscated and seized upon by his oppressor, and El Zagal
was thrust forth, blind, helpless and destitute, upon the
world. In this wretched condition, the late Moorish monarch
groped his way through the regions of Tingitania, until he
reached the city of Velez de Gomera. The king of Velez
had formerly been his ally, and felt some movement of compassion at his present altered and abject state. He gave him
food and raiment, and suffered him to remain unmolested in

---

* Conde, part 4, cap. 41.

his dominions. Death, which so often hurries off the prosperous and happy from the midst of untasted pleasures, spares on the other hand the miserable, to drain the last drop of his cup of bitterness. El Zagal dragged out a wretched existence of many years in the city of Velez. He wandered about blind and disconsolate, an object of mingled scorn and pity, and bearing above his raiment a parchment on which was written in Arabic, "This is the unfortunate king of Andalusia." *

CHAPTER FORTY-FIVE

PREPARATIONS OF GRANADA FOR A DESPERATE DEFENSE

How is thy strength departed, oh Granada! how is thy beauty withered and despoiled, oh city of groves and fountains! The commerce that once thronged thy streets is at an end; the merchant no longer hastens to thy gates with the luxuries of foreign lands. The cities which once paid thee tribute are wrested from thy sway; the chivalry which filled thy Vivarambla with the sumptuous pageantry of war have fallen in many battles. The Alhambra still rears its ruddy towers from the midst of groves, but melancholy reigns in its marble halls; and the monarch looks down from his lofty balconies upon a naked waste, where once had extended the blooming glories of the vega!

Such is the lament of the Moorish writers, over the lamentable state of Granada, which now remained a mere phantom of its former greatness. The two ravages of the vega, following so closely upon each other, had swept off all the produce of the year; and the husbandman had no longer the heart to till the field, seeing that the ripening harvest only brought the spoiler to the door.

During the winter season, King Ferdinand made diligent

* Marmol, de Rebelione Maur., lib. 1, cap. 16. Padraza, Hist. Granat, part 3, c. 4. Suarez, Hist. de Obispados de Guadix y Baza, cap. 10.

preparations for the last campaign that was to decide the fate of Granada. As this war was waged purely for the promotion of the Christian faith, he thought it meet that its enemies should bear the expenses. He levied, therefore, a general contribution upon all the Jews throughout his kingdom, by synagogues and districts; and obliged them to render in the proceeds at the city of Seville.*

On the 11th of April, Ferdinand and Isabella departed for the Moorish frontier, with the solemn determination to lay close siege to Granada, and never to quit its walls until they had planted the standard of the faith on the towers of the Alhambra. Many of the nobles of the kingdom, particularly those from the parts remote from the scene of action, wearied by the toils of war, and foreseeing that this would be a tedious siege, requiring patience and vigilance rather than hardy deeds of arms, contented themselves with sending their vassals, while they stayed at home, to attend to their domains. Many cities furnished soldiers at their cost, and the king took the field with an army of forty thousand infantry and ten thousand horse. The principal captains who followed the king in this campaign were Roderigo Ponce de Leon, the Marques of Cadiz, the Master of Santiago, the Marques of Villena; the counts of Tendilla, Cifuentes, Cabra, and Urena; and Don Alonzo de Aguilar.

Queen Isabella, accompanied by her son the Prince Juan, and by the Princesses Juana, Maria, and Cathalina, her daughters, proceeded to Alcala la Real, the mountain fortress and stronghold of the Count de Tendilla. Here she remained, to forward supplies to the army, and to be ready to repair to the camp, whenever her presence might be required.

The army of Ferdinand poured into the vega by various defiles of the mountains; and, on the 23d of April, the royal tent was pitched at a village called Los Ojos de Huescar, about a league and a half from Granada. At the approach

---

* Garibay, lib. 18, c. 39.

of this formidable force, the harassed inhabitants turned pale, and even many of the warriors trembled; for they felt that the last desperate struggle was at hand.

Boabdil el Chico assembled his council in the Alhambra, from the windows of which they could behold the Christian squadrons glistening through clouds of dust, as they poured along the vega. The utmost confusion and consternation reigned in the council. Many of the members, terrified with the horrors impending over their families, advised Boabdil to throw himself upon the generosity of the Christian monarch: even several of the bravest suggested the possibility of obtaniing honorable terms.

The wazir of the city, Abul Cazim Abdel Melic, was called upon to report the state of the public means for sustenance and defense. There were sufficient provisions, he said, for a few months' supply, independent of what might exist in the possession of merchants and other rich inhabitants. "But of what avail," said he, "is a supply for a few months, against the sieges of the Castilian monarch, which are interminable?"

He produced, also, the lists of men capable of bearing arms. "The number," said he, "is great; but what can be expected from mere citizen soldiers? They vaunt and menace, in time of safety; none are so arrogant, when the enemy is at a distance—but when the din of war thunders at their gates, they hide themselves in terror."

When Muza heard these words, he rose with generous warmth: "What reason have we," said he, "to despair? The blood of those illustrious Moors, the conquerors of Spain, still flows in our veins. Let us be true to ourselves, and fortune will again be with us. We have a veteran force, both horse and foot, the flower of our chivalry, seasoned in war and scarred in a thousand battles. As to the multitude of our citizens, spoken of so slightly, why should we doubt their valor? There are twenty thousand young men, in the fire of youth, for whom I will engage, that in the defense of their homes they will rival the most valiant veterans. Do we want provisions? Our horses are fleet, and our horsemen daring in the foray. Let them scour and scourge the country of those apostate Moslems who have surrendered to the Christians. Let them make inroads into the lands of our enemies. We shall soon see them returning with cavalgadas to our gates; and, to a soldier, there is no morsel so sweet as that wrested with hard fighting from the foe."

Boabdil el Chico, though he wanted firm and durable courage, was readily excited to sudden emotions of bravery. He caught a glow of resolution from the noble ardor of Muza. "Do what is needful," said he to his commanders; "into your hands I confide the common safety. You are the protectors of the kingdom, and, with the aid of Allah, will revenge the insults of our religion, the deaths of our friends and relations, and the sorrows and sufferings heaped upon our land."*

To every one was now assigned his separate duty. The wazir had charge of the arms and provisions, and the enrolling of the people. Muza was to command the cavalry, to defend the gates, and to take the lead in all sallies and skirmishings. Naim Reduan and Muhamed Aben Zayde were his adjutants. Abdel Kerim Zegri, and the other captains, were to guard the walls; and the alcaydes of the Alcazaba, and of the Red Towers, had command of the fortresses.

Nothing now was heard but the din of arms and the bustle of preparation. The Moorish spirit, quick to catch fire, was immediately in a flame; and the populace, in the excitement of the moment, set at naught the power of the Christians. Muza was in all parts of the city, infusing his own generous zeal into the bosoms of the soldiery. The young cavaliers rallied round him as their model; the veteran warriors regarded him with a soldier's admiration; the vulgar throng followed him with shouts, and the helpless part of the inhabitants, the old men and the women, hailed him with blessings as their protector.

* Conde.

On the first appearance of the Christian army, the principal gates of the city had been closed, and secured with bars and bolts and heavy chains: Muza now ordered them to be thrown open: "To me and my cavaliers," said he, "is intrusted the defense of the gates; our bodies shall be their barriers." He stationed at each gate a strong guard, chosen from his bravest men. His horsemen were always completely armed, and ready to mount at a moment's warning: their steeds stood saddled and caparisoned in the stables, with lance and buckler beside them. On the least approach of the enemy, a squadron of horse gathered within the gate, ready to lanch forth like the bolt from the thundercloud. Muza made no empty bravado nor haughty threat; he was more terrible in deeds than in words, and executed daring exploits, beyond even the vaunt of the vainglorious. Such was the present champion of the Moors. Had they possessed many such warriors, or had Muza risen to power at an earlier period of the war, the fate of Granada might have been deferred, and the Moor for a long time have maintained his throne within the walls of the Alhambra.

CHAPTER FORTY-SIX

HOW KING FERDINAND CONDUCTED THE SIEGE CAUTIOUSLY; AND HOW QUEEN ISABELLA ARRIVED AT THE CAMP

THOUGH Granada was shorn of its glories, and nearly cut off from all external aid, still its mighty castles and massive bulwarks seemed to set all attack at defiance. Being the last retreat of Moorish power, it had assembled within its walls the remnants of the armies that had contended, step by step, with the invaders in their gradual conquest of the land. All that remained of high-born and high-bred chivalry was here; all that was loyal and patriotic was roused to activity by the common danger; and Granada, that had so long been lulled into inaction by vain hopes of security, now assumed a formidable aspect in the hour of its despair.

Ferdinand saw that any attempt to subdue the city by main force would be perilous and bloody. Cautious in his policy, and fond of conquests gained by art rather than valor, he resorted to the plan which had been so successful with Baza, and determined to reduce the place by famine. For this purpose, his armies penetrated into the very heart of the Alpuxarras, and ravaged the valleys, and sacked and burned the towns, upon which the city depended for its supplies. Scouting parties, also, ranged the mountains behind Granada, and captured every casual convoy of provisions. The Moors became more daring as their situation became more hopeless. Never had Ferdinand experienced such vigorous sallies and assaults. Muza, at the head of his cavalry, harassed the borders of the camp, and even penetrated into the interior, making sudden spoil and ravage, and leaving his course to be traced by the slain and wounded. To protect his camp from these assaults, Ferdinand fortified it with deep trenches and strong bulwarks. It was of a quadrangular form, divided into streets like a city, the troops being quartered in tents, and in booths constructed of bushes and branches of trees. When it was completed, Queen Isabella came in state, with all her court, and the prince and princesses, to be present at the siege. This was intended, as on former occasions, to reduce the besieged to despair, by showing the determination of the sovereigns to reside in the camp until the city should surrender. Immediately after her arrival, the queen rode forth to survey the camp and its environs: wherever she went, she was attended by a splendid retinue; and all the commanders vied with each other in the pomp and ceremony with which they received her. Nothing was heard, from morning until night, but shouts and acclamations, and bursts of martial music; so that it appeared to the Moors as if a continual festival and triumph reigned in the Christian camp.

The arrival of the queen, however, and the menaced ob-

stinacy of the siege, had no effect in damping the fire of the
Moorish chivalry. Muza inspired the youthful warriors with
the most devoted heroism: "We have nothing left to fight
for," said he, "but the ground we stand on; when this is lost
we cease to have a country and a name."

Finding the Christian king forbore to make an attack,
Muza incited his cavaliers to challenge the youthful chivalry
of the Christian army to single combat, or partial skirmishes.
Scarce a day passed without gallant conflicts of the kind in
sight of the city and the camp. The combatants rivaled each
other in the splendor of their armor and array, as well as in
the prowess of their deeds. Their contests were more like
the stately ceremonials of tilts and tournaments than the
rude conflicts of the field. Ferdinand soon perceived that
they animated the fiery Moors with fresh zeal and courage,
while they cost the lives of many of his bravest cavaliers: he
again, therefore, forbade the acceptance of any individual
challenges, and ordered that all partial encounters should
be avoided. The cool and stern policy of the Catholic sovereign bore hard upon the generous spirits of either army,
but roused the indignation of the Moors when they found
that they were to be subdued in this inglorious manner: "Of
what avail," said they, "are chivalry and heroic valor? the
crafty monarch of the Christians has no magnanimity in
warfare; he seeks to subdue us through the weakness of our
bodies, but shuns to encounter the courage of our souls."

CHAPTER FORTY–SEVEN

OF THE INSOLENT DEFIANCE OF YARFE THE MOOR, AND
THE DARING EXPLOIT OF HERNANDO PEREZ
DEL PULGAR

WHEN the Moorish knights beheld that all courteous challenges were unavailing, they sought various means to provoke the Christian warriors to the field. Sometimes a body

of them, fleetly mounted, would gallop up to the skirts of the camp, and try who should hurl his lance furthest within the barriers, having his name inscribed upon it, or a label affixed to it, containing some taunting defiance. These bravadoes caused great irritation, but still the Spanish warriors were restrained by the prohibition of the king.

Among the Moorish cavaliers was one named Yarfe, renowned for his great strength and daring spirit; but whose courage partook of fierce audacity rather than chivalric heroism. In one of these sallies, when they were skirting the Christian camp, this arrogant Moor outstripped his companions, overleaped the barriers, and, galloping close to the royal quarters, lanched his lance so far within that it remained quivering in the earth close by the pavilions of the sovereigns. The royal guards rushed forth in pursuit, but the Moorish horsemen were already beyond the camp, and scouring in a cloud of dust for the city. Upon wresting the lance from the earth, a label was found upon it, importing that it was intended for the queen.

Nothing could equal the indignation of the Christian warriors, at the insolence of the bravado, and the discourteous insult offered to the queen. Hernando Perez del Pulgar, surnamed "he of the exploits," was present, and resolved not to be outbraved by this daring Infidel: "Who will stand by me," said he, "in an enterprise of desperate peril?" The Christian cavaliers well knew the harebrained valor of Hernando del Pulgar, yet not one hesitated to step forward. He chose fifteen companions, all men of powerful arm and dauntless heart. In the dead of the night, he led them forth from the camp, and approached the city cautiously, until he arrived at a postern-gate, which opened upon the Darro, and was guarded by foot-soldiers. The guards, little thinking of such an unwonted and partial attack, were for the most part asleep. The gate was forced, and a confused and chance-medley skirmish ensued: Hernando del Pulgar stopped not to take part in the affray: putting spurs to his horse, he galloped furiously through the streets, striking fire out of the stones at every bound. Arrived at the principal mosque, he sprang from his horse, and, kneeling at the portal, took possession of the edifice as a Christian chapel, dedicating it to the blessed Virgin. In testimonial of the ceremony, he took a tablet which he had brought with him, on which was inscribed in large characters, "AVE MARIA," and nailed it to the door of the mosque with his dagger. This done, he remounted his steed and galloped back to the gate. The alarm had been given—the city was in an uproar—soldiers were gathering from every direction. They were astonished at seeing a Christian warrior galloping from the interior of the city. Hernando del Pulgar overturned some, cut down others, rejoined his companions, who still maintained possession of the gate by dint of hard fighting, and all made good their retreat to the camp. The Moors were at a loss to imagine the meaning of this wild and apparently fruitless assault; but great was their exasperation, on the following day, when the trophy of hardihood and prowess, the "AVE MARIA," was discovered thus elevated in bravado in the very center of the city. The mosque thus boldly sanctified by Hernando del Pulgar was actually consecrated into a cathedral after the capture of Granada.*

---

* In commemoration of this daring feat, the emperor Charles V., in after years, conferred on Pulgar and his descendants the right of sepulture in that church, and the privilege of sitting in the choir during high mass. This Hernando Perez del Pulgar was a man of letters, as well as arms, and inscribed to Charles V. a summary of the achievements of Gonsalvo of Cordova, surnamed the great captain, who had been one of his comrades in arms. He is often confounded with Hernando del Pulgar, historian and secretary to Queen Isabella.—See note to Pulgar's Chron. of the Catholic Sovereigns, part 3, c. iii., edit. Valencia, 1780.

CHAPTER FORTY-EIGHT

HOW QUEEN ISABELLA TOOK A VIEW OF THE CITY OF
GRANADA—AND HOW HER CURIOSITY COST THE
LIVES OF MANY CHRISTIANS AND MOORS

THE royal encampment lay at such a distance from Granada that the general aspect of the city only could be seen,
as it rose gracefully from the vega, covering the sides of the
hills with palaces and towers.   Queen Isabella had expressed
an earnest desire to behold, nearer at hand, a city whose
beauty was so renowned throughout the world; and the
Marques of Cadiz, with his accustomed courtesy, prepared
a great military escort and guard to protect the queen and
the ladies of the court while they enjoyed this perilous
gratification.

It was on the morning after the events recorded in the
preceding chapter that a magnificent and powerful train
issued forth from the Christian camp.   The advance guard
was composed of legions of cavalry, heavily armed, that
looked like moving masses of polished steel.   Then came the
king and queen, with the prince and princess, and the ladies
of the court, surrounded by the royal bodyguard, sumptuously arrayed, composed of the sons of the most illustrious
houses of Spain; after these was the rear-guard, composed
of a powerful force of horse and foot; for the flower of the
army sallied forth that day.   The Moors gazed with fearful
admiration at this glorious pageant, wherein the pomp of the
court was mingled with the terrors of the camp.   It moved
along in a radiant line, across the vega, to the melodious
thunders of martial music; while banner and plume, and
silken scarf, and rich brocade, gave a gay and gorgeous
relief to the grim visage of iron war that lurked beneath.

The army moved toward the hamlet of Zubia, built on
the skirts of the mountain to the left of Granada, and com-

manding a view of the Alhambra, and the most beautiful quarter of the city. As they approached the hamlet, the Marques of Villena, the Count Urena, and Don Alonzo de Aguilar, filed off with their battalions, and were soon seen glittering along the side of the mountain above the village. In the meantime, the Marques of Cadiz, the Count de Tendilla, the Count de Cabra, and Don Alonzo Fernandez, Senior of Alcandrete and Montemayor, drew up their forces in battle array on the plain below the hamlet, presenting a living barrier of loyal chivalry between the sovereigns and the city.

Thus securely guarded, the royal party alighted, and, entering one of the houses of the hamlet, which had been prepared for their reception, enjoyed a full view of the city from its terraced roof. The ladies of the court gazed with delight at the red towers of the Alhambra, rising from amid shady groves, anticipating the time when the Catholic sovereigns should be enthroned within its walls, and its courts shine with the splendor of Spanish chivalry. "The reverend prelates and holy friars, who always surrounded the queen, looked with serene satisfaction," says Fray Antonio Agapida, "at this modern Babylon, enjoying the triumph that awaited them, when those mosques and minarets should be converted into churches, and goodly priests and bishops should succeed to the Infidel alfaquis."

When the Moors beheld the Christians thus drawn forth in full array in the plain, they supposed it was to offer them battle; and they hesitated not to accept it. In a little while, the queen beheld a body of Moorish cavalry pouring into the vega, the riders managing their fleet and fiery steeds with admirable address. They were richly armed, and clothed in the most brilliant colors, and the caparisons of their steeds flamed with gold and embroidery. This was the favorite squadron of Muza, composed of the flower of the youthful cavaliers of Granada. Others succeeded, some heavily armed, some *à la ginete* with lance and buckler; and lastly came the legions of foot-soldiers, with arquebuse and crossbow, and spear and scimiter.

When the queen saw this army issuing from the city, she sent to the Marques of Cadiz, and forbade any attack upon the enemy, or the acceptance of any challenge to a skirmish; for she was loth that her curiosity should cost the life of a single human being.

The marques promised to obey, though sorely against his will; and it grieved the spirit of the Spanish cavaliers to be obliged to remain with sheathed swords while bearded by the foe. The Moors could not comprehend the meaning of this inaction of the Christians, after having apparently invited a battle. They sallied several times from their ranks, and approached near enough to discharge their arrows; but the Christians were immovable. Many of the Moorish horsemen galloped close to the Christian ranks, brandishing their lances and scimiters, and defying various cavaliers to single combat; but King Ferdinand had rigorously prohibited all duels of the kind, and they dared not transgress his orders under his very eye.

While this grim and reluctant tranquillity prevailed along the Christian line, there rose a mingled shout and sound of laughter near the gate of the city. A Moorish horseman, armed at all points, issued forth, followed by a rabble, who drew back as he approached the scene of danger. The Moor was more robust and brawny than was common with his countrymen. His visor was closed; he bore a huge buckler and a ponderous lance; his scimiter was of a Damascus blade, and his richly ornamented dagger was wrought by an artificer of Fez. He was known by his device to be Yarfe, the most insolent, yet valiant, of the Moslem warriors—the same who had hurled into the royal camp his lance, inscribed to the queen. As he rode slowly along in front of the army, his very steed, prancing with fiery eye and distended nostril, seemed to breathe defiance to the Christians.

But what were the feelings of the Spanish cavaliers, when they beheld, tied to the tail of his steed, and dragged in the dust, the very inscription, "AVE MARIA," which Hernando Perez del Pulgar had affixed to the door of the mosque! A

burst of horror and indignation broke forth from the army.
Hernando del Pulgar was not at hand to maintain his previous achievement; but one of his young companions in arms,
Garcilasso de la Vega by name, putting spurs to his horse,
galloped to the hamlet of Zubia, threw himself on his knees
before the king, and besought permission to accept the defiance of this insolent Infidel, and to revenge the insult offered
to our blessed Lady.   The request was too pious to be refused: Garcilasso remounted his steed; he closed his helmet,
graced by four sable plumes, grasped his buckler of Flemish
workmanship, and his lance of matchless temper, and defied
the haughty Moor in the midst of his career.   A combat took
place in view of the two armies and of the Castilian court.
The Moor was powerful in wielding his weapons, and dexterous in managing his steed.   He was of larger frame than
Garcilasso, and more completely armed; and the Christians
trembled for their champion.   The shock of their encounter
was dreadful; their lances were shivered, and sent up splin-
ters in the air.   Garcilasso was thrown back in the saddle—
his horse made a wide career, before he could recover, gather
up the reins, and return to the conflict.   They now encountered each other with swords.   The Moor circled round his
opponent, as a hawk circles whereabout to make a swoop;
his Arabian steed obeyed his rider with matchless quickness;
at every attack of the Infidel it seemed as if the Christian
knight must sink beneath his flashing scimiter.   But if
Garcilasso were inferior to him in power, he was superior
in agility: many of his blows he parried; others he received
upon his Flemish shield, which was proof against the Damascus blade.   The blood streamed from numerous wounds
received by either warrior.   The Moor, seeing his antagonist
exhausted, availed himself of his superior force, and, grappling, endeavored to wrest him from his saddle.   They both
fell to earth; the Moor placed his knee upon the breast of
his victim, and, brandishing his dagger, aimed a blow at
his throat.   A cry of despair was uttered by the Christian
warriors, when suddenly they beheld the Moor rolling life-

less in the dust. Garcilasso had shortened his sword, and, as his adversary raised his arm to strike, had pierced him to the heart. "It was a singular and miraculous victory," says Fray Antonio Agapida; "but the Christian knight was armed by the sacred nature of his cause, and the holy Virgin gave him strength, like another David, to slay this gigantic champion of the Gentiles."

The laws of chivalry were observed throughout the combat—no one interfered on either side. Garcilasso now despoiled his adversary; then, rescuing the holy inscription of "AVE MARIA" from its degrading situation, he elevated it on the point of his sword, and bore it off as a signal of triumph, amid the rapturous shouts of the Christian army.

The sun had now reached the meridian; and the hot blood of the Moors was inflamed by its rays, and by the sight of the defeat of their champion. Muza ordered two pieces of ordnance to open a fire upon the Christians. A confusion was produced in one part of their ranks: Muza called to the chiefs of the army, "Let us waste no more time in empty challenges—let us charge upon the enemy: he who assaults has always an advantage in the combat." So saying, he rushed forward, followed by a large body of horse and foot, and charged so furiously upon the advance guard of the Christians that he drove it in upon the battalion of the Marques of Cadiz.

The gallant marques now considered himself absolved from all further obedience to the queen's commands. He gave the signal to attack. "Santiago!" was shouted along the line; and he pressed forward to the encounter, with his battalion of twelve hundred lances. The other cavaliers followed his example, and the battle instantly became general.

When the king and queen beheld the armies thus rushing to the combat, they threw themselves on their knees, and implored the holy Virgin to protect her faithful warriors. The prince and princess, the ladies of the court, and the prelates and friars who were present, did the same; and the effect of the prayers of these illustrious and saintly persons was immediately apparent. The fierceness with which the Moors had rushed to the attack was suddenly cooled; they were bold and adroit for a skirmish, but unequal to the veteran Spaniards in the open field. A panic seized upon the foot-soldiers—they turned, and took to flight. Muza and his cavaliers in vain endeavored to rally them. Some took refuge in the mountains; but the greater part fled to the city, in such confusion that they overturned and trampled upon each other. The Christians pursued them to the very gates. Upward of two thousand were either killed, wounded, or taken prisoners; and the two pieces of ordnance were brought off as trophies of the victory. Not a Christian lance but was bathed that day in the blood of an Infidel.*

Such was the brief but bloody action which was known among the Christian warriors by the name of "the queen's skirmish"; for when the Marques of Cadiz waited upon her majesty to apologize for breaking her commands, he attributed the victory entirely to her presence. The queen, however, insisted that it was all owing to her troops being led on by so valiant a commander. Her majesty had not yet recovered from her agitation at beholding so terrible a scene of bloodshed; though certain veterans present pronounced it as gay and gentle a skirmish as they had ever witnessed.

To commemorate this victory, the queen afterward erected a monastery in this village of Zubia, dedicated to St. Francisco, which still exists; and in its garden is a laurel, planted by the hands of her majesty.†

---

* Cura de los Palacios.

† The house from whence the king and queen contemplated the battle is likewise to be seen at the present day. It is in the first street, to the right, on entering the village from the vega; and the royal arms are painted on the ceilings. It is inhabited by a worthy farmer, Francisco Garcia, who, in showing the house, refuses all compensation, with true Spanish pride; offering, on the contrary, the hospitalities of his mansion to the stranger. His children are versed in the old Spanish ballads, about the exploits of Hernando Perez del Pulgar and Garcilasso de la Vega.

CHAPTER FORTY-NINE

CONFLAGRATION OF THE CHRISTIAN CAMP

THE ravages of war had as yet spared a little portion of the vega of Granada. A green belt of gardens and orchards still flourished round the city, extending along the banks of the Xenil and the Darro. They had been the solace and delight of the inhabitants in their happier days, and contributed to their sustenance in this time of scarcity. Ferdinand determined to make a final and exterminating ravage to the very walls of the city, so that there should not remain a single green thing for the sustenance of man or beast. The evening of a hot July day shone splendidly upon the Christian camp, which was in a bustle of preparation for the next day's service—for desperate resistance was expected from the Moors. The camp made a glorious appearance in the setting sun. The various tents of the royal family and the attendant nobles were adorned with rich hangings, and sumptuous devices, and costly furniture; forming, as it were, a little city of silk and brocade, where the pinnacles of pavilions of various gay colors, surmounted with waving standards and fluttering pennons, might vie with the domes and minarets of the capital they were besieging.

In the midst of this little gaudy metropolis, the lofty tent of the queen domineered over the rest like a stately palace. The Marques of Cadiz had courteously surrendered his own tent to the queen: it was the most complete and sumptuous in Christendom, and had been carried about with him throughout the war. In the center rose a stately alfaneque or pavilion in Oriental taste, the rich hangings being supported by columns of lances and ornamented with martial devices. This central pavilion or silken tower, was surrounded by other compartments, some of painted linen lined with silk, and all separated from each other by curtains. It was one of those camp palaces which are raised and demolished in an instant, like the city of canvas that surrounds them.

As the evening advanced, the bustle in the camp subsided. Every one sought repose, preparatory to the next day's trial. The king retired early, that he might be up with the crowing of the cock, to head the destroying army in person. All stir of military preparation was hushed in the royal quarters; the very sound of minstrelsy was mute, and not the tinkling of a guitar was to be heard from the tents of the fair ladies of the court.

The queen had retired to the innermost part of her pavilion, where she was performing her orisons before a private altar; perhaps the peril to which the king might be exposed in the next day's foray inspired her with more than usual devotion. While thus at her prayers, she was suddenly aroused by a glare of light and wreaths of suffocating smoke. In an instant, the whole tent was in a blaze: there was a high gusty wind, which whirled the light flames from tent to tent, and wrapped the whole in one conflagration.

Isabella had barely time to save herself by instant flight. Her first thought, on being extricated from her tent, was for the safety of the king. She rushed to his tent, but the vigilant Ferdinand was already at the entrance of it. Starting from bed on the first alarm, and fancying it an assault of the enemy, he had seized his sword and buckler, and sallied forth undressed, with his cuirass upon his arm.

The late gorgeous camp was now a scene of wild confusion. The flames kept spreading from one pavilion to another, glaring upon the rich armor, and golden and silver vessels, which seemed melting in the fervent heat. Many of the soldiers had erected booths and bowers of branches, which, being dry, crackled and blazed, and added to the rapid conflagration. The ladies of the court fled, shrieking and half-dressed, from their tents. There was an alarm of drum and trumpet, and a distracted hurry about the camp of men half armed. The Prince Juan had been snatched out of bed by an attendant, and conveyed to the quarters of the Count de Cabra, which were at the entrance of the camp. The loyal count immediately summoned his people, and those of his cousin Don Alonzo de Montemayor, and formed a guard round the tent in which the prince was sheltered.

The idea that this was a stratagem of the Moors soon subsided; but it was feared that they might take advantage of it to assault the camp. The Marques of Cadiz, therefore, sallied forth with three thousand horse to check any advance from the city. As they passed along, the whole camp was a scene of hurry and consternation—some hastening to their posts at the call of drum and trumpet; some attempting to save rich effects and glittering armor from the tents, others dragging along terrified and restive horses.

When they emerged from the camp they found the whole firmament illuminated. The flames whirled up in long light spires, and the air was filled with sparks and cinders. A bright glare was thrown upon the city, revealing every battlement and tower. Turbaned heads were seen gazing from every roof, and armor gleamed along the walls; yet not a single warrior sallied from the gates: the Moors suspected some stratagem on the part of the Christians, and kept quietly within their walls. By degrees the flames expired; the city faded from sight; all again became dark and quiet, and the Marques of Cadiz returned with his cavalry to the camp.

CHAPTER FIFTY

THE LAST RAVAGE BEFORE GRANADA

WHEN the day dawned on the Christian camp, nothing remained of that beautiful assemblage of stately pavilions but heaps of smoldering rubbish, with helms and corselets and other furniture of war, and masses of melted gold and silver glittering among the ashes. The wardrobe of the queen was entirely destroyed, and there was an immense loss in plate, jewels, costly stuffs, and sumptuous armor of the luxurious nobles. The fire at first had been attributed to treachery, but on investigation it proved to be entirely accidental. The queen, on retiring to her prayers, had ordered her lady in attendance to remove a light burning near her couch, lest it should prevent her sleeping. Through heedlessness, the taper was placed in another part of the tent, near the hangings, which, being blown against it by a gust of wind, immediately took fire.

The wary Ferdinand knew the sanguine temperament of the Moors, and hastened to prevent their deriving confidence from the night's disaster. At break of day, the drums and trumpets sounded to arms, and the Christian army issued from among the smoking ruins of their camp, in shining squadrons, with flaunting banners and bursts of martial melody, as though the preceding night had been a time of high festivity, instead of terror.

The Moors had beheld the conflagration with wonder and perplexity. When the day broke, and they looked toward the Christian camp, they saw nothing but a dark smoking mass. Their scouts came in, with the joyful intelligence that the whole camp was a scene of ruin. Scarce had the tidings spread throughout the city, when they beheld the Christian army advancing toward their walls. They considered it a feint, to cover their desperate situation and prepare for a retreat. Boabdil el Chico had one of his impulses of valor—he determined to take the field in person, and to follow up this signal blow which Allah had inflicted on the enemy.

The Christian army approached close to the city, and were laying waste the gardens and orchards, when Boabdil sallied forth, surrounded by all that was left of the flower and chivalry of Granada. There is one place where even the coward becomes brave—that sacred spot called home. What then must have been the valor of the Moors, a people always of fiery spirit, when the war was thus brought to their thresholds! They fought among the scenes of their loves and pleasures; the scenes of their infancy, and the haunts of their domestic life. They fought under the eyes of their wives and children, their old men and their maidens, of all that was helpless and all that was dear to them; for all Granada, crowded on tower and battlement, watched with trembling heart the fate of this eventful day.

There was not so much one battle as a variety of battles; every garden and orchard became a scene of deadly contest; every inch of ground was disputed, with an agony of grief and valor, by the Moors; every inch of ground that the Christians advanced, they valiantly maintained; but never did they advance with severer fighting or greater loss of blood.

The cavalry of Muza was in every part of the field; wherever it came, it gave fresh ardor to the fight. The Moorish soldier, fainting with heat, fatigue, and wounds, was roused to new life at the approach of Muza; and even he who lay gasping in the agonies of death, turned his face toward him, and faintly uttered cheers and blessings as he passed.

The Christians had by this time gained possession of various towers near the city, from whence they had been annoyed by crossbows and arquebuses. The Moors, scattered in various actions, were severely pressed. Boabdil, at the head of the cavaliers of his guard, displayed the utmost valor, mingling in the fight in various parts of the field, and endeavoring to inspirit the foot-soldiers in the combat. But the Moorish infantry was never to be depended upon. In the heat of the action, a panic seized upon them; they fled, leaving their sovereign exposed with his handful of cavaliers to an overwhelming force. Boabdil was on the point of falling into the hands of the Christians, when, wheeling round, with his followers, they threw the reins on the necks of their fleet steeds, and took refuge by dint of hoof within the walls of the city.*

---

* Zurita. lib. 20. c. 88.

Muza endeavored to retrieve the fortune of the field. He threw himself before the retreating infantry, calling upon them to turn and fight for their homes, their families, for everything that was sacred and dear to them. It was all in vain—they were totally broken and dismayed, and fled tumultuously for the gates. Muza would fain have kept the field with his cavalry; but this devoted band, having stood the brunt of war throughout this desperate campaign, was fearfully reduced in numbers, and many of the survivors were crippled and enfeebled by their wounds. Slowly and reluctantly Muza retreated to the city, his bosom swelling with indignation and despair. When he entered the gates, he ordered them to be closed, and secured with bolts and bars; for he refused to place any further confidence in the archers and arquebusiers who were stationed to defend them, and he vowed never more to sally forth with foot-soldiers to the field.

In the meantime the artillery thundered from the walls, and checked all further advances of the Christians. King Ferdinand, therefore, called off his troops, and returned in triumph to the ruins of his camp, leaving the beautiful city of Granada wrapped in the smoke of her fields and gardens, and surrounded by the bodies of her slaughtered children.

Such was the last sally made by the Moors in defense of their favorite city. The French embassador, who witnessed it, was filled with wonder at the prowess, the dexterity, and daring of the Moslems.

In truth, this whole war was an instance, memorable in history, of the most persevering resolution. For nearly ten years had the war endured—an almost uninterrupted series of disasters to the Moorish arms. Their towns had been taken, one after another, and their brethren slain or led into captivity. Yet they disputed every city and town, and fortress and castle, nay, every rock itself, as if they had been inspirited by victories. Wherever they could plant foot to fight, or find wall or cliff from whence to lanch an arrow, they disputed their beloved country; and now, when their capital was cut off from all relief, and had a whole nation thundering at its gates, they still maintained defense, as if they hoped some miracle to interpose in their behalf. Their obstinate resistance (says an ancient chronicler) shows the grief with which the Moors yielded up the vega, which was to them a paradise and heaven. Exerting all the strength of their arms, they embraced, as it were, that most beloved soil, from which neither wounds, nor defeats, nor death itself, could part them. They stood firm, battling for it with the united force of love and grief, never drawing back the foot while they had hands to fight, or fortune to befriend them.*

CHAPTER FIFTY-ONE

BUILDING OF THE CITY OF SANTA FE—DESPAIR OF THE MOORS

THE Moors now shut themselves up gloomily within their walls; there were no longer any daring sallies from their gates; and even the martial clangor of the drum and trumpet, which had continually resounded within that warrior city, was now seldom heard from its battlements. For a time, they flattered themselves with hopes that the late conflagration of the camp would discourage the besiegers; that, as in former years, their invasion would end with the summer, and that they would again withdraw before the autumnal rains.

The measures of Ferdinand and Isabella soon crushed these hopes. They gave orders to build a regular city upon the site of their camp, to convince the Moors that the siege was to endure until the surrender of Granada. Nine of the principal cities of Spain were charged with this stupendous undertaking; and they emulated each other with a zeal worthy of the cause. "It verily seems," says Fray Antonio

----

* Abarca, Reyes de Aragon, R. 30, c. 3.

Agapida, "as though some miracle operated to aid this pious work, so rapidly did arise a formidable city, with solid edifices, and powerful walls, and mighty towers, where lately had been seen nothing but tents and light pavilions. The city was traversed by two principal streets in form of a cross, terminating in four gates facing the four winds; and in the center was a vast square, where the whole army might be assembled. To this city it was proposed to give the name of Isabella, so dear to the army and the nation: "But that pious princess," adds Antonio Agapida, "calling to mind the holy cause in which it was erected, gave it the name of Santa Fé (or the City of the Holy Faith); and it remains to this day a monument of the piety and glory of the Catholic sovereigns."

Hither the merchants soon resorted from all points. Long trains of mules were seen every day entering and departing from its gates; the streets were crowded with magazines, filled with all kinds of costly and luxurious merchandise; a scene of bustling commerce and prosperity took place, while unhappy Granada remained shut up and desolate.

In the meantime, the besieged city began to suffer the distress of famine. Its supplies were all cut off; a cavalgada of flocks and herds, and mules laden with money, coming to the relief of the city from the mountains of the Alpuxarras, was taken by the Marques of Cadiz, and led in triumph to the camp, in sight of the suffering Moors. Autumn arrived; but the harvests had been swept from the face of the country; a rigorous winter was approaching, and the city was almost destitute of provisions. The people sank into deep despondency. They called to mind all that had been predicted by astrologers at the birth of their ill-starred sovereign, and all that had been foretold of the fate of Granada at the time of the capture of Zahara.

Boabdil was alarmed by the gathering dangers from without, and by the clamors of his starving people. He summoned a council, composed of the principal officers of the army, the alcaydes of the fortresses, the xequis or sages of the city, and the alfaquis or doctors of the faith. They assembled in the great hall of audience of the Alhambra, and despair was painted in their countenances. Boabdil demanded of them what was to be done in their present extremity; and their answer was, "Surrender." The venerable Abul Cazim Abdel Melic, governor of the city, represented its unhappy state: "Our granaries are nearly exhausted, and no further supplies are to be expected. The provender for the war-horses is required as sustenance for the soldiery; the very horses themselves are killed for food; of seven thousand steeds which once could be sent into the field, three hundred only remain. Our city contains two hundred thousand inhabitants, old and young, with each a mouth that calls piteously for bread."

The xequis and principal citizens declared that the people could no longer sustain the labors and sufferings of a defense: "And of what avail is our defense," said they, "when the enemy is determined to persist in the siege?—what alternative remains but to surrender or to die?"

The heart of Boabdil was touched by this appeal, and he maintained a gloomy silence. He had cherished some faint hope of relief from the soldan of Egypt or the Barbary powers: but it was now at an end; even if such assistance were to be sent, he had no longer a seaport where it might debark. The counselors saw that the resolution of the king was shaken, and they united their voices in urging him to capitulate.

The valiant Muza alone arose in opposition: "It is yet too early," said he, "to talk of a surrender. Our means are not exhausted; we have yet one source of strength remaining, terrible in its effects, and which often has achieved the most signal victories—it is our despair. Let us rouse the mass of the people—let us put weapons in their hands—let us fight the enemy to the very utmost until we rush upon the points of their lances. I am ready to lead the way into the thickest of their squadrons; and much rather would I be numbered among those who fell in the defense of Granada than of those who survived to capitulate for her surrender!"

The words of Muza were without effect, for they were
addressed to broken-spirited and heartless men, or men, perhaps, to whom sad experience had taught discretion.   They
were arrived at that state of public depression when heroes
and heroism are no longer regarded, and when old men and
their counsels rise into importance.   Boabdil el Chico yielded
to the general voice; it was determined to capitulate with the
Christian sovereigns; and the venerable Abul Cazim Abdel
Melic was sent forth to the camp, empowered to treat for
terms.

CHAPTER FIFTY–TWO

CAPITULATION OF GRANADA

The old governor, Abul Cazim Abdel Melic, was received
with great distinction by Ferdinand and Isabella, who appointed Gonsalvo of Cordova and Fernando de Zafra, secretary to the king, to confer with him.   All Granada awaited,
in trembling anxiety, the result of his negotiations.   After
repeated conferences, he at length returned with the ultimate
terms of the Catholic sovereigns.   They agreed to suspend
all attack for seventy days, at the end of which time, if no
succor should arrive to the Moorish king, the city of Granada
was to be surrendered.

All Christian captives should be liberated without ransom.

Boabdil and his principal cavaliers should take an oath
of fealty to the Castilian crown, and certain valuable territories in the Alpuxarra mountains should be assigned to the
Moorish monarch for his maintenance.

The Moors of Granada should become subjects of the
Spanish sovereigns, retaining their possessions, their arms
and horses, and yielding up nothing but their artillery.   They
should be protected in the exercise of their religion, and governed by their own laws, administered by cadis of their own
faith, under governors appointed by the sovereigns.   They

should be exempted from tribute for three years, after which term they should pay the same that they had been accustomed to render to their native monarchs.

Those who chose to depart for Africa within three years should be provided with a passage for themselves and their effects, free of charge, from whatever port they should prefer.

For the fulfillment of these articles, four hundred hostages from the principal families were required previous to the surrender, to be subsequently restored. The son of the king of Granada, and all other hostages in possession of the Castilian sovereigns, were to be restored at the same time.

Such were the conditions that the wazir Abul Cazim laid before the council of Granada, as the best that could be obtained from the besieging foe.

When the members of the council found that the awful moment had arrived when they were to sign and seal the perdition of their empire, and blot themselves out as a nation, all firmness deserted them, and many gave way to tears. Muza alone retained an unaltered mien: "Leave, seniors," cried he, "this idle lamentation to helpless women and children: we are men—we have hearts, not to shed tender tears, but drops of blood. I see the spirit of the people so cast down that it is impossible to save the kingdom. Yet there still remains an alternative for noble minds—a glorious death! Let us die defending our liberty, and avenging the woes of Granada. Our mother earth will receive her children into her bosom, safe from the chains and oppressions of the conqueror; or, should any fail a sepulcher to hide his remains, he will not want a sky to cover him. Allah forbid it should be said the nobles of Granada feared to die in her defense!"

Muza ceased to speak, and a dead silence reigned in the assembly. Boabdil el Chico looked anxiously round and scanned every face; but he read in them all the anxiety of care-worn men, in whose hearts enthusiasm was dead, and who had grown callous to every chivalrous appeal. "Allah Achbar! God is great!" exclaimed he; "there is no God but God, and Mahomet is His prophet! It is in vain to struggle

against the will of Heaven. Too surely was it written in the
book of fate that I should be unfortunate and the kingdom
expire under my rule.''

"Allah Achbar! God is great!'' echoed the viziers and
alfaquis; "the will of God be done!'' So they all accorded
with the king that these evils were preordained; that it was
hopeless to contend with them; and that the terms offered by
the Castilian monarchs were as favorable as could be expected.

When Muza saw that they were about to sign the treaty
of surrender, he rose in violent indignation: "Do not deceive
yourselves,'' cried he, "nor think the Christians will be faithful to their promises, or their king as magnanimous in conquest as he has been victorious in war. Death is the least
we have to fear. It is the plundering and sacking of our
city, the profanation of our mosques, the ruin of our homes,
the violation of our wives and daughters—cruel oppression,
bigoted intolerance, whips and chains, the dungeon, the
fagot, and the stake—such are the miseries and indignities
we shall see and suffer; at least, those groveling souls will
see them who now shrink from an honorable death. For
my part, by Allah, I will never witness them!''

With these words he left the council-chamber, and strode
gloomily through the Court of Lions and the outer halls of
the Alhambra, without deigning to speak to the obsequious
courtiers who attended in them. He repaired to his dwelling,
armed himself at all points, mounted his favorite war-horse,
and, issuing forth from the city by the gate of Elvira, was
never seen or heard of more.* Such is the account given
by Arabian historians of the exit of Muza ben Abel Gazan;
but the venerable Fray Antonio Agapida endeavors to clear
up the mystery of his fate. That very evening, a small
party of Andalusian cavaliers, somewhat more than half a
score of lances, were riding along the banks of the Xenil,
where it winds through the vega. They beheld in the twi·

---

* Conde, part 4.

light a Moorish warrior approaching, closely locked up from head to foot in proof. His visor was closed, his lance in rest, his powerful charger barbed like himself in steel. The Christians were lightly armed, with corselet, helm and target; for, during the truce, they apprehended no attack. Seeing, however, the unknown warrior approach in this hostile guise, they challenged him to stand and declare himself.

The Moslem answered not, but, charging into the midst of them, transfixed one knight with his lance, and bore him out of his saddle to the earth. Wheeling round, he attacked the rest with his scimiter. His blows were furious and deadly; he seemed regardless what wounds he received, so he could but slay. He was evidently fighting, not for glory, but revenge—eager to inflict death, but careless of surviving to enjoy victory. Near one-half of the cavaliers fell beneath his sword before he received a dangerous wound, so completely was he cased in armor of proof. At length he was desperately wounded and his steed, being pierced by a lance, sank to the ground. The Christians, admiring the valor of the Moor, would have spared his life; but he continued to fight upon his knees, brandishing a keen dagger of Fez. Finding at length he could no longer battle, and determined not to be taken prisoner, he threw himself, with an expiring exertion, into the Xenil, and his armor sank him to the bottom of the stream.

This unknown warrior the venerable Agapida pronounces to have been Muza ben Abel Gazan, and says his horse was recognized by certain converted Moors of the Christian camp: the fact, however, has always remained in doubt.

CHAPTER FIFTY-THREE

COMMOTIONS IN GRANADA

The capitulation for the surrender of Granada was signed on the 25th of November, 1491, and produced a sudden cessation of those hostilities which had raged for so many years. Christian and Moor might now be seen mingling courteously on the banks of the Xenil and the Darro, where to have met a few days previous would have produced a scene of sanguinary contest. Still, as the Moors might be suddenly aroused to defense, if, within the allotted term of seventy days, succors should arrive from abroad; and as they were at all times a rash, inflammable people, the wary Ferdinand maintained a vigilant watch upon the city, and permitted no supplies of any kind to enter. His garrisons in the seaports, and his cruisers in the Straits of Gibraltar, were ordered likewise to guard against any relief from the grand soldan of Egypt, or the princes of Barbary. There was no need of such precautions. Those powers were either too much engrossed by their own wars, or too much daunted by the success of the Spanish arms, to interfere in a desperate cause; and the unfortunate Moors of Granada were abandoned to their fate.

The month of December had nearly passed away; the famine became extreme, and there was no hope of any favorable event within the term specified in the capitulation. Boabdil saw that to hold out to the end of the allotted time would but be to protract the miseries of his people. With the consent of his council, he determined to surrender the city on the sixth of January. On the 30th of December he sent his grand vizier, Yusef Aben Comixa, with the four hundred hostages, to King Ferdinand, to make known his intention; bearing him, at the same time, a present of a magnificent scimiter, and two Arabian steeds superbly caparisoned.

The unfortunate Boabdil was doomed to meet with trouble to the end of his career. The very next day, the santon or dervise Hamet Aben Zarrax, the same who had uttered prophecies and excited commotions on former occasions, suddenly made his appearance. Whence he came, no one knew; it was rumored that he had been in the mountains of the Alpuxarras, and on the coast of Barbary, endeavoring to rouse the Moslems to the relief of Granada. He was reduced to a skeleton; his eyes glowed like coals in their sockets, and his speech was little better than frantic raving. He harangued the populace in the streets and squares; inveighed against the capitulation, denounced the king and nobles as Moslems only in name, and called upon the people to sally forth against the unbelievers, for that Allah had decreed them a signal victory.

Upward of twenty thousand of the populace seized their arms and paraded the streets with shouts and outcries. The shops and houses were shut up; the king himself did not dare to venture forth, but remained a kind of prisoner in the Alhambra.

The turbulent multitude continued roaming and shouting and howling about the city, during the day and a part of the night. Hunger, and a wintry tempest, tamed their frenzy; and when morning came, the enthusiast who had led them on had disappeared. Whether he had been disposed of by the emissaries of the king, or by the leading men of the city, is not known: his disappearance remains a mystery.*

The Moorish king now issued from the Alhambra, attended by his principal nobles, and harangued the populace. He set forth the necessity of complying with the capitulation, from the famine that reigned in the city, the futility of defense, and from the hostages having already been delivered into the hands of the besiegers.

In the dejection of his spirits, the unfortunate Boabdil attributed to himself the miseries of the country. "It was my crime in ascending the throne in rebellion against my father," said he, mournfully, "which has brought these woes upon the kingdom; but Allah has grievously visited my sins upon my head. For your sake, my people, I have now made this treaty, to protect you from the sword, your little ones from famine, your wives and daughters from the outrages of war; and to secure you in the enjoyment of your properties, your

---

* Mariana.

liberties, your laws and your religion, under a sovereign of happier destinies than the ill-starred Boabdil."

The versatile population were touched by the humility of their sovereign—they agreed to adhere to the capitulation, and there was even a faint shout of "Long live Boabdil the unfortunate!" and they all returned to their homes in perfect tranquillity.

Boabdil immediately sent missives to King Ferdinand, apprising him of these events, and of his fears lest further delay should produce new tumults. He proposed, therefore, to surrender the city on the following day. The Castilian sovereigns assented, with great satisfaction; and preparations were made in city and camp for this great event, that was to seal the fate of Granada.

It was a night of doleful lamentings, within the walls of the Alhambra; for the household of Boabdil were preparing to take a last farewell of that delightful abode. All the royal treasures, and the most precious effects of the Alhambra, were hastily packed upon mules; the beautiful apartments were despoiled, with tears and wailings, by their own inhabitants. Before the dawn of day, a mournful cavalcade moved obscurely out of a postern-gate of the Alhambra, and departed through one of the most retired quarters of the city. It was composed of the family of the unfortunate Boabdil, which he sent off thus privately, that they might not be exposed to the eyes of scoffers, or the exultation of the enemy. The mother of Boabdil, the sultana Ayxa la Horra, rode on in silence, with dejected yet dignified demeanor; but his wife Zorayma, and all the females of his household, gave way to loud lamentations, as they looked back upon their favorite abode, now a mass of gloomy towers behind them. They were attended by the ancient domestics of the household, and by a small guard of veteran Moors, loyally attached to the fallen monarch, and who would have sold their lives dearly in defense of his family. The city was yet buried in sleep as they passed through its silent streets. The guards at the gate shed tears, as they opened it for their departure.

They paused not, but proceeded along the banks of the Xenil on the road that leads to the Alpuxarras, until they arrived at a hamlet at some distance from the city, where they halted, and waited until they should be joined by King Boabdil.

CHAPTER FIFTY-FOUR

SURRENDER OF GRANADA

THE sun had scarcely begun to shed his beams upon the summits of the snowy mountains which rise above Granada, when the Christian camp was in motion.   A detachment of horse and foot, led by distinguished cavaliers, and accompanied by Hernando de Talavera, bishop of Avila, proceeded to take possession of the Alhambra and the towers.   It had been stipulated in the capitulation that the detachment sent for this purpose should not enter by the streets of the city; a road had therefore been opened, outside of the walls, leading by the Puerta de los Molinos, or the Gate of the Mills, to the summit of the Hill of Martyrs, and across the hill to a postern-gate of the Alhambra.

When the detachment arrived at the summit of the hill, the Moorish king came forth from the gate, attended by a handful of cavaliers, leaving his vizier Yusef Aben Comixa to deliver up the palace.   "Go, senior," said he to the commander of the detachment, "go and take possession of those fortresses, which Allah has bestowed upon your powerful sovereigns, in punishment of the sins of the Moors."   He said no more, but passed mournfully on, along the same road by which the Spanish cavaliers had come; descending to the vega, to meet the Catholic sovereigns.   The troops entered the Alhambra, the gates of which were wide open, and all its splendid courts and halls silent and deserted.

In the meantime, the Christian court and army poured out of the city of Santa Fe, and advanced across the vega. The king and queen, with the prince and princess, and the dignitaries and ladies of the court, took the lead, accompanied by the different orders of monks and friars, and surrounded by the royal guards splendidly arrayed. The procession moved slowly forward, and paused at the village of Armilla, at the distance of half a league from the city.

The sovereigns waited here with impatience, their eyes fixed on the lofty tower of the Alhambra, watching for the appointed signal of possession. The time that had elapsed since the departure of the detachment seemed to them more than necessary for the purpose, and the anxious mind of Ferdinand began to entertain doubts of some commotion in the city. At length they saw the silver cross, the great standard of this crusade, elevated on the Torre de la Vala, or Great Watch-Tower, and sparkling in the sunbeams. This was done by Hernando de Talavera, bishop of Avila. Beside it was planted the pennon of the glorious apostle St. James, and a great shout of "Santiago! Santiago!" rose throughout the army. Lastly was reared the royal standard by the king of arms, with the shout of "Castile! Castile! For King Ferdinand and Queen Isabella!" The words were echoed by the whole army, with acclamations that resounded across the vega. At sight of these signals of possession, the sovereigns sank upon their knees, giving thanks to God for this great triumph; the whole assembled host followed their example, and the choristers of the royal chapel broke forth into the solemn anthem of "*Te Deum laudamus.*"

The procession now resumed its march with joyful alacrity, to the sound of triumphant music, until they came to a small mosque near the banks of the Xenil, and not far from the foot of the Hill of Martyrs, which edifice remains to the present day, consecrated as the hermitage of St. Sebastian. Here the sovereigns were met by the unfortunate Boabdil, accompanied by about fifty cavaliers and domestics. As he drew near, he would have dismounted in token of homage, but Ferdinand prevented him. He then proffered to kiss the king's hand, but this sign of vassalage was likewise declined; whereupon, not to be outdone in magnanimity, he leaned forward and kissed the right arm of Ferdinand. Queen Isabella also refused to receive this ceremonial of homage, and, to console him under his adversity, delivered to him his son, who had remained as hostage ever since Boabdil's liberation from captivity. The Moorish monarch pressed his child to his bosom with tender emotion, and they seemed mutually endeared to each other by their misfortunes.*

He then delivered the keys of the city to King Ferdinand, with an air of mingled melancholy and resignation: "These keys," said he, "are the last relics of the Arabian empire in Spain: thine, oh king, are our trophies, our kingdom, and our person. Such is the will of God! Receive them with the clemency thou hast promised, and which we look for at thy hands."†

King Ferdinand restrained his exultation into an air of serene magnanimity. "Doubt not our promises," replied he, "nor that thou shalt regain from our friendship the prosperity of which the fortune of war has deprived thee."

On receiving the keys, King Ferdinand handed them to the queen; she in her turn presented them to her son Prince Juan, who delivered them to the Count de Tendilla, that brave and loyal cavalier being appointed alcayde of the city, and captain-general of the kingdom of Granada.

Having surrendered the last symbol of power, the unfortunate Boabdil continued on toward the Alpuxarras, that he might not behold the entrance of the Christians into his capital. His devoted band of cavaliers followed him in gloomy silence; but heavy sighs burst from their bosoms, as shouts of joy and strains of triumphant music were borne on the breeze from the victorious army.

Having rejoined his family, Boabdil set forward with a heavy heart for his allotted residence in the valley of Purchena. At two leagues' distance the cavalcade, winding into the skirts of the Alpuxarras, ascended an eminence com-

---

* Zurita, Annales de Aragon.

† Abarca, Annales de Aragon, Rey 30, c. 3.

manding the last view of Granada. As they arrived at this spot, the Moors paused involuntarily, to take a farewell gaze at their beloved city, which a few steps more would shut from their sight forever. Never had it appeared so lovely in their eyes. The sunshine, so bright in that transparent climate, lighted up each tower and minaret, and rested gloriously upon the crowning battlements of the Alhambra; while the vega spread its enameled bosom of verdure below, glistening with the silver windings of the Xenil. The Moorish cavaliers gazed with a silent agony of tenderness and grief upon that delicious abode, the scene of their loves and pleasures. While they yet looked, a light cloud of smoke burst forth from the citadel, and presently a peal of artillery, faintly heard, told that the city was taken possession of, and the throne of the Moslem kings was lost forever. The heart of Boabdil, softened by misfortunes and overcharged with grief, could no longer contain itself: "Allah Achbar! God is great!" said he; but the words of resignation died upon his lips, and he burst into a flood of tears.

His mother, the intrepid Sultana Ayxa la Horra, was indignant at his weakness: "You do well," said she, "to weep like a woman, for what you failed to defend like a man!"

The vizier Aben Comixa endeavored to console his royal master. "Consider, sire," said he, "that the most signal misfortunes often render men as renowned as the most prosperous achievements, provided they sustain them with magnanimity."

The unhappy monarch, however, was not to be consoled; his tears continued to flow. "Allah Achbar!" exclaimed he; "when did misfortunes ever equal mine?"

From this circumstance, the hill, which is not far from the Padul, took the name of Feg Allah Achbar: but the point of view commanding the last prospect of Granada is known among Spaniards by the name of *El ultimo suspiro del Moro;* or, "The last sigh of the Moor."

CHAPTER FIFTY-FIVE

HOW THE CASTILIAN SOVEREIGNS TOOK POSSESSION OF GRANADA

WHEN the Castilian sovereigns had received the keys of Granada from the hands of Boabdil el Chico, the royal army resumed its triumphant march. As it approached the gates of the city, in all the pomp of courtly and chivalrous array, a procession of a different kind came forth to meet it. This was composed of more than five hundred Christian captives, many of whom had languished for years in Moorish dungeons. Pale and emaciated, they came clanking their chains in triumph, and shedding tears of joy. They were received with tenderness by the sovereigns. The king hailed them as good Spaniards, as men loyal and brave, as martyrs to the holy cause; the queen distributed liberal relief among them with her own hands, and they passed on before the squadrons of the army, singing hymns of jubilee.*

The sovereigns did not enter the city on this day of its surrender, but waited until it should be fully occupied by their troops, and public tranquillity insured. The Marques de Villena, and the Count de Tendilla, with three thousand cavalry and as many infantry, marched in and took possession, accompanied by the proselyte Prince Cidi Yahye, now known by the Christian appellation of Don Pedro de Gra nada, who was appointed chief alguazil of the city, and had charge of the Moorish inhabitants, and by his son the late Prince Alnayar, now Don Alonzo de Granada, who was appointed admiral of the fleets. In a little while, every battlement glistened with Christian helms and lances, the standard of the faith and of the realm floated from every tower, and the thundering salvos of the ordnance told that the subjugation of the city was complete.

* Abarca, lib. sup. Zurita, etc.

The grandees and cavaliers now knelt and kissed the hands of the king and queen and the Prince Juan, and congratulated them on the acquisition of so great a kingdom; after which, the royal procession returned in state to Santa Fe.

It was on the sixth of January, the day of kings and festival of the Epiphany, that the sovereigns made their triumphal entry. The king and queen (says the worthy Fray Antonio Agapida) looked on this occasion as more than mortal: the venerable ecclesiastics, to whose advice and zeal this glorious conquest ought in a great measure to be attributed, moved along with hearts swelling with holy exultation, but with chastened and downcast looks of edifying humility; while the hardy warriors, in tossing plumes and shining steel, seemed elevated with a stern joy at finding themselves in possession of this object of so many toils and perils. As the streets resounded with the tramp of steed and swelling peals of music, the Moors buried themselves in the deepest recesses of their dwellings. There they bewailed in secret the fallen glory of their race, but suppressed their groans, lest they should be heard by their enemies and increase their triumph.

The royal procession advanced to the principal mosque, which had been consecrated as a cathedral. Here the sovereigns offered up prayers and thanksgivings, and the choir of the royal chapel chanted a triumphant anthem, in which they were joined by all the courtiers and cavaliers. Nothing (says Fray Antonio Agapida) could exceed the thankfulness to God of the pious King Ferdinand, for having enabled him to eradicate from Spain the empire and name of that accursed heathen race, and for the elevation of the cross in that city wherein the impious doctrines of Mahomet had so long been cherished. In the fervor of his spirit, he supplicated from Heaven a continuance of its grace, and that this glorious triumph might be perpetuated.* The prayer of the pious

---

* The words of Fray Antonio Agapida are little more than an echo of those of the worthy Jesuit father Mariana. (L. 25, c. 18.)

monarch was responded by the people, and even his enemies were for once convinced of his sincerity.

When the religious ceremonies were concluded, the court ascended to the stately palace of the Alhambra, and entered by the great gate of Justice. The halls lately occupied by turbaned Infidels now rustled with stately dames and Christian courtiers, who wandered with eager curiosity over this far-famed palace, admiring its verdant courts and gushing fountains, its halls decorated with elegant arabesques and storied with inscriptions, and the splendor of its gilded and brilliantly painted ceilings.

It had been a last request of the unfortunate Boabdil, and one which showed how deeply he felt the transition of his fate, that no person might be permitted to enter or depart by the gate of the Alhambra through which he had sallied forth to surrender his capital. His request was granted; the portal was closed up, and remains so to the present day—a mute memorial of that event.*

The Spanish sovereigns fixed their throne in the presence-chamber of the palace, so long the seat of Moorish royalty. Hither the principal inhabitants of Granada repaired, to pay

---

* Garibay, Compend. Hist., lib. 40, c. 42. The existence of this gateway, and the story connected with it, are perhaps known to few; but were identified, in the researches made to verify this history. The gateway is at the bottom of the great tower, at some distance from the main body of the Alhambra. The tower has been rent and ruined by gunpowder, at the time when the fortress was evacuated by the French. Great masses lie around, half covered by vines and fig-trees. A poor man, by the name of Matteo Ximenes, who lives in one of the halls among the ruins of the Alhambra, where his family has resided for many generations, pointed out the gateway still closed up with stones. He remembered to have heard his father and grandfather say, that it had always been stopped up, and that out of it King Boabdil had gone when he surrendered Granada. The route of the unfortunate king may be traced from thence across the garden of the convent of Los Martyros, and down a ravine beyond, through a street of gypsy caves and hovels, by the gate of Los Molinos, and so on to the hermitage of St. Sebastian. None but an antiquarian, however, will be able to trace it, unless aided by the humble historian of the place, Matteo Ximenes.

them homage and kiss their hands in token of vassalage; and their example was followed by deputies from all the towns and fortresses of the Alpuxarras, which had not hitherto submitted.

Thus terminated the war of Granada, after ten years of incessant fighting; equaling (says Fray Antonio Agapida) the far-famed siege of Troy in duration, and ending, like that, in the capture of the city. Thus ended also the dominion of the Moors in Spain, having endured seven hundred and seventy-eight years, from the memorable defeat of Roderick, the last of the Goths, on the banks of the Guadalete. The authentic Agapida is uncommonly particular in fixing the epoch of this event. This great triumph of our holy Catholic faith, according to his computation, took place in the beginning of January, in the year of Our Lord 1492, being 3,655 years from the population of Spain by the patriarch Tubal; 3,797 from the general deluge; 5,453 from the creation of the world, according to Hebrew calculation; and in the month Rabic, in the eight hundred and ninety-seventh year of the Hegira, or flight of Mahomet, whom may God confound! saith the pious Agapida.

APPENDIX

FATE OF BOABDIL EL CHICO

THE "Chronicle of the Conquest of Granada" is finished; but the reader may be desirous of knowing the subsequent fortunes of some of the principal personages. The unfortunate Boabdil retired to the valley of Purchena, where a small but fertile territory had been allotted him, comprising several towns, with all their rights and revenues. Great estates had likewise been bestowed on his vizier Yusef Aben Comixa and his valiant relation and friend Yusef Venegas, both of whom resided near him. Were it in the heart of man in the enjoyment of present competence to forget past splendor, Boabdil might at length have been happy. Dwelling in the bosom of a delightful valley, surrounded by obedient vassals, devoted friends, and a loving family, he might have looked back upon his past career as upon a troubled and terrific dream, and might have thanked his stars that he had at length awaked to sweet and tranquil security. But the dethroned prince could never forget that he had once been a monarch; and the remembrance of the regal splendors of Granada made all present comforts contemptible in his eyes. No exertions were spared by Ferdinand and Isabella to induce him to embrace the Catholic religion; but he remained true to the faith of his fathers, and it added not a little to his humiliation, to live a vassal under Christian sovereigns.

It is probable that his residence in the kingdom was equally irksome to the politic Ferdinand, who could not feel perfectly secure in his newly conquered territories, while there was one within their bounds who might revive pretensions to the throne. A private bargain was therefore made, in the year 1496, between Ferdinand and Yusef Aben Comixa, in which the latter, as vizier of Boabdil, undertook to dispose of his master's scanty territory, for eighty thousand ducats of gold. This, it is affirmed, was done without the consent or knowledge of Boabdil; but the vizier probably thought he was acting for the best.

The shrewd Ferdinand does not appear to have made any question about the right of the vizier to make the sale, but paid the money with secret exultation. Yusef Aben Comixa loaded the treasure upon mules, and departed joyfully for the Alpuxarras. He spread the money in triumph before Boabdil: "Senior," said he, "I have observed that as long as you live here you are exposed to constant peril. The Moors are rash and irritable; they may make some sudden insurrection, elevate your standard as a pretext, and thus overwhelm you and your friends with utter ruin. I have observed also that you pine away with grief, being continually reminded in this country that you were once its sovereign, but never more must hope to reign. I have put an end to these evils.   Your territory is sold—behold the price of it. With this gold you may buy far greater possessions in Africa, where you may live in honor and security.''

When Boabdil heard these words, he burst into a sudden transport of rage, and, drawing his scimiter, would have sacrificed the officious Yusef on the spot, had not the attendants interfered and hurried the vizier from his presence.

Boabdil was not of a vindictive spirit, and his anger soon passed away.   He saw that the evil was done, and he knew the spirit of the politic Ferdinand too well to hope that he would retract the bargain.   Gathering together the money, therefore, and all his jewels and precious effects, he departed with his family and household for a port where a vessel had been carefully provided by the Castilian king to transport them to Africa.

A crowd of his former subjects witnessed his embarkation.   As the sails were unfurled and swelled to the breeze, and the vessel parted from the land, the spectators would fain have given him a parting cheering; but the humbled state of their once proud sovereign forced itself upon their minds, and the ominous surname of his youth rose involuntarily to their tongues: "Farewell, Boabdil! Allah preserve thee, *El Zogoybi!*" burst spontaneously from their lips.   The unlucky appellation sank into the heart of the expatriated monarch, and tears dimmed his eyes as the snowy summits of the mountains of Granada gradually faded from his view.

He was received with welcome at the court of his relation Muley Ahmed, king of Fez, and resided for many years in his territories.   How he passed his life, whether repining or resigned, history does not mention.   The last we find recorded of him is in the year 1536, thirty-four years after the surrender of Granada, when he followed the king of Fez to the field to quell the rebellion of two brothers named Xerifes. The armies came in sight of each other on the banks of the Guadiswed, at the ford of Bacuba.   The river was deep, the banks were high and broken; for three days the armies remained firing at each other across the stream, neither venturing to attempt the dangerous ford.

At length the king of Fez divided his army into three battalions; the first led on by his son, and by Boabdil el Chico. They boldly dashed across the ford, scrambled up the opposite bank, and attempted to keep the enemy employed until the other battalions should have time to cross. The rebel army, however, attacked them with such fury that the son of the king of Fez and several of the bravest alcaydes were slain upon the spot; multitudes were driven back into the river, which was already crowded with passing troops. A dreadful confusion took place; the horse trampled upon the foot; the enemy pressed on them with fearful slaughter; those who escaped the sword perished by the stream; the river was choked by the dead bodies of men and horses, and by the scattered baggage of the army. In this scene of horrible carnage fell Boabdil, truly called El Zogoybi or the unlucky—an instance, says the ancient chronicler, of the scornful caprice of fortune, dying in defense of the kingdom of another, after wanting spirit to die in defense of his own.*

DEATH OF THE MARQUES OF CADIZ

THE renowned Roderigo Ponce de Leon, Marques, Duke of Cadiz, was unquestionably the most distinguished among the cavaliers of Spain, for his zeal, enterprise, and heroism

------

* Marmol, Descrip. de Africa, p. 1, l. 2, c. 40. Idem, Hist. Reb. de los Moros, lib. 1, c. 21.

NOTE.—A portrait of Boabdil el Chico is to be seen in the picture-gallery of the Generaliffe. He is represented with a mild, handsome face, a fair complexion, and yellow hair. His dress is of yellow brocade, relieved with black velvet, and he has a black velvet cap, surmounted with a crown. In the armory of Madrid are two suits of armor, said to have belonged to him. One is of solid steel, with very little ornament, the helmet closed. From the proportions of these suits of armor, he must have been of full stature and vigorous form.

in the great crusade of Granada. He began the war by the capture of Alhama; he was engaged in almost every inroad and siege of importance during its continuance; and he was present at the surrender of the capital, which was the closing scene of the conquest. The renown he thus acquired was sealed by his death, which happened in the forty-eighth year of his age, almost immediately at the close of his triumphs and before a leaf of his laurels had time to wither. He died at his palace in the city of Seville, on the 27th day of August, 1492, but a few months after the surrender of Granada, and of an illness caused by the exposures and fatigues he had undergone in this memorable war. That honest chronicler, Andres Bernaldes, the curate of Los Palacios, who was a contemporary of the marques, draws his portrait from actual knowledge and observation. He was universally cited (says he) as the most perfect model of chivalrous virtue of the age. He was temperate, chaste, and rigidly devout; a benignant commander, a valiant defender of his vassals, a great lover of justice, and an enemy to all flatterers, liars, robbers, traitors, and poltroons.

His ambition was of a lofty kind—he sought to distinguish himself and his family, by heroic and resounding deeds; and to increase the patrimony of his ancestors, by the acquisition of castles, domains, vassals, and other princely possessions. His recreations were all of a warlike nature; he delighted in geometry as applied to fortifications, and spent much time and treasure in erecting and repairing fortresses. He relished music, but of a military kind—the sound of clarions and sackbuts, of drums and trumpets. Like a true cavalier, he was a protector of the sex on all occasions, and an injured woman never applied to him in vain for redress. His prowess was so well known, and his courtesy to the fair, that the ladies of the court, when they accompanied the queen to the wars, rejoiced to find themselves under his protection; for wherever his banner was displayed the Moors dreaded to adventure. He was a faithful and devoted friend, but a formidable enemy; for he was slow to forgive, and his vengeance was persevering and terrible.

The death of this good cavalier spread grief and lamentation throughout all ranks, for he was universally honored and beloved. His relations, dependents, and companions in arms, put on mourning for his loss; and so numerous were they that half of Seville was clad in black. None, however, deplored his death more deeply and sincerely than his friend and chosen companion, Don Alonzo de Aguilar.

The funeral ceremonies were of the most solemn and sumptuous kind. The body of the marques was arrayed in a costly shirt, a doublet of brocade, a sayo or long robe of black velvet, a marlota or Moorish tunic of brocade that reached to the feet, and scarlet stockings. His sword, superbly gilt, was girded to his side, as he used to wear it when in the field. Thus magnificently attired, the body was inclosed in a coffin, which was covered with black velvet, and decorated with a cross of white damask. It was then placed on a sumptuous bier, in the center of the great hall of the palace. Here the duchess made great lamentation over the body of her lord, in which she was joined by her train of damsels and attendants, as well as by the pages and esquires, and innumerable vassals of the marques.

In the close of the evening, just before the "Ave Maria," the funeral procession issued from the palace. Ten banners were borne around the bier, the particular trophies of the marques, won from the Moors by his valor in individual enterprises, before King Ferdinand had commenced the war of Granada. The procession was swelled by an immense train of bishops, priests, and friars of different orders, together with the civil and military authorities, and all the chivalry of Seville, headed by the Count of Cifuentes, at that time intendente or commander of the city. It moved slowly and solemnly through the streets, stopping occasionally, and chanting litanies and responses. Two hundred and forty waxen tapers shed a light like the day about the bier. The balconies and windows were crowded with ladies, who shed tears as the funeral train passed by; while the women of the lower classes were loud in their lamentations, as if bewailing the loss of a father or a brother. On approaching the convent of St. Augustine, the monks came forth with the cross and tapers, and eight censers, and conducted the body into the church, where it lay in state until all the vigils were performed by the different orders; after which it was deposited in the family tomb of the Ponces in the same church, and the ten banners were suspended over the sepulcher.*

The tomb of the valiant Roderigo Ponce de Leon, with his banners mouldering above it, remained for ages an object of veneration with all who had read or heard of his virtues and achievements. In the year 1810, however, the chapel was sacked by the French, its altars overturned, and the sepulchers of the family of the Ponces shattered to pieces. The present duchess of Benevente, the worthy descendant of this illustrious and heroic line, has since piously collected the ashes of her ancestors, restored the altar, and repaired the chapel. The sepulchers, however, were utterly destroyed; an inscription in gold letters, on the wall of the chapel, to the right of the altar, is all that denotes the place of sepulcher of the brave Ponce de Leon.

THE LEGEND OF THE DEATH OF DON ALONZO DE AGUILAR

To such as feel an interest in the fortunes of the valiant Don Alonzo de Aguilar, the chosen friend and companion in arms of Ponce de Leon, Marques of Cadiz, and one of the most distinguished heroes of the war of Granada, a few particulars of his remarkable fate will not be unacceptable. They are found among the manuscripts of the worthy padre

---

* Cura de los Palacios, c. 104.

Fray Antonio Agapida, and appear to have been appended to this Chronicle.

For several years after the conquest of Granada, the country remained feverish and unquiet. The zealous efforts of the Catholic clergy to effect the conversion of the Infidels, and the pious coercion used for that purpose by government, exasperated the stubborn Moors of the mountains. Several missionaries were maltreated; and in the town of Dayrin, two of them were seized, and exhorted, with many menaces, to embrace the Moslem faith; on their resolutely refusing, they were killed with staves and stones by the Moorish women and children, and their bodies burned to ashes.*

Upon this event, a body of Christian cavaliers assembled in Andalusia to the number of eight hundred, and, without waiting for orders from the king, revenged the death of these martyrs by plundering and laying waste the Moorish towns and villages. The Moors fled to the mountains, and their cause was espoused by many of their nation, who inhabited those rugged regions. The storm of rebellion began to gather and mutter its thunders in the Alpuxarras. They were echoed from the Serrania of Ronda, ever ready for rebellion; but the strongest hold of the insurgents was in the Sierra Vermeja or chain of Red Mountains, which lie near the sea, and whose savage rocks and precipices may be seen from Gibraltar.

When King Ferdinand heard of these tumults, he issued a proclamation ordering all the Moors of the insurgent regions to leave them within ten days, and repair to Castile; giving secret instructions, however, that those who should voluntarily embrace the Christian faith might be permitted to remain. At the same time, he ordered Don Alonzo de Aguilar and the Counts of Urena and Cifuentes to march against the rebels.

Don Alonzo de Aguilar was at Cordova when he received the commands of the king. "What force is allotted us for

---

* Cura de los Palacios. c. 165.

this expedition?'' said he.   On being told, he perceived that
the number of troops was far from adequate.   ''When a man
is dead,'' said he, ''we send four men into his house to bring
forth the body.   We are now sent to chastise these Moors,
who are alive, vigorous, in open rebellion, and ensconced in
their castles; yet they do not give us man to man.''   These
words of the brave Alonzo de Aguilar were afterward frequently repeated; but though he saw the desperate nature of
the enterprise, he did not hesitate to undertake it.

Don Alonzo was at that time in the fifty-first year of his
age.   He was a veteran warrior, in whom the fire of youth
was yet unquenched, though tempered by experience.   The
greater part of his life had been passed in the camp and in
the field, until danger was as his natural element.   His
muscular frame had acquired the firmness of iron, without
the rigidity of age.   His armor and weapons seemed to have
become a part of his nature, and he sat like a man of steel
on his powerful war-horse.

He took with him, on this expedition, his son Don Pedro
de Cordova, a youth of bold and generous spirit, in the freshness of his days, and armed and arrayed with all the bravery
of a young Spanish cavalier.   When the populace of Cordova
beheld the veteran father, the warrior of a thousand battles,
leading forth his youthful son to the field, they bethought
themselves of the family appellation: ''Behold,'' cried they,
''the eagle teaching his young to fly!   Long live the valiant
line of Aguilar!'' *

The prowess of Don Alonzo, and of his companions in
arms, was renowned throughout the Moorish towns.   At
their approach, therefore, numbers of the Moors submitted,
and hastened to Ronda to embrace Christianity.   Among
the mountaineers, however, there were many of the Gau-
dules, a fierce tribe from Africa, too proud of spirit to bend
their necks to the yoke.   At their head was a Moor named
El Feri of Ben Estepar, renowned for strength and courage.

---

* *Aguilar*—the Spanish for Eagle.

At his instigations, his followers gathered together their families and most precious effects, placed them on mules, and, driving before them their flocks and herds, abandoned their valleys, and retired up the craggy passes of the Sierra Vermeja. On the summit was a fertile plain, surrounded by rocks and precipices, which formed a natural fortress. Here El Feri placed all the women and children, and all the property. By his orders, his followers piled great stones on the rocks and cliffs which commanded the defiles and the steep sides of the mountain, and prepared to defend every pass that led to his place of refuge.

The Christian commanders arrived, and pitched their camp before the town of Monarda, a strong place, curiously fortified, and situated at the foot of the highest part of the Sierra Vermeja. Here they remained for several days, unable to compel a surrender. They were separated from the skirt of the mountain by a deep barranca or ravine, at the bottom of which flowed a small stream. The Moors, commanded by El Feri, drew down from their mountain height, and remained on the opposite side of the brook, to defend a pass which led up to their stronghold.

One afternoon, a number of Christian soldiers, in mere bravado, seized a banner, crossed the brook, and, scrambling up the opposite bank, attacked the Moors. They were followed by numbers of their companions, some in aid, some in emulation, but most in hope of booty. A sharp action ensued on the mountain side. The Moors were greatly superior in number, and had the vantage-ground. When the Counts of Urena and Cifuentes beheld this skirmish, they asked Don Alonzo de Aguilar his opinion: "My opinion," said he, "was given at Cordova, and remains the same; this is a desperate enterprise: however, the Moors are at hand, and if they suspect weakness in us, it will increase their courage and our peril. Forward, then, to the attack, and I trust in God we shall gain a victory." So saying, he led his troops into the battle.*

---

* Bleda. L. 5. c. 26.

On the skirts of the mountain were several level places like terraces; here the Christians pressed valiantly upon the Moors, and had the advantage; but the latter retreated to the steep and craggy heights, from whence they hurled darts and rocks upon their assailants. They defended their passes and defiles with ferocious valor, but were driven from height to height, until they reached the plain on the summit of the mountain, where their wives and children were sheltered. Here they would have made a stand; but Alonzo de Aguilar, with his son Don Pedro, charged upon them at the head of three hundred men, and put them to flight with dreadful carnage. While they were pursuing the flying enemy, the rest of the army, thinking the victory achieved, dispersed themselves over the little plain in search of plunder. They pursued the shrieking females, tearing off their necklaces, bracelets, and anklets of gold; and they found so much treasure of various kinds collected in this spot that they threw by their armor and weapons, to load themselves with booty.

Evening was closing. The Christians, intent upon spoil, had ceased to pursue the Moors, and the latter were arrested in their flight by the cries of their wives and children. Their fierce leader, El Feri, threw himself before them: "Friends, soldiers," cried he, "whither do you fly? Whither can you seek refuge, where the enemy cannot follow you? Your wives, your children, are behind you—turn and defend them; you have no chance for safety but from the weapons in your hands."

The Moors turned at his words. They beheld the Christians scattered about the plain, many of them without armor, and all encumbered with spoil. "Now is the time!" shouted El Feri; "charge upon them, while laden with your plunder. I will open a path for you!" He rushed to the attack, followed by his Moors, with shouts and cries that echoed through the mountains. The scattered Christians were seized with panic, and, throwing down their booty, began to fly in all directions. Don Alonzo de Aguilar advanced his banner, and endeavored to rally them. Finding his horse of no avail

in these rocky heights, he dismounted, and caused his men
to do the same; he had a small band of tried followers, with
which he opposed a bold front to the Moors, calling on the
scattered troops to rally in the rear.

Night had completely closed. It prevented the Moors
from seeing the smallness of the force with which they were
contending; and Don Alonzo and his cavaliers dealt their
blows so vigorously that, aided by the darkness, they seemed
multiplied to ten times their number. Unfortunately, a small
cask of gunpowder blew up near to the scene of action. It
shed a momentary but brilliant light over all the plain, and
on every rock and cliff. The Moors beheld, with surprise,
that they were opposed by a mere handful of men, and that
the greater part of the Christians were flying from the field.
They put up loud shouts of triumph. While some continued
the conflict with redoubled ardor, others pursued the fugitives, hurling after them stones and darts, and discharging
showers of arrows. Many of the Christians, in their terror
and their ignorance of the mountains, rushed headlong from
the brinks of precipices, and were dashed in pieces.

Don Alonzo de Aguilar still maintained his ground; but,
while some of the Moors assailed him in front, others galled
him with all kinds of missiles from the impending cliffs.
Some of the cavaliers, seeing the hopeless nature of the conflict, proposed that they should abandon the height and retreat down the mountain: "No," said Don Alonzo, proudly;
"never did the banner of the house of Aguilar retreat one
foot in the field of battle." He had scarcely uttered these
words, when his son Don Pedro was stretched at his feet. A
stone hurled from a cliff had struck out two of his teeth, and
a lance passed quivering through his thigh. The youth attempted to rise and, with one knee on the ground, to fight by
the side of his father. Don Alonzo, finding him wounded,
urged him to quit the field. "Fly, my son!" said he; "let
us not put everything at venture upon one hazard. Conduct
thyself as a good Christian, and live to comfort and honor
thy mother."

Don Pedro still refused to leave his side. Whereupon Don Alonzo ordered several of his followers to bear him off by force. His friend Don Francisco Alvarez of Cordova, taking him in his arms, conveyed him to the quarters of the Count of Urena, who had halted on the height, at some distance from the scene of battle, for the purpose of rallying and succoring the fugitives. Almost at the same moment, the count beheld his own son, Don Pedro Giron, brought in grievously wounded.

In the meantime, Don Alonzo, with two hundred cavaliers, maintained the unequal contest. Surrounded by foes, they fell, one after another, like so many noble stags encircled by the hunters. Don Alonzo was the last survivor, without horse, and almost without armor—his corslet unlaced, and his bosom gashed with wounds. Still he kept a brave front toward the enemy, and, retiring between two rocks, defended himself with such valor that the slain lay in a heap before him.

He was assailed in this retreat by a Moor of surpassing strength and fierceness. The contest was for some time doubtful; but Don Alonzo received a wound in the head, and another in the breast, that made him stagger. Closing and grappling with his foe, they had a desperate struggle, until the Christian cavalier, exhausted by his wounds, fell upon his back. He still retained his grasp upon his enemy: "Think not," cried he, "thou hast an easy prize; know that I am Don Alonzo, he of Aguilar!"—"If thou art Don Alonzo," replied the Moor, "know that I am El Feri of Ben Estepar." They continued their deadly struggle, and both drew their daggers; but Don Alonzo was exhausted by seven ghastly wounds: while he was yet struggling, his heroic soul departed from his body, and he expired in the grasp of the Moor.

Thus fell Alonzo de Aguilar, the mirror of Andalusian chivalry—one of the most powerful grandees of Spain, for person, blood, estate, and office. For forty years he had made successful war upon the Moors—in childhood by his household and retainers; in manhood by the prowess of his arm, and in the wisdom and valor of his spirit. His pennon had always been foremost in danger; he had been general of armies, viceroy of Andalusia, and the author of glorious enterprises, in which kings were vanquished, and mighty alcaydes and warriors laid low. He had slain many Moslem chiefs with his own arm, and among others the renowned Ali Atar of Loxa, fighting foot to foot, on the banks of the Xenil. His judgment, discretion, magnanimity and justice vied with his prowess. He was the fifth lord of his warlike house that fell in battle with the Moors.

"His soul," observes the worthy padre Abarca, "it is believed, ascended to heaven, to receive the reward of so Christian a captain; for that very day he had armed himself with the sacraments of confession and communion." *

The Moors, elated with their success, pursued the fugitive Christians down the defiles and sides of the mountains. It was with the utmost difficulty that the Count de Urena could bring off a remnant of his forces from that disastrous height. Fortunately, on the lower slope of the mountain, they found the rear-guard of the army, led by the Count de Cifuentes, who had crossed the brook and the ravine to come to their assistance. As the fugitives came flying in headlong terror down the mountain, it was with difficulty the count kept his own troops from giving way in panic, and retreating in confusion across the brook. He succeeded, however, in maintaining order, in rallying the fugitives, and checking the fury of the Moors: then, taking his station on a rocky eminence, he maintained his post until morning; sometimes sustaining violent attacks, at other times rushing forth and making assaults upon the enemy. When morning dawned, the Moors ceased to combat, and drew up to the summit of the mountain.

It was then that the Christians had time to breathe, and to ascertain the dreadful loss they had sustained. Among the many valiant cavaliers who had fallen was Don Fran-

---

* Abacra, Annales de Aragon, Rey xxx. cap. ii.

cisco Ramirez of Madrid, who had been captain-general of artillery throughout the war of Granada, and had contributed greatly by his valor and ingenuity to that renowned conquest. But all other griefs and cares were forgotten, in anxiety for the fate of Don Alonzo de Aguilar. His son, Don Pedro de Cordova, had been brought off with great difficulty from the battle, and afterward lived to be Marques of Priego; but of Don Alonzo nothing was known, except that he was left with a handful of cavaliers, fighting valiantly against an over-whelming force.

As the rising sun lighted up the red cliffs of the mountains, the soldiers watched with anxious eyes if perchance his pennon might be descried fluttering from any precipice or defile; but nothing of the kind was to be seen. The trumpet-call was repeatedly sounded, but empty echoes alone replied. A silence reigned about the mountain summit, which showed that the deadly strife was over. Now and then a wounded warrior came dragging his feeble steps from among the clefts and rocks; but, on being questioned, he shook his head mournfully, and could tell nothing of the fate of his commander.

The tidings of this disastrous defeat, and of the perilous situation of the survivors, reached King Ferdinand at Granada; he immediately marched, at the head of all the chivalry of his court, to the mountains of Ronda. His presence, with a powerful force, soon put an end to the rebellion. A part of the Moors were suffered to ransom themselves, and to embark for Africa; others were made to embrace Christianity; and those of the town where the Christian missionaries had been massacred were sold as slaves. From the conquered Moors, the mournful but heroic end of Alonzo de Aguilar was ascertained.

On the morning after the battle, when the Moors came to strip and bury the dead, the body of Don Alonzo was found among those of more than two hundred of his followers, many of them alcaydes and cavaliers of distinction. Though the person of Don Alonzo was well known to the Moors, being so distinguished among them both in peace and war, yet it was so covered and disfigured with wounds that it could with difficulty be recognized. They preserved it with great care, and on making their submission, delivered it up to King Ferdinand. It was conveyed with great state to Cordova, amid the tears and lamentations of all Andalusia. When the funeral train entered Cordova, and the inhabitants saw the coffin containing the remains of their favorite hero, and the war-horse, led in mournful trappings, on which they had so lately seen him sally forth from their gates, there was a general burst of grief throughout the city. The body was interred, with great pomp and solemnity, in the church of St. Hypolito.

Many years afterward, his granddaughter, Dona Catalina of Aguilar and Cordova, Marchioness of Priego, caused his tomb to be altered. On examining the body, the head of a lance was found among the bones, received without doubt among the wounds of his last mortal combat. The name of this accomplished and Christian cavalier has ever remained a popular theme of the chronicler and poet, and is endeared to the public memory by many of the historical ballads and songs of his country. For a long time the people of Cordova were indignant at the brave Count de Urena, who they thought had abandoned Don Alonzo in his extremity; but the Castilian monarch acquitted him of all charge of the kind, and continued him in honor and office. It was proved that neither he nor his people could succor Don Alonzo, or even know of his peril, from the darkness of the night. There is a mournful little Spanish ballad or romance, which breathes the public grief on this occasion, and the populace, on the return of the Count de Urena to Cordova, assailed him with one of its plaintive and reproachful verses:

> Count Ureña! Count Ureña!
> Tell us, where is Don Alonzo!
>
> (Dezid Conde de Ureña!
> Don Alonzo, donde queda?)*

---

* Bleda. L. 5. c. 26.

Printed in the United Kingdom
by Lightning Source UK Ltd.
102076UKS00001B/6